Anger, Madness, and the Daimonic

SUNY Series in the Philosophy of Psychology
Michael Washburn, editor

Anger, Madness, and the Daimonic

The Psychological Genesis of Violence, Evil, and Creativity

Stephen A. Diamond

Foreword by
Rollo May

STATE UNIVERSITY OF NEW YORK PRESS

Published by
State University of New York Press, Albany

© 1996 Stephen A. Diamond

For information, address State University of New York Press,
State University Plaza, Albany, N.Y., 12246

Production by Marilyn P. Semerad
Marketing by Dana E. Yanulavich

Library of Congress Cataloging-in-Publication Data

Diamond, Stephen A., 1951–
    Anger, madness, and the daimonic : the psychological genesis of
violence, evil, and creativity / Stephen A. Diamond ; foreword by
Rollo May.
        p.   cm. — (SUNY series in the philosophy of psychology)
    Includes bibliographical references and index.
    ISBN 0-7914-3075-8
    1. Anger.   2. Violence—Psychological aspects.   3. Good and evil–
–Psychological aspects.   4. Aggressiveness (Psychology)   5. Creative
ability.   6. Shadow (Psychoanalysis)   I. Title.   II. Series.
BF575.A5D65   1996
155.2'32—dc20   96-27865
                                                          CIP
                10 9 8 7 6 5 4 3 2 1

In Memory of Rollo May

(1909–1994)

Contents

Illustrations

xvii

Acknowledgments

As Freud once said, delving deeply into the dark domain of psychological devils and demons, human destructiveness, violence, and evil is a dangerous and disturbing pastime. But it was not until undertaking the writing of this book that I further discovered firsthand the truth of that old adage: "The devil is in the details." In working on this project, I, for one, have been fortunate during my *nekyia* (or night sea journey into the netherworld) to have found a few fellow travelers who helped me to maintain my equilibrium, lessen my sense of isolation, and keep my feet on terra firma. Indeed, so many people have helped—indirectly or directly—during the past fifteen years in the long, sometimes tedious, and frequently lonely gestation, birth, and rebirth of this book, that I could not possibly list each and every one by name. I hope that any old friends, family, or colleagues inadvertently or of necessity omitted from this brief acknowledgment can forgive my neglecting to mention them: They may no longer figure prominently in my life, or perhaps played no immediate part in the publishing of this book—but they have not been forgotten.

First, I wish to acknowledge my indebtedness to the late Dr. Rollo May for his unswerving receptivity to and support for my germinal conception of this project some fifteen years ago, his generous mentoring and encouragement of my writing over the ensuing decade, and finally, for his foresightful foreword to the book. He will always live in my memory as an inspirational role model, consummate psychotherapist, masterful teacher, and prolific, poetic author. I am also very grateful to his devoted wife and widow, Georgia Lee May, L.C.S.W., for her kind assistance during difficult circumstances.

I further want to thank the following people for participating in a previous incarnation of this project: Sylvia Randall, Ph.D., John Boe, Ph.D., Jeffrey Smith, Ph.D., and Lewis Mehl, M.D., Ph.D., all of whom, at some point, served on my doctoral dissertation committee ("The Daimonic and Depth Psychology: Rollo May's Contribution Reclarified,"

Psychological Studies Institute, Palo Alto, Calif., 1982. Copyright © 1982 by Stephen A. Diamond). I am beholden to Ladson Hinton, M.D., for a great many things, including encouragement par excellence to continue to speak my mind and express my ideas publicly; Robert Hinshaw, Ph.D., founder of Daimon Verlag in Switzerland, for taking keen interest as far back as 1984 in somehow publishing my dissertation in book form; John Beebe, M.D., for his patience, support, and editorial expertise in publishing my professional writings over the years; Jeremiah Abrams, L.C.S.W., for finding my work of sufficient interest to include it as a brief chapter in an excellent anthology he co-edited; Elizabeth Friar Williams, M.S., for believing in the viability of this material as a meaningful contemporary statement, for caringly helping to fashion a formal, effective, professional book proposal, and for editorial work on chapter one; Clay Morgan, my stalwart acquiring editor at SUNY Press, and Michael Washburn, Ph.D., the erudite editor of SUNY's Philosophy of Psychology Series, for seriously valuing this project, taking it on, unflinchingly supporting it, and working closely with me throughout the lengthy revision process to transmute the unrefined, reincarnated manuscript into the best book possible; my consulting literary agent, Laurie Harper, for intelligently coaching me on contract negotiations, lending a knowing, savvy, sympathetic ear, and gently guiding me through the legalistic labyrinth of "permissions"; Dr. June Singer, for sage moral support during the deeply dreaded rewriting process, as well as for reading and editorially critiquing important portions of the manuscript, most notably chapter two; my French tutor, Micheline Le Gall, colleagues Bruce Pither, Ph.D., and Nancy Wesson, Ph.D., and friends Debrah Emerson and Karen Hamilton for reading all or parts of the manuscript at various pre-galley stages and making pragmatic, concrete corrections, and astute comments; Hanni Forester and John Stucky of the Asian Art Museum of San Francisco; Allison Leavens, B.S., of the Virginia Allan Detloff Library of the C. G. Jung Institute, San Francisco, and Michael Flanagin, Ph.D., nurturing curator of the institute's Archive for Research in Archetypal Symbolism (ARAS) collection; the efficient researchers at the remarkable Art Resource, New York; the helpful staff of the Stanford University bookstores and superb library system; and Robert Clark of Minerva Books in Palo Alto. Thank you all for your assistance.

I am also indebted to Jack Rosberg, M.A.—executive director of the Anne Sippi Foundation for Training and Research, Los Angeles—for his enduring enthusiasm for this project, for reading and commenting on certain parts of it, and for graciously contributing the previously unpublished case transcript of "Kelly" in chapter seven; and to Marilyn Menta, M.A., for supportively providing some missing materials, carefully reviewing my synopsis of her collaborative work with former husband Dr. Robert Zaslow, and responding with concrete comments about content and clarity. Special thanks to Mary Buxton, L.C.S.W., for sending me the striking postcard from Japan which more than a decade later would become the dramatic cover art for this book; to Koyo Shimizu of Todaiji-Temple in Nara, Japan, for taking the trouble to track down the particular transparency I requested for use on the cover; and Robert Heffley, M.S., for incomparable, patient, and selfless computer support. My psychology students—both in California and Zürich—have taught me much about presenting this material. Indeed, certain sections of this book were written and presented by me as part of a two-week course at the C.G. Jung Institute, Zürich, in Spring, 1994, called "Psychopathology and Psychodiagnosis." I also wish to thank my family for taking interest in this project, and offering to assist in proofreading the galleys. I am very appreciative of those brave souls who philanthropically allowed me to publish highly personal—yet, hopefully, universally illustrative—case material in this book. Finally, I am forever grateful to my many supportive teachers, supervisors, and especially, countless patients, who, over the course of the past two decades, taught me most everything I know about anger, rage, and the creative art of psychotherapy.

1

The Angry American
An Epidemic of Rage and Violence

Introduction

We live in violent times. The currently raging epidemic of so-called "senseless violence" has become *the* central concern of the American people, dominating news reportage despite the pressing presence of other serious issues, such as the economy and national health care reform. In the grotesque media glare of sickening stories—epitomized most recently by the sensational O. J. Simpson murder case—violence, mayhem, and murder promise to command the lion's share of public attention and focus for the foreseeable future.

The reason for this spotlight on violence in America, by everyone from the media, to the president, to state and local politicians (even those who are not traditional "law and order" advocates), is as stark as it is simple: We are both frightened and fascinated by violence—and by evil in general. "Senseless violence" is the preeminent evil of our day. Citizens who once considered themselves safely cocooned and insulated from such evil now feel vulnerable, as unchecked violence spreads to the once sleepy suburbs, small towns, schools, shopping malls, sporting events, commuter trains, workplaces, and private abodes of middle-class America. Even blasé urban dwellers—no newcomers to a daily diet of destructive violence—are increasingly alarmed and appalled at the apparent trend toward a more visibly violent society. During a period of just two years (1989 to 1991), the chances of becoming a victim of violence in America's besieged cities shot up by 14 percent. We appear to be in the throes of a pernicious outbreak of pathological violence.

Of course, there is controversy as to whether we are in fact *truly* witnessing an advancing avalanche of violence in America today, or whether we might merely be misperceiving this to be the case. Have we succumbed to mass hysteria? Personally, I doubt whether there is any meaningful way to scientifically settle this argument once and for all. Indeed, for most Americans, the matter of statistical proof may be quite beside the point. The growing furor over our national stigma of violence centers substantially less on the question of *quantity* than of *quality:* the quality of life in America has dramatically deteriorated during the past few decades, and is more violent than in almost any other "civilized" society. The United States holds the dubious distinction of having the highest homicide rate of any industrialized Western nation. Obviously, violence is not merely an American problem. At least since Cain slew Abel in anger, the story of humankind has been a violent one, punctuated by war, genocide, mass murder, and malevolence. Destructiveness and violence have proven to be deep-seated—perhaps even archetypal—patterns of human behavior. America itself was the child of violent conflict, conceived and born by way of anger, outrage, and stormy revolt. The subsequent annals of American history are replete with violence: the genocide of Native Americans in the name of "manifest destiny"; the infamous Salem "witch hunts," wherein countless innocent women were pitilessly persecuted; the bloody Civil War, pitting brother against brother, American against American; the vengeful lawlessness of the Wild West; the murderous malice toward blacks (as well as other minority groups), and the reactive, eruptive, incendiary race-riots; the shocking political assassinations; and now, the "senseless" violence we see surrounding us on all sides.

One possibility worth considering is that violence in America is cyclic: it comes and goes in crashing waves, between which there is comparative calm.[1] For many of us, this closing decade before the millennial year two thousand feels like the crest of such a violent wave, one which threatens to radically erode—if not inundate and wash away—the very foundations of civilized society. Americans may have wishfully believed that, as a culture, we had left our violent ways behind, transcended our most primitive tendencies by virtue of technological, psychological, and social enlightenment. We were mistaken. Sadly, there is a surplus of nasty incidents

symbolizing the now sullied American dream: An idolized former foot-
ball star and affable international celebrity stands trial for a bloody double
murder in Los Angeles;[2] in that same beleaguered city, two brothers are
retried (following a hung jury in their first trial) and convicted of the chilling, premeditated murder of their millionaire parents in their posh Beverly
Hills home; thirty-nine-year-old drifter and career criminal Richard Allen
Davis confesses to randomly kidnapping and killing twelve-year-old Polly
Klaas, snatching her from the supposed safety of her suburban bedroom;
the wholesale slaughter at a San Francisco law firm leaves eight dead and
six wounded by an irate gunman, who, for his fitting finale, turns his
weapon against himself; and, in New York City, a man riding on the Long
Island Railroad calmly rises from his seat and methodically massacres fellow
passengers. Such atrocious and seemingly random acts of violence have
become so common as to take their place in the amorphous American
landscape alongside hot dogs, apple pie, baseball, and Budweiser. Violence—brutal, bloody, "senseless" violence—has become a new national
pastime. According to U.S. Justice Department statistics, violent crimes
increased almost 6 percent from 1992 to 1993.[3] By 1994, the situation
had grown sufficiently serious, and was of such grave concern to the
government, that the United States Congress—after considerable debate—
passed a thirty billion dollar national crime bill. On signing the bill,
President Clinton appealed to all Americans to " 'roll up our sleeves to
roll back this awful tide of violence.' "[4]

The workplace has been especially hard hit by this scourge, serving
almost routinely as the gory staging ground for some disgruntled ex-
employee, worker, or customer's deadly revenge. Such violent assaults have
been occurring in offices all across the country—not only in New York
or California. As reported in one recent article, "workplace violence is more
common than most believe. . . . According to a Northwestern National
Life Insurance Company nationwide study on workplace violence from
July 1992 to July 1993, 2.2 million workers were victims of physical attack:
6.3 million were threatened and 16.1 million were harassed."[5] Moreover,
violence is taking its terrible toll on virtually every sector of American
society, including economics: By some estimates, billions of dollars are
being lost because of the negative impact violence has—both directly and
indirectly—on the morale, productivity, and mental or physical health of
American workers.[6]

In his book, *On Being Mad or Merely Angry*, about would-be presidential assassin John Hinckley, Jr., political scientist James Clarke states
that during the past two decades,

instances of occupational frustration being expressed in mass bloodshed are regularly reported. For example, in 1976 a man in Baltimore, angry because of delays in receiving a business permit, shot five municipal employees, killing one; in 1982 an IBM salesman shot five fellow workers, killing three, because he felt that he had been passed over for promotion; in 1986 a disgruntled postal employee in Oklahoma killed fourteen fellow employees before taking his own life; and in 1987 a recently dismissed airline employee shot a pilot, his former boss, and himself, causing the crash of a Pacific Southwestern flight that, incidentally, killed forty other passengers.[7]

Even the sacred refuge of home, that once secure *sanctum sanctorum*, is no longer safe haven. Runaway violence has violated our residences, in forms ranging from stray bullets from drive-by shootings killing innocent family members, to full-blown domestic violence, such as child abuse and spousal battering. Almost one-third of all live-in sexual relationships involve some level of violence between the partners; an estimated one million American children or more are physically or emotionally abused. Domestic violence has become the heated topic of renewed rancor ever since the reported spousal abuse of Nicole Brown Simpson, as well as the indelicate case of Lorena Bobbitt: the woman who cut off her husband's penis with a carving knife, in retaliation for prior mistreatment. The boyish Menendez brothers, who admit to having shotgunned their mother and father to death in their own den, horrified jurors during the first trial with tales of extreme sexual and psychological abuses perpetrated upon them by their wealthy parents, purportedly prompting their violent parricide.

Permit me to cite in some detail Professor Clarke's disturbing conclusions concerning the motivations and mental states that accompany mayhem and murder. He cites one study of mass murderers which found that

> in 75 percent of the 364 cases . . . studied, the killers knew their victims. The motives of mass murderers who know their victims, and are expressing their hostility directly, are usually easier to identify. Often the victims are family members or fellow employees. . . .
>
> For example, in 1987 alone there were at least three such incidents: a former Air Force sergeant killed fourteen members of his family in Arkansas; another man killed his parents, in-laws, wife, and two children in the state of Washington; and another man gunned down seven relatives in Missouri.[8]

In such debacles, says Clarke, "the choice of victims is selective, not random. And in virtually every case there is some frustration, some grievance, that has developed between the killer and his victims which precedes the tragedy" (p. 94).

Then there is the mushrooming number of "random" acts of violence, like James Huberty's mass shooting at a McDonald's in 1984, killing twenty-one unlucky customers:

"Five months after . . . Huberty's rampage in San Ysidro," recounts Clarke,

> Michael Feher barricaded himself atop the stadium at the University of Oregon and shot two people, killing one of them before he was killed. In 1989 another troubled young man, Patrick Edward Purdy, opened fire on a schoolyard full of children in Stockton, California, with an AK-47 assault rifle; he wounded thirty and killed five before he killed himself. . . . All the killers mentioned died at the scene, as they intended to do, their motives remaining obscure. (p. 94–95)

"Such people," Clarke concludes, "kill, it seems . . . simply to make a statement about their disillusionment with their own lives. . . . Most did not appear to be psychotic. Angry, yes, but not mad. Neither . . . inhibited by conscience . . . nor . . . constrained by fear . . . the anonymous mass murderer selects surrogate targets . . . for his rage" (p. 95). In this book, among other things, we will be exploring the intricate interrelationship between anger, rage, "madness," mental disorders, and insanity (see, for instance, chapter six).

Undoubtedly, there is a great deal of disillusionment these days. Shell-shocked citizens who have not yet retreated to the anesthetic safety of what Robert Jay Lifton terms _psychic numbing_—a defensive means of psychologically desensitizing oneself to such terrible carnage—are understandably stunned. Even Europeans, inured as they are to the dark and tragic side of life, look on in utter dismay and disbelief, as they repeatedly see their own touring citizenry savagely assaulted only hours after setting foot on American soil. What on earth is going on there?, they justly wonder. Not that such violent crimes never occur on the Continent, or elsewhere for that matter. One well-publicized case in Liverpool, England, in 1993, involved two ten-year-old boys deliberately killing a two-year-old child, behavior that the disgusted sentencing magistrate labeled unmitigated "evil."[9] In March, 1996, in Dunblane, Scotland, a middle-aged man with a history of strange behavior and a passion for handguns fired on a gymnasium filled with five and six-year-olds, slaying sixteen and seriously wounding a dozen more before committing suicide. And a scant six weeks later, in Tasmania, Australia, a twenty-eight-year-old man armed with a rifle inexplicably massacred thirty-five people en masse, wounding eighteen. It is, however, the furious pace at which these unnerving events are proliferating in America—as well as their sheer viciousness—that has so many of us so worried. Indeed, according to a 1988 study conducted by the United States government, "crimes of violence (homicide, rape, and robbery) are four to nine times more frequent in the United States than they are in Europe."[10]

What are the roots of our malady? Some place the blame on the overabundance and ready availability of firearms in this country (there are almost as many guns in America as people); or on our overwhelmed, underfinanced judicial system; or the gratuitous violence pervading American movies and television programming; or the disintegration of the nuclear family and the demise of traditional "family values"; or on substance abuse; tough economic times; the disenfranchisement of the poor and the uneducated; and so forth. It is no doubt true, for instance, that the troubled "dysfunctional family"—that is, the widespread dissolution of a cohesive, secure container in which children can be adequately loved, cared for, nurtured, protected, and imbued with the collective values of the culture—must be blamed for a great many social ills. (See, for example, the writings of Alice Miller and John Bradshaw.) The family is not only the transmitter of social mores to the next generation; it is the sacred crucible wherein the psychological well-being of each new adult generation is largely determined. Given the violent trend of the past twenty years or so, it seems patently clear that the American family has been failing its children miserably, and is now paying the bloody price for this failure. Problems within the dysfunctional family frequently include parental aggression against children—in the forms of physical, verbal, and sexual abuse—which ultimately begets further aggression and abuses against society. Because we unconsciously or automatically tend to parent our children in ways similar to how we ourselves were parented, abused children often grow up to be abusive adults and parents. Traumatic childhood abuse creates a pathological generation comprised of the "walking wounded": psychologically crippled adults who, while ostensibly functional, can be wickedly cruel to each other, as well as insidiously self-destructive. This vicious cycle must be stopped.

Yet, though I concede that each of these corrosive undercurrents are significant factors contributing to the 11 percent increase in violent crime over the past decade, they seem to me to be symptomatic of a much broader, more pervasive, sinister, and ominous social phenomenon. There is a common thread, a single, latent leitmotif that underlies, runs through, and interconnects these legitimate concerns. It has become the postmodern American Zeitgeist, a feeling which at once divides and unites us. It is our immense *anger* and *rage*. Whether we are willing to admit it or not, *we Americans are an angry people*. We are living not only in an "age of anxiety," as W. H. Auden, Paul Tillich, Rollo May, and other astute students of the twentieth-century psyche have observed, but in an "era of rage" as well. This distressing fact is vividly evident in our daily newspapers, nightly network coverage, radio talk shows, prime-time television, popular music, movies, video games, modern art, literature, and—perhaps most unpleasantly of all—in our own close encounters with the hostility, incivility, and animosity so endemic to modern life as we now know it.

The cultural, interpersonal, and individual problems posed by the potent passions of anger and rage are copious, complex, and highly charged. One such critical outcropping is *violence*, that all-too-frequent offspring of anger and rage. Today we are witnessing the roaring resurgence of our long-simmering anger and rage. Anger and rage—like sexuality in Sigmund Freud's Victorian era—have come to be regarded as evil, sinful, destructive, uncivilized, pagan, and primitive passions, much better buried than openly admitted. The volatile emotions of anger and rage have been broadly "demonized," vilified, maligned, and rejected as purely pathological, negative impulses with no real redeeming qualities. As a result, most "respectable" Americans habitually suppress, repress, or deny their anger—inadvertently rendering it doubly dangerous: The chronic suppression of anger and rage can and does sow the evil seeds of psychopathology, hatred, and violence, as this study strives to demonstrate.

This sweeping denunciation of anger and rage can be found even in the fields of psychology and psychiatry. Most current psychotherapies (including the classic psychoanalytic therapies of Freud and Jung) or cutting-edge psychopharmacological treatments (such as antidepressant drugs or tranquilizers) fail to provide adequate assistance to patients struggling with the powerful "demons" of anger and rage; indeed, in some instances, such treatment approaches may make matters worse. While there has happily been burgeoning interest and research in this area over the past twenty years, the complicated clinical problems presented by anger and rage remain far and away the most confounding Gordian knot still faced in the effective practice of psychotherapy.

One fundamental difficulty has to do with the fact that some psychotherapies do not adequately discriminate between *normal* and *pathological* anger or rage. Many modern clinicians have no appreciation of the nature, meaning, and positive value of *healthy* anger and rage. Psychologists, psychiatrists, and counselors sorely need to reappraise anger and rage, their contributory roles in violence and psychopathology, as well as their central significance in psychotherapy. At the same time, we must more fully recognize the potentially constructive—even creative— power of anger and rage, coexisting side-by-side with its notorious capacity for destructiveness, violence, and evil. Prominent American psychoanalyst Rollo May, almost thirty years ago, articulated this task by pointing out that anger or rage (like other *daimonic* passions) "will always be characterized by the paradox inhering in the fact that it is potentially creative and destructive at the same time. This is the most important question facing modern psychotherapy, and the most fateful also—for on it hinges the lasting and the survival of therapy."[11] We will be delving deeply into the meaning, nature, and clinical implications of the mysterious, classic conundrum called "the daimonic," and its contemporary relevance to anger, rage, evil, violence, and, paradoxically, creativity. In some instances, we will be hearing from May himself— among many others—on these seasonable subjects.

The vexing enigma of violence has now reached epidemic proportions. For this sobering reason, the great challenge of constructively redirecting and rechannelling our anger and rage must be made a national as well as a personal priority. Unless we learn to come to better terms with our wrath, it will no doubt destroy us. Here in America, Pandora's box has blown open and cannot be closed. This explosive state of affairs presents itself, as we will see, with mounting regularity in psychotherapeutic practice. The process of psychotherapy mirrors in so many subtle ways the societal psyche: patients typically reflect in their personal problems precursors of current and coming cultural crises. I propose that the psychological, physical, and spiritual health of American culture depends on how well we can creatively—and therapeutically— harness the prodigious power of these darkest and least accepted of human emotions. This book is intended to be an exploratory step in that direction. It marks a modest attempt to shed some much-needed psychological light on the still obscure subjects of anger, rage, madness, evil, and creativity; make some sense of "senseless" violence; and maybe even provide some moral sustenance in our battle against the raging blight of evil bedeviling us.

Like other notorious acts in a nation with legions of unstable people and 200 million firearms, the things Ferguson is accused of doing . . . —rising in a crowded car, methodically shooting strangers, killing five people and wounding 18 others—appear inexplicable on the surface. . . . [37]

[However,] dozens of interviews with acquaintances, former teachers and employers, public officials, psychiatrists and others have produced a detailed portrait of Ferguson and suggested that the shootings were not the result of a single reverse in his life, but of a long slide of events that took him from a privileged childhood in Jamaica to rejection and failure in America.

. . . . Ferguson had fallen a long way from his origins 35 years ago in Kingston, Jamaica, where the birthright of a cricket-and-private school youth was cut short by the premature death of his parents. Young, articulate, ambitious, he moved to the United States [in 1982] and aspired to the American Dream: college, marriage, jobs with a future.

But it was not to be. In California, he was remembered as brash, arrogant, disdainful of the menial jobs he could find, and critical of whites and even blacks who were not sufficiently militant. Easily offended, acquaintances said, he often twisted meanings to create racial issues where none was intended. After being robbed by two black men, they said, he began carrying a gun in a paper bag.

Later in New York, he became increasingly obsessed with what he saw as ubiquitous racism, and he lashed out angrily. It became a pattern, then a way of life. His wife divorced him in 1988 in what acquaintances called a crushing blow to a psychologically fragile man. . . .

[Black landlord Patrick] Denis, who had heard his lodger take five showers a day and chant mantras at night about "all the black people killing all the white people," said he had feared for some time that Ferguson had become dangerously unstable, . . . had grown tired of his endless racial right-eousness, . . . [and had told him to move out by the end of the month].

"All black people are discriminated against," Denis said. . . . "But you can't take everything in life and say it is the product of racism. He took all his failures in life and gave it a name and made it a cause."[38]

In what became one of the most bizarre courtroom proceedings in American history, Colin Ferguson was found competent to stand trial, and, against legal counsel, chose to act as his own defense attorney.[39] Clearly a highly intelligent, well-educated, and articulate man, Ferguson was allowed to cross-examine during the trial witnesses—some of whom had been wounded on the train—who testified under oath that *he*, the defendant, was indeed the person who had done the shooting. He spoke of himself as someone who had been wrongly charged, denied his guilt, and suggested that the perpetrator was not him, but, rather, some white man. Ultimately, Ferguson was found guilty on most counts, sentenced to life in prison, and reportedly, plans to appeal his case to a higher court.

Now, despite the blatant racial overtones, this was not, at bottom, a cut-and-dried case of racism. It was a case in which chronic feelings of entitlement, frustration, victimization, insignificance, alienation, anger, and rage at *life as it really is* resulted in a despicable act of hatred and retribution. Nor can we simply dismiss this incident as the irrational, aberrant behavior of some madman. For as any serious student of psychopathology soon learns, there is a fine line dividing sanity from insanity, and "normal" responses from "abnormal" ones. Both Freud and Jung discovered that the study of psychopathology provides a great deal of data as to the nature of those ordinary, day-to-day psychological processes to which we are all subject.

There is no doubt in my mind that by the time he committed his heinous acts, Colin Ferguson had been suffering for some time from a severe mental disorder, and was probably psychotic. Nonetheless, this case presents a kind of shadowy caricature reflecting the only-somewhat-more-subtle problems that so many Americans—of varying racial or ethnic backgrounds—daily face: frustration, anger, and sometimes, rage. Ferguson mirrors, in magnified and disfigured form, the American soul-sickness. What was Ferguson so furious about? Many of the same things that infuriate all of us to some degree in this disconcerting day and age! He suffered the traumatic loss of his parents at a relatively tender age, and with this, the loss of the lifestyle to which he had been accustomed. Immigrating to America—as do so many optimistic others—in search of his own success, he discovered only despair, disillusionment, and discontent. Such unexpected and painful twists of fate frequently leave people feeling victimized, frustrated, and angry about the perceived unfairness of life. We Americans in particular seem to be born with or acquire a conscious or unconscious belief that life will be fair, and that goodness will prevail. When we sooner or later learn that this is in fact not always the case, that one cannot be in complete control of one's destiny, and that the vagaries of fate cannot be evaded by virtue, privilege, money, or even prayer, a sort of insidious anger sets in. I suspect this is part of what happened to Colin Ferguson.

Nor can Ferguson's anger be conveniently dismissed as purely pathological, narcissistic rage.[40] While it is certain that he is mentally ill, deranged, or mad, he had not always been so. In all probability, he was predisposed to psychosis prior to his arrival in this country, presumably possessing what might be diagnosed as a "narcissistic," "borderline" or perhaps "paranoid personality disorder." Nonetheless, I would argue that at least some component of his rage can be correctly understood as a normal, existential, or *ontological* part of human experience. The needlessly intimidating term "ontology" refers to the study of both the objective facts and subjective perceptions that universally comprise human existence or *being*. "Ontology," writes Rollo May, "seeks to discover the basic structures of existence—the structures which are given to everyone at every moment."[41] For most present intents and purposes, the terms "ontological" and "existential" can be considered by readers to be interchangeable.

What distinguishes most of us from the Colin Fergusons of the world is the fact that—for various reasons, not the least of which is fear of the likely consequences—we do not literally, as Hamlet states it, "take arms against a sea of troubles." Yet, we are all susceptible to the "slings and arrows of outrageous fortune,"[42] and the frustration, anger, and sometimes even rage that arise when fate deals us a "bad hand." "The concept of destiny makes the experience of anger necessary," writes May. "The kind of person who 'never gets angry' is, we may be sure, the person who also never enounters destiny."[43] *Destiny*, like *fate*, refers to the existential "givens" of life, those aspects of existence that are immutable, inexorable, and inevitable. Destiny differs from "predestination," however, in that destiny exists always in dialectical relationship with human *freedom*. We each have a destiny insofar as we are born into a world at a biologically determined point in time, in a particular place, to specific parents, of a certain gender, and with some unique combination of personal strengths, talents, limitations, and weaknesses. From an existential perspective, we are "thrown" into life without any choice in the mattter. As we mature and develop, what we do with our innate talents, liabilities, tendencies, and sensitivities determines—at least to some significant degree—our destiny or our fate.

Fate is commonly understood as being synonymous with *destiny*. But for psychiatrist Alexander Lowen, "the two words have slightly different meanings. Destiny is related to the word *destination*. It refers to what . . . [we become] , whereas fate describes what one is. Fish are fated to swim as birds are fated to fly, but that is hardly their destiny. . . . The oracle at Delphi did not foretell the destiny of Oedipus, which was to vanish from the earth and find an abode with the gods. He prophesied his fate, which was that he would kill his father and marry his mother."[44] Finding and fulfilling our personal destiny is one of the primary aims of any comprehensive psychotherapy. Destiny, declaims May, "*is the design of the universe speaking through the design of each one of us.*"[45]

The prototypical encounter with fate or destiny, peculiar as it may seem, is the bare fact of being born, or what psychoanalyst Otto Rank referred to as "the trauma of birth."[46] Rank's existential attitude toward the inevitabilities in life, the ontological givens, our destiny, led also to his emphasis on the trauma of separation, beginning with the birth trauma, as well as the need to face death—the ultimate separation experience. Rank, while still under the sway of his mentor, Sigmund Freud, theorized that the experience of birth is a traumatic tearing away of the child from the idyllic womb into a strange, hostile environment, and that the child feels great anxiety and *resentment* toward the mother—and her genitals—for this sudden expulsion from Paradise. Despite the Freudian sexual influence, from which he finally freed himself, Rank emerged as one of the early founders of existential psychotherapy, as will later be elaborated.

Swiss analyst Carl Jung, like Rank, also recognized and commented on this archetypal anxiety and anger regarding separation from the mother and from our originally whole, unconsciously blissful condition, declaring that "a deep resentment seems to dwell in man's breast against the brutal law that once separated him from instinctive surrender to his desires and from the beautiful harmony of animal nature."[47] This "brutal law" to which Jung alludes refers first to the fact of being born, and second, to the necessity of forging an "ego" during the early process of socialization. Acknowledging the resentment we each bear since birth about having been forcefully evicted from the warm, familiar womb and subsequently rent asunder by the collective demands of civilization, Jung, at the same time, wryly critiqued Rank's theory, quipping that to call birth "traumatic" is a gross misuse of that term: Generally speaking, birth is "traumatic" in the same sense that life itself is a traumatic experience! Nevertheless, the existential fact of birth, of being banished from Eden and involuntarily "thrown" into this sometimes unwelcoming, startling, frustrating, and frightening new plane of existence, is perhaps the most primeval root of our ontological resentment, anger, and rage.

Frustration, that exasperating experience of being foiled, thwarted, blocked, or baffled in our best efforts to find satisfaction—or, as Freud said, to seek pleasure and avoid pain—begins at birth and follows us for the rest of our days. Frustration is an existential concomitant of the human condition to which few—if any—are immune.[48] Even in the best of circumstances, infants cannot always be fed at the exact moment they experience hunger pangs, freshly diapered when wet, cuddled, held, and comforted on demand, no matter how loudly or persistently they cry. Much of what infants and children want, they cannot have. With luck, we get what we need to survive and—hopefully—thrive. To some extent, the same may be said of adults: we are not always able to succeed in our endeavors, to attain our goals, or to satisfy our desires, no matter how hard we try. Like infants and children, adults are destined to be disappointed and frustrated, and frequently, to feel angry about being frustrated. Indeed, we *need* to be able to feel angry at life's inevitable frustrations if we are ever to overcome some of them: "When one encounters destiny, one finds anger rising in one, but [ideally] as strength," comments May. "Encountering one's destiny requires strength, whether the encounter takes the form of embracing, accepting, or attacking. . . . Constructive anger is one way of encountering destiny."[49] Constructive anger or rage provides the power and impetus to move beyond the manifold impediments life so predictably presents.

What is the real relationship between frustration and anger? Carol Tavris disputes the widely held notion that frustration leads to anger, rage, and aggressive behavior, a classic psychological theory called the "frustration-aggression hypothesis":[50]

> Frustration *always* causes aggression, these psychologists argued, and aggression is always preceded by frustration. This testable idea sent hundreds of researchers to their laboratories, where they promptly found that some frustrations make you angry, but lots of others do not. If you do not get the job you want or the lover you long for, you are as likely to be disappointed or depressed as angry, and maybe even relieved. Frustration causes many reactions, including a craving for ice cream or a desire to see a mindless movie.[51]

But Tavris here is guilty of cause-and-effect reasoning of the most simplistic, mechanistic, and concrete kind! While frustration surely does not always lead to anger in the form of a reflexively automatic, knee-jerk response, and certainly not to aggressive or violent behavior, Tavris ignores the fact that different individuals have learned different ways of dealing with frustration and anger—which could explain the inconsistencies found in the research. For example, people who, feeling frustrated, crave ice cream or head to the nearest multiplex may well feel angry about being frustrated, but not be aware of it; that is to say, they might be *unconscious* of their anger. The proper inquiry thus turns to how that specific person deals with feelings of frustration and anger—i.e., consciously or unconsciously—instead of whether frustration automatically "causes" anger, or, for that matter, whether anger "causes" aggressive behavior: The ice cream and movies may be means of ameliorating, mitigating, or avoiding angry feelings rather than, as Tavris suggests, hard, scientific "evidence" that no such emotions are universal in the face of frustration.

I hope to have underscored so far that it is not at all unusual, nor in any way "abnormal," to feel frustrated, resentful, or angry about one's life from time to time.[52] In the case of Colin Ferguson, this "ontological" level of frustration and anger spiralled out of control, turning morbid or pathological, a demonic psychological process detailed in chapter six. For now, suffice it to say that Ferguson was unable to cope with his profound frustrations effectively. He let his normal or *existential anger* grow into *neurotic anger,* and then, *psychotic rage,* which he eventually acted out so very violently. What most of us have in common with Colin Ferguson is that we, too, from day to day, are forever forced to cope with our own personal failures, frustrations, limitations, and our resultant anger and rage. So much of the surging tidal wave of anger and rage rampant in our topsy-turvy times is the natural consequence of explosive changes in our perceptions of ourselves, our society, our world, and our most basic presumptions about the nature of life itself. Assailed by the inescapable angst, confusion, and chaos that accompany massive cultural upheaval, we are all apt on occasion to feel outraged at the apparently arbitrary facts of our essentially insecure, often painful, and sometimes, seemingly meaningless, insignificant existence. We rebel—at least inwardly if not outwardly—against our human destiny!

Like Ferguson, or fictional character Bill Foster (Michael Douglas) in the aforementioned film, *Falling Down,* most of us have been culturally conditioned to suppress our rebellious anger and rage, taught that we have no right to be irate about our state, that we stoically ought not cry out against our often outrageous fate. When Foster finally snaps in the film, setting out (again, like Ferguson) on a ruinous rampage, we are reminded that there are limits to the chronic suppression and repression required by social civility; that somehow, despite our deep-seated moralistic, religious, or philosophical proscriptions, we need to find effective, yet salutary ways to depotentiate the destructive power of repressed anger and rage.

Regrettably, the real-life Ferguson, like the fictional Foster, slipped slowly into madness. He was unable to surmount the staggering loss of meaning, purpose, and personal significance he faced in coming to this country; nor the apparently immovable obstacles that destiny so indifferently placed in his path. Feeling utterly frustrated by his inability to fulfill what he took to be his true potential (and possibly his birthright), incapable of realizing the elusive "American Dream," Ferguson aimed his accumulated frustration, rage, and anger at those whom he perceived to be prejudicially impeding his progress. He fell victim to the notorious "victim mentality" so commonly characterizing such cases. As James Clarke concludes,

> the anonymous mass murderer is not motivated by anything his chosen victims have done to him; rather it is what his victims *represent*, or symbolize in his mind, that focuses the diffuse anger and rage of his attack. His alienation has spread like an infection, poisoning his perspective on life, draining away whatever compassion and humanity he might have had. . . .
>
> In a motivational sense . . . that desire to be noticed, . . . to 'make a statement,' to be 'taken seriously' for once in his miserable, pointless life is the goal.[53]

Feeling helplessly victimized by circumstance, society, and fate, perpetrators of "senseless violence" turn the tables, venting their venomous hatred and rage on innocent bystanders. In so doing, the mass killers, unable to assert their power positively in the world, become—if only fleetingly—powerful victimizers as opposed to powerless victims of society.

This leads us to yet another existential source of violence: our sense of alienation, loneliness, and isolation. We are each thrown into the world alone, often must walk through it alone, and we die alone. Most of us frantically do everything in our power to avoid facing this lamentable fact of life. As human beings, we inherit a level of loneliness that can never be completely overcome—though our capacity to connect intimately with others certainly serves to assuage, albeit temporarily, the ineluctable suffering of this existential loneliness. When we are unable to find suitable companionship, solace, support, or love, and are thus frustrated in fulfilling our fundamental need for human warmth and intimacy, a sullen rage can accrue over time, occasionally culminating in destructive violence: "Violence," as May rightly remarks, "is the ultimate destructive substitute which surges in to fill the vacuum where there is no related-ness. . . . When inward life dries up, when feeling decreases and apathy increases, when one cannot affect or even genuinely *touch* another person, violence flares up as a daimonic necessity for contact, a mad drive forcing touch in the most direct way possible."[54]

For some, violence can be a desperate, last-ditch attempt to break out of their self-imposed state of social isolation. In director Martin Scorsese's disturbing film, *Taxi Driver* (1976), starring Robert De Niro and Jodie Foster, Travis Bickle (De Niro) is a lonely, love-starved, frustrated and angry misfit. Striving to transcend his insufferable alienation, he unsuccessfully tries to assassinate a presidential candidate. Finally, he wins some recognition by becoming a vigilante-style killer. John Hinckley, Jr., the confused young man who—in a twisted effort to win the admiration and love of the real-life Jodie Foster—attempted to assassinate President Ronald Reagan in 1981, identified with this pathetic character. Hinckley (like Mark David Chapman, who bitterly gunned down his former idol, famed rock musician John Lennon in 1980) was himself such an isolated, frustrated, and furious soul who—in his own sick way—desperately sought love, attention, and relief from his hellish existence. Once one has publicly committed a high-profile violent crime, he or she is no longer alone, anonymous, and ignored; violence, in such instances, serves as an absurd, evil vehicle to infamy.[55]

One more existential principle worth mentioning at this point pertains to the problem of *meaninglessness*, and what Viennese psychiatrist Viktor Frankl calls "the will to meaning."[56] All people seek some cause, purpose, or raison d'être in life. In lieu of such a central cause, or in the case of the sudden loss or slow erosion of one's sense of purpose, there exists a strong psychological drive toward rediscovering—or, if necessary, recreating—a cause, sometimes any cause, in order to restore some meaningful direction, self-esteem, and sense of purpose. Frankl attributes this tendency to an inherent human need for meaning. The search for meaning is an *existential*—as opposed to a *pathological*—process, though it plays a significant part in the evolution of psychopathological states of mind and madness. Such was the case with Colin Ferguson, a pitifully frustrated man, lost at sea, adrift, buffeted, and bedeviled by the vicious racial undertows and rip tides of American culture. *Meaning*—like some "sense of significance" and "self-esteem"—is essential to human life. We need meaning, much as we need food, water, air, shelter, companionship, sex, and love. When deprived of these natural needs, we are prone to react angrily at this profound threat to our well-being. Our "will to meaning" is an innate inner necessity, the chronic frustration of which can result in anger, rage, despair, and depression. In extreme cases, frustration of the "will to meaning"—what Frankl refers to as "existential frustration"—may engender a deep-rooted rage, that gradually turns into a hard-to-shake hatred of oneself, one's world, and of the people populating it. This bitter resentment toward life—a life devoid of meaning, significance, freedom, dignity, passion, and love—is intimately tied to Sigmund Freud's idea of *Thanatos*, the "death instinct," which drives one to destroy life, as well as to Goethe's satanic "spirit of negation." When we speak of someone as being a "negative" person, we might well be describing the morbid consequences of chronic, unresolved, festering resentments of this sort.

Colin Ferguson, John Hinckley, Jr., and Mark David Chapman each ailed from a distinct lack of meaning in their lives, living as do we all in what Frankl terms the "existential vacuum" of the late twentieth century.[57] When the traditional myths and symbols which once gave meaning and coherence to a culture lose their value, and there are no new myths and symbols to adequately replace them, we are subject to disorientation, a loss of meaning, and a diminished sense of personal and transpersonal significance: "Our particular problem in America at this point in history," opined May more than two decades ago, "is the widespread loss of the sense of individual significance, a loss which is sensed inwardly as impotence. . . . So many people feel they do not and cannot have power, that even self-affirmation is denied them, that they have nothing left to assert, and hence that there is no solution short of a violent explosion."[58] In light of the recent eruption of violent "domestic terrorism" in America—like the fatal, 1995 bombing of a federal building in Oklahoma City, and the lethal attacks of the so-called Unabomber—May's words resonate today. While we know that "absolute power corrupts absolutely," we could consider the contrary also to be true: The absolute absence of personal power can be equally corruptive; powerlessness contributes to the prevalence of violence. Individuals who conceive of themselves as help-less, powerless *victims* of society sooner or later reach the hopeless point of feeling that since they have nothing to lose—no power, influence, prestige, nor status—violence is their sole alternative, their last remaining means of making some potent personal statement. Violence looks like the only voice left to them.

On Rage and Racism

Finally, there lingers the incontestable issue of racism in the Colin Ferguson case. I do not for one moment believe or wish to imply that Ferguson's racial "paranoia" was wholly unfounded. Racial prejudice and discrimination *do* exist in America, alongside other serious social ills, like sexual discrimination—a subject we shall consider in the next chapter. In his frank foreword to the famous book *Black Rage*, first published in 1968, then U.S. Senator Fred Harris had this to say on the still simmering subject of racism in America:

> To be sure, there are many evils which derive from racism that are more easily identified, including the existence of ghetto neighborhoods, joblessness, stultifying classrooms, and poor health. But there should be no mistake about this, for the future of America is too important: the root cause of the black wrath that now threatens to destroy this nation is the unwillingness of white Americans to accept Negroes as fellow human beings. . . . , [and] to [allow them to] do here what all people everywhere must do if they are to develop fully—to find an identity, a sense of worth, to relate to others, to love, to work, and to create.[59]

The prescient insights articulated by this classic work are, in my opinion, even more apropos today than at the racially tumultuous time they first appeared. The authors—both black psychiatrists—place their finger on the pivotal trouble between blacks and whites in America, then and now. What they touched upon but could not possibly have fully anticipated at that time, however, is how this festering rage would slowly snowball and metastasize, spreading like some fatal cancer, beyond all racial bounds, to detrimentally affect—or infect—all Americans, regardless of race, creed, or color. "Aggression," write Grier and Cobbs,

> leaps from wounds inflicted and ambitions spiked. It grows out of oppression and capricious cruelty. It is logical and predictable if we know the soil from which it comes. . . . People bear all they can and, if required, bear even more. But if they are black in present-day America they have been asked to shoulder too much. They have had all they can stand. They will be harried no more. Turning from their tormentors, they are filled with rage. The growing anger of Negroes is frightening to white America. . . . White people have responded with a rage of their own.[60]

These incendiary racial tensions were brought into sharp and undeniable focus in the 1990s by events such as the Rodney King beatings, the Colin Ferguson case, and the divisive O. J. Simpson double-murder trial. Beneath the fragile façade of integration, black rage rumbles relentlessly, despite the intervening decades and the hard-won victories of the civil rights movement. But "black rage" has now been amalgamated with a more democratic form of rage of which we all partake. Blacks no longer have a monopoly on rage in America; though they continue to have ample cause to be angry: "For there are no more psychological tricks blacks can play upon themselves to make it possible to exist in dreadful circumstances," warn Cobbs and Grier. "No more lies can they tell themselves. No more dreams to fix on. No more opiates to dull the pain. No more patience. No more thought. No more reason. Only a welling tide risen out of all those terrible years of grief, now a tidal wave of fury and rage, and all black, black as night."[61] One of the costliest manifestations of black rage has been the "black-on-black" violence tearing apart communities of color. This internecine barbarity bespeaks the despair, frustration, and fury of many African Americans, and their inability to find constructive means of expressing and surmounting it.

Racism—which is rooted in a fundamental fear and defensive resentment of those we deem different, the "other"—and the demonic rage, racial animus, and outright hatred that accompany it, remain among the foremost evils Americans face. Yet, as we shall see, the crucial matter of how an individual—any individual, be they black, white, brown, or yellow, Jew or gentile—deals with such self-evident evils and the frustration, anger, and rage they are destined to provoke, is of paramount importance. Colin Ferguson found his few remaining shreds of meaning and purpose in hating white people, whom he saw as deliberately subverting his success. In the end, he expressed his pent-up rage in a premeditated act of violence, directed against predominantly middle-class caucasian commuters—a despicable and evil act for which he refused, during his first trial, to accept any responsibility.[62] Ferguson's fatal attack, along with the litany of other infamous incidents graphically listed in the preceding pages, demonstrates the devastating impact of violence in its most visible, hideous, and destructive forms. Such revolting violence can be defined, states May summarily, as "an eruption of pent-up passion . . . , an explosion of the drive to destroy that which is interpreted as the barrier to one's self-esteem, movement, and growth."[63] As we have witnessed, it is an outburst that, more often than not, backfires in fatally noxious ways. We can conclude that there was indeed a method to Mr. Ferguson's madness: his victims symbolized the very "devils" he felt had been victimizing *him* all along.

2

Sex Wars
The Animosity Between Women and Men

Hostility between the sexes is very real and very old, . . . and . . . the existing psychoanalytic hypotheses and theories do not sufficiently explain the nature and quality of this hostility, nor do they offer a comprehensive idea as to its origin and development.

—Gregory Zilboorg, "Masculine and Feminine"

In recent years, the proverbial "war between the sexes" has been heating up here in America. This ever-widening schism separating men and women is partially a product of fear, suspicion, mistrust, envy, resentment, and hostility; increasingly, it is also the source of anger, rage, and violence.

Ill will between the sexes can be seen on all planes of social interaction, from politics to personal relations. Some of this animosity was sorely perceptible, for example, during the nationally televised confirmation hearings of Clarence Thomas for the United States Supreme Court in 1992, when attorney Anita Hill accused Judge Thomas of sexual harassment. One side effect of this highly public confrontation was to raise the level of "paranoia"—or of "consciousness" in the positive sense—between the sexes, building an even bigger barrier of mistrust and resentment; or establishing a clearer sense of boundaries, depending upon one's point of view.

Some social pundits insist that there is no more antipathy now between men and women than at any other point in history, blaming the media for blowing the matter out of all proportion. It is true, for instance, that because she had been battered by her husband, O. J. Simpson, the sensational slaying of Nicole Brown Simpson has riveted renewed attention on the widespread but under reported physical abuse of women at the hands of men who supposedly love them. Many—if not most—violent assaults in America stem from some sort of imbroglio between the sexes, such as spurned lovers, quarreling spouses, or vitriolic divorces. These lurid examples mentioned above are not mere anomalies: they are indicative of the tense emotional atmosphere between modern men and women. Animosity—thinly veiled if not flagrant—underlies and undermines heterosexual interactions, creating, for many, a prickly state of affairs that pervades all spheres of social intercourse, from classroom, to boardroom, to bedroom.[1] This animosity is an amplification of an ancient, archetypal tension between the sexes; yet another existential root of anger, resentment, and rage.

Fear, Anger, and Intergender Hostility

What are the dynamics of these heightened hostilities? Some American women are angrily engaged in the political process of dethroning the patriarchal powers that be, in hopes of returning to or approximating a more *matriarchal* society: one at least equally informed by feminine principles, and which values—rather than devalues— the "feminine." Fair enough. Women have been denigrated and denied their equal rights far too long. Women are righteously angry, and are using that anger to actively alter their destinies. They are frustrated and fed up with being mistreated and discriminated against by men and the masculine establishment. Many are channelling their comprehensible outrage into constructive change. To cite feminist author Christine Sommers on this subject:

> Of course, the abuse or slighting of women must be made known and should arouse indignation. Plato himself recognized the role of righteous indignation as a mainspring of moral action. In his metaphor, indignation is the good steed helping the charioteer to stay on the path of virtue by controlling the vicious, wayward steed straining to go its own brutish way. It is the 'spirited element' in the soul that supplies the wise person with the emotional energy, the horsepower, to curb the appetites that he or she may act virtuously.[2]

Most men with at least some modicum of psychological sophistication can see the necessity for this corrective counterbalancing of "masculine" and "feminine" in our lopsided culture. But the fear and antagonism that spring from this escalating power conflict inevitably trickles down to the everyday professional and personal relations between women and men, in what some—of both sexes—find to be an increasingly negative and destructive fashion. In short, men and women may be more *fearful* of each other than ever before; and this burgeoning fear engenders anger, rage, and resentment—which further stoke the flames of fear and hostility, and so on, ad infinitum.

Fight or Flight

Fear—like frustration—is a fundamental factor in the genesis of anger, rage, and violence. As stated in chapter one, our innate, instinctive reaction to fearful situations essentially involves two separate, but related responses: *flight* from the fearful situation, or the arousal of sufficient anger and rage to *fight* against or resist that which frightens us. Physiologist W. B. Cannon (1963) called this fixed Darwinian fact the "fight or flight response."[3] For most—if not all—creatures, including humans, flight is the preferred first response to fright: even rattlesnakes will warn unwary trespassers first, and seek to escape an encounter before striking. Discretion, nature seems to be saying, is indeed the better part of valor. However, in circumstances that are, or at least are perceived to be inescapable, anger and rage arise to aid the organism in fighting for its very survival and that of its progeny.

Humans, being the psychologically complex creatures we are, tend to interpret our circumstances in terms of fight or flight even when no physical threat objectively exists. Therefore, that which we fear—for whatever reason—can quickly become that which angers or enrages us, sometimes eliciting aggressive or violent behavior. In such instances, the conventional sporting wisdom that "the best defense is a good offense" is psychologically accurate. To cite psychiatrist Willard Gaylin: "The most complicated and intricate linkage is the one between anger and fear. It is almost impossible to discuss anger without discussing fear. More important, it is almost impossible to locate either one of these emotions in an instance of human behavior without finding the other lurking in the background."[4]

Fear of Castration

Let us briefly revisit the violently literal and simultaneously symbolic castration of John Wayne Bobbitt by his wife, Lorena, in Manassas, Virginia:

> John Bobbitt, 26, was acquitted November 10 [1993] of charges that he raped Lorena Bobbitt, who is 24. During the trial, Lorena Bobbitt testified that she cut off his penis [with a kitchen knife while he slept] in retaliation for years of alleged abuse.[5]

Bobbitt's penis was surgically reattached. His wife was tried and found not guilty of "malicious wounding" due to diminished mental capacity. This case struck deep chords of anger and animosity toward men in women—some of whom openly celebrated the castration—and of anxiety, vulnerability, and fear of women in men.

Castration anxiety—not the physical kind, of course, but rather the symbolic kind—underlies much of men's fears and ensuing hostility toward women. Castration is a primal male fear. Freud (1938), in what was destined to become one of his most critically repudiated sexist speculations, postulated that prior to the age of five, little boys, upon first viewing the female genitalia, believe that all females once had a penis which was for some reason removed (*castration complex*). For factors that seem all too obvious, this conviction, said Freud, causes substantial anxiety in the boy, which peaks a short time later as part of the famous Oedipus complex, during which the boy's budding sexuality is directed toward mother and threatened with castration by father—his principal opponent and rival for mother's affections. Although it is the father who is actually seen as the castrating threat during the Oedipal conflict, it should be noted that the dread of castration, and the overwhelming anxiety that accompanies it, is engendered at first by the boy's initial interest in the opposite sex (mother). This powerful early association between sexual feelings for females and fear of castration (castration anxiety) remains with the boy into manhood, manifesting most often in an unconscious fear of women and of the "feminine" in general. This deep-seated dread, however, does not typically manifest as a physical fear of castration as Freud contended—though that too may sometimes be present (and, apparently, in certain cases like the one cited above, prove quite appropriate!). More often, it manifests as a symbolic, psychological fear or anxiety associated with the opposite sex, sometimes conceived of by psychoanalysts as the castrating, devouring *vagina dentata* (the dangerous vagina with teeth).[6]

For some men, it is this typically unconscious castration complex that compels their hostility toward women, and generates their rage. As Jungian analyst Eugene Monick explains in *Castration and Male Rage*:

> To remove, damage or insult phallos is to remove, damage or insult a man's deepest sense of himself as a male person . . . . Castration as a metaphor refers to a man's deepest fear that his manhood might be lost or seriously compromised. . . .
>
> Male rage, and the heralds of rage—discomfort, depression, dark moods, nastiness, anxiety and anger, to say nothing of hurt—are ubiquitous. Rage lurks beneath the surface of every man's composed behavior, ready to erupt when the appropriate button is pushed. No man is exempt, no matter how evolved his sensibilities, how contained his emotions, how educated his mind. Rage and its harbingers are not peculiar to men, to be sure, but there is a quality, a character, to male rage that is directly related to the ominous import of castration as a peculiarly male terror.[7]

Masculine vs. Feminine

As early as 1932, psychoanalyst Karen Horney, in a paper entitled "The Dread of Woman: Observations on a Specific Difference in the Dread Felt by Men and by Women Respectively for the Opposite Sex," disputed Freud's notion of "penis envy" on the part of the female. She maintained, notes Monick, that "male dread of the vagina . . . is not rooted in castration anxiety—from knowing there is genitalia without penis—but rather refers back to the mystery of motherhood from which the male is excluded."[8] On this point, Horney—one of the first female psychoanalysts— differs from Freud, coming closer to Carl Jung's more metaphorical interpretation of castration, and mirroring his equally controversial conceptions of *masculine* and *feminine*. Horney held that

> one of the exigencies of the biological differences between the sexes is this: that the man is actually obliged to go on proving his manhood to the woman. There is no analogous necessity for her. Even if she is frigid, she can engage in sexual intercourse and conceive and bear a child. She performs her part

by merely *being*, without any *doing*—a fact that has always filled men with admiration and resentment. The man on the other hand has to *do* something in order to fulfill himself. The ideal of 'efficiency' is a typical masculine ideal.[9]

Horney was one of the first feminist critics of Freud's—and, for that matter, almost everyone else's—"masculine" view of women from the monocular perspective of a "male-dominated western world, oriented toward the materialistic, the mechanistic, toward action based on a universe divided into subjects and objects in opposition."[10] However, despite the heroic efforts of Horney and Jung to rehabilitate the "feminine," American women—wishing, as always, to be à la mode with the current cultural trend—have today adopted the more "masculine" mode of "doing," abandoning "being": most American women now work, in addition to keeping house and assuming primary responsibility for child-rearing. Hence, they—like most other busy Americans—have scant opportunity for "wasting time" or simply just "being." We universally devalue the "feminine" mode, which is why we tend to devalue females, as feminists rightly point out.

While there has been ongoing debate as to the causes for the growing antagonism between the sexes, it seems to me that one of the most fruitful means of making sense of this phenomenon addresses the inherent, psychobiological differences between women and men in terms of the above-mentioned "masculine" and "feminine" principles. Jung used the confusingly ambiguous terms "masculine" and "feminine" not to describe rigidly dogmatic, gender-specific personality traits, but rather to connote two opposite—yet complementary—modes of being-in-the-world, two elemental qualities of existence. The "feminine principle" corresponds to the twenty-five-hundred-year-old Taoist symbol, *yin*, and refers to a more unconscious, emotional, instinctual, fertile, earthy, organic, irrational, receptive, rhythmic, natural, non-judgmental, soft, sensual, subjective, passive, poetic attitude toward life; the ancient Chinese "masculine principle," *yang*, denotes a more conscious, competitive, logical, intellectual, linear, rational, analytical, objective, forceful, active, willful, mechanistic, firm, unyielding, goal-directed, and aggressively controlling attitude. In Taoist religious symbolism, both yin and yang are depicted as two fish—one black, the other white—which together comprise a whole circle or sphere. The eternal harmonic tension between these two commingled modes of being depicts the dynamic polarity of life.[11]

Jungian analyst Irene Claremont de Castillejo distinguishes the "masculine" from the "feminine" as follows:

If we realize that on the whole the basic masculine attitude to life is that of focus, division and change; and the feminine (in either sex) is more nearly an attitude of acceptance, an awareness of the unity of all life and a readiness for relationship, then we can accept a rough division of the psyche into masculine and feminine. But today, when masculine and feminine characteristics are so interwoven in people of both sexes, it may be clearer to speak of 'focused consciousness' on the one hand and 'diffuse awareness' on the other, knowing that these qualities belong to both men and women in varying degrees.[12]

In Claremont de Castillejo's terms, "focused consciousness" gets the job done; "diffuse awareness" allows one to enjoy and appreciate the process: one complements the other.

"Focused consciousness" is penetrating, linear, analytical, and can be exemplified by the dogged, undistracted training of conscious awareness on the completion of a particular task, to the relative exclusion of all else. This is an aspect of the yang, or *masculine principle*, involving the process of actively doing something. "Diffuse awareness," on the other hand, is an unfocused form of being, in which one allows one's attention to drift freely without rational interference, and can be seen in the states of daydreaming, musing, or merely "being" instead of "doing." Whereas women, claims Claremont de Castillejo, tend naturally toward "diffuse awareness," men are more inclined to "focused consciousness." Both ways of being-in-the-world are vital to both men and women; each are useful and necessary ways of being able to perceive and respond to the world within and around us. In the practice of psychotherapy, for example, the "feminine" and "masculine" modes of being-in-the-world are equally important, regardless of the therapist's gender. There are times to be quiet and passive as the patient tells his or her story; and there are times to be active, firm, and even forceful in responding to specific symptoms or critical situations. Sensing when to shift from one mode to another comprises no small part of the art of psychotherapy.

Animus and Anima

The usually repressed and therefore underdeveloped "feminine" qualities in men are what Jung termed the *anima*; the "masculine" qualities in women were named the *animus*. "What is especially interesting," writes

Rollo May, "is that this term 'animus' means both a feeling of hostility, a violent, malevolent intention (animosity) and also *animate*, to give spirit, to enliven. All of these terms have their root in the Latin, 'anima,' soul or spirit."[13] As we will see, what Jung really meant by "anima" or "animus" is at the very root of resentment, anger, hostility, and sometimes, violent rage arising between the sexes; but it is equally responsible for romance and sexual love.

Of late, Jung and his followers have come under increasing fire from feminist therapists regarding the use of what they consider to be such "sexist" terminology. Indeed, there are numerous theoretical and practical pitfalls presented by the Jungian notions of anima and animus. Not the least of these concerns the proclivity to reify these amorphous, mythological symbols, turning them into "things"—bearing concrete, immutable, and biologically predetermined traits—rather than retaining their intended psychological utility as metaphorical concepts signifying the mental attitude most opposite, complementary, and compensatory to one's conscious personality. (As discussed later, in chapter four, some of these same snares apply also to the Jungian doctrine of the "shadow.") One common criticism has to do with the notion that only men have "anima," or "soul." Why, some psychologists want to know, can women not have anima also? And why should it be assumed that certain traits are by definition "masculine" or "feminine" per se? Why even draw such distinctions? Jung, it is justifiably argued, was a victim of his unconscious cultural biases toward women, just as was Freud. As James Hillman explains:

> Today the notions of "masculine" and "feminine" are in dispute. This dispute has helped differentiate gender roles from social ones, and even to differentiate kinds of gender identity, i.e., whether based on primary or secondary, manifest or genetic, physical or psychic gender characteristics. It has become difficult to speak of the anima as inferior femininity, since we are no longer certain just what we mean with "femininity," let alone "inferior" femininity.[14]

Certain feminist analysts in particular find fault in Jung for referring to the functions of "anima" and "animus" as "inferior." They feel insulted and demeaned by the "fact" that Jung found femininity "inferior" in men, while, at the same time, finding women's masculinity also "inferior." Jung stands charged by some with judging the feminine—and therefore, women—to be inferior to the masculine (i.e., men). Consider, for example, the following comments by one female psychologist and analytic training candidate:

[Can] . . . a theory, system and analytic mode set up by a man, whose view of women clearly has been affected by the socio-cultural prejudices of his age, . . . ever be suitable for the healing of women wounded by these very things[?] I was already chafing at what seemed a contradiction, a woman's finding herself through a psychology which, though stressing individuation and wholeness, often seems to have a subtext which states . . . she can be "healthy" and "normal" only when being one half of what is possible for a human (e.g., feeling, passive, related, yin—the things on the other side being given to men, her unconscious and her animus). . . .

. . . Jung often equates thinking with masculinity and feeling with femininity and then sees both, ipso facto, as inferior when present in the "wrong" sex.[15]

What some feminist critics seem to forget, however, is that Jung—whose position on such matters is certainly not beyond reproach—used the term "inferior" not as some final negative value judgment of the "feminine," and therefore, of women. He used "inferior" merely to reflect the undisclosed and therefore "underdeveloped," unrefined, or crude quality of the unconscious in general. Due, by definition, to the relative unconsciousness of anima and animus, we tend automatically to project our unknown, nebulous, mysterious "inner woman" or "inner man" onto the opposite sex, or in some cases, onto the same sex. This commonplace unconscious projection of anima and animus becomes the source not only of "romantic" love or infatuation with an idealized partner, but of bitterness as well in our sometimes stormy relations with the opposite sex. For one thing, it is impossible for the beloved to live up to the idealized, inhuman image of anima or animus, sooner or later leading to mutual feelings of frustration and resentment. Moreover, when the repressed qualities of anima or animus are sufficiently negative, demonization of the other may occur, often in jarring juxtaposition to idealization. In *demonization*, as will be detailed forthwith, we project all of our most negative feelings about ourselves onto someone we recognize to be our opposite. Since men and women are of opposite gender, we naturally make excellent targets on which to cast our most rejected, repudiated personal qualities, our contrasexual shadow. The result: instant animosity.

Fear of the Feminine

For men, one source of contrasexual animosity is what the Jungian analyst Erich Neumann (1905–1960) referred to as "fear of the feminine." Neumann believed that male children, in psychologically separating from their mothers in order to establish an "ego" or masculine identity of their own, come to perceive the "feminine" qualities of the mother as fearful and threatening: "The fear of the feminine normally appears as fear of the Terrible Mother, the witch."[16] In "normal" development, the boy rejects the "feminine," and heroically learns to identify with the father, shifting his allegiance from matriarchal to patriarchal values. We witness signs of this transition in the refusal of most boys to play with dolls like girls do, preferring instead the stereotypical activities of their male peer group. Failure to accomplish this Herculean labor, held Neumann, produces men who have never properly separated from their mothers, are unable to create intimate connections with other women, lack the requisite aggression to assert themselves in the world, distrust their masculine instincts, are unable to commit, or, perhaps his most controversial contention, are interested only in homosexual relationships.[17] This is, said Neumann, "pathological fear of the feminine,"[18] the psychological defense against which, I would add, consists not infrequently of contempt for the opposite sex. (Demonstrating once again that old dictum, "the best defense is a good offense.") Men's hostility toward women more often than not hides their fear of the feminine.

Neumann further suggests that women, as well as men, must also psychologically separate from the mother—albeit to some lesser degree—and, failing to do so, may similarly suffer from "fear of the feminine." In such cases, women may subtly or outrightly reject their natural femininity in favor of a more "masculine" mentality and persona.

Fear of the Masculine

What Neumann—and so many other Jungians— for some unknown reason forgets to discuss is women's *fear of the masculine*. In many ways, "fear of the masculine" in women is the contemporary cultural counterpart to "fear of the feminine" in men. Today, it is broadly believed by analytical psychologists that the female infant does not separate from the feminine field of the mother nearly as much as does the male; nor does she need to. On the contrary, it is essential for the female child to retain her close connection and affiliation with the feminine (nature) and the mother, for the mother provides the developing female with a "feminine identity" or "sense of self" (not simply persona) via the psychological processes of *mirroring* and *modeling.*[19] This lastingly intimate intermingling with the mother and matriarchal values, states Neumann, "increases the contrast to and fear of the patriarchal world."[20] Men and the masculine—especially when there has been little or mostly negative contact with them—come to connote something strange and alien, fostering in females a sort of sexual xenophobia. Hence we have one of the existential determinants of the female's more or less unconscious fear, distrust—and sometimes, defensive contempt—of the potentially overpowering masculine, which must be consciously overcome if autonomy, self-reliance, independence, and the capacity for healthy heterosexual intimacy are to be achieved.[21] The same may be said of men's defensive stance toward women. In other words, each sex must strive to become more aware of the psychological source of our mutual apprehension, mistrust and hostility in order to transcend it. Placing the blame on each other for our own problems with intimacy simply will not do.

Of course, some apprehensions must be seen in perspective: research statistics confirm that women have very real physical— not just psychological or emotional—reasons to fear men. According to one source, "34 percent to 59 percent of women reported sexual assault by their husbands. . . . In addition, severe and lethal violence against non-married women partners appears to be on the rise, . . . [having] increased quite sharply between 1976 and 1987."[22] Depending upon whose statistics one chooses to believe, three to six million American women are physically abused by men each year.[23]

Sexual Demonization

One of the most persistent forms of demonization in human history has been the misogynistic demonization of women by men. Man has always (it seems) projected some evil upon womankind—seeing in her his own "negative anima" or "shadow"—from Adam and Eve to the presently polarized state of American gender relations. The Inquisition of the early Middle Ages persecuted women as "witches," accusing them of worshipping the devil; those found "guilty" of such charges (almost all of them) were tortured and put to death in the most diabolical ways imaginable:

Who can contemplate without indignation and holy wrath the instruments of torture used by inquisitors in their infamous vocation? There are thumbscrews, there are black-smith's tongs and pincers to tear out the finger nails or to be used red-hot for pinching; there is the "Scavenger's Daughter," also the "Iron Virgin," a hollow instrument the size and figure of a woman, with knives inside which are so arranged that, when closing, the victim would be lacerated in its deadly embrace.[24]

By some estimates, the number of "witches" tormented and then murdered during the sixteenth through eighteenth centuries easily exceeds thirty-thousand, and may be in the millions.[25]

Such sadistic practices against women persist today, albeit in somewhat more secretive, clandestine, or covert forms. For instance, *clitoridectomy*—the primitive ritual of mutilating or removing the clitoris—is one notable and not-so-subtle rite de passage still widely practiced in certain cultures. From the aforementioned medieval torture devices, some readers might have recognized a few of the modern methods utilized in sexual sado-masochism, which at times include women permitting men to act out their hostile fantasies. As feminists have emphasized, women in this country are constantly derided, degraded, derogated, and devalued by men. Due largely to the numinous force that female sexuality exerts over men—coupled with the female's comparatively close contact with nature, the unconscious, and the so-called "irrational" sphere of intuition, instinct, and emotions—most men relate to women with a mixture of intense fear, animosity, and profound fascination. "All of this generates hostility toward the woman on the man's part," admits May:

> But "good" men repress this hostility—perhaps under a Victorianlike code of putting women on a pedestal—even though this hostility is shown in semirecognizable form in men's groups, men's humor, and so on. Male anger arises from the situation in which the woman seems to hold power over his own glands, some secret influence over his internal organs that may be shown in his involuntary erections. This at first surprises him, then bewitches (the word is apt) him, and finally enrages him.[26]

As previously defined in chapter one, rage is the natural, psychobiological response to that which we experience as threatening to our well-being and personal security. We each—whether woman or man, though men probably moreso—wish to maintain and thus actively seek some sense of control over our selves and our immediate environment. As the founders of Alcoholics Anonymous knew, there are some aspects of existence over which we can gain ascendancy, and some over which we cannot; and the ability to distinguish between the two is a true measure of mature wisdom. One realm in which we often find our "will to control" challenged or completely thwarted is in our romantic entanglements. When one's sense of control is lost or compromised in his or her erotic encounters, fear or anxiety can rapidly turn to resentment, anger, or rage. Sexual attraction and love can be experienced as a frightening loss of control for either sex: sexual surrender or true intimacy requires a conscious lowering of one's defenses, a courageous relinquishing of control. For both sexes, there is an instinctive fear of such potentially fateful encounters. At bottom, it is a dread of the unknown: we fear being irrevocably affected—in a sense "infected"—by the mysterious "other." We fear losing rational control over ourselves and our behavior. In some instances, we fear losing control over the beloved's behavior, believing that by controlling or manipulating him or her, we can also master our own emotions. Such attempts at domination—and both sexes have developed different techniques for dominating the other—are doomed to failure, since they are based on a thoroughly illusory premise: We cannot control other people's feelings; nor can we control the behavior of others for very long before they begin feeling resentful.[27]

For most men, women symbolize sexuality, and sexuality has long been linked to fate, temptation, sin, and evil (fig. 1). In the biblical Garden of Eden, it was the satanic snake—that daimonic symbol of libido, eros, or raw sexual energy—which convinced the first female, Eve, to taste the "forbidden fruit," and through her, caused our prototypes to be permanently cast out of Paradise. The precipitous expulsion of Adam and Eve marks the first introduction of evil to human consciousness: prior to eating from the Tree of Knowledge, humankind, like animals, knew nothing of evil. Ever since, partiarchal cultures have looked askance upon sexuality—and, by association, women, those dangerous seducers of men—as tempting, serpentine sources of evil. But such negative attitudes are by no means unique to Western culture, as Oxford professor Wendy O'Flaherty informs us: "The connection between procreation and evil, the implication that sexual creation is the epitome of sin, recurs constantly in the Hindu mythology of evil; women are not only the abstract cause of a number of evils and sins in the world, they are also used as the specific instrument of the gods to corrupt individual sages and demons."[28]

Fig. 1. Winged Sumerian demoness with talons (circa 2,000 B.C.). She is at once alluring and dangerous; angelic and demonic. From the collection of Colonel Norman Colville. Warburg Institute, London, England.

Men's prejudicial perception of the opposite sex has a long and sordid history. Consider the story of Samson, the long-haired, Hebrew Hercules, and his beautiful, shear-happy downfall, Delilah; the ever-present wicked witches in world folklore and fairy tales; the notoriously treacherous, yet unendurably desirable femme fatale; the enchanting Lorelei of Germanic legend; or the similar Grecian sirens, whose irresistably seductive song lured unsuspecting sailors to their sudden demise in Homer's Odyssey:

> First you will come to the Sirens, who bewitch every one who comes near them. If any man draws near in his innocence and listens to their voice, he never sees home again, never again will wife and little children run to greet him with joy; but the Sirens bewitch him with their melodious song. There in a meadow they sit and all round is a great heap of bones, mouldering bodies and withering skins.[31]

So strong was the attraction of the sirens' song that Odysseus ordered his men to plug their ears with wax, and—having refused the wax in order to hear for himself their excruciatingly exquisite singing—to bind him securely by ropes to the ship's mast in order to avoid disaster. The devouring Hindu goddess Kali is sometimes depicted with human skulls dangling from her belt as she demonically dances on dead men, presumably her unwary victims (fig. 2). And, of course, as every school child learns, it was Pandora, that far-too-curious female, who—like her scriptural counterpart, Eve—unwittingly released evil into the world by imprudently prying open the infamous forbidden box. According to one version of the Greek myth, Pandora was the first woman, supposedly sent by Jupiter "to Prometheus and his brother, to punish them for their presumption in stealing fire from heaven; and man, for accepting the gift." Endowed by the gods with unearthly beauty and grace, Pandora was "seized with [and succumbed to] an eager curiosity" to view the contents of a certain mysterious jar:

> Forthwith there escaped a multitude of plagues for hapless man,—such as gout, rheumatism, and colic for his body, and envy, spite, and revenge for his mind,—and scattered themselves far and wide. Pandora hastened to replace the lid! but, alas! the whole contents of the jar had escaped, one thing only excepted, which lay at the bottom, and that was hope.[30]

Fig. 2. The Hindu deity Kali. Divine and diabolical, she is both demonic and benign. From Paul Carus, *The History of the Devil and the Idea of Evil* (La Salle, Ill.: Open Court, 1974), p. 97.

Fig. 3. Gorgon. Detail of an Attic vase. Louvre, Paris, France. Courtesy Giraudon/Art Resource, New York.

Last, but certainly not least, were the hideous Greek Gorgons (fig. 3), the most fearsome feminine symbols of demonic evil:

"And they are three, the gorgons, each with wings
And snaky hair, most horrible to mortals.
Whom no man shall behold and draw again
The breath of life,"
for the reason that whoever looked at them was turned instantly into stone.[31]

Each of these female images of evil is primarily a male *projection*—an unconscious psychological defense mechanism in this case made use of by men to displace their pronounced fear of, and defensive hostility toward, the feminine. Of course, in point of fact, they exist in every one of us, in the form of denied daimonic tendencies.

Objectification of women—perceiving them mechanistically as sexual objects to be used and possessed by men—is a popular method of demonization. It is a manifestation of unconscious or conscious hostility, a sexual defense designed to make women seem sub-human. Sam Keen, in his book *Faces of the Enemy*, describes and demonstrates this psychological process of dehumanizing the enemy in war, as well as in the battle between the sexes: "In the patriarchal tradition, which has created the warrior psyche, both the female and the feminine virtues have been degraded. Women and all things feminine must be kept in control. As Nietzsche said, 'When you go to a woman do not forget the whip.' "[32] Here, Nietzsche, who never married, covertly confesses his own deep-seated dread—and compensatory contempt—of women and the feminine.

Is it any wonder that such derisive treatment and negative attitudes on the part of men toward women has ignited such fulminating rage in some women against men? Yet, while women's deserving indignation has in recent times led to more equality and many positive social changes, it has now sunk, in some quarters, to an unprecedented level of nastiness, testiness, and volatile overreactivity. This fairly palpable upsurge of feminine rage and sexual/political hypersensitivity is gradually giving rise to the vengeful demonization of men by resentful women. To cite one self-proclaimed "First Wave" feminist, Christina Hoff Sommers, from her recent critique of what she deems this "Second Wave" of fuming "gender feminists": "Theirs is a feminism of resentment that rationalizes and fosters a wholesale rancor in women that has little to do with moral indignation. Resentment may begin in and include indignation, but it is by far the more abiding passion. Resentment is 'harbored' or 'nurtured';

it 'takes root' in a subject (the victim) and remains directed at another (the culprit)."[33] Sommers refers to such mean-spirited purveyors of ill-will toward men as "resenter feminists, . . . [who speak bitterly] of backlash, siege, and an undeclared war against women" (p. 45). And in response to this putative threat, this internecine civil war, these women are fighting back. More angry women are making increasingly contentious accusations about those "evil" men. As affirmed in the following chapter, there is indeed a preponderance of evil in our epoch. Admittedly, most of their allegations are, at least to some extent, true, warranting the outrage of the victims—and the full force of the judicial system. The fact that women—at least prior to the previously mentioned Simpson verdict—are feeling more supported and encouraged by the system to speak out on such long-standing injustices and abuses is a positive development. Yet, the sheer volume and vehement tone of some complaints is suspicious; it suggests the presence of an underlying enmity and vindictive antipathy toward *all* men, and has become, in my view, yet another destructively polarizing propensity in an already antagonistic culture. Having been made scapegoats (much like the Jews or the blacks) for so many centuries, some spiteful women are now doing to men—sometimes innocent men—what has for so long been wrongly done to them. *Scapegoating* is indeed a sort of demonization: we project our deepest fears, darkest impulses, least acceptable qualities, and most despicable, malicious motivations onto another person, an organization, a religious or ethnic group, a country, a gender, or an entire race—and we hate them. By demonizing the "other," we imagine them less human, and hence, easier to despise, defame, and, if need be, even to kill.[34] While I am relieved to say that intergender hostilities have not yet approached such slaughterous proportions, as Sommers reports, vicious gender politics are especially prominent on the contemporary university campus, where so-called "political correctness" (p.c.) is wielded as a sexist weapon by certain parties to empower women and emasculate men.[35] Chauvinism is alive and well in America—on *both* sides of the gender aisle.

Gender, Rage, and Violence

The unassailable facts that most mass murderers are men, and that men commit the overwhelming majority of violent crimes, do not necessarily mean that women are any less cantankerous than their male counterparts. National surveys of domestic violence indicate that women assault their partners at about the same frequency as do men.[36] However, due to the discrepancy in physical strength between most men and women, women are usually the more seriously injured party during these donnybrooks. Perhaps stemming less from a lack of violent intent than what Freud once referred to in children as "weakness of limb," women still find themselves at a distinct disadvantage in this very literal "battle of the sexes." To cite psychologist and criminologist Anne Campbell: "Maleness and aggression have become linked to the point where it is easy to forget about women's aggression. It takes place far less often than men's, and it rarely makes headlines. It is private, unrecognized, and frequently misunderstood."[37] Campbell, whose research included interviewing women in both the United States and England, contends that women have different styles of perceiving and thinking about their own anger and rage than do men, and therefore, tend to deal with it differently. She points out that on the whole, women experience greater guilt and anxiety about their anger, causing them to suppress it more so than men. As socially unacceptable as the expression of anger or rage may be for middle class American men, it appears to be the least acceptable in women. Angry men, as the absurd stereotype goes, are typically not seen as "bullies," but, instead, are "aggressive"; angry women are all vixens, shrews, or "castrating bitches." Especially prone to inhibiting, "swallowing," or concealing their anger, women—like men—may also be driven to violent behavior, albeit much more slowly: "The vast majority of homicides committed by women are of their husbands or lovers, specifically those who have physically abused them."[38] In such situations, years or decades of passivity and restraint culminate in a violent eruption of chronically repressed rage. Even in the profusion of cases wherein women remain passive rather than becoming violent, Campbell concludes—correctly, in my opinion—that "the personal distress that . . . [their lack of self-assertion] causes women, and their higher rates of both neurosis and depression, are symptoms of the internal turmoil that comes with the daily stifling of one's anger."[39]

For many modern women, the only visible alternative to such suffocating passivity, slavery, and perennial victimhood has been to get angry, very angry, to begin venting their smoldering rage. The target for this resurgent rage is men, their presumed enemy. Women's anger and rage have proven to be positive forces for much-needed changes and corrections in men's mistaken attitudes toward them. Unfortunately, the proverbial pendulum now seems for growing numbers to have swung from one extreme of feminine passivity and acquiescence to an altogether opposite—and equally unviable—pole of resentment and retribution. Such

vituperative tactics serve only to aggravate the vicious circle of fear, defensive backlash, and animosity between women and men. Under these warlike conditions, where battle lines are drawn exclusively on the basis of gender, the festering resentment, hostility, and contempt harbored by some women toward men for so long can contaminate even the most conscientious efforts at constructive self-assertion. But if women are willing to bear this in mind as they go about righting the wrongs they see, maybe some new, more moderate middle ground can be found upon which to securely stand. We men, as is widely known, have our own notorious difficulties dealing with anger and rage, and do not make desirable role models in these matters. Women must find their own way.

For men are markedly the more violently aggressive of the two sexes, and, throughout history, have made precious little progress in peacefully managing anger and rage. It has been mainly men who wage wars, pillage cities, rape women, and do irrevocable violence to the environment. Men have always been the greatest mongers of aggression and violence. We men must get better at mitigating these tendencies. Nevertheless, modern women—as they become more conscious of their own anger and rage—must also, like men, learn to confront their *equal* capacity for negative aggression, hostility, and even violence. Continuing to project these "masculine" tendencies onto men—either individually or as a gender—is a dangerously outmoded female defense mechanism. Women are not immune to the destructive predisposition historically associated with men: equality pertains also to the inherent potentialities for evil in either sex. In this perilous age of guns, bombs, and other high-tech killing devices, violence can no longer be conceived of as simply a function of brute strength. Moreover, violence—like evil in general—comes in various forms and subtle gradations. Violence also has its feminine face.

We are all—both women and men—required to come to terms with our daimonic tendencies. Refusal to do so will lead only to the further erosion of our already brittle gender relations—and beyond. Anger and rage are daimonic forms of power. And along with the intoxicating concomitants of power comes the very real human responsibility for consciously choosing how to employ this power: Shall we exercise it in the pursuit of good or evil; self-assertion or self-serving villainy; cooperation or coercion; reconciliation or revenge? That is the foremost question facing men and women today. And, in the broadest sense, it is this common quest toward which the remainder of this book is dedicated.

3

The Psychology of Evil
Devils, Demons, and the Daimonic

Evil has become a determinant reality. It can no longer be
dismissed from the world by a circumlocution. We must learn to
handle it, since it is here to stay. How we can live with it without
terrible consequences cannot for the present be conceived.
— C. G. Jung, *Memories, Dreams, Reflections*

Anger was regarded in the ancient world as something
pre-eminently evil, stirred up like the violence of thunder
and lightning by powerful supernatural forces.
—*Encyclopedia of Witchcraft and Demonology*

The belief in a supernatural source of evil is not necessary;
men alone are quite capable of every wickedness.
—Joseph Conrad, *Under Western Eyes*

Hostility, hatred, and violence are the greatest evils we have to contend with today. Evil is now—ever has been, and ever will be—an
existential reality, an inescapable fact with which we mortals must reckon.
In virtually every culture there has existed some word for *evil*, a universal, linguistic acknowledgment of the archetypal presence of "something

that brings sorrow, distress, or calamity . . . ; the fact of suffering, misfortune, and wrongdoing."[1] Yet another of Webster's traditional definitions links the English word *evil* with all that is "angry, . . . wrathful, . . . [and] malignant."[2] The term *evil* has always been closely associated with anger, rage, and, of course, violence. But today we seem uncomfortable with this antiquated concept. Our discomfort resides largely in the religious and theological implications of evil, based on values, ethics, and morals that many today find judgmental, dogmatic, and passé. In a secular society like ours, we Americans have tended to avoid biblical characterizations such as "sin," "wickedness," "iniquity," and "evil."[3] Nevertheless, as Jungian analyst Liliane Frey-Rohn rightly remarks: "Evil is a phenomenon that exists and has always existed only in the human world. Animals know nothing of it. But there is no form of religion, of ethics, or of community life in which it is not important. What is more, we need to discriminate between evil and good in our daily life with others, and as psychologists in our professional work. And yet it is difficult to give a precise definition of what we mean psychologically by these terms."[4]

Evil is an actuality, whether or not we choose to deny it. In their 1971 anthology, *Sanctions for Evil,* social psychologists Nevitt Sanford and Craig Comstock cogently justify resurrecting the religiously tainted term "evil": "In using the word *evil,* we mean not that an act or pattern of life is necessarily a sin or a crime according to some law, but rather that it leads to damage or pain suffered by people, to social destructiveness of a degree so serious as to call for use of an ancient, heavily freighted term."[5] When employed in this sense, *evil* is synonymous with "senseless violence." But, on a still subtler level, evil can be considered *that tendency which—whether in oneself or others—would inhibit personal growth and expansion, destroy or limit innate potentialities, curtail freedom, fragment or disintegrate the personality, and diminish the quality of interpersonal relationships.*

The fact that evil, as defined above, exists more or less throughout our world seems incontrovertible. We see evil every day in its infernally multifarious forms. First, there are the cosmic, supernatural, transpersonal, or natural evils like floods, famine, fire, drought, disease, earthquakes, tornadoes, hurricanes, and harmful, unforeseeable accidents that wreak untimely death havoc, and unmentionable suffering on humanity. This is the metaphysical or "existential evil" with which the biblical Book of Job concerns itself, and which religions worldwide try mightily to explain. Existential evil is an ineluctable part of our human destiny, and one with which we must reckon as best we can, without closing ourselves off to its tragic, intrinsic reality. But there is, of course, another kind of evil at large: human evil, "man's inhumanity to man" in the most panoramic sense. By "human evil," I mean *those attitudes and behaviors that promote excessive interpersonal aggression, cruelty, hostility, disregard for the integrity of others, self-destructiveness, psychopathology, and human misery in general.* Human evil can be perpetrated by a single individual (personal evil) or by a group, a country, or an entire culture (collective evil). The Nazi atrocities directly or indirectly engaged in by the German people dramatically exemplify the latter.

The most pernicious form of evil today (as further discussed in chapter six), may be madness, mental illness, or psychopathology: It is evil in this guise, and in its most radical manifestation—destructive violence—that has now become the target of such intense psychological scrutiny and treatment. With escalating urgency, contemporary culture calls upon the psychologist and psychiatrist to do battle with this evil: to explain, control, or "cure" bedeviled individuals who tend to be homicidal, suicidal, sexually perverted, assaultive, abusive, addicted, anorexic, alcoholic, or otherwise violently destructive to themselves and/ or others. *This*—I am speaking here of the suffering, not the sufferers— is the true reality of evil today! And it raises the following question: How can the skilled psychologist—let alone the average citizen—even begin to effectively cope with evil without more fully comprehending its fundamental nature?

Though it may seem to some an anachronistic throwback to a by-gone era, my preoccupation with the psychology of evil is not without twentieth-century precedent. Sigmund Freud, for instance, wrestled with this thorny issue, as have many other notable psychologists and psychiatrists, including Carl Jung, Erich Fromm, Bruno Bettelheim, Viktor Frankl, Karl Menninger, Robert Lifton, Rollo May, and most recently, M. Scott Peck.[6] Freud's somewhat pessimistic solution took the eventual form of an evil "death instinct" (Thanatos) doing eternal battle with a good "life instinct" (Eros), with evil ever-dominating this tragic duel. C. G. Jung, drawing upon Nietzsche's existential philosophy, spoke of the "shadow" to portray the problem of personal and collective evil. His position, summarized here by Frey-Rohn, was that social morality can never be considered the causal source of evil: it only "becomes negative [i.e., evil] whenever the individual takes its commandments and prohibitions as absolutes, and ignores his other impulsions. It is not the cultural canon itself, therefore, but the moral attitude of the individual which we must hold responsible for what is pathological, negative, and evil."[7] Frey-Rohn refers to the subjective relativity of "good" and "evil," and, more importantly, the individual's personal responsibility for deciding what is good or evil for themselves rather than relying solely on external laws, rules, and regulations.[8]

It is admittedly tempting to dismiss the reality of evil entirely due to its inherent subjectivity and relativity. As that wise bard William Shakespeare bade Hamlet speak: "For there is nothing either good or bad, but thinking makes it so."[9] This recognition of the relativity of good and evil, and its basis in egoistic evaluations of right and wrong, positive and negative, has a time-honored tradition in Asian religion and Oriental philosophy. But as Jung said, the fact that the conceptions of "good" and "evil" are limited inventions of the human mind (ego consciousness), convenient cognitive categories into which we try to neatly sort the stuff of life, does not detract from the vital importance of properly discerning between them. For without such psychological distinctions, what ethics will serve to guide our daily behavior? On what moral ground can we stand in making the many minor and major day-to-day decisions modern life demands? To cite Justin Martyr on this matter: " 'The worst evil of all is to say that neither good nor evil is anything in itself, but that they are only matters of human opinion.' "[10]

Evil has an archetypal—or universal—quality. "There is no religion in the world," writes philosopher Paul Carus, "but has its demons or evil monsters who represent pain, misery, and destruction." To those who would deny the reality of evil, its existential facticity, arguing that its relativity ("One man's meat is another man's poison") and subjectivity (what I view as evil, another sees as good) render it illusory, Carus responds: "Evil and good may be relative, but relativity does not imply non-existence. Relations are facts too."[11] To merrily dismiss evil as merely a mental illusion (or "Maya" as Buddhists term it) is to cowardly duck the difficult task and fateful human accountability for consciously coming to know good and evil.[12] Evil is a very real phenomenon. But it is not a "thing," with physical properties of its own apart from those human actions which comprise it; nor is it an "entity" with a will of its own, as the traditional doctrine of the devil advocates. Evil is a *process* in which we humans more or less inevitably participate. Indeed, it is a psychological—or spiritual, if you prefer—*process of negation*. By "negation" I do not, however, mean non-existence. Negation is as real a force in the world as affirmation; negative and positive are simply two opposite poles of one, single reality. (Consider, for example, a magnet with its two opposing yet integrally related poles.) As Jungian analyst and Episcopal priest John Sanford puts it, the Christian doctrine of *privatio boni* (the "nothingness" of evil) put forth by Augustine (354–430 A.D.), "does not deny the reality of evil but states what evil is. It says that while evil exists it can only exist by living off the good and cannot exist on its own."[13] Of course, the same may be said of the "good," which cannot exist on its own either, without some reference and comparison to that which is "evil."

But, if finally we accept the necessity of discerning between evil and good, who then shall be the crowning connoisseur of good and evil? The individual? The community? The court? The State? The priest, rabbi, or psychotherapist? How can we make constructive, humane use of such categories? To whom shall they apply? And for what purpose?

Psychiatrist M. Scott Peck, whose perspectives will be explored further in chapter seven, proclaims "that [human] evil can be defined as a specific form of mental illness and should be subject to at least the same intensity of scientific investigation that we would devote to some other major psychiatric disease."[14] He defines "evil" as a negative force "residing either inside or outside of human beings, that seeks to kill life or liveliness" (pp. 42–43). For Peck, the primary root of most human evil is "malignant narcissism" (p. 78), a term taken from Erich Fromm.[15] Peck identifies evil people not "by the illegality of their deeds or the magnitude of their sins" (p. 71), nor by their evil acts, for then "we should all be evil, because we all do evil things" (p. 70). It is rather "the consistency of their sins" (p. 71), says Peck, that makes people 'evil' or 'not evil.' In other words, it is the chronic self-deception, ego-inflation, and "unsubmitted will" (p. 78), the constant lying to themselves and others, and their rabid refusal to confront their own flaws that characterize Peck's "people of the lie."

Peck's equation of human evil with one specific sort of psychopathology—*pathological narcissism*—is accurate up to a point. Pathological or malignant narcissism is indeed a variant of human evil, as we shall later see. But human evil can never be simply distilled to one particular psychiatric diagnosis, as Peck proposes. Were such a thing possible—which it is not—we might, like Peck, be enticed to "diagnose" the "evil ones" around us, and—like the witches or Jews—try to "treat," isolate, sterilize, or exterminate them. The problem with Peck's perception of evil, in my view, is his proclivity to project evil exclusively onto some small segment of the population, instead of acknowledging its imminent presence in each of us. Peck pathologizes evil, seeking to turn the term "evil" into a formal psychodiagnostic category specifically describing particular character traits.[16] Yet, in a very real sense, I submit that *all psychopathology is a sort of evil,* insofar as it entails serious human suffering. While it may be very tempting to succumb to Peck's argument that evil insidiously manifests itself most commonly in deceptively well-functioning but sub-tly pathological personalities—or in blatant caricatures of evil like Ted Bundy, Jim Jones, Charles Manson, or Richard Allen Davis—we would do well to remember that evil remains an ever-present, archetypal poten-tiality in each of us. To naively or narcissistically think otherwise is tan-tamount to denying the personal capacity for evil—the permanent presence of the "shadow" or the "daimonic"—forever dwelling in the fathomless depths of each and every fallible human being. Such denial is evil of the most insipid, prosaic, and dangerous kind.

Prefiguring Peck, Rollo May long held that here in America—with its youthful optimism and naiveté—we comprehend little of evil's true nature, and are thus pitifully ill-prepared to contend with it. As a psycho-therapist, May mostly concerned himself with the problem of personal or *individual evil*. While fully recognizing the grave risks (such as war) and intrapsychic influences of group or *collective evil* on the individual, May maintained that even in the often crushing influences of collective pres-sures, we must be mindful of the crucial role played by the individual in evil: "Evil is certainly not exclusively within the self—it is also the result of our social interrelationships—but the participation of the self in evil cannot be overlooked."[17]

Whence comes evil? To what extent are we witting or unwitting participants in evil? What is the psychological process by which we par-ticipate in evil? And what can be done—if anything—to derail this destruc-tive process and, to some degree, decrease personal and collective evil? These are a few of the age-old questions we turn to next.

Demons

From time immemorial, spirits, devils, or demons have been believed to be the source, and sometimes the personification, of evil (see fig. 4). Sigmund Freud suggested that our forebears—who apparently had no short supply of their own anger, rage, and resentments—projected their hostility onto imaginary demons (fig. 5). Such superstitions as the belief in the existence of demons, said Freud, derive "from suppressed hostile and cruel impulses. The greater part of superstition signifies fear of impending evil, and he who has frequently wished evil to others, but because of a good bringing-up, has repressed the same into the uncon-scious, will be particularly apt to expect punishment for such unconscious evil in the form of a misfortune threatening him from without."[18] What

Fig. 4.   Pazuzu, evil male demon, has the stinging tail of a scorpion
(Mesopotamian, circa 500 B.C.). Louvre, Paris, France.

Fig. 5. Asmodeus, ancient Hebrew demon of anger, rage, and lustful violence (Tobit 3:8). Considered the king of demons, his main function was to promote marital discord. Courtesy of Ernst and Johanna Lehner, *A Picture Book of Devils, Demons and Witchcraft* (New York: Dover, 1971), p. 22.

is more, Freud considered it "quite possible that the whole conception of demons was derived from the extremely important relation to the dead," adding that "nothing testifies so much to the influence of mourning on the origin of belief in demons as the fact that demons were always taken to be the spirits of persons not long dead."[19]

Demons served as ready scapegoats and repositories for all sorts of unacceptable, threatening human impulses, such as anger, rage, guilt, and sexuality. Moreover, writes theologian Gerardus van der

Leeuw, "horror and shuddering, sudden fright and the frantic insanity of dread, all receive their form in the demon; this represents the absolute horribleness of the world, the incalculable force which weaves its web around us and threatens to seize us. Hence all the vagueness and ambiguity of the demon's nature. . . . The demons' behaviour is arbitrary, purposeless, even clumsy and ridiculous, but despite this it is no less terrifying."[20] (See fig. 6.) For this reason, demons are deemed evil, designated by us to carry all of those dreaded aspects of human

Fig. 6.   Murderous Assyrian-Babylonian demon of disease, death, and other earthly evils. Courtesy of Ernst and Johanna Lehner, *A Picture Book of Devils, Demons and Witchcraft* (New York: Dover, 1971), p. 1.

nature we find too abominable, despicable, and monstrous to bear. But the popular, one-sidedly negative view of demons is simplistic and psychologically unsophisticated. For Freud informs us that those identical demons felt to be angry spirits of recently deceased relatives, though feared at first by our forebears, played an important part in the mourning process: once confronted and psychologically assimilated by the bereaved mourners, these same evil demons were "revered as ancestors and appealed to for help in times of distress."[21] We know from psychotherapy that survivors of the death of loved ones can suffer a great deal of guilt, and anger at having been abandoned. Perhaps our primitive predecessors came to terms with their own projected anger by accepting and befriending the furious "demons" of their dead: by so doing, they, in effect, psychologically transformed their own wrathful feelings from menacing foes to friendly emotional forces and spiritual allies.

It is entirely possible, from what little we understand of their practice of *trephining,* that inhabitants of the Stone Age, some five hundred thousand years ago, were attempting to release evil spirits from the physically or mentally ill by surgically excising sizable sections of their skulls. *Demonology*—the belief in the existence of spirits, demons, or devils—is probably the primeval prototype of the modern science of *psychopathology*: both paradigms seek to make sense of mental illness and aberrant human behavior. "The view that demons . . . are responsible for the origin of evil," writes mythologist Wendy Doniger O'Flaherty, "is found in its purest form in Manicheanism, a religion originating in Persia in the third century A.D., composed of Gnostic Christian, Mazdean, and pagan elements, and representing Satan as coeternal with God."[22] The far-reaching influence of demonology can be found in the ancient cultures of the Hebrews, Chinese, Egyptians, and Greeks, as well as in medieval Europe and colonial America. Physician-turned-philosopher Karl Jaspers defined *demonology* as follows: "We call demonology a conception which makes being reside in powers, in effective form-constituting forces, constructive and destructive, that is in demons, benevolent and malignant, in many gods; these powers are perceived as directly evident, and the perceptions are translated as a doctrine."[23]

Our modern English terms "demon" and "demonic" are derived from the Latin spelling popularized during the Middle Ages: *daemon* and *daemonic.* Carl Jung, referring to the medieval concept of the *daemonic,* professed that "from the psychological point of view demons are nothing other than intruders from the unconscious, spontaneous irruptions of unconscious complexes into the continuity of the conscious process. Complexes are comparable to demons which fitfully harass our thought and actions; hence in antiquity and the Middle Ages acute neurotic disturbances were conceived as [daemonic] possession."[24] Indeed, prior to the seventeenth-century philosophical revelations of René Descartes—which later spawned the scientific objectivism that so characterizes the contemporary study of psychopathology—it was commonly believed that an emotional disorder, madness, lunacy, or insanity was literally the work of evil demons, who in their winged travels would inhabit the unwitting body (or brain) of the unfortunate sufferer. This archetypal imagery of invasive flying entities with supernatural powers is still evident today in such colloquialisms for insanity as having "bats in the belfry," and in the delusional patient's obstinate belief about being manipulated by "aliens" in flying saucers.[25]

Even Hippocrates (5 B.C.), the father of modern medicine, was first trained as an exorcist. Bernard Dietrich explains that in ancient Greece, "the period of personal gods was preceded by that of a belief in daemonism or animism: each occurrence and experience in human life was attributed to the agency of a daemon. But these daemons, in the beginning, were not imagined as personal beings, but as abstract forces in the neuter gender. . . . "[26] The original, archaic Greek word for one of these wondrous beings, described by Hesiod and others as "invisible and wrapped in mist," was *daimon* (δαίμων).[27]

The Daimonic

Rollo May made use of the classical Greek idea of the daimon to provide the basis for his mythological model of the *daimonic*. "The daimonic," wrote May,

> is *any natural function which has the power to take over the whole person*. Sex and eros, anger and rage, and the craving for power are examples. The daimonic can be either creative or destructive and is normally both. When this power goes awry, and one element usurps control over the total personality, we have "daimon possession," the traditional name through history for psychosis. The daimonic is obviously not an entity but refers to a fundamental, archetypal function of human experience—an existential reality. . . . [28]

Moreover, May maintained that violence "is the daimonic gone awry. It is 'demon possession' in its starkest form. Our age is one of transition, in which the normal channels for utilizing the daimonic are denied; and such ages tend to be times when the daimonic is expressed in its most destructive form."[29] Senseless violence, as will be demonstrated, is the daimonic run amuck.

The genesis of the idea of the "daimon"—pronounced "di-mone"— is decidedly difficult to pin down. We do know that Empedocles, the fifth-century B.C., pre-Socratic Greek philosopher, employed this term in describing the psyche or soul; to be even more precise, he identified daimon with *self*. Reginald Barrow reports that the

> histories of Greek Religion or Philosophy do not usually say much, if anything, about daemons. Though the idea occurs as early as Homer, it plays little or no part in recognised cults; for it had no mythology of its own; rather it attached itself to existing beliefs. In philosophy it lurks in the background from Thales, to whom "the universe is alive and full of daemons", through Heraclitus and Xenophanes, to Plato and his pupil Xenocrates, who elaborated it in detail. . . . In Hesiod the daemons are the souls of heroes of past ages and now kindly to men; in Aeschylus the dead become daemons; in Theognis and Menander the daemon is the guardian angel of the individual man and sometimes of a family.[30]

Some classical scholars say that the term "daimon" was used by writers such as Homer, Hesiod, and Plato as a synonym for the word *theos,* or *god*; still others, like van der Leeuw, point to a definite distinction between these terms: The term "daimon" referred to something indeterminate, invisible, incorporeal, amorphous and unknown, whereas "theos" was the *personification* of a god, such as Zeus or Apollo. The daimon was that divine, mediating spiritual power that impelled one's actions and determined one's destiny. It was, in the judgment of most scholars, inborn and immortal, embodying all innate talents, tendencies (both positive and negative), and natural abilities. Indeed, one's daimon manifested as a sort of fateful "soul" which spurred one on toward good or evil.

The earliest pre-Christian conception of daimons or *daimones* (δαίμονες) considered them ambiguous—rather than exclusively evil— beings, and predates even the great philosophers of ancient Greece. This latter view coincides with that of M. L. von Franz, who writes that "in pre-Hellenic Greece the demons, as in Egypt, were part of a nameless collectivity."[31] It further corresponds with May's own conception of the daimonic as an essentially undifferentiated, impersonal, primal force of nature. "Because," says Barrow,

> the daemons have left few memorials of themselves in architecture and literature, their importance tends to be overlooked. . . . They are omnipresent and all-powerful, they are embedded deep in the religious memories of the peoples, for they go back to days long before the days of Greek philosophy and religion. The cults of the Greek states, recognised and officially sanctioned, were only one-tenth of the iceberg; the rest, the submerged nine-tenths, were the daemons. They lurk behind the Hebrew scriptures in spite of the careful revision in the interests of monotheism, and in the post-exilic literature vague supernatural beings abound. The New Testament is full of them. . . . It is the Christian writers, from Justin onwards, who haul the daemons out into the open and battle with them; they leave no doubt about the dimensions of the evil they were combating; and they were not fighting with shadows.[32]

Minoan (3,000–1,100 B.C.) and Mycenaean (1,500–1,100 B.C.) daimons were seen as attendants or servants to deities, rather than as deities themselves, and were imagined and represented as half human/half animal figures, such as the fearsome Minotaur (figs. 6 and 7). It was believed during Homer's day (around 800 B.C.) that all human ailments were brought about by daimons. But daimons could also cure, heal, and bestow the blessings of good health, happiness, and harmony. Though there is some debate as to its pre-Homeric presence, E. R. Dodds indicates that the idea of the daimon appears in both the *Iliad* and the *Odyssey*. "The most characteristic feature of the *Odyssey* is the way in which its personages ascribe all sorts of mental (as well as physical) events to the intervention of a nameless and indeterminate daemon or 'god' or 'gods.' "[33] Plato (428–347 B.C.) later alluded to the daimonic realm in his writings, referring to the great god of love, Eros, as "a daimon," and relating the story of the *daimonion* of Socrates: that supposedly supernatural "voice" inside the head of Socrates, which spoke to him whenever he was about to make some mistaken decision. In Plato's *Symposium*, wise woman Diotima of Mantineia describes the daimonic this way:

Fig. 7.   Mithraic deity, Aion, both monstrous and beneficent (second century). Museo Gregoriano Profano, Vatican Museums, Vatican State. Courtesy Alinari/Art Resource, New York.

"All that is daemonic lies between the mortal and the immortal. Its functions are to interpret to men communications from the gods—commandments and favours from the gods in return for men's attentions—and to convey prayers and offerings from men to the gods. Being thus between men and gods the daemon fills up the gap and so acts as a link joining up the whole. Through it as intermediary pass all forms of divination and sorcery. God does not mix with man; the daemonic is the agency through which intercourse and converse take place between men and gods, whether in waking visions or in dreams."[34]

Plutarch, who declared that the Egyptian deities Isis and Osiris were themselves distinguished daimons, also wrote of the "daimonic sign" of Socrates, says Dodds, speculating that "pure souls on occasion can come into contact with spiritual power, can hear a spiritual, but wordless, voice and be guided accordingly. For this spiritual power the word is daemon, but a theory of daemons is not further elaborated."[35] Whether it was indeed a humanlike voice which spoke to Socrates since childhood, or some less distinct, "wordless," more amorphous mental phenomenon, is impossible to say. In any case, it was in fact his fervent faith in this guiding spirit or "guardian angel"—his treasured *daimonion*—which eventually brought about the indictment, trial, and death of Socrates for teaching his students "false *daimonia*." The Athenians found his philosophy sacreligious, and threatening to the established order, not unlike the Pharisaical objections to the preachings of Jesus some four centuries hence. During his heyday, however, Socrates attributed to this uncanny daimonion his success (or failure) as a philosophical instructor:

"For there are many whom it resists. They cannot benefit from intercourse with me, and I am not capable of such intercourse. In many cases, it presents no obstacle to companionship, but the persons concerned derive no aid from it. But if the . . . [daimonic] power participates helpfully in the relationship, the companions immediately find themselves on the path of progress."[36]

The possible implications of this statement for the practice of psychotherapy are profound. In the words of one insightful scholar, "Plutarch reveals to us the function of these *daimones*. They are the source in us of emotions good and bad."[37] It is of no small significance that Socrates seems to have experienced his daimonic guidance always in the form of a warning or resistance or opposition to some possible course of action; this was later, as we shall see, also to become the role of the Judeo-

Christian conception of Satan: to oppose, obstruct, accuse, or lead astray the sinner—or the potential sinner. Both were adversarial "voices": the Socratic daimonion doing good; Satan doing evil.

The "precise definition of the vague terms 'daemon' and 'daemonios' was something of a novelty in Plato's day," according to Dodds, "but in the second century after Christ it was the expression of a truism. Virtually everyone, pagan, Jewish, Christian or Gnostic, believed in the existence of these beings and in their function as mediators, whether he called them daemons or angels or aions or simply 'spirits.' "[38] In Greece, "there were two types of daemon," writes B. C. Dietrich:

> One was a group of spirits who were imagined to exist within nature, above the earth, and who had deep roots in popular fancy throughout the world and were live figures in national mythology. These were the nymphs. . . . and even [the] Muses. . . . The second group consisted of the spirits that lived beneath the earth, or perhaps within it. They represented the forces of growth in nature, her phenomena, and her great power of good and ill for man. Allied to these nature spirits were the daemons of the dead and of the underworld.[39]

M. L. von Franz observes that "the word *daimon* comes from *daiomai*, which means 'divide,' 'distribute,' 'allot,' 'assign,' and originally referred to a momentarily perceptible divine activity, such as a startled horse, a failure in work, illness, madness, terror in certain natural spots."[40] As Jung put it, "the Greek words *daimon* and *daimonion* express a determining power which comes upon man from outside, like providence, or fate, though the ethical decision is left to man."[41] Daimons, at first, were potentially both good and evil, constructive and destructive, depending in part upon how the individual would relate to them. But it was one of Plato's students, Xenocrates, writes historian Jeffrey Burton Russell, who "established the negativity of the term by dividing the good gods from the evil demons and shifting the destructive qualities of the gods onto the demons. . . . The negative meaning was further set in the second century B.C.E. by the Septuagint translation of the Hebrew Bible into Greek, which used *daimonion* to denote the evil spirits of the Hebrews."[42]

Thus began the gradual degradation of the daimon into our modern misunderstanding of the *demon* as exclusively evil, and the ascendancy of the Judeo-Christian conception of the *devil* as evil incarnate. During "the Hellenistic and Christian eras," writes May, "the dualistic split between the good and evil side of the daimon became more pronounced. We now have a celestial population separated into two camps—devils and angels, the former on the side of their leader, Satan, and the latter allied to God. Though such developments are never fully rationalized, there must have existed in those days the expectation that with this split it would be easier for man to face and conquer the devil."[43] Around the rise of Christianity, the old daimons started to disappear, their Janus-like nature torn asunder. "Evil" and "good" were neatly divided, and the daimons, now isolated from their positive pole, eventually took on the negative meaning and identity of what we today term demons. These destructive demons were believed by the Church to be commanded by that veritable embodiment of all evil: the devil (figs. 8 and 9).

Fig. 8.   St. Michael slaying the dragon of sin (Revelation 12: 9), from an eleventh-century bible. From Ernst and Johanna Lerner, *A Fantastic Bestiary: Beasts and Monsters in Myth and Folklore* (New York: Tudor, 1969), p. 13.

Fig. 9.   The Tempter (Satan) in the form
of a winged serpent whispering into the ear
of St. Martin (eleventh century). Courtesy
of Ernst and Johanna Lehner, *A Picture
Book of Devils, Demons and Witchcraft* (New
York: Dover, 1971), p. xvii.

The Devil

Jeffrey Burton Russell, who has written extensively on the history of Satan,
informs us that "the word 'Devil' comes indirectly from the Hebrew *satan*,
'one who obstructs,' and [that] the Devil and Satan are one in origin and
concept." He further explains, however, that

> the origins of the Devil and of the demons are quite distinct.
> The demons derived from the minor evil spirits of the Near
> East, whereas the Devil derives from the Hebrew mal'ak, *the
> shadow of the Lord* [my emphasis], and the Mazdaist principle

of evil itself. The New Testament maintained the distinction by differentiating between the terms *diabolos* and *daimonion*, but it was a distinction that was often blurred, and many English translations muddle it further by translating *daimonion* as "devil." . . . By the first century of the Christian era . . . evil spirits usually went by the name of *daimonia*, "demons." This Hellenistic classification would lump Satan with the other evil spirits in the category of *daimonia*.[44]

But according to a different authority, "the word *devil* is a diminutive from the root *div* and from it we get the word *divine*; devil merely means 'little god.' "[45] This multiplicity of "little gods" can be found in the New Testament, demonstrated in this "case history" of Jesus curing a demoniac:

> When he [Jesus] had come out of the boat, there met him out of the tombs a man with an unclean spirit, who lived among the tombs; and no one could bind him any more, even with a chain; for he had often been bound with fetters and chains, but the chains he wrenched apart, and the fetters he broke in pieces; and no one had the strength to subdue him. Night and day among the tombs and on the mountains he was always crying out, and bruising himself with stones. . . . [Jesus] said to him, "Come out of the man, you unclean spirit." And Jesus asked him, "What is your name?" He replied, "My name is Legion; for we are many." (Mark 5:2–9)[46]

Professor Elaine Pagels of Princeton University points out that in the Hebraic tradition, a *satan* was always an angel (from the Greek *angelos*), a celestial messenger sent by god in the form of an obstacle or obstruction to human action. But this "satan," states Pagels, "is not necessarily malevolent. God sends him like the angel of death, to perform a specific task, although one that human beings may not appreciate. . . . Thus the *satan* may simply have been sent by the Lord to protect a person from worse harm." Prior to its being employed as a pejorative term denouncing and demonizing the perceived enemies of early Christianity, or anthropomorphized into the supernatural essence of evil, a satan was merely one of the many daimones, or "spirit energies," writes Pagels, "the forces that energize all natural processes. . . ."[47]And, as Jungian analyst James Hillman notes, for the almost two millennia since this distortion of the originally ambiguous daimones into evil demons, devils, or Satan, "the denial of daimons and their exorcism has been part and parcel of Christian psychology, leaving the Western psyche few means but the hallucinations of insanity for recognizing daimonic reality."[48] The epoch-making Cartesian approach of the late Rennaissance separated mind and body, subject and object, and deemed "real" only that aspect of human experience which is objectively measurable, or quantifiable. This advance led, notoriously, to the abject neglect of "irrational," subjective phenomena. Descartes' seventeenth-century breakthrough was a dubious development in human thought: It enabled us to rid the world of superstition, witchcraft, magic, and the gamut of mythical creatures—both evil and good—in one clean, scientific sweep.

But at what spiritual or psychological cost was the daimonic done away with during the Enlightenment? What the well-intentioned creators and perpetuators of this artificial dichotomy overlook, is that we can hardly hope to conquer devils and demons simply by expelling and destroying them—the latter being impossible without maiming ourselves in the process. The daimons cannot be eradicated, as though they were some unwanted pests invading one's fields or home. We might succeed in dispelling them temporarily; but they have only gone underground, burrowing into our rich psyches like cicadas, waiting to be reborn when the time is right. To drive the daimons away, to banish them from consciousness, is to impoverish ourselves and our world; to build a world no longer animated and alive, but dead, disenchanted, and inanimate. A more psychologically or spiritually sound solution may be achieved only by confronting and meaningfully assimilating what these daimons symbolize for us today into our selves and our daily lives. Pagan peoples managed to maintain a proper relationship with the daimonic realm, and, in some isolated cases—such as the Aborigines of Australia or certain primitive Amazonian tribes still miraculously untouched by civilization—continue to do so even today. For such simple natives, as for their forebears, says van der Leeuw, "each Thing has its own mysterious and incalculable aspect, each experience of Nature its own demon: pixies, moss and wood fairies, elves, dwarfs, *etc.*, inhabit waters and forests, fields and the subterranean caverns of the mountains, . . . and to this analogies can be found everywhere."[49] Naive, innocent minds perceive all of nature to be alive and animated with every manner of specter, sprite, gnome, bogey, fairy, and hobgoblin imaginable. Each spirit has its place in life, and is the object of worshipful veneration—and fear. But for most of us today, this natural *participation mystique* has become a lost way of being-in-the-world from which we are far removed—even with our own newly found "gods" of

science, technology, psychology, and New Age spiritualism. We have deliberately excommunicated the daimons, and hence, forfeited direct contact with our innermost selves and with nature. In exiling the "evil" side
of the daimonic—so-called "demons"—we also banished the "angels." But
the daimons have by no means desisted in touching our lives. Quite the
contrary.

Mephistopheles in America

Professor David Manning White comments that "concomitant with the
presence of evil as the sum force of mankind's negativity, the concept of
the devil has from earliest times played an integral part in religious thought.
Although men and women probably had their personal demons from the
very beginning of their perplexity about the nature of their existence, it
wasn't until Zoroaster named the evil force Ahriman that the devil became a central part of a religion."[50] In several religious systems since then,
including the Judeo-Christian tradition, the devil has come to virtually
personify evil.

Though there is scant mention of Satan as some supernatural presence in the Old Testament, the New Testament is replete with references
to Satan or the devil. "The English 'Devil,' like the German *Teufel* and
the Spanish *diablo,* derives from the Greek *diabolos,*" writes Russell.
"*Diabolos* means 'slanderer' or a 'perjuror' or an 'adversary' in
court. . . . Although the concept of the Devil—a single personification of
evil—does not exist in most religions and philosophies, the problem of
evil exists in every world view except that of radical relativism."[51]

Eventually, the devil became a preeminent image of evil (see, for
instance, fig. 10). But while it is almost certainly an archetypal or universal
symbol appearing in the myths and legends of many different generations
and cultures, Russell reminds us that "the concept of the Devil is found
in only a few religious traditions. There was no idea of a single personification of evil in ancient Greco-Roman religions, for example, and there
was and is none in Hinduism or Buddhism. Most religions—from Buddhism
to Marxism—have their demons, but only four major religions have had
a real Devil. These are Mazdaism (Zoroastrianism), ancient Hebrew religion (but not modern Judaism), Christianity, and Islam" (p. 4).

For the early followers of these four religions, the idea of the "devil"
must have held tremendous significance—as it does still for some today.
But for many others in our iconoclastic culture, the devil has been deflated

Fig. 10.   *Bouc de La Goétie Basphomet,* the androgynous goat incarnation of Satan. Courtesy of Ernst and Johanna Lehner, *A Picture Book of Devils, Demons and Witchcraft* (New York: Dover, 1971), p. 24.

to a relatively lifeless concept sorely lacking the numinous authority it once so widely enjoyed. For rising numbers of individuals disenchanted with organized religion, Satan has become a diluted *sign*—no longer a true symbol—of a rejected, unscientific, and superstitious religious system no longer seen as spiritually significant. Nevertheless, as revealed by at least one major survey published in 1988, here in the secular United States, a 66 percent majority of us "believe in the Devil," as compared to only 30 percent or fewer of the population in European nations like Great Britain, Norway, Sweden, France, and Italy.[52] And, the following year, as if to confirm this fascinating fact, *Life* magazine decided to "give the Devil his due" by dedicating a full-color layout to the venerable "Prince of Darkness," introduced as follows: "Primordial and familiar, fantastic and credible, most ancient and foul seducer—his presence is once again among us, the stuff of grisly headlines. A being of many names, we call him the evildoer, mischief-maker, Lucifer, demon, tempter, serpent, fiend, Beelzebub, Baal, the devil and . . . SATAN."[53] This surprising resurgence of Mephistopheles in America is not confined to "born-again" Christians, Satanists, or New Age subculture; it is also being seen in the consulting rooms of psychotherapists across the country.

Sigmund Freud—who believed the devil to be a symbol for the father[54]—speculated some seventy years ago that "the fact that we so seldom in analysis find the devil probably indicates that in those we analyze the role of this medieval, mythological figure has long since been outplayed. For various reasons the increase in skepticism has affected first and foremost the person of the devil."[55] "This would seem to be confirmed," suggests psychoanalyst Louis Berkowitz almost half a century later,

> by the relatively sparse references to the devil in current psychological literature. Yet, with no fewer than four analysands within the past eight years, the writer [Berkowitz] has been confronted with the unmistakable vivid image of the devil himself or his derivative. All these patients were relatively well educated and sophisticated, and in each instance the devil came upon the scene suddenly and unexpectedly, leaving the analysand incredulous at the fact that it was indeed his own devil.[56]

In one such case, a hostile but fairly high-functioning female imagined something " 'growing' in her . . . from a part of her body in the middle region. It was growing bigger and bigger and then it took the form of a little black devil with horns and a tail, the entire body growing larger and smaller, between twelve inches and six inches in size, . . . [with] a sarcastic smile. . . . " Another patient dreamed of attempting to kill an elusive, black tapeworm which turned into " 'a tiny black devil with horns . . . '. "[57]

What can we make of this far-fetched phenomenon? The once maligned and scientifically repudiated symbol of the devil seems to be making a comeback. Why? How can we interpret this dramatic return of the devil to the late-twentieth-century psyche? Permit me to propose at least a partial reply to my own question: We Americans need desperately to better understand, constructively relate to, and meaningfully communicate about the perennial problem of evil. In the absence of adequate symbols and myths to express and contain our modern experience of evil, we must either modify our existing myths or create completely new, symbolic conceptualizations of evil. Failing to do so forces us into a reactionary and regressive return to outdated myths like the "devil." Symbols and myths have always provided a means of making sense of evil, and putting it in its proper perspective. Symbols and myths make a meaningful niche for evil in our world-view; without them, we cannot contextually grasp the gross reality of evil; nor can we comprehend its psychological significance. Hence, the indispensable role of wicked stepparents, witches, ghosts, and other malevolent creatures in traditional children's fairy tales, and in all myths and legends of lands far and near, each one symbolizing some salient aspect of evil.[58]

Amidst the current atmosphere of anger, rage, and violence, we Americans find ourselves faced with the forbidding countenance of unveiled evil. We have closed our collective eyes to evil for so long, we can hardly recognize it, let alone make sense of it. Dazed, frightened, and confused, some of us—for want of a more psychologically accurate, integrating, and meaningful myth—seize blindly upon the timeworn symbol of the devil, in order to somehow express this disturbing encounter with the dark, destructive side of the daimonic. Our desperate desire to resurrect the devil as the author of evil may manifest in a morbid fascination with demonology, demonstrated by the disquieting proliferation of satanic cults in this country and elsewhere. Current trends toward Satanism in America, in my estimation, are a tragically misguided attempt to discover some missing sense of personal power and significance, community, and a deeper connection with the daimonic domain. The pursuit of such legitimate goals via perverse—sometimes even murderous—behavior bespeaks all too clearly the collective plight that plagues us: the problem resides in the presumed division between good and evil still promulgated by Western religious tradition, a rigid dualism that condemns the daimonic as evil, and evil only. The daimonic has in our day been confused with the *demonic*.

The Demonic vs. the Daimonic

Like many of his contemporaries, Rollo May—who served briefly as a Congregational minister before becoming a psychologist—came to consider the Judeo-Christian notion of the "devil" an anachronistic concept lending itself far too readily to evading our own participation in and personal responsibility for evil. As he saw the situation, "the common personalized term [for evil] which has been used historically, namely the devil, is unsatisfactory because it projects the power outside the self. . . . Furthermore, it always seemed to me a deteriorated and escapist form of what needs to be understood about evil."[59] The devil no doubt does make a convenient scapegoat upon which to heap our disowned evil tendencies (fig. 11). What we lack—and what the archetypal model of the daimonic provides—is a new, or renewed vision of that valid realm of reality betokened by the "devil," one which can also include the *constructive* side of this elemental power. For, when properly interpreted, the symbol of the devil holds truly a *coincidentia oppositorum*—a coincidence of opposites. This highly significant fact is contained in the etymology of our English term "devil," which, as May explains,

> comes from the Greek word *diabolos;* "diabolic" is the term in contemporary English. *Diabolos,* interestingly enough, literally means "to tear apart" (*dia-bollein*). Now it is fascinating to note that this diabolic is the antonym of "symbolic." . . . There lie in these words tremendous implications with respect to an ontology of good and evil. The symbolic is that which draws together, ties, integrates the individual in himself and with his group; the diabolic, in contrast, is that which disintegrates and tears apart. *Both of these are present in the daimonic.* [my emphasis][60]

There is, indeed, a tremendous difference between the *demonic*—connoting that which is purely negative and evil—and the *daimonic*, which contains the creative seeds of its own redemption. The daimonic—unlike the more polarized, and thus, comprehensible ideas of the demonic or the devil—transcends the dualism of "good" and "evil," deriving as it does

Fig. 11. *The Scapegoat* by M.C. Escher. The artist's symmetrical image depicts the pitfalls of artificially dividing the daimonic into distinct polar components. Copyright ©1995 M. C. Escher/Cordon Art-Baarn-Holland. All rights reserved. Courtesy Cordon Art.

from what theologian Paul Tillich termed "the ground of being": that indivisible and ineffable state wherein the cosmic polar opposites co-exist as potentialities, the realization of which depends in some measure on the mediating human will. In contrast to the demonic, the daimonic includes the *diabolic* as well as *divine* human endowments, without making them mutually exclusive; it is that numinous aspect of being and of nature that is both beautiful and terrible at the same time. In this regard, the daimonic resembles certain tenets of pre-Christian monistic religions like Hinduism, which holds that both good and evil stem from the the identical, ultimately inseperable, divine principle (Brahman): "The great gods of India," writes Russell, "including Kali, Shiva, and Durga, manifest opposite poles in a single being: benevolence and malevolence, creativity and destructiveness. . . . Hebrew religion originally attributed all that is in heaven and earth, whether constructive or destructive, to the one God [Yahweh]. . . . He was both light and darkness, construction and destruction, good and evil."[61] (See figs. 12 and 13.) This inseperable ambiguity is also very much in keeping with the earliest conception of Satan as Lucifer—the "light-bearer"—who, to paraphrase Mephistopheles in Goethe's *Faust*, seeking to do evil, inevitably effects some good in the process.[62]

Hence, we have seen that "the daimonic" has been known throughout history by many names. German novelist Hermann Hesse, for instance, in *Demian*, refers to this numinous, archetypal, transcendent, *coniunctio oppositorum* as Abraxas:

> "This name occurs in connection with Greek magical formulas and is frequently considered the name of some magician's helper such as certain uncivilized tribes believe in even at present. But it appears that Abraxas has a much deeper significance. We may conceive of the name as that of a godhead whose symbolic task is the uniting of godly and devilish elements." . . .
>
> . . . [Demian] said that we had been given a god to worship who represented only one arbitrarily separated half of the world (it was the official, sanctioned, luminous world), but that we ought to be able to worship the whole world; this meant that we would either have to have a god who was also a devil or institute a cult of the devil alongside the cult of god. . . . Abraxas was the god who was both god and devil.[63]

"Abraxas, the Anguipede" or serpent-footed deity, dates back to at least the earliest days of Christianity, and was particularly popular among the Gnostics (fig. 14). This ancient configuration of the daimonic bears

Fig. 12.   The mercurial daimon of the alchemic philosophers. From Giovanni Battista Nazari's *Della Transmutatione Metallica* (Brescia, 1589). Courtesy of Ernst and Johanna Lehner, *A Picture Book of Devils, Demons and Witchcraft* (New York: Dover, 1971), p. 20.

Fig. 13.   Buer, mandala-like daimon of philosophy, medicine, and holistic healing. From *Dictionnaire Infernal* by J. A. S. Collin de Plancy (Paris: Henri Plon, 1863; reprint, Genéve: Slatkine Reprints, 1980), p. 123.

Fig. 14. "Abraxas, the Anguipede" depicted as a composite of diverse symbolic, cosmic qualities, including serpentine legs. Greco-Roman amulet (circa 250 A.D.).

some similarities in function to the Christian figure Lucifer. But above all, Abraxas is a myth, which like "the daimonic," surpasses the polarities of most of our accepted, dualistic ideas of the divine, and defies form. As Pistorius professes in *Demian:* " 'Abraxas . . . is God and Satan and he contains both the luminous and the dark world.' "[64]

Like the Greek hero Perseus—whom the goddess Athena helped to behead the Gorgon (see fig. 3), Medusa, by handing him a shiny shield to safely mirror her horrific image—we will always require some means of consciously reflecting on the reality of evil and making sense of it; this is the main function of enduring myths and symbols like Abraxas, or the devil, or the daimonic. Without such pragmatic intellectual props—which really are divine gifts—we could not live very long in a world so thoroughly riddled with evil. For we cannot too long "gaze into the face of absolute evil"[65] unaided by some mythological, theological, or philosophical filter, or reflective, cognitive mechanism. Myths and symbols serve such protective purposes for the vulnerable human psyche; they buffer and deflect the devastating impact of radical evil, and imbue it with meaning.

But this important theme of "mirroring" and "reflection" in the myth of Perseus and Medusa contains an additional clue for more clearly apprehending evil. Much of the evil we see "out there" in the world, and in others, is in some measure a reflection of ourselves: our own human potential for, and unavoidable participation in evil. The myth counsels that the only meaningful—and ultimately, viable—way of comprehending and combatting evil is to understand it as a mirroring of the daimonic elements eternally present in nature and in all humanity. We are the primary progenitors of evil: we not only define it, but, as we shall see, we wittingly or unwittingly create and perpetuate it. Therefore, it is we who are responsible for much of the evil in the world; and we are each morally required to accept rather than project that ponderous responsibility—lest we prefer instead to wallow in a perennial state of powerless, frustrated, furious, victimhood. For what one possesses the power to bring about, one has also the power to limit, mitigate, counteract, or transmute. Recall that as a result of Perseus' courageous encounter with Medusa, Pegasus, that magnificent, winged, white steed, arose from her vital lifeblood; and the now reenergized Perseus rode on triumphantly to conquer more monstrous demons, and marry the beautiful maiden, Andromeda. Good can come from defiantly facing evil. But evil, alas, will always find another face.

Fig. 15. *Head of the Medusa* by Caravaggio. Uffizi, Florence, Italy. Courtesy of Alinari/Art Resource, New York.

4

Myths of the Unconscious
The Id, the Shadow, and the Daimonic

In describing the living processes of the psyche, I deliberately and
consciously give preference to a dramatic, mythological, way of
thinking and speaking, because this is not only more expressive but
also more exact than an abstract scientific terminology, which is wont
to toy with the notion that its theoretic formulations may one fine
day be resolved into algebraic equations.
—C. G. Jung, *Aion*

Models, Myths, and Symbols

For most modern readers, the intangible idea of "the daimonic" may
be difficult to grasp. This is due in part to a deep-seated desire to
deny our intrinsic capacity for anger, rage, violence, and evil in general.
Another reason is our immoderate rationalism and materialism.[1] We
believe that unless we can weigh, measure, or otherwise objectively
quantify the subject of our study, it must not exist. Moreover, we tend
toward a more "masculine,"[2] scientific view of the world, wherein
we pigeonhole and categorize reality in terms of "black" or "white,"
"good" or "bad." Something or someone is either fish or fowl, saint
or sinner, this or that, but never simultaneously *both*. But the daimonic
is a *myth*; it supersedes such simplistic dichotomies. Or, maybe more
accurately, it permits us to see beyond our own dichotomous, materialist perceptions.

87

Perhaps the best way to comprehend the daimonic concept is to more fully appreciate its historical context as a psychological model or myth. Psychology and psychiatry—much as they may pride themselves on being scientific—are rife with myths. The daimonic, for example, is but one among many myths of "the unconscious," as we shall soon see. But what exactly do we mean here by "myths"?

Myths and symbols serve similar purposes: they express existential truths that defy logical or rational explanations. Myths are by no means notions untrue, as common usage has it. On the contrary, myth is one way we attribute meaning to our existence—no myth, no meaning. In psychological terms, *myth*, writes Rollo May, is "a way of looking at oneself including one's body in relation to the world."[3] May goes on to add that "whether the meaning of existence is only what we put into life by our own individual fortitude, as Sartre would hold, or whether there is a meaning we need to discover, as Kierkegaard would state, the result is the same: myths are our way of finding this meaning and significance."[4] We can also think of symbols and myths as psychological *models* or *paradigms*. These are cognitive constructs we create in an endeavor to understand our universe and our selves. As Jungian analyst Aniela Jaffé notes,

> the construction of models in science is nothing out of the ordinary. Every science when confronted with irrepresentible realities, is compelled to project models of them. The atom is in itself an entity that cannot be represented in time and space, but the physicist constructs a model of it from its observable effects. The biologist does the same thing in cases where he can study directly only the outside of the object, the inner processes of the organism remaining inaccessible to him.[5]

Paradigms or models of reality can be more or less elegant. The more elegant, the more power they have to capture and hold the imagination, to fascinate, and to convey vital meaning. Like myths and symbols, they speak to us not merely intellectually, but on several different levels of experience at once. They are synthetic, bringing sometimes highly disparate components together into one, inclusive concept. They have universal appeal, transcending differences of language or culture. They generally arise out of intense conflict and struggle, and provide new perspectives on old problems. So long as scientific models and paradigms retain the power to grasp us in this way, to demand some responsive, subjective stand toward them, they remain mythic or symbolic in quality. Hence, they enjoy longevity.

Creative ambiguity is one key characteristic of myths and symbols: They always contain some measure of mystery, an inherent impenetrability capable of inducing a sense of wonder or awe in the beholder. The real significance of symbols and myths—as well as elegant psychological models or paradigms—resides in their uncanny ability to take hold of us, to touch us, even move us, and to speak to those places in ourselves where words or rational formulations fail to reach. To borrow Rudolf Otto's phrase, they contain the propensity to stimulate in us some sense of the *mysterium tremendum*. Indeed, they are typically a response to that which Otto terms the *numinous*, the "holy" or the "awful" experience of "daemonic dread."[6] The greatest hindrance in apprehending potent myths like the daimonic has to do with how unprepared we really are to psychologically confront and come to conscious terms with them, and their sometimes disturbing implications.

The archetypal human capacity to create symbols, myths, or models as means of describing phenomenological experience is crucial to theology, philosophy, psychology, and practically every other scientific, artistic, or intellectual pursuit. It is a way of conferring form to chaos. Carl Jung once said that "since every scientific theory contains an hypothesis, and is therefore an anticipatory description of something still essentially unknown, it is a symbol."[7] Let us more closely examine now some of the most prominent models, symbols, or myths upon which the modern field of depth psychology is founded.

The Unconscious

Depth psychology is that specialized branch of psychotherapy that concerns itself with the phenomenology of the "unconscious." Swiss psychiatrist Eugen Bleuler (1857–1939)—who supervised Jung's psychiatric residency during the dawning days of Freud's fin de siècle psychoanalytic discoveries—is "commonly credited with having coined the term *Tiefenpsychologie* (depth psychology)."[8] Consider Freud's ironic comments from 1922 on the subject of "depth psychology," and their uncanny pertinence to the presently muddled state of affairs in the affiliated fields of psychopathology and psychotherapy:

> Psychiatry is at present essentially a descriptive and classificatory science whose orientation is still towards the somatic rather than the psychological and which is without the possibility of

giving explanations of the phenomena which it observes. Psycho-analysis does not, however, stand in opposition to it, as the almost unanimous behaviour of the psychiatrists might lead one to believe. On the contrary, as a *depth-psychology*, a psychology of those processes in mental life which are withdrawn from consciousness, it is called upon to provide psychiatry with an indispensable groundwork and to free it from its present limitations.[9]

The predominance during the nineteenth century of the organic or *somatogenic* model in psychopathology (which scientifically sought to replace medieval demonology with a more rational mythology) took a direct hit with the publication in 1895 of *Studies on Hysteria*, by Freud and the Viennese physician Josef Breuer. Assimilating the findings of Franz Anton Mesmer, French physicians A. A. Liebault, Hippolyte Bernheim, Jean Charcot, and Pierre Janet—as well as psychological precursors like Kant, Nietzsche, Schopenhauer, C. G. Carus, and Eduard von Hartmann— Freud and Breuer put forth a powerful argument for a *psychogenic* (or primarily psychological) model of mental illness, based on the hypothesized existence of the "unconscious." The term "*un*-conscious" conveys exactly its meaning: it refers to that portion of subjective experience of which we are unaware or not conscious; it is that which is obscured, invisible to consciousness—at least, " '*at the moment*.' "[10] One simplistic analogy made use of by Fechner, Freud, and Jung, might call to mind an iceberg floating in a vast, uncharted ocean: the "tip" of the iceberg is consciousness; all that cannot be seen below the surface of the dark sea—as well as the sea itself—is "the unconscious."

Breuer, Freud's astute senior colleague and coauthor, theorized that the unconscious or "split-off mind is the devil with which the unsophisticated observation of early superstitious times believed that . . . patients were possessed. It is true that a spirit alien to the patient's waking consciousness holds sway in him; but the spirit is not in fact an alien one, but a part of his own."[11] Freud himself, at first, took the concept of "the unconscious" quite literally, as can be seen in the following statement from his now famous *Introductory Lectures on Psychoanalysis*, first delivered in Vienna between 1915–1917:

> I confess that for a long time I was willing to accord Janet very high recognition for his explanation of neurotic symptoms, because he regarded them as expressions of "*idées inconscientes*" possessing the patient's mind. Since then, however, Janet has

taken up an attitude of undue reserve, as if he meant to imply that the Unconscious had been nothing more to him than a manner of speaking, a makeshift, *une façon de parler*, and that he had nothing "real" in mind.[12]

For Freud at that time, "the unconscious" was no mere metaphor; it was a palpable and scientifically demonstrable structure in the human psyche.

Freud's eventual "psychology of the unconscious" sought to scientifically explain not only those phenomena previously attributed to demonism or neurological disease, but the entire problem of human evil as well. (Indeed, as suggested earlier, "psychopathology" can be conceived of as an insidious form of evil afflicting the human psyche.) The *unconscious* became Freud's psychobiological model of the unknown human mind, a vast, veiled repository for repressed instinctual experience: "The division of mental life into what is conscious and what is unconscious is the fundamental premise on which psycho-analysis is based; and this division alone makes it possible for it to understand pathological mental processes. . . . Psycho-analysis cannot accept the view that consciousness is the essence of mental life, but is obliged to regard consciousness as one property of mental life, which may co-exist along with its other properties or may be absent."[13] Freud's original use of the term "unconscious" referred to those myriad mental phenomena that are hidden, " 'concealed', . . . or . . . 'inaccessible to . . . consciousness'." [14]

Carl Jung, in his extensive exploration of the hitherto uncharted territory happened upon by Freud, mapped out this newly developed model of the "unconscious" in considerably more detail. For Jung, the unconscious consisted of

> everything of which I know, but of which I am not at the moment thinking; everything of which I was once conscious but have now forgotten; everything perceived by my senses, but not noted by my conscious mind; everything which, involuntarily and without paying attention to it, I feel, think, remember, want, and do; all the future things that are taking shape in me and will sometime come to consciousness: all this is the content of the unconscious.[15]

In addition to these psychic contents, which are always capable of becoming conscious at some point, says Jung,

> we must include all more or less intentional repressions of painful thoughts and feelings. I call the sum of all these

contents the "personal unconscious." But, over and above that, we also find in the unconscious qualities that are not individually acquired but are inherited, e.g., instincts as impulses to carry out actions from necessity, without conscious motivation. In this "deeper" stratum we also find the . . . *archetypes*. . . . The instincts and the archetypes together form the "collective unconscious." I call it "collective" because, unlike the personal unconscious, it is not made up of individual and more or less unique contents but of those which are universal and of regular occurrence.[16]

Jung further subdivided the territory of the unconscious into various "archetypal" aspects, each with their own peculiar qualities, characteristics, and influences.

While deeply admiring the seminal contributions of Freud and Jung, May, a formally trained neo-Freudian psychoanalyst, expressed serious concerns regarding how we have since come to think about "the unconscious," suggesting that, over the trans-Atlantic miles and the years, their brilliant, metaphorical models of the unconscious have been distorted by dogmatic disciples. Indeed, many psychologists today reject "the unconscious," viewing it as a fragmenting, concretized, overly deterministic concept fostering a fundamental misperception of people as purely passive recipients and helpless victims of autonomous "unconscious" forces beyond their control. "Now it must be admitted," avows May,

that the doctrine of the unconscious has played most notoriously into the contemporary tendencies to rationalize behavior, to avoid the reality of one's existence, to act as though one were not himself doing the living. (The man in the street who has picked up the lingo says, "My unconscious did it") . . . . But this is the "cellar" view of the unconscious, and objections to it should not be permitted to cancel out the great contributions that the historical meaning of the unconscious had in Freud's terms. Freud's great discovery and perdurable contribution was to enlarge the sphere of human personality beyond the immediate voluntarism and rationalism of Victorian man, to include in this enlarged sphere the "depths," that is, the irrational, the socially repressed, the hostile and unacceptable urges, the forgotten aspects of experience, ad infinitum. The symbol for this vast enlarging of the domain of personality was "the unconscious."[17]

From Freud and Breuer's initially crude hypothesis of "the unconscious" evolved subsequent variations on this enigmatic theme, including Freud's revised idea of "the id," Jung's misty conception of "the shadow," and, more recently, May's classical model of "the daimonic."

The Id

Long-time Freudian disciple Otto Rank—whose contributions to existential psychotherapy and the psychology of creativity will be briefly considered in chapter seven—asserts that "Freud did not discover the unconscious, as has been erroneously claimed by his followers; he merely rationalized this nebulous conception typical of German romantic philosophy. Those philosophical romanticists of post-Napoleonic Germany conceived of the Unconscious as the irrational element in human nature manifested in racial folk-tradition." Moreover, Rank claims that Freud, following Nietzsche, developed his concept of the "id" only reluctantly, and in direct response to Jung's "discovery" of the "collective unconscious":

> Thus originated the famous theory of the "unconscious," a term designating the most vital force of human behaviour as a mere absence of consciousness. Such a negative conception at the basis of the whole psychoanalytic system betrays not only Freud's purely rationalistic approach but also his moralistic philosophy. Originally conceived of as the receptacle of the individual's "badness," the unconscious became a kind of private hell which housed the evil self. Only after Jung had extended its content beyond the repressed material in the individual was it christened with the broader but quite neutral term, "id"—unfittingly borrowed from Nietzsche's intuitive philosophy of self-expression ("id thinks, in me," as opposed to the psychological notion, "I think.").[18]

Freud credited author and physician Georg Groddeck with prompting his decision to dub that most archaic, primitive, instinctual part of the unconscious mind the "Id."[19] "Groddeck himself," noted Freud, "no doubt followed the example of Nietzsche, who habitually used this grammatical term for whatever in our nature is impersonal and, so to speak, subject to natural law."[20] The Latin word *id* was employed by Freud's English translators to stand in for the original German term *Es*, meaning "it." The "it" or "id," then, is that which is antithetical to the *ich*, the original German term for the conscious "I" or the personal "ego": "The ego represents what we call reason and sanity," wrote Freud, "in contrast to the id which contains the passions" (p. 30). Despite Freud's final theoretical dividing line between *superego, ego* and *id*, he recognized that this hypothetical boundary is, in reality, osmotic, and that "the ego is not sharply separated from the id; its lower portion merges into it" (p. 28). He appears to have been at least partially aware of the limitations and impracticalities of theoretical artifices like those used by himself and others to dissect and compartmentalize the inherently indivisible, organically whole human psyche.

The primitive "passions" of the id are most simply defined as any powerful feeling, impulse, or emotion, such as sexuality, love, or hate. As we have seen, these same irrational human passions also preoccupied the early Greeks, spawning their deeply ambivalent conception of them as daimones. According to psychiatric historian Henri Ellenberger, Groddeck's prototypical "description of the id reflected, to an extreme degree, the old Romantic concept of an irrational unconscious. He conceived of the id as impersonal and full of aggressive and murderous impulses, and believed each drive had its obverse."[21] Freud himself compared the id to a metaphorical horse whose superior power must be simultaneously partaken of, harnessed, and carefully controlled by its overmatched rider—the much weaker ego.[22] The "ego" had the unenviable task of serving as "an intermediary between the id and the external world in the service of the pleasure principle, to protect the id from the dangers of the external world,"[23] as well as from the internalized superego. Freud described the inscrutable id as "the dark, inaccessible part of our personality; what little we know of it we have learnt from our study of the dreamwork and of the construction of neurotic symptoms, and most of that is of a negative character. . . . We approach the id with analogies: we call it a chaos, a cauldron full of seething excitations."[24] Since the id is, by definition, "amoral," it is not the least bit concerned about such insignificant matters as good and evil; existentially, it antedates even the most basic polarities of what we decree to be "positive" or "negative." Hence, the ego—with the help of the superego or "social conscience"—must protect the external world from the dangers of the id as well as vice versa. In Freud's paradigm, both Eros and Thanatos may be said to be primal instinctual forces at least partially comprising the id, which, at bottom, is inextricably embedded in human biology.

Freud posited the mythic theory of Thanatos opposing Eros just three years prior to first introducing his idea of the id in 1923.[25] He was sixty-seven, and seems to have been moving during this period away from his earlier mechanistic, materialist model of the mind, toward a more poetic, mythological conceptualization of the unconscious. The id—along with Eros and Thanatos—was but one feature of Freud's replacement of his former topographic model (the unconscious, preconscious, and conscious) with his later tripartite structural model (the id, ego, and superego). Because Freud presumed that both the ego and superego depend solely upon the primordial energy of the id for their effective functioning, this structural model demonstrates once again that he intended his theoretical compartmentalization of the essentially insubstantial psyche to be more figurative than concrete. But for some reason, Freud never further elaborated on his nebulous symbol of the id prior to his death in 1939; nor did he adequately differentiate it from his landmark conception of the "unconscious." What may have been Freud's final recorded thought on the matter (1938) alludes paradoxically to a topic he had consistently tried to exclude from psychoanalysis at all costs: " 'Mysticism—the obscure self-perception of the realm outside the Ego, the Id.' "[26]

The Shadow

As mentioned earlier, the onerous task of further mapping the "unconscious" was left for Freud's free-thinking former protégé, Swiss psychiatrist Carl Jung: "I cannot say where I could find common ground with Freud when he calls a certain part of the unconscious the Id. Why give it such a funny name? It is the unconscious and that is something we do not know. Why call it the Id?," wondered Jung in 1935.[27] For all intents and purposes, the answer to Jung's query, in my opinion, was that Freud had begun to distinguish different levels or strata of "the unconscious": instinctual, primal, and even mythological versus personal or psychological contents. That is, Freud discerned the necessity to further refine and delineate the gross phenomenon he had uncovered, up until then known generically as the "unconscious." Carl Jung sensed precisely the same imperative.

Jung's approach—in addition to dividing the unconscious into *personal* and *collective* contents, the latter presumably being most closely correlated with Freud's id—was to adopt from philosopher Friedrich Nietzsche what some might see as an equally "funny name" for the unconscious: the *shadow*. For Jung, "the shadow" was mainly a metaphorical means of addressing the prominent role of "the unconscious" in the problem of evil. "The SHADOW," said Jung, is "that hidden, repressed, for the most part inferior and guilt-laden personality whose ultimate ramifications reach back into the realm of our animal ancestors and so comprise the whole historical aspect of the unconscious."[28] Depending in part upon the prevailing cultural canons and social mores imposed upon a person, these "inferior" personality traits include such unacceptable, sinful, or "evil" passions as sexual lust, anger, or rage. The shadow is "the inferior part of the personality," states Jung's associate, Aniela Jaffé, the "sum of all personal and collective psychic elements which, because of their incompatibility with the chosen conscious attitude, are denied expression in life. . . ."[29] Jung additionally differentiated between the so-called "personal shadow" (i.e., individual evil) and the "archetypal shadow" (i.e., transpersonal and collective evil).

Nonetheless, differing with Freud, Jung maintained that the compensatory effects of this shadowy and much despised aspect of the unconscious could be *positive* as well as negative: "If it has been believed hitherto that the human shadow was the source of all evil, it can now be ascertained on closer investigation that the unconscious man, that is, his shadow, does not consist only of morally reprehensible tendencies, but also displays a number of good qualities, such as normal instincts, appropriate reactions, realistic insights, creative impulses, etc."[30] For Jung, the "shadow" should never be mistaken and immediately dismissed as merely evil or *demonic*; it has its positive potentialities, too.

Jung's correlation (above) between the shadow and "the unconscious man" as such lends support to my thesis that in developing this concept, he sought a more highly differentiated, phenomenologically descriptive version of the "unconscious" or the "id" than had been previously proffered by Freud. But foremost for Jung was finding a way of articulating symbolically the psychological problem of evil, and the prodigious dangers of excessive unconsciousness. He was especially concerned with those peculiar mental states traditionally believed to be "demonic possession." Jung's psychological symbol of "the shadow" served as a secular stand-in for yet another, more senior symbol of personal and transpersonal evil: "the devil." As J. B. Russell writes, Jung

> argued that the traditional theory of evil as privation [the Augustinian religious doctrine of *privatio boni*] diverted us from identifying and dealing with the real darkness of the human personality. . . . If the enormously powerful cosmic

energy represented by the Devil is denied and repressed, it will burst forth with a destructiveness proportional to the degree of its repression. But if it is integrated, its energy can be turned toward the greater good. . . . By "Devil" Jung meant a mythical, psychological symbol, not a metaphysical entity in the Christian sense.[31]

Extremely well-read and erudite, Jung had been exposed to and profoundly influenced by the classical idea of the daimonic; he frequently refers to it throughout his prolific writings, and evidently wished to capture and assimilate its vitally equivocal quality in his own enigmatic myth of the shadow. As the son of a Swiss parson, Jung was steeped in the Protestant mythos, had fully digested the rich symbolism of Catholicism, and intensively studied several other great religious and philosophical systems. However, he preferred to employ the relatively banal—and therefore, more rational—terms "the shadow" and "the unconscious," as he once said, "knowing that I might equally well speak of 'God' or 'daimon'. . . . When I do use such mythic language, I am aware that 'mana,' 'daimon,' and 'God' are synonyms for the unconscious."[32] By Jung's own admission, terms such as "the shadow" or "the unconscious" were "coined for scientific purposes, and [are] far better suited to dispassionate observation which makes no metaphysical claims than are the transcendental concepts, which are controversial and therefore tend to breed fanaticism" (p. 336).

The shadow, pithily comments one psychiatric colleague of Jung's, "is the sum of those personal characteristics that the individual wishes to hide from . . . others and from himself. But the more the individual desires to hide it from himself, the more the shadow may become active and evil-doing. . . . At times too, owing to the influence of alcohol or some other cause, the shadow can temporarily take hold of an individual, who later might be quite surprised that he was capable of such evil behavior."[33] *Possession* by the "shadow"—a phenomenon further described in the following chapter—is not, however, something that occurs only at an individual or personal level; it also includes the possibility of group possession by the "collective shadow." Jung derived his psychological hypotheses of individual and collective possession in part from an historical knowledge of *demonism*, which he defined formally in 1945:

Demonism (synonymous with daemonomania=possession) denotes a peculiar state of mind characterized by the fact that certain psychic contents, the so-called complexes, take over the

control of the total personality in place of the ego, at least temporarily, to such a degree that the free will of the ego is
suspended. . . . Demonism can also be epidemic. . . . The epidemic
form includes the induced collective psychoses of a religious or
political nature, such as those of the twentieth century.[34]

Two cataclysmic World Wars and the epidemic violence we bear witness
to today testify to the truth of this terrifying collective phenomenon.

The Daimonic vs. the Shadow

Carl Jung's amorphous symbol of the *shadow* and Rollo May's classical
model of the *daimonic* are undeniably similar paradigms. But these two
timeless myths also contain noteworthy differences. Let us first elucidate
some subtle distinctions, before stating the obvious similarities.

Distinctions

"The daimonic," wrote Rollo May in 1969, eight years after Jung's
death,

is the urge in every being to affirm itself, assert itself, perpetuate and increase itself. The daimonic becomes evil when it
usurps the total self without regard to the integration of that
self, or to the unique forms and desires of others and their need
for integration. It then appears as excessive aggression, hostility, cruelty—the things about ourselves which horrify us most,
and which we repress whenever we can or, more likely, project
on others. But these are the reverse side of the same assertion
which empowers our creativity. All life is a flux between these
two aspects of the daimonic.[35]

(We will turn our attention to the much neglected *creative* side of the
daimonic a little later, in chapter eight.)

May—an existential analyst who studied with Alfred Adler in Vienna
during the early 1930s—was (like the earliest Jung) a *phenomenologist*. As
such, he spoke out against materialist trends in psychology, trends that
tend to reduce dynamic symbols or myths of the psyche—such as "the
unconscious," "the id," or "the shadow"—to prefigured, dogmatic doctrine. May credited his long-time mentor and friend, theologian Paul

Tillich (1886–1965), with having been "the contemporary thinker . . . chiefly responsible for bringing the daimonic to our attention today."[36] Tillich, an émigré from Nazi Germany, understood the daimonic, and sometimes alluded to it in his philosophical lectures and writings.[37] In some respects, both Tillich's and May's controversial reintroduction of the antediluvian daimonic myth into modern religion and psychology was an effort to counteract and correct tendencies toward misusing, mechanizing, or otherwise misinterpreting Jung's seminal metaphor of the "shadow," with its enormous psychological, spiritual, and social significance—especially regarding the nature of human evil. "In the daimonic," comments May, "I . . . want to state the problem of evil in such a way that psychologists will not be able to derogate it simply as a *lack* of something, for example, a lack of growth or as simply immaturity, or as a process which depends always on something else, such as the doctrine of the shadow in Jungianism."[38] Evil is an existential actuality, and cannot be attributed to the mere absence of "good," or "family values," or neurochemical "normalcy," or even "consciousness." The responsibility for personal evil ought not be sloughed off onto any thing or person outside nor inside us, other than ourselves. Therefore, we need sophisticated psychological models or myths that permit us to better apprehend the problem of evil, and our own participation in it. Jung stated the case as follows:

> Today we need psychology for reasons that involve our very existence. . . . We stand face to face with the terrible question of evil and do not even know what is before us, let alone what to pit against it. . . . *We* have no imagination for evil, but evil *has us in its grip.* . . . That is the psychological situation in the world today: some call themselves Christian and imagine that they can trample so-called evil underfoot by merely willing to; others have succumbed to it and no longer see the good. . . . One half of humanity battens and grows strong on a doctrine fabricated by human ratiocination; the other half sickens from the lack of a myth commensurate with the situation. . . .
> Our myth has become mute, and gives no answers.[39]

Jung's own answer to this muteness was, of course, the "shadow" myth.

Now, one of the clinically counterproductive consequences of concretizing into rigid doctrine Freud's or Jung's "topographical," "structural," or "archetypal" models of the human psyche, says May, is that in so doing, we psychotherapists are "playing directly into the patient's neurosis to the extent that we teach him new ways of thinking of himself as a mechanism. This is one illustration of how psychotherapy can reflect the fragmentation of the culture, structuralizing neurosis rather than curing it."⁴⁰ The overall effect is one of unwittingly taking part in and reinforcing the patient's already precarious state of psychic dis-integration and powerlessness, instead of promoting his or her psychological integration, unity, and empowerment.

Consider, for example, Jung's characterization of the unconscious—including the personal complexes, the ego or persona, the archetypes of anima, animus, and the shadow—as "behaving autonomously," beyond any conscious control. The shadow, writes Aniela Jaffé, is a "relatively autonomous 'splinter personality,' . . . [which] behaves compensatorily to consciousness."⁴¹ Another of Jung's first followers, Frey-Rohn writes: "Time and again one can ascertain that, in coming to terms with the personal shadow, the individual arrives inevitably at the point where he is confronted with autonomous powers which are simply superior to his will . . . , at first . . . experienced as an overwhelming threat to one's being. Accordingly, the affects and projections associated with it are characterized by an obstinacy which we cannot modify either by feeling or by insight."⁴² Or again, in Jung's own words: "When one analyses [*sic*] the psychology of a neurosis one discovers a complex, a content of the unconscious, that does not behave as other contents do, coming or going at our command, but obeys its own laws, in other words it is independent or, as we say, autonomous. It behaves exactly like a goblin that is always eluding our grasp." And regarding the unconscious in general: "We must assume that the unconscious . . . has an independent function. This is what I call the autonomy of the unconscious." In short, for Jung, "the unconscious is an autonomous psychic entity."⁴³ Finally, there are the following remarks, again from Frey-Rohn, concerning the inherent human capacity to divide consciousness via the defense mechanism of *dissociation*. She emphasizes that in such circumstances,

> the dissociated content . . . in no way loses its efficacy, as the pioneers of depth psychology—Janet, Charcot, and Freud—have demonstrated. Quite the contrary; the deeper the repression, the more active the dissociated content. From its background in the unconscious, like a hidden kobold, it contrives all kinds of negative effects in the outer world. It can unexpectedly invade consciousness, and assume complete control of the unconscious personality. In such cases one often has the impression that the psyche is being controlled by a "stranger" who appears as a "voice," as a "spirit," or even as

an "overrated idea." This kobold, or "stranger" in the psyche, is at the root of every neurosis. It is also the fundamental cause of the individual's experience of evil—and, indeed, of the experience of his own individual-evil.[44]

Note that for Frey-Rohn, "it"—what Jung refers to as the "autonomous unconscious" or "shadow"—is seen as the culprit, as opposed to the person him- or herself. But who is it that bears the responsibility for "dissociating" these undesirable contents—these daimons—in the first place? And who continues to entomb them?

Extreme instances such as those described above by Frey-Rohn may be seen in psychosis or dissociative disorders involving "multiple personalities"—though the way in which such dissociative phenomena manifest in "garden variety," or what we might deem "normal neurosis," is infinitely more nondescript and subtle. Nonetheless, the "shadow" or the generic "unconscious" is considered by most Jungians to be an objective, independent, separate *entity*, with a will and "mind of its own," a foreign resident distinct and different from the conscious personality. The most obvious hazard in this sort of radical anthropomorphism—despite its sometimes indisputable phenomenological accuracy—is the temptation of the patient, therapist, or both, to displace all that is evil in one's self onto this fragmentary figment of imagination known metaphorically as "the shadow." This mental deed being done, the patient (via his or her defense attorney) may now claim—as do so many murderers and other violent offenders these days—that "the unconscious," or "the shadow" made them behave as they did, rendering them wholly irresponsible for their actions.

Admittedly, such an anthropomorphic approach in psychotherapy has merit. In confronting persistently bedeviling psychological problems, patients must establish some cognitive framework for conceptualizing their inner experience. Envisioning their difficulties as "demons" or "devils" to be grappled with, or as the "shadow" with which one must morally wrestle, can be quite useful during this daunting process. But the strictly allegorical nature of this symbolic language must always be borne in mind by both patient and therapist. As May explains: "My slightly anthropomorphic terminology comes out of my work as a therapist and is not out of place there. Though the patient and I are entirely aware of the symbolic nature of this (anxiety doesn't *do* anything, just as libido or sex drives don't), it is often helpful for the patient to see himself struggling against an 'adversary.' "[45] From this metaphorical perspective, the pragmatic clinical value of mythical concepts like the "unconscious," the "id," the "shadow," and the "daimonic" becomes exceedingly clear. The Jungian goal of meeting, accepting, and integrating the personal shadow, for instance, is a poetic expression of a healing myth. But such potentially therapeutic myths will only be truly healing when presented in ways that recognize the participatory role of the individual in human evil and most psychopathology, and emphasize the all-important part played by personal choice in the mitigation or perpetuation of one's own pathological symptoms.

The practical difficulties encountered even with so secular, neutral, and nebulous an image as the "shadow," are identical with those of the equally mercurial metaphysical idea of the "devil": we tend to *reify*, make concretely or materially "real," what was meant to be symbolic, metaphorical, or metaphysical. May does not dispute the phenomenological fact of Freud's diffuse description of the unconscious per se; but he does object to the literal interpretation of Freud's "topographical" paradigm of the mind: "It is always inaccurate to speak of *the* unconscious, *the* preconscious or subconscious: these are never *places*. But we must be able to include *unconscious experience* [in psychotherapy]. This is a problem not yet adequately dealt with."[46] He further argues that the inherent "split" in consciousness reflected by both the Freudian and Jungian doctrines of the "unconscious," and so often observed clinically in severe neurosis and psychosis, is more an artifact of major psychopathology than an accurate picture of the natural psyche. In reality, the psyche is normally characterized by a considerably more fluid and permeable boundary betweeen consciousness and unconsciousness. To amend my aforementioned "iceberg" analogy, not only can the iceberg bob higher or lower in the sea (unconsciousness), revealing at times more or less of itself; but, depending on conditions, fog frequently obscures visibility of the "tip" (consciousness).

Indeed, May defines "unconsciousness" as *"the potentialities for awareness and experience which the individual is unable or unwilling at that time to actualize."* Like Jung, he holds that "unconscious experience itself is intentional, moves toward meaning"[47]; that is to say, it is *teleological*. But in contradistinction to Jung's attribution of "autonomy" to unconscious contents, May contends that, in actuality, "neither the ego, nor the unconscious, nor the body can be autonomous. Autonomy by its very nature can be located only in the *centered self*."[48] May's use of the term "self," however, is not to be confused with the splintered and defensive fragment of personality referred to by Freudians as the "ego," or by Jungians as the "persona." Rather, the existential "self" is that indivisible point of centered integration presumed to exist at some level of the personality, from which we can objectively observe our own behavior in the world. Simultaneously, the "self" is the subjective side—in polar relationship with the objective world—of human existence. The subjective experience of *self, sense of self, centered self,* or a sense of *being* in the individual marks the momentous—and therapeutically indispensable—discovery of that unifying perception that "constitutes this infinitely complex set of deterministic factors into a person to *whom* the experiences happen and who possesses some element, no matter how minute, of freedom to become aware that these forces are acting upon him."[49] Absolutely central to the continuous process of creating and maintaining this "centered self," is the much-maligned matter of human *will*; that is, the ever-present presumption of a potentially autonomous "self" that, in Tillich's terms, "acts from the centered totality of its being."[50] It is only from this pivotal standpoint that an individual can ethically choose how he or she will respond to the blind, obliging, psychobiological urgings of the daimonic; and willingly assume the responsibility for the consequences.

In May's existential psychology, further defined in chapter seven, the *self* is the indivisible sphere from which we decide or will what to become conscious of from moment to moment. It is we—and no one else—who create or negate our own consciousness, an unavoidable and essential psychological process. "Otherwise," says May, "there would be no consciousness. For every thought destroys as it creates: To think this thing, I have to cut out something else; to say 'yes' to this is to say 'no' to that and to have a 'no' in the very ambivalence of the 'yes.' To perceive this thing I have to shut out other things. For consciousness works by way of either/or: it is destructive as well as constructive."[51] This innate human capacity for creating or destroying consciousness is the birthplace of the perennial problem of evil. As authors of our own consciousness we possess—at least to some degree—the power and responsibility for choosing to expand consciousness, or to contract it through the use of various psychological defense mechanisms, such as dissociation or *denial.* The inherent paradox of human consciousness is that it "*implies always the possibility of turning against one's self, denying one's self.* The tragic nature of human existence inheres in the fact that consciousness itself involves the possibility and temptation at every instant to kill itself."[52] This congenital self-destructive tendency comprises one inextricable side of the daimonic, and can be roughly correlated with Freud's *Thanatos.* Though not directly equivalent to it, Freud's *Eros* is also fused with the daimonic, which "inhabits the underground realms as well as the transcendent realms of eros."[53] But beyond this dualistic conception of human consciousness is the inbred capacity of consciousness—with the assistance of the unconscious—to surpass the usual either/or polarity of rational, linear thinking. Jung's felicitous term to describe this extraordinary process is the *transcendent function*: "The cooperation of conscious reasoning with the data of the unconscious is called the 'transcendent function.' . . . This function progressively unites the opposites,"[54] says Jung, yielding a symbolic solution that transcends and resolves the original irreconcilable conflict.

Nevertheless, perhaps we can now begin to see why May so strenuously objected to the Jungian "concept of the '*autonomy* of the unconscious mind',," which he felt artificially and unnecessarily "lead to a dichotomy between the 'rational' and 'irrational'."[55] Such clear and unambiguous boundaries simply do not exist in the phenomenologically fluid psyche, as they do not exist between body and mind: it represents only a partial truth based, at best, upon a magnified mirroring of our current state of self-fragmentation. But in fairness to Jung, it is important to note his deliberate—if not consistent—use of the term "partial" when speaking of the autonomous behavior of unconscious contents: the shadow, in actuality, is not totally independent, but only partially autonomous; or as Jaffé (above) states it, "relatively" autonomous. This is a crucial distinction, with far-reaching clinical implications, as we shall see. Still, as in the Judeo-Christian tradition, Jung's underlying presumption of the "autonomy of the unconscious" can, in overly literal analytical interpretations, lend itself to disowning and projecting our daimonic capacity for evil: not, this time, onto some external entity, such as the "devil," but instead, onto that more or less "autonomous stranger" residing deep within us—namely, the compensatory "shadow." In this sort of misguided Jungianism—practiced perhaps by uninitiated dilettantes, dogmatic neophytes, or fundamentalist disciples—unconscious "complexes" like the shadow could be viewed as practically impossible to govern, control, or personally impact, permitting the patient to apathetically and irresponsibly resign him- or herself to perpetual victimization by these invincible "archetypal" powers. With such a passive or pessimistic attitude on the part of the patient—and possibly the analyst as well—what real motivation could be mustered in fighting against these foreign forces? What hope could there be of gaining some greater measure of control and discipline over one's irrational or destructive behavior? The psychological "battle" would be lost before it ever began; and patients would be enabled to persist in their not uncommon efforts to, as May says, "relinquish . . . [their]

position as the deciding agent . . . , [and] to search for everything else as responsible for one's problems rather than one's self."[56] While there is obviously a plethora of problems external to us in life, beyond our control, we humans must still bear the weighty responsibility for choosing how we respond to them.

In his model of the daimonic, May seeks to minimize this fragmenting evasion of integrity, freedom, and personal responsibility by retaining "a decisive element, that is, the choice the self asserts to work for or against the integration of the self."[57] What he means is that no matter how "possessed," or "pushed," or "driven" we may be by the "shadow" or the "daimonic" at any given moment, there is always potentially some degree of freedom—minuscule as it might seem—to consciously choose one's personal response or one's attitude toward these awesome powers. Indeed, the dynamic forces of the daimonic are acting upon us all the time—and we, in turn, are interacting regularly with them—whether we are aware of this fact or not. Implicit in the daimonic model is the inherent and ineluctable participation of the *self*: that indivisible center from which individuals can either unconsciously resign themselves to be destructively governed by their anger and rage, for instance, or consciously learn to experience the daimonic, pause, and then decide how, when, where, or even whether to act on these compelling impulses. Hence the individual is by no means forever "doomed" to domination (or damnation) by the daimonic, as in the more deterministic Freudian model; or as per some currently popular biochemical theories. There is always the psychological possibility for freedom and self-determination. Such freedom, though, exists only *in potentia*: *freedom* and *will* are human functions that must be constantly and courageously exercised lest we lose them. The daimonic is our destiny, our precious human heritage; it cannot be gotten rid of, erased, eradicated, or enduringly exorcised. It is an existential truth, a phenomenological fact. We can, however, participate constructively in the daimonic insofar as we are willing to work towards its integration into consciousness—a never-ending process until death. The inherent human faculty for such an elemental decision to do so transcends all allegedly "autonomous" urges, blind pushes, archetypal possessions, biological drives, instincts, etc.; it contains the omnipresent possibility of consciously exercising our freedom and will even in the face of what may at times persuasively seem to be autonomous psychic or psychobiological forces. Ultimately, our conscious choices can at least alter or abate the negative influences of the daimonic; and, they can redirect the daimonic into more positive pursuits, as shall later be illustrated.

Much of the negative power of the daimonic derives not from biologically predetermined instincts, aberrations, or autonomous entities in the psyche, but rather, from the conscious suppression or unconscious repression of our most basic human tendencies.[58] If we can take full responsibility for having repressed or denied the daimonic, thereby amplifying its "relative autonomy," we can start to come to better terms with it. For freedom—true autonomy, the liberty to choose, to consciously decide how to relate to the daimonic—is to be found not in the absence of psychobiological determinism or quasi-autonomous "complexes," but in spite of them: *"Freedom,"* affirms May, "is thus not the opposite to determinism. Freedom is the individual's capacity *to know that he is the determined one,* to pause between stimulus and response and thus to throw his weight, however slight it may be, on the side of one particular response among several possible ones."[59] This does not imply that the daimonic represents a less-than-formidable force with which to be reckoned. Far from it. As an archetypal function, the daimonic derives its prodigious power from "those realms where the self is rooted in natural forces which go beyond the self and are felt as the grasp of fate upon us."[60] But the deceptively convincing subjective state of being "grasped" or "driven" or "possessed" by irresistible, impersonal, fatalistic forces cannot be considered some final, irreversible fait accompli, precluding personal responsibility. In contrast to Freud's pessimistic id system, the daimonic model presumes—with tempered optimism—the individual's potential to constructively stand up to and ameliorate the negative influences. And to do so with dignity, integrity, and creativity. The daimonic, like the shadow, can be met, atoned, and meaningfully integrated—albeit often with great toil, risk, and psychic upheaval.

The daimonic is a psychobiological admixture that includes and incorporates Jung's conception of the shadow, as well as the archetypes of anima, animus, and Self. Whereas Jungian doctrine differentiates the shadow from the Self, and the personal shadow from the collective and archetypal shadow, May makes no such presuppositions. His existential, ontological, or phenomenological method recalls a caution from one of Jung's most famous disciples, M. L. von Franz:

> We should be skeptical about attempts to relate some of these "souls" or "daimons" to the Jungian concepts of shadow, anima, animus and Self. It would be a great mistake, as Jung himself often emphasized, to suppose that the shadow, the anima (or animus), and the Self appear separately in a person's unconscious, neatly timed and in definable order. . . .

If we look for personifications of the Self among the daimons of antiquity, we see that certain daimons are more like a mixture of shadow and Self, or of animus-anima and Self, and that is, in fact, what they are. In other words, they represent the still undifferentiated "other," unconscious personality of the individual.[61]

In clinical practice, the daimonic paradigm always supposes the presence and participation of the self, in no matter what multifarious forms it may manifest; it refers to this naturally alloyed, phenomenologically undifferentiated, unadulterated subjective experience as it truly exists—prior to intellectual compartmentalization, partitioning, or analysis. As a comprehensive psychological model *sui generis*, the "daimonic" supersedes, subsumes, and transcends the "shadow." It is rooted in that existential "ground of Being" which those holiest of Hindu scriptures, the Upanishads, refer to as "Brahman," and which Carl Jung came to call the Self: an essentially unknowable organic center in the personality that is "not only the centre but also the whole circumference which embraces both conscious and unconscious; it is the centre of this totality, just as the ego is the centre of the conscious mind." The concept of the Self, said Jung, "designates the whole range of psychic phenomena in man. It expresses the unity of the personality as a whole."[62] This same unifying quality is found also in the idea of the daimonic, which refers traditionally to the aggregate gestalt of one's innate, indissolvable individuality.

Indeed, the daimonic myth is designed to resurrect the incorruptible reality residing beneath the neurotic fragmentation marring modern psychology, by bridging "*the cleavage between subject and object which has bedeviled Western thought and science since shortly after the Renaissance.*"[63] The trick to doing so, suggests May,

> is always to see both sides of the daimonic, to see phenomena of the inner experience of the individual without psychologizing away our relation to nature, to fate, and to the ground of our being. If the daimonic is purely objective, you run the danger of sliding into superstition in which man is simply the victim of external powers. If, on the other hand, you take it purely subjectively, you psychologize the daimonic; everything tends to be a projection and to become more and more superficial; you end up without the strength of nature, and you ignore the objective conditions of existence, such as infirmity and death.[64]

Similarities

Despite the subtle—yet significant—disparity between the shadow and the daimonic, both paradigms bring a hopeful message about human existence. Both are unifying symbols serving to reconcile the sundering imposed upon us by the existential conflict of opposites. Both make us more aware of the latent reality of evil—not only in others, but most importantly, in ourselves. Facing and consciously assimilating the daimonic—or the shadow—forces the recognition of a totality of being composed of good and evil, rational and irrational, masculine and feminine, conscious and unconscious features. Both the daimonic and shadow become evil (i.e., *demonic*) when we begin to deem them so, and subsequently suppress, deny, drug, or otherwise strive to exclude them from consciousness. In so doing, we either unwittingly or purposely participate in the *process of evil*, potentiating the violent eruptions of anger, rage, social destructiveness, and assorted psychopathologies that result from their reasserting themselves—with a vengeance—in their most negative forms. However, as Jung said of the shadow, when we choose instead to constructively integrate the daimonic into our conscious personality, we participate in the metamorphic *process of creativity.* For evil— or creativity, as we shall later see—seldom, if ever, consists of some single, isolated act, in the absence of any prior relevant psychological context. Both evil and creativity are byproducts of a profound psychological process. Psychotherapy—especially depth psychology—is very much concerned with this cryptic process. Or, at least, it should be.

Both models recognize the collective—as opposed to purely personal—problem of evil. "In a repressive society," writes May, " individual members, representatives of the daimonic of their times, express vicariously . . . atrocities for the society as a whole."[65] This systemic, transpersonal phenomenon corresponds to what Jung called the "collective shadow." Psychologically and otherwise, we exist not as totally isolated monads, but as separate-yet-related components of a human ecosystem, wherein we are continually affected by—and individually capable of affecting, for better or worse—our culture and each other. But the formidable interpersonal and collective forces impinging incessantly upon and seeking expression through the individual in no way relieve us of our personal responsibility for dealing with the daimonic or shadow. Both Jung (who, as a consequence of confronting and redeeming his own psychological devils and demons, became a "daimonic man"[66]) and May (who had his own intimate knowledge of the daimonic realm) believed that there is an implicit ethical and moral obligation to choose our responses to the daimonic or shadow carefully and conscientiously. "Bringing the shadow to consciousness," finds Frey-Rohn, who could just as well be speaking of the daimonic,

> is a psychological problem of the highest moral significance. It demands that the individual hold himself accountable not only for what happens to him, but also for what he projects. . . . Without the conscious inclusion of the shadow in daily life there cannot be a positive relationship to other people, or to the creative sources in the soul; there cannot be an individual relationship to the Divine.[67]

The last, but assuredly not least important similarity, as will be embellished upon in the next chapter, is the potential power of both the shadow and the daimonic to take "possession" of the person—in both positive and negative forms. For, as we shall learn as we proceed, above and beyond its similarities to Jung's concept of the shadow, the daimonic model holds far-reaching theoretical and clinical applications for the fields of psychology and psychiatry. As a modern psychological myth par excellence, the daimonic lends itself superbly to better understanding and addressing today's pressing problems of pathological anger, rage, and violence. Applying this serviceable paradigm, we could correctly comprehend such devilishly destructive behaviors as negative types of "daimonic possession." Possession of this subversive, injurious sort, as analyst John Sanford suggests, may be "the worst form of evil."[68]

5

The Possession Syndrome
Demonic or Daimonic?

We are lived by Powers we pretend to understand.
—W. H. Auden

Obsession and Possession

Despite the enduring and well-documented record of possession phenomena occurring in every era around the world,[1] Jungian analyst Esther Leonard De Vos notes that "in the main body of psychiatric and psychological literature, . . . it is easy to find articles which describe *obsession* [my italics], few or none which describe *possession*. According to Webster, the words 'possession' and 'obsession' have similar meanings. The word 'obsession' originally meant 'to be under the influence of an evil possession.' . . . The history of obsession [can be] traced back to an account of possession recorded in the fifteenth century."[2] Indeed, the term "obsession" was first used by the Catholic Church to describe the more mild forms of demonic possession. As Roman Catholic priest Montague Sommers specifies: "By obsession is meant that the demon attacks . . . from without; possession is meant that he assumes control . . . from within."[3] (See fig. 16.)

Parisian neurologist Pierre Janet (1859–1947) later adopted this term "obsession," recounts Carl Jung, to refer to "certain ideas that had taken possession of the patient's brain. . . . The medieval theory of possession (toned down by Janet to 'obsession') was . . . taken over by Breuer and

111

Fig. 16. *Saint Benoit delivre un clerc possédé du démon* (Saint Benoit saves a clergyman possessed by a demon). From *Les Démoniaques dans l'Art* by J. M. Charcot and Paul Richer (Paris: A. Delahaye and E. Lecrosnier, 1887).

Freud in a more positive form, the evil spirit—to reverse the Faustian miracle—being transmogrified into a harmless 'psychological formula.' "[4]

Today, the now standard psychiatric term "obsession" is officially defined as a recurrent, intrusive, and persistent thought, impulse, or image subjectively experienced as unwanted, unacceptable, or inappropriate, and, therefore, deeply disturbing: as though some alien idea, impulse, or emotion has forcibly assailed one's mind against one's will. The obsessive symptom "is experienced as being foreign to the person's experience of himself or herself as a psychological being [i.e., it is "ego-alien"]. . . . Obsessions are recurrent ideas that are . . . not voluntarily produced . . . , but, rather . . . invade consciousness . . . ."[5] Obsessive symptoms may be manifested in many different mental disturbances, including psychosis, depression, and anxiety disorders. But despite its conspicuous absence in the current psychiatric and psychotherapeutic texts, it must be admitted that the mysterious phenomenon known for millennia as "demonic possession" persists today in differing forms and varying degrees; what has changed is the way in which we now attempt to explain it.

Freud first became fascinated with devils and demons when working closely with neurologist Jean-Martin Charcot (1825–1893) at the Salpêtrière hospital during the mid-1880s on cases of supposed possession. Charcot contended that so-called "diabolic" or "demonic" possession is primarily a psychological rather than metaphysical syndrome. So bewitched was Freud with these bizarre phenomena that he subsequently wrote an essay (1923) entitled "A Neurosis of Demoniacal Possession in the Seventeenth Century," wherein he analyzes a medieval recounting of a demonic possession reported to have occurred soon after the sudden death of the affected man's father. Concluding in his study that "the Devil is an image of the father and can act as an understudy for him,"[6] Freud's final position was that possession is not caused by external, supernatural, evil spirits inhabiting the human body, but by neurosis: irreconciled, internal, repressed emotional or psychological conflicts.

Jung more or less concurred with Freud on this central point:

> There can be no doubt that mental illnesses play a significant part in causing belief in spirits. Among primitive peoples these illnesses, so far as is known, are mostly of a delirious, hallucinatory or catatonic nature, belonging apparently to the broad domain of schizophrenia, an illness which covers the great majority of chronically insane patients. In all ages and all over the world, insane people have been regarded as possessed by evil spirits, and this belief is supported by the patient's own hallucinations: they hear "voices." Very often these voices are

those of relatives or of persons in some way connected with the patient's conflicts. To the naive mind, the hallucinations naturally appear to be caused by spirits.[7]

Is there any difference between what our ancestors saw as "demonic possession" and what we in the modern world refer to as "psychopathology"? This question is the thorny subject of ongoing theoretical wrangling between secular scientists and twentieth-century theologians. But by far the more pertinent inquiry is not whether "possession" survives as a contemporary phenomenon, for it undeniably does exist in our day. The crucial question, at least for our purposes, concerns the *etiology* of possession—that is, its actual cause or causes—as well as its subjective meaning for the "possessed" person. I would go so far as to argue that practically all manner of what we psychologists and psychiatrists daily diagnose as "mental disorders," may, even in this hyper-rational era, be alternatively viewed as a variety of *daimonic*—not *demonic*—*possession.*

Types of Possession

Sommers, in his *History of Witchcraft and Demonology,* reports that "the ancient Egyptians . . . held that some diseases were due to the action of evil spirits or demons, who in exceptional circumstances had the power of entering human bodies and vexing them in proportion to the opportunities consciously or unconsciously given to their malign natures and influences.[8] We see here a recognition by the Egyptians of at least some participation on the part of particular patients in the presumed possession process. In classical Greece, writes theologian Morton Kelsey, the verb *daimonizomai* meant

> to be possessed by a demon or demons. . . . People possessed by demons, according to Thayer's Lexicon, are those suffering from. . . . especially severe diseases, either bodily or mental (such as paralysis, blindness, deafness, loss of speech, epilepsy, melancholy, insanity, etc.), whose bodies demons had entered, and so held possession of them as not only to afflict them with ills, but also to dethrone the reason and take its place themselves; accordingly the possessed were wont to express the mind and consciousness of the demons dwelling in them; and their cure was thought to require the expulsion of the demon.[9]

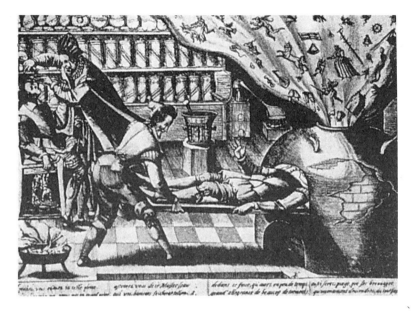

Fig. 17. Expulsion of the demons (seventeenth century, anonymous). From Carl Jung, *Symbols of Transformation*, vol. 5 of *The Collected Works of C. G. Jung* (Princeton, N.J.: Princeton University Press, 1967), plate 1a.

This was very much the methodology of Jesus in dealing with "demoniacs," described in the New Testament as suffering from myriad mental and physical symptoms: "They brought unto him all that were diseased, and them that were possessed with devils . . . And he healed many that were sick of divers diseases, and cast out many devils" (Mark 1:32, 34).[10] (See fig. 18.)

Such serious syndromes—when not demonstrably organic in origin—are nowadays accorded sanctimonious, scientifically sanctioned diagnostic terms like "conversion disorder," "depression," or "psychosis": specific categories of what we generically call "psychopathology." As Jung said in 1927:

Three hundred years ago a woman was said to be possessed of the devil, now we say she has a hysteria. Formerly a sufferer was said to be bewitched, now the trouble is called a neurotic dyspepsia. The facts are the same; only the previous explanation, psychologically speaking, is almost exact, whereas our

Fig. 18.   Jesus casting out devils (after Schnorr von Carolsfeld). From Paul Carus, *The History of the Devil and the Idea of Evil* (LaSalle, Ill.: Open Court, 1974), p. 158.

rationalistic description of symptoms is really without content. For if I say that someone is possessed by an evil spirit, I imply that the possessed person is not legitimately ill but suffers from some invisible psychic influence which he is quite unable to control.[11]

Let us consider some clinical illustrations of contemporary "possession." One of the most dramatic of these syndromes is technically termed "dissociative identity disorder,"[12] more commonly known as "multiple personality disorder." There is a great deal of disagreement surrounding this disorder, the appropriate application of the diagnosis, and its true etiology. Though once believed to be rare, in recent years the reported incidence of MPD (as it is conveniently called) in the United States is rising, presumably in conjunction with what one psychologist calls the generally "skyrocketing prevalence of dissociative disorders"[13] seen in this country. Classic cases of MPD have been depicted in popular books and films such as *The Three Faces of Eve, Sybil,* and *When Rabbit Howls.*

According to the American Psychiatric Association, *multiple personality disorder* involves "the presence of two or more distinct identities or personality states (each with its own relatively enduring pattern of perceiving, relating to and thinking about the environment and self). At least two of these identities or personality states recurrently take control of the person's behavior." Or, to put it somewhat more graphically, these so-called "subpersonalities" (they can number from two to more than one hundred!) actually take *possession* of the afflicted person's thoughts and actions. "The personality that presents itself for treatment often has little or no knowledge of the existence of the other personalities. . . . Studies have demonstrated that various personalities in the same person may have different physiologic characteristics and different responses to psychological tests. Different personalities may, for example, have different eyeglass prescriptions, different responses to the same medication, and different I.Q's."[14] What credible sense can we make of these incredible cases? Once having witnessed such strange symptoms, it is easily understood how this impressive phenomenon might well be interpreted as "demonic possession."

Psychiatrist Henri Ellenberger explains that throughout human history, there have been "two different types of possession, the somnambulic and the lucid. The individual in *somnambulic* possession suddenly loses consciousness of his self and speaks with the 'I' of the supposed intruder; after regaining consciousness, he remembers nothing of what 'the other one' has said or done." This precisely portrays the rapid transition from one personality to another typifying MPD, as well as the patient's inability to recall what the so-called 'alter' said or did during their period of domination. "In cases of *lucid* possession [my italics]," continues Ellenberger, "the individual remains constantly aware of himself, but feels 'a spirit within his own spirit,' struggles against it, but cannot prevent it from speaking at times. In both forms possession is experienced as a kind of intrapsychic parasitism: just as a tapeworm can live in the body, so can a parasitic spirit live in the soul."[15]

From the perspective of *analytical psychology,* MPD may be the most convincing demonstration of Jung's notion of the comparative "autonomy" of the unconscious "complexes." Elaborating on the early discoveries of Freud and Breuer, Jung postulated that *complexes* "are psychic fragments which have split off owing to traumatic influences or certain incompatible tendencies."[16] Jung often spoke of the complexes as behaving like "secondary or partial personalities possessing a mental life of their own."[17] When chronically repressed or dissociated, these "splinter person-alities" can become sufficiently powerful to usurp the entire personality, causing a temporary condition of acute possession. Hence, it is not unusual for MPD patients to insist that they are possessed by another person, a spirit, or some other sort of intrusive foreign entity.

In MPD, the personality is compartmentalized into walled-off subpersonalities (complexes), each containing encapsulated unconscious contents too traumatic, painful, or morally unacceptable for the person to consciously acknowledge. Robert Louis Stevenson's masterful story *The Strange Case of Dr. Jekyll and Mr. Hyde* is an archetypal tale of possession by an unconscious "alter ego" or "complex." The mild-mannered, civi-lized, sophisticated physician, Dr. Henry Jekyll, discovers and drinks a potion—that is, psychologically speaking, a method or mechanism of *disinhibition*, like drugs, alcohol, or self-induced trance—by which his dissociated alter ego, his "shadow," is brought to light and allowed to be lived out. This process could be correctly equated to so-called "arti-ficial" or "voluntary possession," a practice about which we shall soon be saying more. Edward Hyde, the ugly, hateful, and evil opposite of Jekyll's kind and gentle public persona, having finally gotten a taste of freedom, gradually grows stronger, to the point of being able to emerge and take over at will—but now, against the conscious wishes of the good Dr. Jekyll. The consequences, of course, are catastrophic: mayhem, murder, and suicide ensue.[18]

The *International Classification of Mental and Behavioural Disor-ders* contains yet another diagnostic category called "Trance and Posses-sion Disorders." These include those relatively rare cases where "the individual acts as if taken over by another personality, spirit, deity, or 'force.' "[19] One extreme example of such a "possession disorder" is the Malayan "amok syndrome," in which the person is suddenly and irresistably possessed by a blinding, homicidal rage. This "running amok," as it is traditionally known, in which the possessed person more or less indiscrimi-nately attacks and kills others—after which he or she typically has no memory of what transpired and sometimes commits suicide—sounds remarkably similar to some of the lethally violent outbursts incrementally occurring in American culture. Presumably, the affected individual—due to cultural, moral, or religious prohibitions—has repressed his or her aggression, anger, and rage to such a deleterious degree as to become violently predisposed to destructive possession by the long-dissociated fury. Frequently, the precipitating trigger for these fatal outbreaks of formerly suppressed rage is some stress-induced state of *abaissement du niveau mental* (reduction of consciousness), in which the dissociative ego defense mechanisms seem to suddenly dissolve. Regrettably, we are now seeing such horrific homicidal rampages multiply here in America, contributing to our notoriously high rates of violent crime noted in chapter one. We are fast becoming a nation of emotional "time-bombs," poised to explode at the slightest provocation.

In striving to comprehend various syndromes once understood as "possession," *daemonomania,* or "demonism,"[20] modern psychiatry and psychology have sought to provide a scientific alternative to traditional demonology. The ubiquitous belief that invasive, invisible entities—demons—are to blame for bizarre human cognitions and behaviors prevailed well beyond the post-Cartesian age of Enlightenment. Depth psychology has endeavored valiantly to provide new paradigms for such phenomena, as we witnessed in the preceding chapter. Most recently, instead of invisible devils or the "unconscious," medical science (psychiatry) has substituted a belief in the influence of biochemical entities (called "neurotransmitters"), microscopic "demons" deemed responsible for mental illness. Yet, amidst all the latest medical discoveries, one thing remains constant: *we still seek to detect and identify the concealed sources of evil.*

Psychoanalyst D. J. Henderson provides a more psychodynamic perspective on the past and present state of affairs:

Popular concepts of mental disorder have come full circle. Medieval beliefs in possession by devils and demons gave way to the nineteenth century medical model of mental disorder. The "illness" model was followed by Freud's psychoanalytic schema in which he conceptualized the various forms of psychopathology as derivatives of repudiated, repressed instinctual impulses. . . . However, many therapists became dissatisfied with the classical psychoanalytic schemata and tried to create new systems based on culture or religion or interpersonal process rather than on instinct and the personal unconscious. Although undoubtedly good therapeutic work was performed on the basis of these "new schools," there was the general feeling that the culturalists, interpersonalists, and perhaps even the Jungians were not getting down to bedrock. . . . From the work of object-relations psychologists has come an emerging synthesis founded on the firm footing of classical tradition, but incorporating concepts of "possessing forces." The new possessing forces are not, of course, the demons and witches of medieval times, but rather the good and bad objects of inner psychic reality.[21]

Much like the above-mentioned biologically-biased focus on neurotransmitters, for many students of "object relations," these internal representations and images have become prime suspects in producing pathological states of mind. But just what are these "good and bad objects of inner psychic reality"? Modern "ego psychology," an outgrowth of Freudian psychoanalytic theory, observes that we create and maintain symbolic, inner representations of outer objects and our relationship to them, starting with that most significant "object" for every infant: the mother. As we mature, we "introject" and unconsciously carry around these frequently confused, polarized, or distorted "objects," which—when "projected" onto the present environment—can negatively affect our interpersonal relationships. When, for example, in adulthood, the inner object representing mother remains polarized or "split" into a "good mother" and a "bad mother," psychopathology may result. As Henderson states, "what is needed to link [demonology] to the psychodynamic viewpoint is an awareness that the persecuting forces are not the evil supernatural forces of medieval times but rather the internalized persecuting bad objects of Klein (1932) and Fairbairn (1943)."[22] We shall delve no further here into the sometimes impenetrably intricate and dryly mechanistic theory of "object relations."[23] However, some readers may have already recognized the resemblance between these "possessing forces of inner psychic reality," and Jung's much earlier theory of unconscious "complexes" and "archetypes," both of which he believed to contain "a specific energy which causes or compels definite modes of behavior or impulses; that is, they may under certain circumstances have a possessive or obsessive force (numinosity!). The conception of them as *daimonia* is therefore quite in accord with their nature."[24] Whatever terminology clinicians today choose to apply to the phenomenon once so widely known as "demonic possession," it seems self-evident to some, like May, that "in discarding the false 'demonology,' we accepted, against our intention, a banality and shallowness in our whole approach to mental disease."[25] We have reduced mental disorders to the most materialist and mechanistic terms possible; and in so doing, we have stripped them of any spiritual significance or existential meaning.

For instance, if you were to witness what we would today term an "acute psychotic episode," you would be perfectly correct in calling it "possession." For in this highly intensified state, the profoundly psychotic person is likely to exhibit several of the following florid features: She or he may hear voices when there is no other person present; see visions of various sorts invisible to others; exhibit religious or sexual preoccupation, violent behavior, "super-human" strength, spitting or projectile vomiting (particularly when physically restrained). In addition, identification of oneself or others as the devil, demons, or God; the subjective sense of being externally controlled or influenced by satanic forces; severe agitation, confusion, disorientation, and, frequently, post-episodic amnesia are all commonly occurring symptoms of acute psychosis, more customarily called "madness."

Now compare the preceding brief clinical sketch of full-blown psychosis to the following description of demoniacal possession: "Demoniacal possession presents a bizarre and repulsive set of symptoms that may be marked by subsequent amnesia. Once the so-called entities take control of the demoniac, the central characteristic of the syndrome is its malignancy and the fact that the possessed appears to lose control and awareness of his ego and superego functions: he is 'taken over' as if by an outside force capable of powers far beyond his own."[26] T. K. Oesterreich notes that, in addition to these startling objective symptoms, the possessed person typically manifests markedly different facial features as well as altered speech patterns, in which the "new" voice speaks for the possessing entity: "[The] first and most striking characteristic is that the patient's organism appears to be invaded by a new personality; it is governed by a strange soul. This is what has given to these states, from the earliest times . . . up to the most recent, the name of 'possession.' "[27]

Genuine Possession, Pseudo-Possession, and Psychosis

In his popular book *People of the Lie: The Hope for Healing Human Evil,* psychiatrist M. Scott Peck draws a definite distinction between human evil and supernatural, metaphysical, or "demonic evil," the latter being the cause, he contends, of *genuine* possession. Peck further distinguishes satanic possession from mental illness, stating that though in such cases "there has to be a significant emotional problem for the possession to occur in the first place, . . . the proper question to pose diagnostically would be: 'Is the patient just mentally ill or is he or she mentally ill and possessed?'"[28] It is true that in certain religious circles, serious attempts are made to differentiate "genuine possession" from "pseudo-possession" or mere mental illness, the former being defined as a legitimate "metaphysical claim . . . [that] the individual is taken over by some supernatural entity."[29]

During one clinical study (1980) of sixteen patients confined in an acute psychiatric hospital, all of whom sincerely believed themselves to be "possessed," British researchers discovered that, though severely ill, these patients did not in fact exhibit the traditional trademarks of "genuine" possession. Instead, they simply *believed* themselves to be possessed. In the case history of each patient studied, the researchers found that "there had been exposure to beliefs likely to include a belief in the devil," as well as evidence that "the idea of possession was directly suggested to some patients."[30] Indeed, according to Oesterreich, "the appearance of possession, particularly in its gravest forms, is always . . . associated with belief in the devil."[31] Hence, the extremely heightened suggestibility of such patients is highly suspect in the so-called "pseudo-possession syndrome" of psychotic patients. Since we are all suggestible to some degree, depending in part upon personality, experience, and circumstances, the term "hypersuggestibility" seems most suitable to describe the central dynamic of this syndrome.

Hypersuggestibility is one of the most common concomitants of psychosis. It is a psychological state induced by a void demanding fulfillment; an intellectual vacuum inherently abhorrent to human nature; a desperate desire to decode, decipher, or attach significance to intolerable chaos and confusion; an anxious grasping at straws of missing meaning. Prior to, during, and just after an acute psychotic episode, patients are extraordinarily suggestible, due to decimating emotional, physical, and psychological upheaval. It is no great mystery—nor solely some negativistic resistance to standard psychiatric drug treatment, as some clinicians presume—why so many patients, utterly perplexed and bewildered by their symptoms, reject outright the banal medical or behavioral models of mental disorder and powerful pharmaceutical remedies foisted upon them by well-meaning physicians and psychotherapists. These mainstream biochemical myths of mental illness are of very limited value to such patients. Most do not "buy" biologically-based explanations of their shattering subjective experience; they instinctively repudiate them. By comparison, the outmoded (though evidently still very meaningful) myths of the "devil" or of "demons" provide a far more viable (yet still woefully inadequate) alternative hypothesis to hang on to. And hang on they do, as the dogged persistence of such treatment-resistant delusions so dramatically demonstrates.

It must be confessed, however, that in the cases of floridly psychotic patients—prior to the introduction of tranquilizing drugs—one often sees an unmitigated madness far surpassing any intellectual belief in or simple suggestion of possession: such patients *are possessed!* Consider, for example, the following case: A thirty-one-year-old former European boxing and wrestling champion

> was noticed by his friends to be undergoing a change in personality. They had always regarded him as shy and timid, but now he began to brag that he was becoming stronger, even "invincible." . . . On the other hand, . . . [his friends] noticed that he sometimes had periods, lasting minutes to hours, when he seemed extremely anxious and depressed, during . . . [which] he spoke of being controlled by Stalin and Hitler. . . . He believed that yellow cars were a "special sign of the devil."
>
> After a fight with his landlady, . . . [he] went out on his balcony and addressed her with a moving speech, . . . [explaining] that the voices of Goebbels, Hitler, Stalin, Gandhi, and Jesus were talking through his mouth, one after the other. After the tirade, he walked to the church, where he asked for absolution and insisted on sharing the host with the priest, . . . talking endlessly about being threatened by the devil. . . .
>
> . . . Aggressive and agitated, . . . he describes his thoughts as being broadcast aloud, says he is Jesus, hears voices, [and] sees "strange things."[32]

Psychosis or possession? Under our present system of psychiatric nosology this person is said to be "psychotic"; the formal diagnosis, given this patient's history, would, in all probability, be "bipolar disorder," better known as manic-depressive illness, from the same origin (*maniacus*) as the colloquial term, "maniac." "Schizophrenia" might be another possibility. But having once uttered this lofty, pseudo-scientific pronouncement, what have we really said about the subjective, psychological experience of the suffering soul standing before us? The so-called "schizophrenic psychoses," for instance, are a specific group of similar syndromes "in which there is a fundamental disturbance of personality, a characteristic distortion of thinking, often a sense of being controlled by alien forces, . . . disturbed perception, . . . [and] delusions, to the effect that natural and supernatural forces are at work to influence the schizophrenic person's thought and actions in ways that are often bizarre. . . . Hallucinations, especially of hearing, are common."[33] (See fig. 19.) In schizophrenia—and in psychosis in general—the prevalence of what we clinicians call "religious preoccupation" is striking: psychotic patients regularly report hearing the voice of God or of the devil. Commonly, they are

Fig. 19. Bizarre—perhaps hallucinatory—apparition of the devil. From *Dictionnaire Infernal* by J. A. S. Collin de Plancy (Paris: Henri Plon, 1863; reprint Genéve: Slatkine Reprints, 1980), p. 213.

convinced, beyond all rational argument, that they are somehow being controlled by someone or something other than themselves, either through mechanical, psychic, or supernatural means; not infrequently, they confess to being possessed by spirits, demons, or Satan himself. This is a universal phenomenon found virtually in every culture. What might it really mean?

The riddle of psychosis—its causes and significance—remains unsolved. It is a syndrome still shrouded in confusion, not only for those afflicted by it, but for those of us who attempt to minister to them.

Theories professing to reveal the roots of psychosis include organic, genetic, neurological, biochemical, cultural, socioeconomic, psychosocial, behavioral, cognitive, and psychodynamic models—to mention just a few of the multifarious factions. Of these, the most ascendant and widely accepted explanation for psychotic conditions such as schizophrenia or bipolar disorder (manic-depressive illness) is the *biochemical model,* which presumes that there is an inherited, biochemical abnormality in certain people predisposing them to psychosis.

Now, I will not dispute that there probably is *some* genetic predisposition or biological substrate to certain types of psychosis—and possibly to many other much less severe mental disorders. But to blithely attribute such a vitally intense, dynamic, and dramatic phenomenon as psychosis solely to imbalanced neurotransmission or maladaptive behavior (as do many modern clinicians) is a gross oversimplification of a highly complex, multidetermined syndrome. This is certainly not to imply that the appropriate use of "anti-psychotic" medications has no place in the treatment of psychosis: medication can curtail psychotic behavior and symptomatology. But biochemical intervention does not actually "exorcise" the psychological "demons"; it only drugs them into relative tranquility. One inherent danger in a purely biochemical approach to psychosis—or to most neurotic conditions, for that matter—is the promotion of a permanent state of mind-numbing emotional anesthesia or apathy: The daimons of which we have spoken so much are pharmacologically deadened and depotentiated; and along with them, the patient's natural vitality and daimonic drive. When psychosis (or the "possession syndrome") is understood instead in terms of the daimonic, the basic level of biological aberration is seen to be a simultaneously occurring consequence rather than the primary cause of the disorder; though there is also ample recognition that this physiological component of the illness can—and must in most cases—be more or less temporarily controlled biochemically: not in order to extirpate the offending daimons, but rather to render them less incapacitating, permitting the patient an opportunity to more gamely grapple with the daimonic in psychotherapy. In reality, a few do make this Herculean effort; most, however, do not, due to finances, fear, and discouragement from both within and without.

I propose that what some call "genuine possession" can correctly be seen as daimonic possession or madness, and properly defined as the most acute phase of a psychotic episode. Patients in this severest state of madness do not simply verbalize about believing themselves to be possessed: They scream it, bellow it, act it out, live it in the white-hot core of their being, in all its holy terror and intensity; they are wholly and deliriously clutched in the gut-wrenching grips of the daimonic. Any individual going into or coming out of this kind of direct encounter with the daimonic is completely disoriented and extraordinarily susceptible—more than willing to accept any sort of explanation coming close to making sense of their terrifying, inexplicable experience. Many, feeling possessed, manipulated, or controlled by something foreign to themselves, reflexively latch on to the literalized idea of the "devil" or "demons" in order to bestow meaning on their bewildering inner battle. Even after hospitalization and symptom-reducing medications, some patients retain their delusion of devilish possession because they have not to their own satisfaction been presented with a more feasible interpretation of subjective reality. Thus, say the previously cited British researchers, even in the post-episodic period "the metaphysical question is likely to loom large for the patient, who almost inevitably believes or at least has believed in the devil. A medical view of the situation may have been urged upon the patient when he [or she] was obviously unwell and irrational. This may have been necessary in order to persuade the patient to accept treatment. However, even if a medical view has been accepted as an expedient, *the problem remains for the patient of reintegrating his [or her] view of the world.* [my emphasis]"[34] Without a viable alternative viewpoint to having been virtually possessed body and soul by the devil or demons, adrift and disoriented patients cling desperately to their delusions like so many stunned shipwreck survivors to wreckage, thus reinforcing and perpetuating their debilitating derangement.

Neurosis and Romance as Possession

Those of us lucky ones who have not personally undergone the splintering experience described above may become complacent in the comforting illusion that possession is something associated solely with psychosis or severe psychopathology. Let me now lay that naive notion to rest: There is no clear dividing line separating "psychosis" from "neurosis"; both categories are considered "mental disorders," though, by definition, neurosis is typically far less crippling than psychosis. Since psychopathology can accurately be conceived as comprising a wide spectrum of varying degrees of mental health or illness, it is safe to say that there are few of us—if any—who are free of neurotic symptoms of some sort or another.

You may recall that obsessive symptoms—such as those found in certain neurotic disorders—were once considered by Catholicism to be mild signs of demonic possession. *Obsessions* are like harassing little mental "demons," in the form of unwanted thoughts, ideas, or feelings that invade our minds against our conscious will. *Phobias,* another neurotic symptom, involve overwhelming anxiety and sometimes panic-inducing fear of—as well as wishes to avoid at all costs—certain situations or objects; often these fears are felt by the sufferer to outstrip all conscious control. Acute anxiety, insecurity, or loneliness can be excruciatingly painful, compelling emotional demons from which we flee by means of substance abuse, promiscuity, workaholism, and so forth. And the metaphorical demon *depression* can seize one's soul from "out of the blue," vampirically draining life of its vitality, meaning, and beauty. These racking emotions are not purely pathological or neurotic, for they may appear in presumably "normal" people too, manifesting as minor fluctuations in mood, edginess, anxiety, irritability, hypersensitivity, apathy, guilt, psychic inertia, and so on. Surely, no one—not even the saints—is immune to the powerful inner "demons" of anger, rage, sex, power, and erotic infatuation or romantic love. (See fig. 20.)

The unforgettable, intoxicating experience of "falling in love" is one form of daimonic possession almost everyone can relate to. Falling in love feels very much like being physically invaded or infected by some external spirit or entity. As Cole Porter lyrically says in his standard love song, "I've got you under my skin," admitting that the mysterious "other" has somehow magically broached the protective barrier of the skin and psyche, as might a bacterium or virus—or a demon! Briefly after exposure to the beloved, at least some of the classic "symptoms" ensue: anxiety, sleeplessness, agitation, appetite disturbance, obsessive longing, compulsive behavior, alternating elation and apprehension, and countless other little signs and symptoms lovers learn to live with. We have been deeply and irrevocably affected by encountering another, and are made aware of a powerful, unbidden, irrational process being—for better or worse—inexorably set into motion within us. We are possessed! Which is why Plato referred to Eros—more commonly conceived of as Cupid—as the mischievous daimon he really is.

These then, are a few of the familiar psychological demons that plague every person from time to time. They have grown legion in the contemporary psyche, so much so that it has become part of popular parlance to speak of someone's being figuratively beset, driven, or dragged down by his or her "demons." (See fig. 21.) Possession by these

Fig. 20.　*St. Anthony Tormented by Demons.* Engraving by Martin Schongauer (fifteenth century, German). Courtesy The Metropolitan Museum of Art, New York. Rogers Fund, 1920 (20.5.2).

Fig. 21. Two demons dragging some tortured soul down to hell. Michelangelo Buonarroti, *The Last Judgement,* detail from Sistine Chapel, Vatican Palace, Vatican State. Courtesy Alinari/Art Resource, New York.

comparatively pedestrian demons can be deceptively subtle, as in the case of people who simply seem to have "bad luck" in their business or personal affairs. We say they are "jinxed"; "born under a bad sign"; "cursed"; "hoodooed," etc. Such ill-fated patterns of behavior or negative responses to one's attitude by others can sometimes be traced back to a stubborn yet stealthy state of possession: our attitudes and actions are sufficiently latently influenced—in the detrimental sense—to sabotage even our most conscientious efforts. Unconscious hostility or "passive-aggressive" behavior are but two possible examples of such negative possession states. It is my belief that, of all the demons bedeviling us today, repressed, unresolved anger and rage are by far the most dangerous, destructive, and difficult to regulate. We cannot wish them away; nor can we exorcise them lastingly without losing something precious in ourselves. They are here to stay, and we had better learn to deal with them. This is the reason Rollo May declared that "the daimons are here. Surely not as entities, but as symbols of tendencies within ourselves that obsess us."[35]

Voluntary vs. Involuntary Possession

As we have seen, the age-old phenomenon of possession has a well-earned reputation for being associated with evil, destructiveness, psychopathology, and violence. This distinctly negative quality of possession will always be present to the extent that the possessing daimons are disconnected from consciousness. In such a situation, the daimonic drives us blindly and uses us to achieve its own goals, regardless of the undesirable consequences. As Jung points out:

> Probably no one imagines this state as being particularly harmless, and there is in fact no difference in principle between a slip of the tongue caused by a complex and the wildest blasphemies; it is only a difference of degree. The history of language provides innumerable illustrations of this. When some one is in the throes of a violent emotion we exclaim: "What's got into him today?" "He is driven by the devil," . . . etc. In using these somewhat worn metaphors we naturally do not think of their original meaning, although it is easily recognizable and points without a doubt to the fact that naiver and more primitive people did not "psychologize" disturbing complexes as we do, but regarded them as beings in their own right, that is, demons.[36]

Conversely, there has always existed another type of possession—"voluntary" or "benevolent possession"—in which the individual consciously chooses to invite the daimonic forces for constructive purposes, like religious rituals or artistic creativity. *Benevolent possession* is a state of mind during which the person is guided by supposedly divine and beneficent—as opposed to demonic and maleficent—spirits or daimons. Our popular mythology about "angels" reflects this helpful, protective, and instructive side of the daimon. Jungian analyst Alfred Ribi writes that

> we can learn much from primitive peoples about the positive function of possession. In this extraordinary ecstatic state in which the ordinary consciousness is more or less disabled, even paranormal feats, which are often used for the welfare of the community, become possible. (Genuine seances with mediums approach this quite closely.) Ecstatic states have always been considered an exceptional religious condition and play a major role in many religions throughout the world. The oracles of the Pythia in Delphi or the soothsaying Germanic seeresses should be seen in this light. . . . The techniques for reaching such a state are many and varied—from chemical drugs to monotonous rhythms. In every case, there is an *abaissement du niveau mental,* a lowering of the mental level, which makes it easier for unconscious contents to cross over.[37]

Psychoanalyst Erich Fromm relates this ecstatic, rage-inducing initiation rite known traditionally by some Teutonic tribes as "going berserk," during which

> the male youth was induced into a state of identification with a bear. [The term "berserk" may be literally translated as "bear shirt."] The initiated would attack people, trying to bite them, not speaking but simply making noises like a bear. To be in this trancelike state was the highest accomplishment of this ritual, and to have participated in it was the beginning of independent manhood. The expression *furor teutonicus* implies the sacred nature of this particular stage of rage. . . . It is rage for the sake of rage, not directed against an enemy or provoked by any damage or insult. It aimed at a trancelike state which in this case is organized around the all-pervasive feeling of rage. It may be that the induction of this state was helped by

drugs. . . . The unifying force of absolute rage was required as a means to arrive at the experience of ecstasis.[38]

We are reminded here of Zaslow's remarks in chapter one about the positive value of rage. Sacred rites des passages such as these permitted participants to fully immerse themselves in rage, redeeming it from repression, and infusing it with a positive rather than only negative power.

As to the use of psychogenic drugs such as peyote, psilocybin, mescaline, lysergic acid diethylamide (LSD), hashish, marijuana, or that old standard—alcohol—to deliberately induce states of daimonic possession, there is no debating the Dionysian and mind-altering effects produced by their ingestion. Alcohol has long been utilized by artists to lubricate creativity by artificially inducing the daimonic. Psychedelic drugs, popularized by Timothy Leary during the 1960s, are apparently having a renascence. Some "New Age" scientists, like anthropologist Terrance McKenna, are calling for a return to "archaic" consciousness through the increased use of psilocybin mushrooms: He claims that certain "entities" speak to him under the influence of this drug, seemingly much in the manner of Socrates' daimonion, or those ancestral spirits of the dead we discussed in chapter three.[39] At all events, the insidious dangers of psychoactive drug use—even for well-intentioned "spiritual" or "religious" purposes—must not be underestimated: the daimonic is definitely not something to be naively toyed with by dilettantes.

During the Middle Ages, the knights sought out such ecstatic experiences by way of voluntarily surrendering themselves spiritually—though not physically—to the love of a fair damsel, who became the revered object of adoration, worship, and "inspiration, the symbol of all beauty and perfection, the ideal that moved him to be noble, spiritual, refined, and high-minded."[40] Throughout history, the beneficial, restorative, and invigorating effects of "falling in love" are legendary—as are the all-too-familiar pitfalls. As stated earlier, these are forms of "erotic possession."

Benevolent possession can occur in the creative process as well. The artist allows herself or himself to be swept up in the raging current of primordial images, ideas, intuitions, and emotions emanating from the daimonic; while, at the same time, retaining sufficient conscious control to render this raw energy or *prima materia* into some new creative form. Such a voluntary surrender to the daimonic, says May, must not "be thought of merely as a Bacchic 'letting go': it involves the total person, with the subconscious and unconscious acting in unity with the conscious.

It is not, thus, *irrational;* it is, rather, suprarational. It brings intellectual, volitional, and emotional functions into play together."[41] We will be delving deeply into the intimate relationship between the daimonic and creativity in chapter eight.

Voluntary possession can be a constructive, integrating, even healing experience. But its inducement demands specific attributes, discipline, and skills, including adequate ego strength to withstand and meaningfully structure (rather than succumbing to) daimonic chaos. The boundary between benevolent and *malevolent possession* is perilously permeable, and may be abruptly or imperceptibly breached. In the absence of such essential personal qualities—as well as the much-needed external matrix of family, friends, and community support—voluntary possession can quickly deteriorate into destructive, *involuntary possession*, otherwise known as madness or psychosis. This is, for example, one way of thinking about *mania* in bipolar disorder, formerly manic-depressive psychosis: "The very name . . . given by the Greeks to madness was derived from the root-word *man, men,* which occurs in the Latin *Manes,* and indeed the Romans thought that a madman was tormented by the goddess Mania, the mother of the Lares, the hallucinations of lunatics being taken to be spectres who pursued them."[42]

Manic-depressive psychosis was observed at least as far back as 400 B.C. by Hippocrates, and has always been associated with possession, madness, and creativity. Clinical psychologist Kay Redfield Jamison—who herself suffers from manic-depressive disorder—makes a compelling (if not completely convincing) biological argument for the genetic and biochemical determinants of bipolar disorder, in conjunction with its close correlation to the "artistic temperament."[43] But bipolar disorder can also be conceived as a psychological and emotional process of voluntary and involuntary possession, comprising alternating polar extremes of destructiveness and creativity. In its manic or "high" phase, it is the prototype of "creative madness," or daimonic possession. Many artists with this syndrome—especially those who are extraordinarily talented—seek to intentionally *invite* possession by the daimon of Mania (or by the Muse, yet another daimonic myth) in order to enhance their creative powers. While this barely controlled, voluntary state of benevolent possession—sometimes referred to today as "hypomania"—can be abundantly productive and fruitful, it too often turns into manic psychosis: the person is swamped, inundated, swept away, and sometimes drowned by the daimonic. Or, mania may just as swiftly turn to its opposite—psychotic depression—yet another state of negative possession about which we will have more to say in the next chapter.[44]

Nonetheless, when considered within certain cultural contexts, claims one author, "possession by benevolent, mystical spirits is a socially acceptable expression of psychological conflicts that functions to provide the agent with a source or abreaction, communication, status, and resolution of cognitive and emotional stress."[45] Daimonic possession, as we have seen, can be beneficial, cathartic, and even therapeutic in some instances. There are societies existing today (in Haiti and Mexico, for example) that do not consider the possession phenomenon pathological, but rather encourage their citizens to ceremoniously, ritually, voluntarily invite the daimonic to take temporary possession of them, in sincere hopes of resolving their psychological and spiritual problems.

One excellent example of the therapeutic practice of voluntary possession is Voodoo, an ancient religion still popular in West Africa, the West Indies, Haiti, Brazil, and—perhaps surprisingly—some sections of the United States.[46] Speaking of the occult belief-system of Voodoo, psychologist Esther Leonard De Vos explains that Voodoo hinges on the belief in the existence of powerful, yet invisible spiritual forces: "The belief that there are invisible forces that can affect the lives and behavior of man is one of the oldest and most prevalent beliefs. In a much earlier time these invisible forces were called gods or demons. . . . These forces are not physical nor visible, and because of this they are referred to by the Haitian who practices Voodoo as *les invisibles*. Being invisible does not make them less real; they are considered to be true and correct."[47]

De Vos goes on to say that a person may invoke the deities or *loa* for assistance in difficult times or circumstances with the aid of the Voodoo priests or shamans; but on occasion, these "invisible forces" can take possession of the troubled person, precipitating a "possession crisis phenomenon." She describes this dramatic event as follows:

> The possession crisis itself is brief in duration, usually lasting from five to eight minutes, and manifests itself in three distinct phases. The first stage is hyperventilation during which the person remains conscious but experiences distortions in perceptions, including hallucinations and loss of equilibrium. . . . The second phase follows immediately, and is typified by psychomotor agitation. . . . During this phase consciousness is lost. The third stage is marked by the collapse of the person possessed, after which he soon regains consciousness. There is always amnesia for the duration of the possession crisis.[48]

This vivid depiction resembles a highly condensed version of what we psychologists call a "brief psychotic episode." But the author, a Jungian analyst, arrives at the following conclusion: "In contrast to analysis, where individuality is retained and developed, the possession crisis ceremony brings people together in a common ritual with a prescribed goal. The individual abandons himself to the group in a kind of ecstasy or act of surrender. Something greater than the individual emerges; . . . the energy released is channelled toward . . . healing." And finally: "Possession in Christianity is not dissimilar from possession in Voodoo, except that in Christianity the only possession sought is by the Holy Ghost; all other possessions are considered works of the devil."[49] Voluntary possession is indeed similarly practiced by some Christians, as De Vos points out; particularly Christian fundamentalists, for whom possession by the "Holy Ghost" or "Holy Spirit" is something to be enthusiastically encouraged within the supportive context of the congregation, and highly valued for its presumed healing powers, both spiritual and physical.

Voluntary possession also holds a place of major importance in the time-honored tradition of shamanism. Ribi reports one such self-induced initiatory experience related by a South Dakotan medicine man, during which he was visited in a sublime vision by what would later become his "helping spirits," or *spiritus familiares*—the "winged ones": "supernatural beings, somewhat comparable to our angels. . . . If he follows these destiny fraught powers, they will show him their helpful side. If he struggles against them, they will turn their demonic, destructive side to him."[50] We will touch lightly on the topic of "angels" and their psychological significance in a forthcoming chapter.

But to sum up for now the potentially positive, cathartic, creative, integrating, and therapeutic uses of daimonic possession, I enlist the aid of yet another distinguished Jungian analyst, M. Esther Harding, who states succinctly that

> in the orgiastic religions, in which awe of the god and inspiration by him were experienced as part of the ritual, the goal of the religious practices was the attainment of an ecstasy in which the worshipper felt himself *to be possessed* by his god. . . . The wild and prolonged dancing of the dervishes of Mohammedan countries produces an ecstatic, trancelike condition. Ascetic practices are also undertaken for the same purpose, as among the medicine men of some American Indian tribes, and also among Eskimos, who become nearly

crazed from fasting, loneliness, and self-inflicted pain. The latter practice played a part also in the ritually produced ecstasy of the *flagellantes* of mediaeval times, whose cult has survived even to the present day. . . . In India, the yogin seeks this ecstatic state, called *samadhi,* through meditation and other yogic practices. . . . Drugs such as hashish, . . . marijuana, or peyote, in addition to alcohol, have been used in widely separated parts of the globe in connection with religious rituals to induce states of trance. . . .[51]

There has always been a connection linking creativity—and religiosity—with the transforming phenomenon of daimonic possession. "In such experiences of inspiration and rapture," writes Harding,

the poets of all times have felt themselves to be filled with a divine influx. . . . For a short space of time such an individual feels himself to be made whole through *submitting* to possession of his being by a power greater than himself. . . .

There is no doubt that life is renewed through contact with these instinctive depths, dangerous though such a contact [can be]. . . . Individuals who have had such experiences assert that they attained a sense of redemption . . . through such a consummation of union with the daemonic force, which they conceived of as God.[52]

6

Madness, Mental Disorders, and the Daimonic

The Central Role of Anger and Rage in Psychopathology

We know from a treatise in the Hippocratic Corpus . . . that mental
disturbance often showed itself in dreams or visions of angry daemons.
—E. R. Dodds, *The Greeks and the Irrational*

The human rage reaction has not been adequately evaluated
from a psychiatric or psychological point of view, even though
it is a central phenomenon in violence . . . , psychosis,
[and a multitude of other mental disorders].
—Robert W. Zaslow, *The Psychology of the Z-Process*

The Daimonic and Depth Psychology: Discovering Repressed Rage

Friedrich Nietzsche

Philosopher Friedrich Nietzsche (1844–1900), one of the intellectual
forerunners of modern depth psychology, foresaw Freud's idea of
the "death instinct," Jung's conception of the "shadow," and Alfred
Adler's emphasis on the "will to power." He also anticipated existential

psychiatrist Viktor Frankl's central presumption of an inherent and transcendent "will to meaning."[1] Moreover, Nietzsche appears to have predicted our present predicament regarding the daimonic emotions of anger and rage. As Ellenberger writes: "A conspicuous feature of Nietzsche's psychology is the importance he ascribes not only to aggressive but also to self-destructive instincts."[2] "Nothing," notes Nietzsche himself in *Ecce Homo*,

> consumes a man more quickly than the emotion of resentment. . . .
> It involves a rapid using up of nervous energy, an abnormal increase of harmful secretions, as, for instance, that of bile into the stomach. Resentment should above all be forbidden the sick man—it is *his* special danger: unfortunately, however, it is also his most natural propensity. This was perfectly understood by that profound physiologist Buddha. His "religion," which it would be better to call a system of hygiene, . . . depended for its effect upon the triumph over resentment: to free the soul from it—that was the first step towards recovery.[3]

Nor was the concept of what Sigmund Freud later termed "sublimation" new in Nietzsche's time: it was applied by Nietzsche not only to the sexual instincts, but—in even greater measure—to the aggressive impulses as well. "The word 'resentment,' which comprehended all sorts of feelings of rancor, spite, envy, grudge, jealousy, and hatred," adds Ellenberger, "was given a new meaning by Nietzsche. When such feelings are inhibited and therefore become unconscious to the subject, they manifest themselves in disguised forms, notably false morality."[4] Overly moralistic, rigid, fundamentalist religious or spiritual leaders who tend to deny their own daimonic impulses—and hence, fall prey to them—perfectly exemplify Nietzsche's point. In addition to denying the sexual component of the daimonic, there is also the traditional belief among such self-righteous poseurs and their followers "that religious or spiritual people are not personally aggressive. Hate, power drives, resentment, and jealousies are unspiritual feelings belonging to the non-religious."[5] Such high-minded "spiritual" people tend to hold the daimonic in contempt, considering it despicable, diabolic, unholy, and irretrievably evil.

Sigmund Freud

Sigmund Freud (1856–1939), the undisputed "father" of depth psychology, at first paid little attention to the role of repressed anger and rage in psychopathology. For Freud, prior to the early 1920s, the root of all evil was limited to the repression of our instinctual sexuality or *libido*.

However, fateful events as Freud grew older—for instance, the first World War, and his painful personal struggle against palatal cancer—forced him to confront, reconsider, and theoretically incorporate the problem of human aggression, destructiveness, death, and evil.

At the advanced age of sixty-four, in *Beyond the Pleasure Principle*, Freud first posited what later came to be called "Thanatos," the "death instinct"; and, in 1922, he published the following bold statement:

> Though psycho-analysis endeavours as a rule to develop its theories as independently as possible from those of other sciences, it is nevertheless obliged to seek a basis for the theory of the instincts in biology. On the ground of a far-reaching consideration of the processes which go to make up life and which lead to death, it becomes probable that we should recognize the existence of two classes of instincts, corresponding to the contrary processes of construction and dissolution in the organism. On this view, the one set of instincts, which work essentially in silence, would be those which follow the aim of leading the living creature to death and therefore deserve to be called the *'death instincts'*; these would . . . manifest themselves as *destructive* or *aggressive* impulses. The other set of instincts would be those which are better known to us in analysis, the libidinal, sexual or life instincts, which are best comprised under the name of *Eros*.[6]

Just where these elusive "aggressive impulses" had been hiding during the course of countless Freudian analytic treatments until then remains a serious matter with far-reaching implications for current psychotherapies, as we shall see.

In 1927, subsequent to Freud's rather vague recognition of the role of aggressive impulses like anger and rage in psychopathology, psychoanalyst Karl Abraham astutely postulated the unconscious presence of repressed violent impulses in manic-depressive patients. Though "bipolar disorder" is today almost globally believed to be due to some ill-defined "biochemical imbalance" and successfully controlled with lithium, my own clinical observation (as well as that of others) confirms that there is in fact often an inordinate amount of overt anger, rage, resentment, and hostility during—and, to some lesser but still significant degree, even in the interim between—the "manic" phases of this misunderstood mental disorder.[7]

A few years later, Freud further explained how his two proposed instincts—Eros and Thanatos—are not in fact distinct and separate drives, but rather converge and overlap, as though partaking of some common spring of irreducible primal energy:

> According to our hypothesis human instincts are of only two kinds: those which seek to preserve and unite—which we call 'erotic,' exactly in the sense in which Plato uses the word 'Eros' in his *Symposium,* or 'sexual,' with a deliberate extension of the popular conception of 'sexuality'—and those which seek to destroy and kill and which we class together as the aggressive or destructive instinct. As you see, this is in fact no more than a theoretical clarification of the universally familiar opposition between Love and Hate. . . . [However,] we must not be too hasty in introducing ethical judgments of good and evil. Neither of these instincts is any less essential than the other; the phenomena of life arise from the operation of both to-gether, whether acting in concert or opposition. It seems as though an instinct of the one sort can scarcely ever operate in isolation; it is always accompanied—or, as we say, alloyed—with an element from the other side, which modifies its aim or is, in some cases, what enables it to achieve that aim. Thus, for instance, the instinct of self-preservation is certainly of an erotic kind, but it must nevertheless have aggressiveness at its disposal if it is to fulfill its purpose. So, too, the instinct of love, when it is directed towards an object, stands in need of some contribution from the instinct of mastery if it is in any way to possess that object. The difficulty of isolating the two classes of instinct in their actual manifestations is indeed what has so long prevented us from recognizing them.[8]

This nearly Nietzschean allusion to the "alloying" or "con-fusion" of Eros and Thanatos—that is, of sexual instinct with other instincts in a coalescence of forces transcending any possible "ethical judgments of good and evil"—approaches Adler's "confluence of drives" model, Jung's unifying primal libido theory proposed in 1912, as well as May's post-Freudian paradigm of the daimonic as a phenomenologically undifferen-tiated, primal force of nature.[9] But it was not until 1937, two years before his death, that Freud finally "discovered"—proclaiming his debt to the pre-Socratic Greek philosopher, Empedocles—his "new," dualistic theory of Eros and Thanatos: "[Empedocles] taught that there were two prin-ciples governing events in the life of the universe as in that of the mind, and that these principles were eternally in conflict with each other. . . .

These powers . . . he . . . conceived of as 'natural forces working like instincts, and certainly not intelligences with a conscious purpose.' "[10] But beyond his increasingly mythological and philosophical formulation of these two great and opposing archetypal principles at work in the cosmos and in the human psyche, Freud said surprisingly little on the specific problem of anger and rage in psychopathology and psychoanalysis.

Psychoanalyst Michael Stone, in a valuable review of the psychoanalytic literature on rage and aggression, reminds us of Melanie Klein's presumption (1937) that "the complex attitudes of hate and aggression were already well differentiated practically at birth." Another Freudian disciple, Otto Fenichel, says Stone, in 1945 theorized that states of rage could be humanly endured only "for a short time without discharge, but must then be released, no matter at whom . . . —alluding to the pathological and exaggerated nature of this emotion." And Freudian analyst Sandor Rado spoke in 1956 of the so-called "emergency" emotions of "rage and 'retroflexed' rage, as [found] in depressive conditions. Outbursts of rage Rado understood as attempts to rid ourselves of 'excessive emergency emotions'."[11] Stone himself speculates that "violence—in effect, the pathology of aggression—is peculiar to mankind and is not seen in the animal kingdom. This difference is to be accounted for in large measure, I believe, by the unique ability thanks to our memory and language, to think about the past and the future. For over and above temporal lobe epilepsy, serotonin deficiency, hyperandrogenization, and so on, that may provoke violent outbursts, there is learning and anticipation."[12]

"Hitler's life," writes Stone,

> makes an illustrative example. His father, Alois, beat Hitler's older brother "unmercifully with a hippopotamus whip," once rendering him unconscious. . . . The father was still harsher with Adolf, who, as the more rebellious son, was savaged every day—till at age 11 he refused to give his father the satisfaction of crying, even after 32 lashes. . . . Here are the seeds of Hitler's ungovernable hatred, ragefulness, and quest for revenge. Hitler's seething hatred did not die when, three years later, his father died; instead it sought satisfaction from the customary target of the day.[13]

Stone here refers, of course, to those seemingly perennial scapegoats, the Jewish people. The enormous stores of anger, rage, and resentment fueling Adolf Hitler's pathological hatred of Jews are also hinted at by Erich Fromm, who cites Hitler's barely controlled, intensely intimidating *"attacks of anger."*[14]

Alfred Adler

Austrian physician Alfred Adler (1870–1937) proposed, in 1908—almost two decades prior to Freud's paying any attention to it—that there exists a primary, powerful, and distinct aggressive drive which cannot be accounted for by mere sexual frustration: "From early childhood," wrote Adler,

> we can say from the first day (first cry), we find a stand of the child toward the environment which cannot be called anything but hostile. If one looks for the cause of this position, one finds it determined by the difficulty of affording satisfaction for the organ [i.e., frustration]. This circumstance as well as the further relationships of the hostile, belligerent position of the individual toward the environment indicate a drive toward fighting for satisfaction which I call "aggression drive."[15]

Adler further felt that "inferiority feelings"—a phrase he first coined—in the form of "increased dependency and the intensified feeling of our own littleness and weakness, lead to inhibition of aggression and thereby to the phenomenon of anxiety."[16] What he called "masculine protest" consisted of a compensatory striving for superiority (to counteract feelings of inferiority), aggression, ambition, avarice, and envy, coupled with constant "defiance, vengeance, and resentment." For Adler, "fighting, wrestling, beating, biting, and cruelties show the aggression drive in its pure form" (p. 35). The "refinement" (or what Freud called "sublimation") of the aggressive instinct, according to Adler, resulted in such diverse—and often destructive—human activities as competitive sports, strivings for interpersonal power and social dominance, racial, religious, and international hostilities, and war. Moreover, he maintained that the myriad "manifestations of the aggression drive are found again in the neuroses and psychoses," describing how

> we find pure expressions of the aggression drive in temper tantrums and attacks of hysteria, epilepsy, and paranoia. Phases of the turning round of the drive upon the self are hypochondria, neurasthenic and hysterical pain, the entire syndrome of complaints in neurasthenia, hysteria, accident neurosis, ideas of reference and persecution, self-mutilation, and suicide. . . .
> . . . The various forms of anxiety come about because the aggression drive, which is at the basis of anxiety, can take hold of various systems. It may enervate motor systems (tremor,

shaking, cramps, catatonic phenomena, functional paralysis as inhibition of aggression). It may also excite the vasomotor system (heart palpitations, paleness, blushing) or other tracts, so that we may find perspiration, incontinency and vomiting, or prevention of secretion as an inhibition phenomenon. (pp. 36–37)

Adler's legendarily keen powers of observation foreshadowed the future field of psychosomatic medicine.

What Adler, a contemporary and colleague of Freud, sought in his psychological theory amounts to no less than a holistic or unified model of personality, based on his so-called "confluence of drives" hypothesis: He claimed that there was a natural "confluence," or coming together of several drives such as sexuality (libido in Freud's model), aggression, and the Nietzschean will to power ("masculine protest") into a relatively undifferentiated, superordinated force. By "superordinated," Adler meant that these diverse, dynamic drives or impulses could be collectively controlled and function as one when usurped and directed by an over-riding drive like aggression. (Readers will note the clear similarity between Adler's early concept of drive confluence and May's model of the daimonic, recalling, perchance, that May briefly studied under Adler.) Although Adler was later to stray from his theoretical focus on the primacy of aggression in normal human behavior, write apostles Ansbacher and Ansbacher, he "retained it as the basis of his understanding of abnormal behavior, and . . . considered every symptom as an act of aggression aimed at a single opponent, or society at large."[17] His theory of aggression had a profound and lasting influence on Freud and the future of psychoanalysis. Edward Hitschmann, one of the first Freudians, finds it "a very interesting event in the history of science, that one man [Adler] finds a certainly all-important impulse in the human mind and considers the fate of this impulse in the development of men with great intelligence, but relinquishes the problem again entirely. And that a man of Freud's genius hesitated twenty-two years to accept the aggression-impulse, but does it then in full extent, admitting his failure finally in his seventy-fourth year!"[18] Hitschmann, who overstates Adler's "abandonment" of the aggression theory, none-theless correctly points to the presence of some primal, unconscious fear or resistance—operating even in the rigorous minds of the most penetrating depth psychologists—which interferes with the ready recognition of this dark and dangerous side of the human psyche. It is as though some civilized part of us refuses to see—or cannot look at for too long without hastily averting our gaze—the harsh and disturbing reality of the daimonic: "See no evil; hear no evil; speak no evil."

Finally, Freud—who fell victim to this prosaic variety of "psychic blindness" through the penultimate decade preceding his death—publicly "confessed" his "sin" as follows: " 'A powerful measure of desire for aggression has to be reckoned as part of the instinctive endowment of men. *Homo homini lupus* . . . I can no longer understand how we could have overlooked the universality of non-erotic aggression and destruction and could have omitted to give it its due significance in our interpretation of life . . . '."[19] Today, we clinicians continue to suffer from much this same sort of psychic blindness regarding the prominent role of repressed anger and rage in psychopathology. For the most part, we wish it would magically disappear, without our having to hear, see, or speak of it.

Carl Gustav Jung

Like Adler, Carl Jung (1875–1961) could not accept Freud's dogmatic definition of libido (i.e., sexuality) as the predominant instinctual drive above all others, preferring to consider "libido" a far more diffuse, generalized, and heterogeneous form of "psychic energy." "Libido," argued Jung, "from the genetic point of view, . . . is bodily needs like hunger, thirst, sleep and sex, and emotional states or affects. . . . "[20] Fatefully, he dared to differ with Freud on this most sacred psychoanalytic point, feeling that "the motive forces at the back of neurosis come from all sorts of congenital characteristics and environmental influences, which together build up an attitude that makes it impossible . . . to lead a life in which the instincts are satisfied. . . . Hence there can be no *sexual* theory of neurosis, though there may very well be a *psychological* one" (p. 139). In Freud's defense, however, Jung adds that "despite his definition of libido as sexuality, Freud does not explain 'everything' in terms of sex, as is commonly supposed, but recognizes the existence of special instinctual forces whose nature is not clearly known. . . . At the back of all this lies the hypothetical idea of a 'bundle of instincts,' in which the sexual instinct figures as a partial instinct" (p. 132).

Readers may once again note the recurring subterranean theme of some undifferentiated and indivisible, instinctually based dynamic force underpinning—implicitly if not explicitly—Freud's sexual paradigm, Adler's "power" paradigm, and Jung's generic "libido" paradigm. In much the same fashion as Adler—and Otto Rank, another of Freud's closest collaborators—the heretical Jung held "libido" to consist of what other psychiatrists and psychologists had once called "will," or "tendency," or "striving."[21] Jung believed that libido is comprised of many different instinctual needs and drives, including sexuality and aggression; and that the repression or dissociation of these sometimes unacceptable, "shadow" impulses could lead to various species of psychopathology. Regrettably, however, he did not—despite his prolific writings—deem it necessary to speak directly to the role of repressed anger and rage in mental disorders. Nevertheless, even in his embryonic conception of libido, Jung was fully cognizant of the capacity for certain dissociated "complexes" to "possess" or enslave the libido in the service and bidding of some singularly irrational symptom or behavior: "As a power which transcends consciousness the libido is by nature daemonic: it is both God and devil."[22]

Wilhelm Reich

Viennese psychiatrist Wilhelm Reich (1897–1957), a great admirer of Freud, tried his best to loyally conform to Freud's libido theory, scientifically researching the role of repressed sexual energy or "libido" in psychopathology. Reich came to call this quantifiable, biosexual, libidinal energy "orgone." Orgone, when chronically blocked or inhibited in the body, caused symptoms, and hence, claimed Reich, required physical liberation by way of cathartic expression. Reich became convinced that the early depth psychologists (Freud, Adler, Jung, Rank, Stekel, Ferenczi, et al.) "came to grief upon the *one* question which determines *every* psychotherapeutic situation: *What shall the patient do with his natural sexuality once it is liberated from repression?*"[23] Reich's radical solution was to encourage the patient's full expression of his or her suppressed sexuality via uninhibited sexual orgasm during intercourse, love-making, or masturbation. But simplistic as this may sound, sexual satisfaction proved elusive for most neurotic patients. "What was overlooked," writes Reich, "was the fact that the essence of a neurosis is the *inability of the patient to obtain gratification*. The focal point of this . . . problem is '*orgastic impotence.*' My first relevant observation was the fact that genital satisfaction relieved symptoms. However, clinical observation showed also that only very rarely is genital energy available in the necessary amount. It was necessary to look for the places and mechanisms in which this energy was bound up or misdirected" (ibid.).

Undeterred by these roadblocks, Reich pressed on in his crusade to liberate the natural sexuality and orgasmic potency of his patients,

employing physical manipulation and deep-breathing, among other unorthodox methods. In so doing, he unexpectedly stumbled upon a startling discovery: Whenever he began breaking through the patient's rigidly
defensive "body armor"—the term Reich used to describe chronic muscular contractions presumed to inhibit the desired "orgasm reflex"[24]—he
was befuddled to find that "the energy that held the armor together consisted mostly in destructiveness which had become bound. This was shown
by the fact that destructiveness would be set free as soon as the armor began
to crack. Whence came this destructive and hateful aggression?"[25]

Whence indeed! Confronted with this never-before reported phenomenon, Reich, still undaunted, proved both brilliant and brave in
exploring this dark and previously uncharted dimension of human personality, observing that

> people reacted with intense hatred to any attempt to disturb
> the neurotic equilibrium which was maintained by their armor.
> This inevitable reaction proved a major obstacle in the path
> of the investigation of character structure. Destructiveness itself
> was indeed never free. It was always covered up by opposing
> character attitudes. Where life situations really called for ag-
> gression, action, decision, for taking a stand, there was instead
> consideration, politeness, restraint, false modesty; in short all
> kinds of character traits which enjoy high esteem as human
> virtues. But there was no doubt: *they paralyzed every rational
> action, every living active impulse* in the individual.[26]

Reich recognized that the raw, repressed anger, rage, and aggressive impulses he touched upon in therapy remained, for the most part,
unconscious, dormant, defensively bound up in the patient's constrictive
"body armor" and rigid character structure. "And if it happened that there
appeared some aggression, it was confused, aimless, and seemed to cover
up a deep feeling of insecurity or a pathological egotism. In other words,
it was *pathological,* not healthy, rationally directed aggression." Consistently faced with these irrefutable facts, Reich "began to comprehend the
latent hatred which is never lacking in patients."[27] Gradually, he further
inferred that if sexuality, libido, or "orgone" was ever to be fully liberated, it would first be necessary to somehow safely and therapeutically
release this repressed anger, rage, and hatred. (We shall survey some of
Reich's controversial techniques for doing so in the next chapter.)

But ultimately, in true Freudian fashion, Reich concluded that human
evil, or "pathological destructiveness—or simply human malice quite

generally—proved to be one . . . misdirection of genital energy" (p. 128). Deciding to frame his radical findings in the Freudian libido theory of the day—subordinating anger and rage to sexuality—Reich regrettably missed the revolutionary meaning of his inadvertent discovery. Nonetheless, despite his subsequent personal and legal problems after immigrating to the United States, Reich played a premier part in revealing the latent role of anger and rage in psychopathology.

Hostility, Anxiety, and the Daimonic

In his highly recommendable book *The Meaning of Anxiety*, first published in 1950, American psychologist Rollo May pondered the poorly understood relationship between anxiety and hostility, in an effort to discern which of these two phenomena contribute most to functional psychopathology. By "hostility," he meant the repression of hostile impulses such as anger, rage, or resentment, and its pervasive psychological and physiological effects. May concluded that "in neurotic patterns, including the special group of these patterns termed psychosomatic illnesses, anxiety is the primary etiological phenomenon. In this sense anxiety is the *psychic* common denominator of all disease as well as of all behavior disturbances."[28] He arrived at this arguable premise on grounds that anxiety accompanies all types of psychological repression—be it the denial of sexuality or of hostility—and thus plays the most pivotal role in the process of psychopathology. Moreover, May maintained that "clinical experience has proved to psychologists and psychiatrists alike that the central problem in psychotherapy is the nature of anxiety. To the extent we have been able to solve that problem, we have made a beginning in understanding the causes of integration and disintegration of personality."[29] May articulated in America what became known as the "spectrum theory" of psychopathology, which, according to one of its prominent opponents, perceived "all psychopathology . . . [as] secondary to anxiety, which in turn was caused by intrapsychic conflict. Psychosis was considered the result of such an excess of anxiety that the ego crumbled and regressed, and neurosis, the result of a partially successful defense against anxiety that led to symptom formation."[30]

At the time of its mid-century publication, May's comprehensive study—originally a doctoral dissertation overseen by his chairperson, Paul Tillich—joined the ranks of only a few prior major psychological treatises on the specific problem of anxiety, including Sören Kierkegaard's *The*

Concept of Dread (first published in Danish in 1844 and in English in 1944), and Freud's *Inhibitions, Symptoms, and Anxiety* (1927). Freud and his followers had been focused on the problem of traumatic infantile sexuality, Victorian sexual suppression in adults, and, belatedly, the long-denied, primary aggressive drive. Each of these areas were seen as highly conflictual sources of "signal anxiety": a defensive symptom set off to alert the ego to the increased proximity to consciousness of such threatening unconscious contents. But, by the middle of the chaotic twentieth century, the problem of anxiety itself had, for some psychotherapists, surpassed in importance the presumed primacy of both sexuality and aggression as *the* most pressing psychological symptom of the day:

> Every alert citizen of our society realizes, on the basis of his own experience as well as his observation of his fellow-men, that anxiety is a pervasive and profound phenomenon in the twentieth century. From 1945 and the birth of the atom bomb, anxiety shifted from a covert to an overt problem. . . .
>   . . . One had the impression in the middle decade of this century the explorations and investigations in such diverse fields as science and poetry, religion and politics were converging on this central problem of anxiety. Whereas the period of two or three decades before might have been termed the "age of covert anxiety," . . . the middle of our century may be called, as Auden and Camus called it, the "age of overt anxiety."[31]

May's attention to anxiety—in both its normal and pathological manifestations—reflects accurately the collective mood or Zeitgeist of this tense "cold war" period. Pent up aggression had been massively, collectively vented in the pandemonium[32] and devastating global destructiveness of World War II. The proverbial "genie" (an idea probably derived from the Arabic words *djinn,* connoting the devil, *jinniy,* meaning "demonic spirit," or the alternate Latin term *genii,* meaning daimones) had been released from, and then, blessedly, returned to its bottle—at least, for the time being. Freudian sexuality became the common stuff of cocktail conversation; and the impending "sexual revolution" of the 1960s was slowly gestating. All this created a much-needed window of opportunity for philosophers and psychotherapists to turn their attention to anxiety. May's position as to the primacy of anxiety in mental disorders was strongly influenced by the European existentialists, like Nietzsche, Kierkegaard, Camus, Sartre, and May's mentor, Tillich. Psychoanalytically, he corroborated the work of Karen Horney, who, unlike Freud, placed anxiety anterior to the instinctual drives. Horney saw anxiety—not sexuality or aggression—as the dominant drive in certain cases, and believed that "basic anxiety" is inseparably linked with hostility. She felt, for instance, that aggressive impulses such as anger and rage are repressed by children due to anxiety; furthermore, that this anxiety pertains to the child's fear of losing desperately depended upon parental support should she or he dare to openly express such hostile feelings.[33]

But I, for one, take a somewhat different stance than do May and Horney on the intersecting subject of anxiety and psychopathology. I agree with May that anxiety is an ontological and incontestable aspect of the human condition; and, with both he and Horney that, especially when repressed or avoided, anxiety plays an important part in spawning psychopathology. But anxiety is not today, in my opinion, the primary culprit in most types of psychopathology. *The preeminent problem in contemporary psychopathology is not anxiety, but repressed anger and rage.*

Nonetheless, there can be little question of the inextricable link between anger and rage, resentment or "hostility," and anxiety. For instance, May notes Horney's emphasis "on the *reciprocal relation of hostility and anxiety*," reporting that "except in unusual cases, her experience has been that anxiety which on superficial observation is related to sexual impulses often turns out to have its source in hostile or counter-hostile feelings about the sexual partner."[34] Hence she saw that anxiety may sometimes be *symptomatic of suppressed anger or rage* as well as sexuality. Horney had discovered that dogmatic preoccupation with Freudian sexuality provides a perfect "smokescreen" for the denial of a different facet of the daimonic lurking beneath the patient's symptomatic anxiety: not libido or eros, but rather repressed anger and rage, resentment, or hostility. Ironically, this same fact had been observed by Freud himself as early as 1917:

> When we subject to analysis the situation in which the anxiety, or the symptom accompanied by anxiety, arose, we can as a rule discover what normal mental process has been checked in its course and replaced by a manifestation of anxiety. . . . This process would have been accompanied by a particular affect and now we discover, to our astonishment, that this affect . . . is in every case replaced by anxiety, no matter what particular type it had previously been. So that when we have a hysterical anxiety condition before us, its unconscious correlative may be . . . apprehension, shame, embarrassment; or, quite as pos-

sibly, a 'positive' libidinal excitation; or an antagonistic, aggressive one, such as rage or anger. Anxiety is thus general current coin for which all the affects are exchanged. . . . [35]

There exists, as Freud unexpectedly found, a direct correlation between anxiety and the daimonic, deriving from the intrapsychic conflict the daimonic tends to cause. The resurgence of suppressed daimonic elements engenders what Freud dubbed "signal anxiety." For most of his life, however, Freud—and hence, his followers—remained fixated on the erotic side of the daimonic. But the daimonic can never be reduced or exclusively identified with just one—or even two—particular human tendencies. Sexuality and eros represent but one component of the daimonic; the teeming passions of anger and rage make up yet another of paramount importance. We could further add that *any* basic human emotion, need, or experience—like loneliness, tenderness, the existential striving for significance, meaning, spirituality, and personal power—which we deliberately deny or evade, becomes part of the daimonic. This includes, of course, the painful (and therefore, assiduously avoided) experience of anxiety, which, when systematically suppressed, can itself become daimonic.

Existential psychology and psychotherapy place special emphasis on the phenomenon of anxiety—both in its "normal" (or ontological) and "neurotic" (or pathological) forms. May, the foremost American proponent of existential therapy, was one of the first to "de-pathologize" the experience of anxiety, debunking the definition of "mental health" as being devoid of all anxiety. He drew a distinction between "normal" and "neurotic" or "psychotic" anxiety, suggesting that *pathological anxiety* results from the repression of normal, existential or *ontological anxiety.* May defines anxiety as "the *experience of Being affirming itself against Nonbeing.* The latter is that which would reduce or destroy Being, such as aggression, fatigue, boredom, and ultimately death."[36] This decidedly humanistic notion in no way discounts or negates Freud's understanding of anxiety as a *signal* to the ever-vigilant ego that some unconscious, unacceptable, and therefore previously suppressed drive, idea, or emotion is pressing its way toward consciousness. It simply means that not all anxiety is symptomatic of psychopathology. In many cases, anxiety can be a naturally occurring concomitant to *la condition humaine:* a nebulous but numinous feeling of "daemonic dread," to invoke Rudolf Otto's phrase. Or, in Sören Kierkegaard's terms, a dreadful "fear and trembling" in the face of the daimonic facts of life.[37] Such *existential anxiety,* said May, "is essential to the human condition."[38] It is normally found in fundamental human processes, like personal growth, maturation, and creativity. This sort of anxiety is not "neurotic"; it is part and parcel of the normal, natural course of evolving human consciousness, as we shall see, and a bona fide route toward rediscovering the daimonic. However, as with any other truly daimonic element, when we ignore, avoid, deny, drug, or suppress our ontological or existential anxiety, we unwittingly set the stage for the unwelcome appearance of neurotic—or, in some cases, even psychotic—states of *daimonic anxiety.* "Panic disorder," for example—an extremely painful and disabling seizure of neurotic anxiety—may be viewed as a temporary "possession" of daimonic anxiety, resulting from the habitual repression or avoidance of "normal," existential anxiety.

Freud's seminal concept of "signal anxiety" corresponds to Kierkegaard's conviction about anxiety being our "best teacher." By taking the experience of phobic or "free-floating" anxiety as a cue that something is amiss, not quite "right," that some wayward content of the unconscious is at play, our anxiety can be utilized like an Ariadnean thread,[39] leading us through the daimonic depths to the "demons" residing there. Carl Jung was cognizant that anxiety, appearing, as it does, in manifold forms such as physical symptoms, fantasies, nightmares, or severe states of panic, could occasionally herald an imminent invasion of (or possession by) the unconscious, and possible psychosis. He also knew, along with Kierkegaard, that the necessary task of coming to terms with the contents of the unconscious is always accompanied—with very good reason—by dreadful anxiety, apprehension, a primordial, instinctive fear of the daimonic; and, that all attempts to block off or dissociate these daimonic contents are neurotic, and finally, futile. To confront the dreaded demons of anger and rage, we must be equally willing to do battle directly with the frightful demon of anxiety, the infamous dragon of dread. For inevitably, anger, rage, and anxiety go hand in hand, and can never be entirely disentangled.

Narcissistic Rage

Psychoanalysts such as Erich Fromm, Heinz Kohut, and Otto Kernberg have related the problem of hostility, anger, and rage to an underlying matrix of neurotic narcissism. *Pathological narcissism* is certainly one of the most pervasive, insidious human evils, and, like anxiety, is highly correlated with anger and rage. According to Kohut, Kernberg, and various developmental psychologists, pathological narcissism stems from inadequate, insufficient, or traumatic parenting or surrogate parenting prior to five years of age, i.e., during the pre-Oedipal period. Deprivation or emotional trauma during this delicate developmental milestone renders severe psychic wounding in children, resulting in distorted perceptions of both themselves and the world. When we perceive our parents or caretakers to be unloving, rejecting, or hostile, we respond by concealing our so-called "true self," replacing it with what we believe those around us want us to be. We thereby create a "false self." As psychologist Stephen Johnson succinctly summarizes: "Even though narcissism comes from the Greek myth superficially understood to represent self-love, exactly the opposite is true in the narcissistic personality disorder or narcissistic style. The narcissist has buried his [or her] true self-expression in response to early injuries and replaced it with a highly developed, compensatory, 'false self.' "[40] A great deal of what neurotic narcissism disguises—and few of us are fully free from it—is our unresolved infantile anger, resentment, and rage.

As mentioned earlier, Horney noted that despite the pain and anger about not being loved—or, at least, never as well loved as one would like—children dare not demonstrate their feelings for fear of further frustration, rejection, retribution, or, far too frequently, physical or psychological abuse. This vicious cycle can repeat itself throughout one's life, sometimes causing a deep-seated neurotic condition characterized by compensatory grandiosity, hypersensitivity, and a long-buried, pathological rage. The typically well-camouflaged yet intense and overreactive neurotic anger of the narcissistic character is referred to as *narcissistic rage*. "Narcissistic rage," writes Kohut,

> belongs to the large psychological field of aggression, anger, and destructiveness . . . and occurs in many forms; they all share, however, a specific psychological flavor which gives them a distinct position within the wide realm of human aggression. The need for revenge, for righting a wrong, for undoing a hurt by whatever means, and a deeply anchored, unrelenting compulsion in the pursuit of all these aims, which gives no rest to those who have suffered a narcissistic injury—these are the characteristic features of narcissistic rage in all its forms and which sets it apart from other kinds of aggression.[41]

In a recent book addressing the "primacy of psychic structure and aggression in determining psychopathology," Kernberg recognizes that "hatred derives from rage, the primary affect around which the drive of aggression clusters," and that this hatred is "the core affect of severe psychopathological conditions, particularly severe personality disorders, perversions, and functional psychoses."[42] But the infantile anger and rage associated with narcissism is not limited to the pathological condition we clinicians call "narcissistic personality disorder." Nor is it limited to the numerous other mental disorders in which pathological narcissism plays some part. Neurotic narcissism is a pervasive, endemic aspect of modern life, and exists to varying degrees in each and every one of us. A great deal of the destructive anger, rage, and violence, the animosity between the sexes, and the hypersensitivity to any and all perceived slights beset- ting the collective American psyche springs from pathological narcissism.

Confessing the close—and often causal—tie between narcissism, anger, and rage, we remain in a quandary regarding the proverbial "chicken or egg" question: Which really comes first, narcissism or rage? Some psychoanalysts suggest (mistakenly, in my opinion) that the majority of anger and rage is pathological, and must therefore be therapeutically rooted out. This is most conspicuously so in the matter of severe narcissistic rage: "Our therapeutic aim with regard to narcissistic rage," clarifies Kohut, "is neither the direct transformation of the rage into constructive aggression nor the direct establishment of controls over the rage by the autonomous ego. Our principal goal is the gradual transformation of the narcissistic matrix from which the rage arises."[43] Kohut, who modified and expanded Freud's original ideas about narcissism, suggests that pathological narcis- sism is an arrest or distortion of normal, pre-Oedipal development, during which the infant's natural, normal, healthy, primitive or "primary narcis- sism" is deficiently dealt with or unempathically "mirrored" by the pri- mary caretakers—in most cases, the parents, particularly the mother. This so-called "narcissistic wounding" or frustration results in the neurotic perseveration of unresolved, primitive, infantile narcissism into childhood and adulthood. Narcissism in adults may represent a form of "healthy" narcissism never allowed adequate expression or gratification during childhood, and hence, never outgrown. It can also signify an infantile egoism never sufficiently socialized, and therefore, never moderated.

Rollo May sheds some much-needed light on this murky matter when he notes that *narcissism has its origin in revenge and retaliation.*[44] *Neurotic* narcissism is rooted in anger, rage, and resentment—the *normal* human response to disappointment, hurt, rejection, betrayal, abuse, or abandonment. There is nothing the least bit pathological about an infant or child feeling angry, outraged, or resentful when emotionally or physi- cally mistreated; indeed, it would be a pathological cause for concern if one could not react with anger at such insults.[45] Therefore, before we rush to attribute all anger and rage to pathological narcissism, let us first discriminate normal, healthy, or ontological narcissism from that which is unhealthy, morbid, and destructive.

Normal Narcissism

In "normal narcissism," writes one analyst, we have "realistic ambitions and an adequate sense of self-esteem. . . . We are all in continual need for recognition, of having our existence and our worth acknowledged by others."[46] *Healthy narcissism* includes the essential capacity to defend oneself when mistreated or unfairly attacked; to stand up for oneself and one's self-worth; to respect oneself and require respect from others; to believe in, recognize, and pursue—against all obstacles—the actualization of one's own creative potentialities; to assert oneself in the world and to affirm one's own personal boundaries and birthright to be in the world; to say what one really wants; to reasonably value (rather than overvalue) oneself and to value—and maturely love—appropriate others. It incorporates the capacity to be selective in the relationships we choose; to say "no" to others when and where necessary; and, when personal boundaries or self-esteem are persistently violated, to feel correspondingly angry or outraged at the offending person or situation, and to assertively voice such feelings. Normal narcissism is necessarily counterbalanced in the non-pathological personality by an equally well-developed, deep and abiding respect for the feelings, rights, and integrity of others. It entails an acceptance of personal limitations, foibles, and the fact that frustration—and failure—is a universal phenomenon.

Neurotic Narcissism

"Neurotic narcissism," on the other hand, is a perverted caricature of "normal narcissism." It begins as normal, healthy infantile narcissism; but, because of a hostile, inadequate, rejecting, or indifferent environment during infancy and childhood, the individual is so deeply injured that he or she, comprehensibly, becomes angry. This utterly natural, appropriate anger is in turn rejected, repudiated, and not infrequently, punished—as are the developing child's normal narcissistic needs for love, acceptance, and admiration. The child is thus forced to repress not only the healthy narcissism, but also the healthy (or ontological) anger about being rejected, spawning the rage-soaked seeds of neurosis or psychosis. For at bottom, neurotic narcissism is the sad story of rejection, and the indelible pain and bitterness of being rebuked.

Neurotic narcissism, paradoxically, involves the vengeful, hostile, compulsive rejection of the same human love, warmth, affection, and acceptance that was so painfully denied one during childhood. In some instances, such seemingly senseless, self-destructive behavior serves the subconscious purpose of causing the other person (or persons) to experience the same painful rejection as did we with our parents.[47] May reminds us that this unfortunate fact is illustrated touchingly in the tragic tale of Narcissus and Echo. Echo, the sweet nymph, falls madly in love with Narcissus at first sight, only to be rudely rejected by him: "Echo then pines away," adds May, "leaving behind only her melodious voice. . . . *But in her need for revenge*, she calls upon the gods to punish Narcissus *by making him also the victim of unrequited love*. It is only then that he falls in love with his own reflection."[48] The fatal self-absorption of Narcissus is a dire, neurotic reaction designed to fend off potential rejection via the hostile rejection of others. It is an angry, vindictive, preemptive repudiation of all further future snubs; a raging refusal to risk romantic rejection. Indeed, it consists of a well-orchestrated, offensive onslaught aimed at precluding any reminders or repetitions of the stinging reminiscences of unreciprocated passion.

Another myth illuminating the bitter, vengeful quality of narcissism is the Grimm's fairy tale *Little Briar Rose*, better known to most Americans as *Sleeping Beauty*. The mythic motif of rejection, resentment, and rage may be found from the first: When the king and queen invite the famous "wise women" to a great feast celebrating the birth of their daughter, Briar Rose, they make the mistake of excluding one of them. Feeling snubbed, she shows up in a snit, irately casting an acrimonious curse on the innocent child: "The King's daughter shall in her fifteenth year prick herself with a spindle, and fall down dead."[49]

"Hell hath no fury like a woman scorned," as folk wisdom—and William Congreve—warns us.[50] Fortunately, one of the invited wise women softens the intemperate blow by modifying the death sentence to a century-long sleep. Despite their best efforts, Briar Rose's parents are inevitably unable to protect her from the evil spell. On her fifteenth birthday, the vindictive curse is finally fulfilled: Moments after sensing the slight wound inflicted, as prophesied, by the sharp spindle, sleep overtakes poor Briar Rose—as well as every other sentient being throughout the palace. Even the restless wind ceases to blow, and the hearth fire refuses to flame.

"But round about the castle there began to grow a hedge of thorns, which every year became higher, and at last grew close up round the castle and all over it, so that there was nothing of it to be seen, not even the flag upon the roof."[51] Perhaps the reader recognizes this metaphorical "hedge of thorns" in some prickly person he or she knows. Such hostile defense mechanisms serve to protect the insecure, vulnerable, narcissistically injured individual—female or male—in much the same way as real thorns protect the rose's delicate petals: We may successfully fend off those persons by whom we could be hurt emotionally; but simultaneously, we imprison ourselves within barbed wire walls of our own making. Though this fairy tale is typically interpreted psychoanalytically as symbolizing the onset of menstruation and sexual maturation during adolescence, it may be aptly applied to adult development as well; for, as we know, chronological age and physical *maturation* do not necessarily mirror one's psychological and emotional *maturity*. The narcissistic wounding which so often occurs initially during the pre-Oedipal period, and is then reactivated during the dramatic throes of adolescence, can inhibit, or—as in the case of Sleeping Beauty—stunt one's emotional growth well into biological adulthood. The unconscious "sleep" of Briar Rose, resembling a sort of "suspended animation," symbolizes this psychological state of defensive fixation, insulation, or retarded emotional development. As psychoanalyst Bruno Bettelheim has said: "If we do not want to change and develop, then we might as well remain in a deathlike sleep. During their sleep the heroines' beauty is a frigid one; theirs is the isolation of narcissism. In such self-involvement which excludes the rest of the world there is no suffering, but also no knowledge to be gained, no feelings to be experienced."[52]

As the legend spread throughout the land of this lovely sleeping beauty, all manner of eager young men make efforts to penetrate the thorny hedge surrounding her: "But they found it impossible, for the thorns held fast together as if they had hands and the youths were caught in them, could not get loose again, and died a miserable death."[53]

About this myth, May comments that "we can assume . . . there will be rage in Briar Rose that she is so completely blocked off from life. . . . Her rage shows itself in the fact that the briars around the castle *kill the suitors*. In every neurotic pattern others are dragged down and made to suffer by virtue of the anger—in this case, Briar Rose's anger."[54] Yet, we must remember that Briar Rose's narcissistic rage does not derive merely as an angry reaction to her self-imposed isolation; her rage presumably began at a much earlier point in her psychological development—symbolized by the narcissistic vulnerability of the wounded wise woman—and has been building ever since. Her "briars" or thorny defenses by which she fatally repels potential suitors are symptomatic of her repressed anger, rage, and hostility toward others—especially men. The grotesque image of these luckless suitors impaled on bloody thorns and suffering an agonizing fate bespeaks the poignant experience of every man or woman who has tried in vain to love a prickly person like Briar Rose. Such people—female or male—are still so unconsciously angry about prior rejections, disappointments, and narcissistic injuries that they are simply not psychologically ready for any real relatedness or true emotional intimacy. Sex, of course, may be another matter entirely!

This question of emotional or psychological "readiness" is central to the story of Sleeping Beauty, the problem of narcissism, and today's thorny relations between men and women. (See chapter two.) Many—if not all—men and women, have been narcissistically injured to some degree or another; we still carry around the hurt and anger of our old wounds, bringing this emotional "baggage" into our adult relationships. We unconsciously continue this compulsive pattern until we become ready for *true intimacy*. True intimacy requires tremendous courage. It takes true courage to create intimate relationships, since we all have our share of protective prickliness to penetrate. Even in the case of certain "well-adjusted," ostensibly "open" individuals who, at least superficially, seem to have comparatively few defenses or boundaries to traverse, one often arrives at a frustrating point beyond which no further entry is permitted; and the originally alluring pseudo-openness—or, more accurately, the lack of appropriate personal boundaries—proves itself to be yet another neurotic "briar patch," a deceptive *pseudo-intimacy*.

We can see a vivid example of the courage and impeccable timing necessary to overcome these exceedingly common neurotic defenses in the happy ending of our Briar Rose myth. A brave young prince, undaunted by the grisly lot of her previous suitors, decides—against all wise counsel to the contrary—to seek out the comely yet inaccessible Briar Rose:

> But by this time the hundred years had just passed, and the day had come when Briar Rose was to awake again. When the King's son came near to the thorn-hedge, it was nothing but large and beautiful flowers, which parted from each other of their own accord, and let him pass unhurt. . . . [55]

Not only is the fortunate prince granted ingress to the forbidding palace: he unknowingly kisses the sleeping princess at precisely the moment she was destined to reawaken after her prolonged slumber. The timeless myth suggests that one must have not only great courage, but good timing (or "luck," as we sometimes say) to successfully connect deeply with another. Both participants must be consciously ready—and willing—to bravely relinquish their hostile, narcissistic defenses if true intimacy is to occur. Intimacy—in the deepest sense of selectively allowing another entry into one's usually well-defended fortress—always involves a choice, a fateful, fundamental decision.

Depression and Anger

Depression is another common emotional disorder long believed by depth psychologists to correlate closely with repressed anger and rage. Freud felt that frustrated sexual instincts—libido—lead to anger, which, instead of being consciously expressed toward the frustrating object, is unconsciously turned inward against one's self, in the form of self-hatred, neurotic guilt, and a severely punitive "superego." In the view of Freudian W. R. D. Fairbairn, "since the depressive reaction has its roots in the late oral phase, it is the disposal of his hate . . . that constitutes the great difficulty of the depressive individual." Fairbairn and other "object relations" analysts believe "that loss of the [loved or needed] object is the basic trauma underlying the depressive state,"[56] and hold that the reactive and generally repressed rage around this loss drives many classic depressive symptoms such as neurotic self-criticism, negativism, and apathy.

   Apathy may be understood as a denial of the daimonic so sweeping that almost all "negative" emotions have been suppressed by the patient in order to survive. Depression is in actuality not a distinctive feeling or emotion so much as an absence of deep passion, a superficial substitute for the intense daimonic emotions that underlie depression: anger, rage, despair, pain, sadness, grief, discouragement, loneliness, powerlessness, fear, etc. But in disallowing or distancing ourselves from these feelings, we have unwittingly diminished our capacity to feel much of anything at all— negative or positive. In a sense, we are possessed by the same daimonic passions and impulses we seek to dispel. When seriously depressed, we say that we feel ourselves "in the grips" of depression, "seized" by it, enveloped, entombed, overcome, or overwhelmed. Jung alluded to this phenomenological fact—and to the importance of trying to discover the meaning of depression—when he wrote that depression should "be regarded as an unconscious compensation whose content must be made conscious if it is to be fully effective. This can be done only by consciously regressing along with the depressive tendency and integrating the memories so activated into the conscious mind—which was what the depression was aiming at in the first place."[57]

One uses depression as one utilizes anxiety: by blindly following its lead into—and, hopefully, out of—the daimonic labyrinth. Depression—like anxiety—does, when correctly related to, redirect the individual back toward his or her suppressed daimonic passions, and thus, to life. Some intimate connection to the daimonic is essential to satisfactory functioning in the world. Denial of the daimonic cuts us off from the incandescent source of vital energy needed to creatively contend with the never-ending challenges of life. If, for example, someone is depressed, and unable to feel sufficiently angry or outraged at an intolerable or destructive life-situation, what on Earth will incite them to do something to change it? As May remarks, "many people who come for therapy have lost their freedom because of their repression of anger, a repression generally caused by their learning early in life that any anger will be severely punished."[58] This truism is supported experimentally by psychologist Martin Seligman's "learned helplessness" hypothesis.[59] Seligman proposes that depression is primarily a learned response to certain circumstances, and to life in general. He conducted laboratory studies on dogs who were electrically shocked each time they tried to escape from their cage. Eventually, discouraged and fearful, the dogs simply gave up on their escape efforts, apathetically resigning themselves to their severely limited world despite the fact that the electricity had been disconnected—making freedom an ever-present possibility. We cannot, of course, anthropomorphically conclude that these poor animals learned not to get angry. We can, nonetheless, safely surmise that their aggressive attempts at asserting their freedom and will were stymied, and then abandoned, due to an overriding fear of punishment—in much the same manner as the abused child or the battered spouse learns to surrender his or her right to self-assertion, anger, outrage, righteous indignation, and finally, freedom itself.

But what of the two other currently favored explanations for depression: the *biochemical* and the *cognitive* models? Let us begin with the latter. "Cognitions"—or, put in plain language, thoughts—clearly play a major role in the etiology and prolongation of clinical depression, as they do in most other mental disorders. This seems obvious: How we think affects how we feel, as well as how we behave in various situations—and vice versa. Cognitive or cognitive-behavioral therapists like Aaron Beck and Albert Ellis believe that depression and other mental disorders are the consequence of "cognitive distortions" (Beck) or "irrational beliefs" (Ellis), such as a negative world-view or self-concept.[60] When events are interpreted—generally, automatically, without awareness—on the basis of these false or irrational presumptions, depression ensues. "Cognitive therapy" focuses to some extent on "restructuring" this faulty myth, or what Alfred Adler referred to as one's "guiding fiction," or "life-style." "Life-style," as one Adlerian defines it, "refers to the convictions individuals develop early in life to help them organize experience, to understand it, to predict it, and to control it. . . . Consequently, a *life-style* is neither right nor wrong, normal or abnormal, but merely the 'spectacles' through which people view themselves in relationship to the way in which they perceive life."[61]

Though some may be loath to admit it, what cognitive therapists like Ellis do is a kind of remedial philosophizing: they are aware of the immense importance of one's underlying—and typically unexamined—*Weltanschauung*, or world-view, in constructively dealing with the inevitable stresses and strains of life. Philosopher Arthur Schopenhauer (yet another significant forerunner of modern depth psychology) concurred with Epictetus, the first-century A.D. Stoic who held that *"men are not influenced by things, but by their thoughts about things."*[62] In my view, any psychotherapy worth its salt must include at least some emphasis on how patients think about themselves; perceive the ponderous things that happen to them; interpret their responses to those inner and outer events; and endeavor to make sense of life in general. For without some conscious recognition and cognitive restructuring of one's subjective mythology about oneself, no lasting therapeutic transformation can take place.

The "irrational" or "negativistic" thought patterns so common in clinical depression can be considered destructive "demons," which must be deliberately brought to light and cognitively "restructured." But from whence come these cognitive "demons"? They derive, in part, from parental influences and training, to be sure. But they also indicate underlying daimonic affects. For instance, severe self-criticism or abuse cannot be said to be simply a learned cognition or behavior; it can also spring from a deep-seated self-hatred or unresolved rage. Psychoanalytic theory explains that

> under ordinary circumstances a person experiences in consciousness both the affect and the imagery of an emotion-laden idea, whether it be a fantasy or the memory of an event. When [the defense mechanism of] isolation occurs, the affect and the

impulse of which it is a derivative are separated from the ideational component and pushed out of consciousness. If isolation is completely successful, the impulse and its associated affect are totally repressed, and the patient is consciously aware only of the affectless idea that is related to it.[63]

Consider, for example, the fact that neurotic obsessions—which, as we know, can be defined as intrusive, irrational thoughts or cognitions commonly associated with "obsessive-compulsive disorder"—frequently contain a *preoccupation with aggression.* This lends support to the theory that irrational cognitions can be symptomatic of "isolated" or suppressed anger, and sometimes murderous or suicidal rage. Among the classic earmarks of "madness" or psychosis are *delusions:* fixed, false, irrational beliefs or ideas (i.e., cognitions), firmly adhered to despite objective evidence to the contrary. Such rigidly held and ofttimes bizarre cognitions can occur in cases of severe depression, mania, schizophrenia, and other psychotic disorders such as acute drug intoxication. These *idées fixes subconscientes,* as Janet termed them, take hold of the person's mind and refuse to let go. The delusional patient is, for all intents and purposes, veritably possessed by these demonic ideas, and cannot be dissuaded by rational debate. Delusions are perhaps the most devilishly difficult "cognitive demons" to deal with therapeutically—though their stubbornness may sometimes be abated by use of certain anti-psychotic medications.

Of course, any time we proffer some diagnosis, make an interpretation, or speak with patients about a particular paradigm by way of which we—and, much more importantly—they might better comprehend their symptoms or psychological predicament, we are addressing the cognitive aspect of the problem. To the extent we also direct ourselves to the patient's behavior—as again, any psychotherapy to some extent must, in order to help the patient to modify or gain greater control over it—we are now attending to the *cognitive-behavioral* levels of the disorder. But these do not comprise the entire problem because they do not include the whole person. Cognitive-behavioral approaches confine themselves to attacking one or two specific parts of the patient's problem, while tending to neglect or even avoid others—especially repressed anger and rage. This rational, pre-programmed approach brings to mind the mythological hero Hercules, who, in fighting the indefatigable, nine-headed Hydra, found that as soon as he lopped off one of the monster's serpentine heads, two more immediately appeared to take its place. (See fig. 22.) It was not until Hercules conquered the immortal head at the Hydra's center—which he could not kill but merely buried alive beneath an enormous stone—that his harrowing labor was completed. Cognitive-behavioral therapists may temporarily aid patients on an intellectual, rational, logical level, but the central, indestructible daimonic core or passionate heart of the matter—the "irrational" anger and rage—remains typically untouched, overlooked, or ignored. The same may be said, in my estimation, of most other current psychotherapies, including even the prolonged, intensive labors of orthodox Freudian analysis.

A similar critique can also be made about the widespread use of potent psychopharmacological agents like Prozac for the sole and primary treatment of depression. Clinical depression does, of course, occur on a biological level, including classic vegetative symptoms such as sleep and appetite disturbance, psychomotor retardation, and a general diminution of vitality or libido. Antidepressant drugs serve to alleviate such symptoms, providing the patient with some additional stamina and energy essential for coping with their daily difficulties. Helpful as it is in providing symptomatic relief, however, the pharmacological approach—when relied upon instead of psychotherapy—is yet another unidimensional, mechanistic attack on but one of the metaphorical Hydra's heads; it fails to address the problem of depression at its daimonic crux. Such symptom-oriented treatment rather tends—with some success—to further dampen the daimonic, to drug the deleterious demons into a state of relative tranquility and impotence. But as May cautions: "It is the failure of therapy, rather than its success, when it drugs the daimonic, tranquillizes it, or in other ways fails to confront it head on."[64]

In "major depression"—a serious but typically non-psychotic disorder—neurotransmitters have similarly been suspected of causing some of the most crippling symptoms, such as insomnia or hypersomnia, severe weight loss or gains, lethargy, apathy, and gloomy outlook. Clinical depression is believed to be associated with a deficiency of certain neurotransmitters called "catecholamines" in the brain. Since many (but not all) depressed patients respond well to psychotropic medications that increase catecholamines, such as *dopamine* and *norepinephrine*, it had been assumed that depression is caused by a deficiency of these substances. Surprisingly, however, one of the most popular antidepressant drugs, Prozac, "has almost no effects on norepinephrine or dopamine neurotransmission."[65] Yet, for significant numbers of people, it works!—at least, inasmuch as it counteracts some of the obstinate symptoms from which seriously depressed patients suffer. Prozac (fluoxetine) works—and with purportedly fewer side effects than its pharmacological predecessors—by blocking the reuptake (i.e., by increasing the available amounts) of a totally different neurotransmitter: *serotonin*. Serotonin has been directly linked with aggression, anger, and rage in both monkeys and humans! Low levels of serotonin are associated with depression, aggression, and violence—including violence against oneself, suicide—while higher levels are associated with adaptive and effective social functioning.

One recent study demonstrates the co-existence of and correlation—if not the causal connection—between anger and depression in some patients, as well as the mollifying effects of Prozac on both: "We have recently reported a series of illustrative cases in which [clinically depressed] patients presented with 'anger attacks,' sudden spells of anger resembling panic attacks but lacking the affects of fear and anxiety. . . . These anger attacks were experienced as uncharacteristic, were inappropriate to the situations in which they occurred, and responded well to treatment with antidepressants [Prozac]."[66] Irritability is a well-known symptom of clinical depression, though overt expressions of anger and rage are typically not considered part of the standard clinical picture. Yet, in this study of seventy-nine (mostly female) patients diagnosed as suffering from major depression, thirty-four concurrently reported "anger attacks." Like "panic attacks," which involve a sudden seizure of uncontrollable anxiety, these "anger attacks" in clinically depressed patients can be interpreted as temporary states of "daimonic possession," during which the patient's previously stifled rage erupts unexpectedly and uncontrollably, and, just as rapidly, subsides. Prozac apparently diminishes the frequency and power of these "anger attacks," in similar fashion to the way certain other drugs effectively control "panic attacks."

Paradoxically, there are at the same time reports about depressed patients being prescribed Prozac and, uncharacteristically, becoming angry, as in this anecdote from psychiatrist Peter Kramer's book, *Listening to Prozac:* "After two months [on Prozac, Sally] . . . felt less depressed and much more angry."[67] What Kramer and others find especially puzzling are the occasional reports of patients on Prozac becoming not just very angry, but violently assaultive, and sometimes suicidal. Aside from the plain fact that drugs such as Prozac can, indeed, profoundly impact a person's perceptions, mood, attitude, and behavior—for better or worse—what further implications can we infer? One credible explication for such cases would require conceding that Freud and the psychoanalysts were right all along: depression is a condition in which the person's anger and rage have been habitually repressed or suppressed. As a result, the subdued rage festers unconsciously, negatively affecting how we feel and think about ourselves. Once the dampering lid of the depressed mood is artificially, biochemically lifted, the dangerous, daimonic genie of rage is released. Thus, it may be that in some cases, so-called "mood brighteners" like Prozac and its pharmaceutical successors, run the risk of emancipating the daimonic—that is, the patient's repressed anger, rage, or self-hatred—prematurely, prior to the patient's (and/or the doctor's) preparedness to deal with it. It is common clinical knowledge that, contrary to what one might assume, depressed and suicidal patients are most at risk for acting on their suicidal impulses during the days and months *after* the depression starts to lift. Presumably, this is due to the increased energy the dissipating depression makes accessible to nonetheless still suicidal patients, enabling them to carry out their self-destructive plans. We could call this potentially perilous—yet absolutely indispensable—"energy" *chi*, as do the Chinese; or *élan vital*, following the vitalistic French philosopher Henri Bergson; or "will" as did Schopenhauer; or "libido" in the generic, Jungian sense. Or, we could dub it, as I do, "the daimonic," though this does not necessarily render each of these terms identical. For instance, whereas Bergson's idea of *élan vital* alluded to a predominantly biological "vital energy," both May, in his paradigm of "the daimonic," and Jung, in his broad conception of "libido," prefer a considerably less biological and more psychological interpretation of this elemental force. Embodying—but not limited to—Plato's idea of Eros, the daimonic contains the irrepressible, predetermined, biologically based urge in all beings everywhere not only to survive, but to exuberantly assert, advance, and reproduce themselves. When this psychobiological urge is repeatedly frustrated or inhibited, be it in animals or humans, depression generally follows.

Drugs and the Daimonic

What lies behind the burgeoning popularity of legal and illegal drugs like alcohol, cocaine, marijuana, Xanax, Valium, and Prozac? On the one hand, some drugs dampen down the daimonic. Most illicit drugs provide a temporary, transitory escape from some of the more unpleasant, disturbing, existential facts of life, and our subjective reactions to them: anxiety, pain, suffering, loneliness, meaninglessness, death, anger, and rage. Psychiatric medications may be—and often are—used to control the patient's problematic symptoms or behavior by tranquilizing or squelching the daimonic. The standard use of lithium carbonate in the treatment of bipolar disorder or manic-depressive illness is a good example. During the "manic" phase of this syndrome—in which intense irritability, anger, and rage frequently inform the clinical picture—patients are possessed by these daimonic powers in positive and negative ways. Despite the fact that lithium can control—though not cure—the ecstatic episodes so characteristic of this crippling disorder, many patients vehemently resist taking lithium prophylactically, fearing (with some justification) that their lives will become banal, boring, and sterile if forever rendered devoid of the daimonic. Typically, such patients have an intuitive appreciation of the daimonic and its valuable qualities—despite all the trouble it causes them. Indeed, many—if not most—seriously mentally ill patients are quite resistant to taking psychiatric medications. They seem to sense—to paraphrase the lyric poet, Rainer Maria Rilke—that once their demons are dispatched, the "angels" will be too. That is, they fear losing touch with the positive, creative aspects of the daimonic. Some patients seemingly prefer living with their bedeviling symptoms to the bland tepidity of "normalcy" or "social adjustment" promulgated by mainstream psychiatry and psychology.

On the other hand, certain antidepressants, such as the "energizing" drugs Prozac or Zoloft, actually seem to biochemically stimulate the daimonic—sometimes with dangerous consequences. The same may be said of "street drugs" like "crack" cocaine, methamphetamine, or PCP: these powerful substances, when taken in massive doses, magnify the daimonic. Uncontrollably belligerent patients brought into the hospital emergency room in psychotic states induced by these drugs manifest many of the symptoms of so-called "demonic possession" noted in the preceding chapter, including "superhuman" strength: sometimes as many as six police officers or attendants are required to contain the violent behavior of such enraged patients. As also mentioned previously, hallucinogenic drugs like LSD, mescaline, psilocybin, hashish, and marijuana have been employed throughout history to invoke the daimonic for spiritual or religious purposes. Such sacred rituals, when properly performed, are almost always highly structured, secure, supportive, and take place within a highly controlled social context capable of safely containing the conjured daimonic energies.

But for the most part, psychotropic medications and street drugs share at least one common purpose: they are used—for better or worse—in an effort to alleviate suffering, either by dispersing disturbing symptoms such as depression and anxiety, or by briefly escaping from life's problems into ecstasy. Ecstasy, as earlier stated, is a specific form of daimonic possession easily induced by drugs and alcohol. This ecstatic state

of mind is sought out not only by religious sorts, artists, and other creative individuals, but also by people who have buried or lost touch with
the daimonic, and wish to resurrect it. Drugs or alcohol are the quick-
est—and potentially, most destructive—means of either disinhibiting or
depressing the daimonic. When we therapists say that a patient has been
"self-medicating"—using illicit drugs or alcohol to manage their psychological demons or their apathy—we are referring to this simple psychophysiological fact.

Let us first consider *alcoholism*, the commonly used term for a mental
disorder marked by the chronic, excessive use of alcohol. Alcohol—the
most widely used and abused psychoactive substance in the world—is a
central nervous system depressant, though its initial effects (as most of
us know) are feelings of stimulation, euphoria, well-being, and disinhibition. Due to this legendary disinhibiting quality, alcohol—in addition
to its aphrodisiacal stimulation of the erotic side of the daimonic—"is
frequently associated with the commission of criminal acts. More than one-
half of all murderers and their victims are believed to have been intoxicated at the time of the act. One study indicates that about one fourth
of all suicides occur while the person is drinking alcohol."[68] The aforementioned tale of Dr. Jekyll and Mr. Hyde demonstrates that the daimonic
can not only be controlled or subjugated by means of scientific potions,
but can also be chemically induced. The dramatically transformative drug
imbibed by Dr. Jekyll is described by Stevenson as "a blood-red liquor,
which was highly pungent to the sense of smell, and seemed to . . . contain
phosphorous and some volatile ether." To this mysterious tincture, Jekyll
added a "crystalline salt of a white color,"[69] similar in appearance to
cocaine, and proceeded to drink the untested mixture:

> I came to myself as if out of a great sickness. There was
> something strange in my sensations, something indescribably
> new, and, from its very novelty, incredibly sweet. I felt younger,
> lighter, happier in body; within I was conscious of a heady
> recklessness, a current of disordered sensual images running
> like a mill race in my fancy, a solution of the bonds of obli-
> gation, an unknown but not an innocent freedom of the soul.
> (p. 102)

But beyond and beneath this rejuvenating ecstasy, Jekyll discovered
something sinister: "I knew myself, at the first breath of this new life, to
be more wicked, tenfold more wicked . . . ; and the thought, in that
moment, braced and delighted me like wine" (p. 102). You might have

observed that, on occasion, normally mild-mannered, passive people, when intoxicated, can become belligerent, angry, aggressive, and even violent; they act completely "out of character," as we say. In rare instances, technically termed "pathological" or "idiosyncratic" alcohol intoxication, the typically meek, submissive person turns suddenly hostile and assaultive "within minutes of ingesting an amount of alcohol insufficient to induce intoxication in most people."[70] Regarding the relationship between violent behavior and alcohol, some researchers report "that alcoholics as a group exhibit more violent behavior than do nonalcoholics, especially when drinking." However, these same psychologists also confess that "there is no clear understanding of the mechanisms by which alcoholism and aggression might be linked. . . . One school of thought proposes that the ingestion of alcohol serves as a signal that aggression may be acceptable; another postulates that the pharmacological actions of alcohol may function to directly elicit aggressive behavior."[71] At all events, it must be admitted that our cognitions, moods, emotional states, and even behavior can be dramatically influenced by such readily available psychoactive agents. Moreover, we must further concede that basic human emotions such as anger and rage appear to have specific biochemical correlates in the brain and nervous system: a characteristic biochemistry of anger and rage, as it were, over which selected psychoactive substances exercise some sway. Yet, at the same time, let us carefully resist the temptation to leap to rash conclusions concerning causality: the observation that a correlation exists between biochemistry and anger or rage does not necessarily translate into cause and effect. One could effectively argue that anger and rage cause alterations in body chemistry, rather than vice versa. Biochemistry—in most cases—is an integral component of anger and rage, rather than its cause.

Furthermore, there remains the confounding fact that many violent behavioral syndromes bear an uncanny resemblance to Dr. Jekyll's climactic experience of being possessed by Mr. Hyde without even ingesting the identity-altering drug. For example, there are clinical reports of cases wherein sudden, impulsive, uncharacteristic violence is the primary symptom even when the patient is not under the immediate influence of drugs or alcohol. These episodically violent offenders are seen frequently enough to prompt at least one psychologist some years ago to propose a new diagnostic category to specifically describe them: "The Berserker/Blind Rage Syndrome," hypothesized to have "existed for centuries and therefore . . . very likely to be the basis for the famous Berserker Vikings. . . ."[72] In these instances, the usually nonviolent, peaceable patient savagely assaults others (often strangers); experiences amnesia during episodes of "blind rage"; angrily overreacts to an actual external stimulus toward which the rage is directed; episodically exhibits extraordinary physical strength and relative immunity to injury; and is, by definition, not under the influence of drugs or alcohol, brain damaged, nor suffering from some other major mental illness. Today—since no such diagnostic category has yet been adopted by the American Psychiatric Association—this syndrome might still be labeled "intermittent explosive disorder."[73] There is currently a mushrooming movement afoot, however, based on recent research, to formally include specific "anger disorders" in the forthcoming revision of the American Psychiatric Association's diagnostic manual of mental disorders.[74]

Here is an example of one such case:

A divorced, Caucasian male, devoid of any previous acts of serious violence, has been recently dating his exwife. They have expressed a desire to remarry. One night the patient stops at her house to drop off a package. There is no answer at the front door. Since her car is in the driveway, he thinks she cannot hear the doorbell, so he goes to the back of the house. Looking into the large window of the den, he sees his exwife nude, having sexual intercourse with a man. "The next thing I know, I'm inside, covered with glass—but without a scratch—on top of my wife, having beaten her to death." Upon arrest for the woman's murder, the patient is bewildered at what has happened and insists he cannot remember the movements of that transitional period. The woman's lover indicates that the patient crashed through the window, beat him off, and proceeded to beat the woman to death.[75]

What causes such catastrophic, Jekyll and Hyde behavior? No alcohol or drug ingestion just prior to or during this deadly episode was reported; chemical intoxication was not the culprit. What, then, takes place in impulsive perpetrators of what we commonly—and legally—call "crimes of passion"? Could such violent, often murderous behavior be caused, as some scientists believe, by a genetic deficiency or endogenous biochemical imbalance? It is true that violent seizures of rage have been surgically, and in other ways, artificially induced in laboratory animals,[76] and that inappropriate aggressive behavior in humans is sometimes seen in cases of organic brain syndrome or temporal lobe epilepsy. But, in the above-mentioned syndrome, "the Berserker/Blind Rage patients show no history of epilepsy of any type." Moreover, "aggression as a result of such [epileptic] seizures is extremely rare and such aggression, when it does occur, is extremely limited in scope."[77] Could it be that these violent individuals carry around with them a characterologically concealed rage so pervasive, secretly lurking beneath their passive personae, that the most minuscule degree of alcohol-induced disinhibition—or merely some minor insult—is sufficient to spontaneously trigger a destructive state of "daimonic possession"? Let us also bear in mind the distinct possibility that particular patients—though not intoxicated at the precise time of such a violent episode—might nevertheless have a history of sporadic or habitual drug or alcohol abuse. This suppressive, self-medicating style of dealing with their anger, of pacifying their raging "demons," could conceivably set the stage later for eruptive violence with or without an exogenous chemical catalyst being ingested.

The Biological Basis of the Daimonic

In the final analysis, the daimonic may be said to have a biological substrate. But having made such a banal, scientific statement, what do we really mean by it? There has been an obvious—and ominously regressive—trend in psychiatry and psychology during recent decades toward the "organic" or "medical" model of mental disorders. Such a paradigm places excessive emphasis on the biological components of mental illness, thereby downplaying the significance of psychological or sociological sources of emotional suffering. Proponents of this materialist model seek, as far as possible, to reduce all so-called "mental disorders" to their biological bases, in hopes of discovering not only their biogenetic causes, but their psychopharmacological or biological cures. Bolstering their claims are myriad research findings linking aggression (at least in animals) with testosterone, progesterone, dopamine, and epinephrine levels.[78] Studies comparing aggressiveness in monozygotic against dizygotic twins are said to support the role of heredity, as does the existence of certain chromosomal and metabolic disorders associated with aggressive personality traits. Finally, some research suggests a correlation between brain damage and violent behavior.

The portentous discovery during the 1950s of psychotropic drugs efficacious in reducing the symptoms of many bedeviling mental disorders revolutionized the field of psychiatry and psychology—and, slowly but surely, severely eroded the practice of psychotherapy. Today, the prevailing attitude of most mainstream American mental health providers—

and, without exception, the insurance companies that must pay for their services—assumes that the vast majority of mental disorders embody at least some biological or biochemical imbalance, and will therefore most expediently be ameliorated by medication and, possibly, some supportive, time-limited, "brief therapy."

This predominantly pharmacological treatment approach pertains especially—though is definitely not limited to—the most severe and disabling mental conditions, such as schizophrenia, bipolar disorder, panic disorder, and major depression. These first two conditions comprise what humankind from time immemorial has colloquially called "madness," "possession," or "insanity." Today, we term such sufferers "psychotic," or "mentally ill." *Schizophrenia,* for instance, is the most common form of psychosis, affecting approximately 1 percent of the world's population across diverse cultures. While it seems certain that what we now scientifically label as "schizophrenia" was seen historically as "demonic possession," the nineteenth-century physicians who studied this baffling syndrome—then called *dementia praecox*—believed there was a biological (or *organic*) basis to this syndrome. The introduction of effective, "antipsychotic" drugs during the mid-twentieth century seemed to support this hypothesis.

Yet, despite our mind-boggling technological advances in medicine during the past hundred years, there is still very little conclusive evidence to sustain the increasingly strident claims of modern psychiatry that schizophrenia is essentially an inherited, biochemical disease directly affecting the brain's normal functioning. Those who subscribe to this theory (and it is merely one widely held view, not a foregone conclusion), again point emphatically to (inherently flawed) research on twins, demonstrating a much higher statistical incidence of schizophrenia (up to 50 percent) in *monozygotic* (identical) twins than is found in *dizygotic* (or fraternal) twins.[79] They further surmise that since schizophrenic symptoms are controlled (though not eliminated) by drugs called "phenothiazines," and phenothiazines block the uptake of the neurotransmitter dopamine, schizophrenic patients must have too much dopamine in their brains. This hypothesis has since been disputed on several fronts, one of which is the fact that phenothiazines have proven "effective in treating virtually all psychotic and agitated patients, regardless of diagnosis."[80] In considering the generalized effects of this and other anti-psychotic drugs, I would remind readers that these remedies were originally referred to generically as "major tranquilizers," an extremely apt description if ever there was one of their phenomenological effects: they suppress the psychotic patient's pervasive anxiety—and, indeed, the daimonic in general—thereby modulating anxiety-driven symptoms such as agitation, delusions, and hallucinations. *Lithium*, that highly effective, naturally occurring salt commonly used in the treatment and prevention of *mania* (a classic kind of "madness"), is one notable exception. Of all the psychotropic medications, lithium seems to control and moderate the daimonic most directly, attacking it on a yet little-understood neurobiological level, without the heavy sedation (or side effects) caused by most other anti-psychotic drugs.

Anger, rage, madness, and the daimonic no doubt have biological roots reaching down deeply into the neurophysiology, biochemistry, and even molecular makeup of man. Indeed, without its biological and physical foundations, human existence would cease to be. But *soma* and *psyche* can never be completely separated; they are two aspects of a fundamentally indivisible ground of being upon which human existence stands, and from which the daimonic emanates. It is for this reason that "madness" will never be reduced to pure biology—or to pure psychology for that matter. As psychiatrist and psychoanalyst Willard Gaylin states it: "All biologically trained physicians and psychologists assume that *all* body functions, motor and perceptive, have a final end point that involves the chemistry and physics of the body. . . . [But] chemistry is not an alternative to psychodynamics, only an alternative language."[81] Modern psychiatry's current culprit or "demon" *du jour* now deemed responsible for psychosis and other mental disorders, is the tiny *neurotransmitter*: microscopic molecules that regulate the rate of neuronal firing and receptivity. By restoring the normal balance of these unruly "devils," mental illness may be conquered once and for all! Or so many had hoped. Notwithstanding the initial enthusiasm—and significant attenuation of psychotic symptoms like hallucinations and delusions—schizophrenia and other psychoses such as mania are still maddeningly mysterious afflictions, the true origins of which remain obscure.

Anger, Rage, and Madness

In contradistinction to the above-articulated biochemical perspective, psychosis—or "madness," as it is more commonly called—has always been closely associated with anger and rage. In English, this enduring relationship may be seen in the synonymous use of the term "mad" for "angry." Carol Tavris tells us that the poet Horace, around the time of Christ, wrote that anger " 'is a brief madness,' succinctly noting the affinity between 'mad' and 'angry.' The match is psychological as well as linguistic," writes Tavris, "because in many cultures (including our own) an enraged individual and an insane one are both regarded as being out of control, unable to take responsibility for their actions."[82] But Tavris disputes the validity of this interrelationship, posing an important question: "What role does the *belief* in the similarity between rage and madness play?" (p. 57). She points out that "other cultures, such as the Eskimo, distinguish the two conditions: a person who is legitimately insane cannot be expected to control himself, but one who is merely angry can and must control himself" (ibid.). She also argues that syndromes such as the aforementioned "running amok" in Malayan culture—during which a period of depression and brooding is abruptly followed by a furious outburst of violent rage, mayhem, and murder—is not a "true" madness or psychosis at all. Tavris bases her opinion on the fact that the *pengamok* (those who actually run amok) are sometimes dissuaded from acting on these destructive impulses by the threat of capital punishment; and on a study in which "the victims of the *pengamok* proved to be 'rational' choices: a wife suspected of infidelity, a quarrelsome neighbor, an oppressive religion teacher. The Malay who killed . . . five customers of coffeehouses had carefully assured that his victims were Chinese: as his record showed, he had harbored anger at the Chinese who had killed some Malays several years before" (p. 59).

In my estimation, the crucial fact here is that this man had harbored his anger and rage to the point of hatred, and hence, became prone to a violently explosive expression of that fetid hatred. The only thing proven by Tavris' analysis is precisely what I have herein striven to suggest: There is meaning in madness. This meaning may be found not only in the subjective symptoms of madness, but in the bizarre or impulsive behaviors of the madman or madwoman. A polite, well-mannered Malay man, with no previous history of violence, "out of the blue" takes up traditional weapons and slaughters five people for no apparent reason; an Australian, Scottish, or American man in a decidedly different culture strides into an office building, restaurant, post office, school yard, or train, and guns down everyone in sight; a former soldier, angry with the government, apparently bombs a building, killing or maiming hundreds inside; an international celebrity's estranged ex-wife and her friend are found brutally butchered, in what one prosecuting attorney describes as "a case about anger, revenge, and retribution." *Be this not madness?* If not, then what is?

But having designated such behavior "madness," what does this really mean? Is there a difference between "madness," "mental illness," "psychosis," or "insanity"? Tavris seeks to draw such a distinction, noting that "the so-called psychotic symptoms of the *pengamok* vanish within a month or two of the episode, which is hardly the case for true psychotics."[83] I do not know how much experience Tavris—a "social" as opposed to "clinical" psychologist—has with psychotic patients (very little, if any, I suspect); but she is simply mistaken. There are in fact several types of "true" psychosis in which the symptoms appear suddenly and—just as suddenly—remit. For instance, in "schizophreniform disorder," the symptoms last "at least one month, but less than six months."[84] "Brief psychotic disorder" has a duration of "at least one day and no more than one month, with eventual full return to [the] premorbid level of functioning."[85] Both major depressive and manic episodes may be sufficiently severe, bizarre, and disabling to be deemed psychotic, yet of relatively brief duration, as is postpartum psychosis. And substance-induced psychotic disorders like cocaine or amphetamine psychosis can occur quite quickly and resolve equally rapidly. The *Synopsis of Psychiatry* states that the *pengamok* to which Tavris refers may, subsequent to their murderous rampage, "require treatment for a chronic psychotic condition which may have been the underlying cause."[86] Some—though not all—of these outbursts of anger, rage, and hatred, are associated with what we in Western culture call "psychosis."[87]

At the same time, Tavris is right in recognizing that one can be angry—even violently enraged—and not technically "psychotic" or "insane." (The mere fact that someone behaves bizarrely or destructively or murderously does not, in and of itself, make them "psychotic," "insane," or, if we equate these terms, "mad.") "Psychosis" is a psychiatric term of dubious definition. The two traditional hallmarks of psychosis are delusions and hallucinations. But beyond these characteristic symptoms, the definition of psychosis becomes murky. The *International Classification of Diseases* defines the *psychoses* as specific mental disorders "in which impairment of mental function has developed to a degree that interferes grossly with insight, ability to meet some ordinary demands of life or to maintain adequate contact with reality. It is not an exact or well defined term."[88] The American Psychiatric Association has stated that "the term *psychotic* does not apply to minor distortions of reality that involve matters of relative judgment. For example, a depressed person who underestimates his achievements would not be described as psychotic, whereas one who believes he has caused a natural catastrophe [e.g., an earthquake] would be so described."[89] Psychosis can be caused by organic, physiological conditions, like brain damage, drug intoxication, and systemic disease; or it may be caused primarily by psychological or emotional stress and trauma; and, in many cases—though clearly, the minority—some combination thereof. The critical question as to the relationship between the daimonic, madness, psychosis, insanity and *responsibility* touched on by Tavris will be returned to in the closing chapter.

Psychosomatic Disorders

Let us next take a cursory look at the correlation between anger, rage, and certain bodily symptoms. The "demons" of suppressed anger and rage have long been suspected of playing a central role in what we commonly call "psychosomatic" disorders, such as tension or migraine headaches, asthma, essential hypertension, ulcers, irritable bowel syndrome, colitis, neurodermatitis, psoriasis, and urticaria.[90] For instance, according to the *Synopsis of Psychiatry*, patients with high blood pressure (hypertension) "appear to be outwardly congenial, compliant, and compulsive; although their anger is not expressed openly, they have much inhibited rage. There appears to be a familial genetic predisposition to hypertension; that is, when chronic stress occurs in a genetically predisposed compulsive personality who has repressed and suppressed rage, hypertension may result."[91] In traditional Chinese medicine, many of these disorders are attributed to some diminution or blockage of the *chi* energy referred to earlier: the basic, homogeneous life force coursing through and animating body and mind.

One study reviewed in a recent book, *Anger Kills: Seventeen Strategies for Controlling the Hostility that Can Harm Your Health*, observed men, half of whom had been designated highly "hostile personalities." By "harassing" the participants, researchers discovered "that as anger and irritation increased, blood-pressure and muscle blood flow responses increased *only* among the high . . . [hostility] men; there was no association between anger and irritation and physiologic reactivity in the low . . . [hostility] men."[92] This finding seems to corroborate my thesis that chronic suppression or repression of rage predisposes people to overreact to environmental stressors that individuals without such "reservoirs" or "lowered thresholds" for rage usually let "roll off their backs."

As concerns yet another classic psychosomatic syndrome—ulcers—there has been new medical research suggesting that ulcers are caused not (as many psychologists and physicians believe) by "stress," but rather by bacteria. Even if this proves to be true after all the data is in (which it is not) common sense dictates that being in a constant state of barely suppressed rage or chronic hostility could have an overstimulating effect on the production of gastric acid, which—in addition to attacking the overwhelmed stomach lining—might lower the patient's immunological resistance to such opportunistic organisms. The archaic association between *bile* (a greenish secretion of the liver), *spleen* (another gland-like abdominal organ located adjacent to the stomach), and *gall* (a yellowish bile secreted by the gallbladder) with anger, resentment, rancor, bitterness, ill-humor, hostility, latent malevolence, spite, impetuous temper, irascibility, and violent rage reveals an intuitive—if not quite anatomically accurate—understanding of the role of repressed anger and rage in digestive system disorders in general.

When we speak of "stress," which has been scientifically linked to lowered immune system functioning, it is important to bear in mind the ambiguous and generic nature of the term. In popular parlance, "stress" is used to describe feelings of subjective strain due to any number of challenging environmental or psychological situations, such as starting a new job, divorce, natural disasters, or the loss of a loved one. In most stress-related mental disorders and psychosomatic syndromes, anger or rage is frequently part of the clinical picture. Why is this? If one analyzes such situations carefully, these unresolved feelings of frustration, anger, and rage can be seen to comprise a significant portion of what most people generally refer to as "stress." Zaslow and Menta, for instance, citing the work of Hans Selye, suggest that repressed rage is a central source of chronic systemic stress, contributing not only to psychosomatic illness, but to "hyperactivity and other pathological 'stress' disturbances."[93] It requires considerable effort and energy to keep anger or rage constantly in check: the body must always be "on guard" against any possibility of becoming visibly angry or violent. This results in a continuing state of tension, an inability to relax, and habitual hyperstimulation of the "fight or flight" response, which, over time, takes a toll on the body. So-called *chronic fatigue syndrome*, for example, could prove to be at least partially caused by such a state of constant inner conflict, pressure, and tension stemming from too much suppression of the daimonic.

Headaches are one of the most common medical complaints. According to one recent study,

> the role of personality traits in the etiology of headache has long been the focus of much attention. One of the personality traits that most often has been linked to tension headache is anger and hostility. In fact, Adler and Adler went so

far as to state, "If one had to accord primacy to a single emotion in tension headache . . . it would be anger." Most theoretical formulations emphasize the relationship of anger and hostility to anxiety and depression, particularly as they involve the patient's family or other important interpersonal relationships. As feelings of resentment and hostility toward a loved one are repressed, anxiety and depression often are the result. As these emotions build and the threat that hostility will be expressed increases, the turmoil can give rise to physical symptoms.[94]

These researchers found that tension headache subjects differed

from controls in their experience and expression of anger and hostility, . . . [and were] prone to feelings of resentment, suspicion, mistrust, and antagonism in their interpersonal relations. They are also disposed to perceive situations as annoying or frustrating, and . . . are aroused to anger more often than controls. When it comes to the expression of anger, headache subjects do not differ from controls in their tendency to express their anger toward other people or objects in the environment, but they are more likely to suppress their angry feelings.[95]

The fact that tension headache sufferers seem more susceptible to hostility suggests that their characteristic tendency to suppress anger creates a lowered threshold of tolerance for frustration, and a pervasive characterological hostility that detrimentally affects how they perceive themselves and others. Hostility—hidden or overt—is the characterological consequence of chronically suppressed anger and rage.

One of the early pioneers of psychosomatic medicine, psychoanalyst and physician Franz Alexander, felt that

the common introduction of the migraine attack is a state of repressed rage. The most striking observation is the sudden termination of the attack almost from one minute to another after the patient becomes conscious of his hitherto repressed rage and gives expression to it in abusive words. . . .

According to Cannon, the blood flow to the brain remains ample and is relatively increased in states of violent emotion. In inhibited rage, when muscle action is blocked and blood flow to the muscles does not increase, . . . the blood flow to the cranium probably becomes even greater. This may be the physiological basis of the migraine attack. Increased muscle tonus and elevation of blood pressure are other components of the rage syndrome.[96]

We have since learned that genetic predisposition and various sorts of generic anxiety and "stress" probably also play a major part in the phenomenon of migraine headaches. Nevertheless, the potential presence of repressed anger or rage in migraine patients—as in so many other psychosomatic syndromes—cannot be overlooked as a likely contributing factor.

The Anatomy of Passion

Bearing upon the biological or biochemical aspects of the daimonic, madness, and other mental disorders, Willard Gaylin synopsizes the situation well:

> We know little of the anatomy of human anger and aggression, [and] we know less of its chemistry. . . .
> . . . Nothing—let me repeat, nothing—can be definitively said at this point about the chemistry of emotion, despite all the claims and counter claims. . . .
> And so, after all this, the biological models are only a hope of the future—assuming that the rampant changes in our sociology, economics and politics allow us an extended future. They offer us little practical use today [in controlling or channelling our anger and rage].[97]

But despite Dr. Gaylin's desire for some physiological or even surgical solution to what he sees as our antiquated, outmoded, and obsolete "mechanisms of anger" (p. 168), I strongly doubt that any purely biological paradigm or palliative for anger, rage, violence, or, for that matter, most mental disorders, will ever prove viable. This, however, is no nihilistic pessimism on my part. Rather, it is due to the fact that I, unlike Gaylin and others, do not consider what Freud described as a "desire for [destructive] aggression" to be a primary or independent drive. I see such daimonic impulses and tendencies as reactive yet archetypal potentialities inherent in human nature; existential by-products of the frustrations, injurious losses of love, nurturance, meaning, support and significance, and countless other emotional woundings, traumas, and stressors that constitute the human condition. Much as we might like to rid ourselves of the unseemly responses of anger or rage, nipping them in their organic or biochemical buds, in so doing we would destroy a precious piece of that which makes us most human. Or, as one French philosopher tersely expressed it: " '*Un homme sans passion et désires [sic] cesserait d'etre un homme.*' ('A man without passions or desires would cease to be a man.')"[98]

Neo-Freudian analyst and social philosopher Erich Fromm arrived at a similar conclusion in his classic study, *The Anatomy of Human Destructiveness:* "My thesis," said Fromm, " . . . is that destructiveness and cruelty are not instinctual drives, but passions rooted in the total existence of man."[99] These daimonic "passions" are not identical to "instincts." For Fromm,

> *instincts* are answers to man's *physiological needs,* [whereas] man's character-conditioned *passions* are answers to his *existential* needs and they are specifically human. . . .
>
> . . . Although not directly serving physical survival they are as strong—and often stronger—than instincts. They form the basis for man's interest in life, his enthusiasm, his excitement; they are the stuff from which not only his dreams are made but art, religion, myth, drama—all that makes life worth living. (pp. 26–29)

Unlike Freud, or ethologist Konrad Lorenz, Fromm views human destructiveness—or evil—as arising from *characterological* rather than predetermined, innate, physiological or instinctual programming. Fromm further equates human cruelty and destructiveness in general with "malignant aggression," a kind of "character-bound," psychopathological perversion. He prefers the poetic term "passions" to describe many aspects of the daimonic; yet, curiously, makes almost no mention at all in his bulky book of the burning passions of anger and rage.

Finally, a comment concerning my own metaphorical use of the terms "reservoir," "bottling up," "erupting," and so on when referring to the repression or suppression of anger and rage. I am by no means promulgating a hydraulic, materialist model of emotions, like Freud and most of his contemporaries followed, but, rather, much prefer a phenomenological one. Such language is for me simply a *façon de parler* used to describe certain human experiences. I utilize this terminology in a phenomenological, qualitative, or descriptive, not physical, quantitative, or mechanistic manner. Notwithstanding the irrefutable physiological foundations of human life and of the daimonic, we are not mere machinery, governed solely by the laws of physical science. The sometimes deterministic influences of the daimonic, the driving passions, the inestimable "powers of nature," as Goethe called them, or the instincts, do not reduce us to direct comparison to machines, computers, or animals. Instincts in animals are reflexive, inherited, immutable, and—in contrast to human passions—can never be consciously, subjectively apprehended and evaluated (though it is true that some instinctual behaviors in animals may be modified by learning or conditioning). Nor are we creatures unequivocally controlled by the principles of learning and conditioning, as behaviorist B. F. Skinner believed. We are first and foremost *human* beings, and, in addition to creaturely instincts, carry human qualities unique in all of nature. In attempting to perceive and comprehend the *whole* person, the comprehensive human being before us, we must create—rather than transpose from other fields of study—models that mirror and describe our subjective human experience. This is also why Rollo May, in accord with existential philosophers Gabriel Marcel and Jean-Paul Sartre, insisted that "when you see a person as a composite of drives and deterministic forces you have everything except the one to whom these experiences happen, everything except the *existing person him [or her] self.*"[100] What makes us most human is not whether we are or are not biologically driven and determined beings; but, rather, *how we respond to this relative truth.* The conscious choices we make in relating to the dynamic, psychobiological forces of the daimonic define our humanity.

Human models like "the daimonic" must be *humanistic,* not mechanistic or animalistic, or even scientific. *Science* is the creation by humans of a particular paradigm and methodology for discovering truth and understanding reality. Hence it can never fully reflect the hidden face of humanity, its creator, in the same sense that a computer can never become fully human or know what it means to be human: however sophisticated, these machines will forever remain mere artifacts of humanity. Insofar as computers cannot agonize over how to best come to terms with the instinctual and psychobiological inclinations of the daimonic, they will never know both the bane and the blessing of human existence. They can never know daimonic passion.

7

Redeeming Our Devils and Demons

Dealing with Anger and Rage in Psychotherapy

Contemporary depth psychology does not agree on the
way to achieve catharsis [therapy] because it does not agree
on the nature of the human situation.
—David L. Miller, "Orestes: Myth and Dream as Catharsis"

Resentment—in its various manifestations—is perhaps the central
problem of psychological development and psychotherapy.
—Edward F. Edinger, *Melville's Moby-Dick*

The task of the therapist is to conjure up the
devils rather than put them to sleep.
—Rollo May, "Psychotherapy and the Daimonic"

Psychotherapy's Current Identity Crisis

The daimonic passions of anger and rage pose a perennial problem for
psychotherapists of all persuasions. I am speaking not only of the
sometimes violent spleen of patients in psychotherapy, but also of the
clinician's own rancor. Unfortunately, there is precious little agreement

among the many different schools of psychotherapy as to how—or, for that matter, even whether—to contend with these dangerous emotions; so much depends on the specific orientation subscribed to by any given therapist, as well as his or her unresolved personal issues surrounding rage and anger. When it comes to addressing their patients' wrathful feelings, therapists tend—either consciously or unconsciously—to either dissuade the overt expression of anger; simply ignore it; intellectually analyze it; promote its full physical or emotional ventilation; rationalize or cognitively "restructure" it; focus on controlling or modifying its outward behavioral manifestations; and/or employ psychotropic medications to chemically allay the patient's anger or rage. In practice, most apply some combination of these and other techniques in an attempt to appease, assuage, or mollify the daimonic. It has become commonplace these days for therapists to find themselves treating very angry, often violent, patients. Increasingly, clinicians are expected—and pressured—by insurance companies and health maintenance organizations to remedy such serious symptoms in what has euphemistically been termed "brief therapy": a time-limited treatment modality traditionally consisting of from three to twenty sessions.

Many readers may already be aware that contemporary psychotherapy is in a state of acute crisis and chaos. As theologian David Miller observes, there is scant concurrence among psychiatrists, psychologists, and other mental health professionals as to the causes, and consequently, the most efficacious treatment for mental disorders—even at this highly touted, technologically advanced state of the art.[1] Perusing the incredibly contradictory literature or attending some cacaphonous, multidisciplinary conference on psychotherapy reveals a total disarray, a virtual "Tower of Babel": each camp clings to and dogmatically proclaims the correctness of their own paradigm, model, myth, or *Weltanschauung*, to the exclusion of all other alternative viewpoints. It is reminiscent of the ancient Hindu story of the wise men and the elephant: As I remember it, each sage was blindfolded, brought before an elephant, and then told to identify the nature of that which he touched but could not see in its entirety. One was allowed to touch the elephant's ear; another its tail; yet another, its trunk. When asked, separately, to describe the undisclosed object, each sage waxed poetic regarding the specific, isolated part he had personally encountered. Yet not one of these wise men was able to recognize the object of his study as an elephant. Because of their blindfolds—which we could think of as arrogant psychological preconceptions—they were unable to discern, despite their well-known wisdom, the proverbial "forest for the trees." We are faced today with a similar situation in the field of psychotherapy. For the *whole*—in this case, the whole human being, the suffering individual—can never be fully comprehended (or, for that matter, effectively "therapized") when perceived only in part, and out of context. This fact comprises the fundamental philosophy of "holistic" (or, more accurately, "wholistic") healing, whether in the fields of medicine or psychotherapy.[2]

In hopes of resolving at least some of this theoretical divisiveness, I propose a redefinition of that endangered form of psychotherapy referred to traditionally as "depth psychology." I would redefine "depth psychology" *to include the various forms of psychotherapy that deal directly with the daimonic, and encourage its constructive integration into consciousness.*

Practitioners of "depth psychology"—including Freudians, Jungians, and other psychodynamically oriented therapists—are a dying breed. It is true, for instance, that Jungian analysis has enjoyed a well-deserved resurgence during the past decade, and that there are more Jungian analysts in practice and training today than ever before. But overall, the trend is just the reverse in mainstream psychiatry and psychology. *Pharmacotherapy*—the use of psychotropic medication—has far outstripped psychotherapy as the treatment of choice for most mental disorders. Even when psychotherapy *is* seen as valuable and appropriate, non-depth psychologies like cognitive-behavioral therapy or brief, supportive therapy (individual or group) are now the preferred treatment modality for health maintenance organizations and, hence, for most pragmatic mental health providers.

There are numerous subtle and not-so-subtle reasons for this dramatic shift at this particular point in the evolution of psychotherapy as a science and profession. To name but a few: enormous economic pressure to provide "cost-effective" services; the speed and efficacy of new medications in controlling the crippling symptoms (but, typically, not the true causes) of psychosis, depression, anxiety, and other mental disorders; and recent research findings suggesting the supposed superiority of certain sorts of psychotherapy over others in the treatment of specific syndromes.[4] In truth, however, the motivations for this troubling trend are at least as much a matter of *philosophy* as of finances. In America, our approach to therapy reflects our fundamental philosophy of psychology, psychotherapy, and life in general. And, as we all know, the unstated yet omnipresent American philosophy—whether in eating habits, work ethic, or psychotherapy—can be accurately summed up in two simple sentences, the first being: *Rapidity is valued over quality.* We Americans crave speed and convenience: We want whatever it is we want right now, whether it be burgers or emotional unburdening. The second—and, for me, far more insidious—guiding principle can be stated as follows: *Deny the daimonic at all costs.* Harvard psychiatrist Michael Sperber observed some twenty years ago that

> our society does not encourage the daimonic, in part because of its destructive aspects. In fact, in this age of conformity, there is rather a tendency to repress the daimonic. The task of mental health professionals is to resist the temptation to use refine-ments in psychotechnology (psychopharmacology, electroshock therapy, and behavior modification) in order to suppress the daimonic, and instead to cultivate its emergence and integra-tion in the individual.[5]

While I wish to point out that though the techniques mentioned by Sperber can have clinical value in some cases, clearly, this temptation to which he refers, rather than being resisted, has today become a prime directive of the dominant American philosophy of psychotherapy. Why? For one thing, dealing with the daimonic can be dangerous. Most psychotherapists—re-gardless of their professional credentials—are justifiably fearful of the daimonic. Rather than encouraging (or, at least, not dis-couraging) patients to recognize their anger or rage during a psychotherapy session, there may instead be the propensity on the part of therapists to wittingly or unwit-tingly avoid, minimize, or rationalize these raw, unrefined, frightening feelings. Some psychotherapists, for instance, might dread—should they ever permit the patient to verbally express rage—the imminent possibility of physical violence directed either at themselves or others. Indeed, this is a serious and realistic concern, since there are increasing accounts of psycho-therapists being assaulted by their patients, or, of patients acting out their rage in the community.[6] There may also be grave concern that patients could become even more self-destructive or actively suicidal than they already are. The operative philosophical principle presumes that, since the daimonic is potentially destructive, it is always, therefore, safer *not* to deal with it; moreover, should the rage begin to break through the patient's defensive denial, and intensify beyond the comfort levels of either patient or thera-pist, the patient must be drugged, in order to dampen down the daimonic. The daimonic is misperceived as purely evil (i.e., demonic) and, therefore, must be subdued by whatever means deemed medically necessary. This governing philosophical prejudice generally applies to the undesirable ap-pearance of any daimonic emotions on the part of the therapist, too, as shall be explained presently.

The trouble with the foregoing clinical philosophy is that, ultimately, it causes more problems than it circumvents; it all-too-frequently turns into a self-fulfilling prophecy. It is iatrogenic: it reinforces the process of suppressing the daimonic, which not only perpetuates the patient's underlying problems, but in turn may produce, over time, a violently destructive explosion or implosion of daimonic rage. For the patient's anger or rage does not magically dissipate due to being ignored, derogated, denounced, or drugged. It merely goes underground, where it grows all the more dangerous, and from where, eventually, it will likely erupt into some sort of violence—be it directed outwardly or inwardly. The daimonic—especially when persistently repressed over long periods of time—can be compared to dynamite: it is powerful, volatile, explosive, and deadly if mishandled. When treated properly, however, by an expert with the requisite respect, skill, care, courage, and consciousness, it can become a constructive, transformative force. Paradoxically, the destructive power of dynamite has helped humankind create great cities, towns, and superhighways, in addition to waging war. But, like dynamite, when handled with ignorance, negligence, carelessness, irresponsibility, disrespect, or maliciousness, the daimonic can prove fatally destructive to all within its purview. To the extent psychotherapy promotes the demonization and subjugation of the daimonic, it becomes not curative, but yet another contributing factor to the current epidemic of violence. On the contrary, the more we psychotherapists can learn about constructive ways of confronting and coming to terms with the daimonic— both in our patients and ourselves—the better we get at defusing violence where it begins: within the *individual*. For it would best be admitted by anyone truly interested in violence and its prevention that "all the highest achievements of virtue, as well as the blackest villainies, are individual."[7] Ironically, earnest effort toward vanquishing runaway violence in America at this microcosmic, *personal* level, is probably the most viable—yet least valued—course of action available to us.

Catharsis and the Daimonic

We continue our stated task of redefining "depth psychology" with a discussion of *catharsis*. "Catharsis" is a term derived from the Greek word *katharsis*, sometimes used synonymously for "therapy." *Katharsis*, which came from *kathairein*, "to clean or purify," was "used by Aristotle in his description of the effect of tragedy," and implies any "purification or purgation of the emotions . . . that brings about a spiritual renewal or a satisfying release from tension." In modern psychotherapy, *catharsis* refers to "the process of bringing repressed ideas and feelings into consciousness, especially by the technique of free association as employed in psychoanalysis, [with] drugs or hypnosis sometimes being used as adjuvants."[8]

According to David Miller,

> metaphorically, *katharsis* presents seven pictures. (1) In one ancient papyrus *katharsis* is "clearing," as when a person is clearing the land of twigs and stones. (2) In another papyrus *katharsis* is "winnowing," as in the thrashing of grain. (3) Diocles used the term as the image of "cleaning" when he described the process of cleaning food by cooking it. (4) Theophrastus, in his essay "On Plants," meant "pruning" when he used *katharsis* in relation to trees. (5) Both Philodemus . . . and Epicurus . . . used the same word to picture the "clarification" achieved by explanation. (6) Galen, of course, used *katharsis* to signify the "healing" of an illness by the application of medicine. And (7) Chrysippus' *katharsis* was the "purifying" of the universe by fire.[9]

Evidently, even some two thousand years ago, "catharsis" could mean different things to different people!

Catharsis is commonly—though incorrectly—understood today as solely connoting emotional "release" and therapeutic "expression" of pent-up, previously suppressed or repressed feelings, like anger, rage, or crying. But the diverse practice of catharsis can be traced back to primitive healing rituals, exorcism, and *confession*, the latter having been employed at one time by the Incas and Aztecs of Mexico, and, of course, the Catholic Church, where it continues today. In more recent times, confession as a means of catharsis had been utilized by the medical profession, even prior to turn-of-the-twentieth-century psychoanalytic discoveries. For instance, several decades before Breuer and Freud began publishing their *Studies on Hysteria* (in 1893–1895), Austrian physician Moritz Benedikt "showed that the cause of many cases of hysteria and other neuroses resides in a painful secret, mostly pertaining to sexual life, and that many patients can be cured by the confession of their pathogenic secrets."[10] Physicians throughout history have known of the cathartic, healing qualities of confession, and made good use of it. The best physicians still use it. Not until the tail end of this dehumanizing century did medical doctors start to abandon this intimate practice in favor of a more clinical, technological, and impersonal approach to treating patients. We have all experienced first hand the impoverishing results of this sterile, mechanistic movement in modern medicine, which strives vainly to separate body from mind, psyche, or soul.

The conception of catharsis as *purgation* can be found in Dante's early fourteenth-century masterpiece, the *Divine Comedy,* wherein Dante and his faithful guide, Virgil, descend down into the Stygian depths of Hell, their subsequent ascent to Heaven being possible only by way of Purgatory. Psychologically, *purgatory* can be compared to part of the psychotherapeutic or cathartic process, the confronting and confessional purging of our disturbing devils or demons: "The 'Inferno'—or hell— consists," says Rollo May, "of suffering and endless torment that produces no change in the soul that endures it and is imposed from without. But in the 'Purgatorio' suffering is temporary, a means of purification, and is eagerly embraced by the soul's own will. Both must be traversed before arriving at the celestial 'Paradiso.' "[11] The daimonic cannot be circum- vented, sidestepped, or spiritually "transcended," making the journey through one's own personal "heart of darkness" needless—much as we might wish it possible. This is one of the subtle perils of the "transpersonal" psychology movement: some who are drawn to mysticism, metaphysics, and New Age spiritualism—both patients and therapists—naively perceive this psychotherapeutic approach as a means of attaining to 'Paradiso' directly, without the dirty work of first facing our personal demons on the mundane, gritty, Earth-bound level rather than the transcendent, spiritual, or *trans*personal plane. But the daimonic brooks no shortcuts or convenient evasions. All who dare venture into the true "spiritual" realm—the passionate domain of the daimons—must be prepared to meet the metaphorical dark deities, forces, powers, or spirits, "abandoning all hope" of finding just angelic ones. Many, alas, are not. Herein lies the danger.

But the question remains as to precisely what comprises purgation, catharsis, or psychotherapy: What makes therapy "therapeutic"? Is simply speaking about one's "demons" sufficient to "exorcise" them? During the 1960s, classical psychoanalytic or "talk" therapy came under heavy attack, accused of being an overly intellectual and introspective exercise that failed to provide true emotional catharsis, and required far too much time and money. Ironically, this criticism arose from the perceived discrepancy between Freud's original theories of catharsis or *abreaction,* and the actual practice of psychoanalysis by his followers. In practice, as Otto Rank[12] recognized, psychoanalytic psychotherapy had become desiccated and detached from the emotional power of the daimonic, despite the beneficial effects of affective "abreaction" observed by Breuer and Freud:

> The fading of a memory or the losing of its affect depends on various factors. The most important of these is *whether there has been an energetic reaction to the event that provokes an affect.* By 'reaction' we here understand the whole class of voluntary and involuntary reflexes—from tears to acts of revenge—in which, as experience shows us, the affects are discharged. If this reaction takes place to a sufficient amount a large part of the affect disappears as a result. Linguistic usage bears witness to this fact of daily observation by such phrases as 'to cry oneself out' *['sich ausweinen'],* and to 'blow off steam' *['sich austoben',* literally 'to rage oneself out']. If the reaction is suppressed, the affect remains attached to the memory. An injury that has been repaid, even if only in words, is recollected quite differently from one that has had to be accepted. . . . The injured person's reaction to the trauma only exercises a completely 'cathartic' effect if it is an *adequate* reaction—as, for instance, revenge. But language serves as a substitute for action; by its help, an affect can be 'abreacted' almost as effectively.[13]

By "language," what Freud and Breuer refer to is *verbalizing* feelings and impulses, as opposed to acting on them, as in the case of talionic retribution. But in order to be "cathartic," or therapeutic, the patient must experience—or re-experience—these emotions as profoundly as possible, rather than endlessly discussing them in some superficially detached, rational fashion. True catharsis, it was later claimed—mostly by the so-called "me generation"—consists not of arid conversation, interminable intellectual analysis, and inaction, but requires active ventilation, or unbridled expression of long-locked up passions. Alternative approaches, like Arthur Janov's "Primal Therapy," popularized this point of view, encouraging patients to stop passively talking about their problems, so as to be able to *relive* and *re-experience* their repressed "Primal Pain."[14] Janov's revolutionary Primal Therapy served as the stimulus or prototype for several later psychotherapies, some of which will be selectively reviewed in this chapter.

In popular culture, *sexuality*—not the far less palatable "Primal Pain"—was, of course, the first American taboo to be fully "ventilated," in a collective surge of libido which lead to what was soon to be called the "sexual revolution" of the 1960s and 1970s. Patients were routinely encouraged by their therapists to explore and experiment with their sexuality, and, in general, to liberate themselves from their puritanical sexual "hang-ups" or inhibitions. "Free love" became the counter-cultural credo of "hippies"—and inevitably, of countless others—during those titillating times. The widespread use of hallucinogenic drugs like marijuana, mescaline, and LSD fueled the "free love" movement, as well as prying open what visionary poet William Blake once described as the "doors of perception."[15] The psychological aftermath of this heady decade has been far more formative than most people realize; the philosophical repercussions are still being felt in all quarters of American culture. Along with just about everything else, the field of psychotherapy was forever changed. Carol Tavris critically comments that as a result, today, "the ventilationist view is widespread not only among clinical psychologists and psychiatrists, but also among the general populace as well. . . . A majority of adults endorse the catharsis notion. . . . Never mind whether your emotional release makes those around you feel worse, or fails to solve the problem. If you can do what you want, it must be good for you. That's the American way, after all."[16]

By the time I began studying and practicing psychotherapy in the mid-1970s, the sexual genie had already been freed from its fetters, and this issue no longer proved to be what patients most wanted or needed to talk about. Instead, *spirituality*—spurred simultaneously by its massive suppression in secular American society as well as by the eye-opening, "mind-altering" psychedelic drug "trips" of the late 1960s—surfaced as the pressing issue that most preoccupied my peers. The Woodstock generation, having been sexually liberated, now sought spiritual liberation. There was a tremendously exciting spirit of self-exploration and self-discovery, leading many of us not only to new or "alternative" types of therapies, but toward Oriental philosophy and religion. We were searching for something more in life than the bland materialism for which most of our parents had seemingly settled. We were seeking "God," meaning, the "spiritual life"—though most of us, in our youthful naiveté, had no real conception of what "spirituality" actually entails.

Both in my psychological studies and didactic personal therapy, it soon became plain to me that something had gone wrong with our whole approach to anger and rage in American culture. "Spirituality," for instance, had turned for most into a one-sided, "blissed-out" affair, in which all "negative" impulses or emotions such as jealousy, envy, anger, or rage were judged "unspiritual" or "anti-spiritual," and hence, suppressed as antithetical to the spiritual journey. We aspired to be "good," "mellow," "enlightened" men and women, without malice. But, in so doing, we had denied the daimonic. We were suffering from *pseudoinnocence*, a childish naiveté which, as May writes, "does not lead to spirituality but rather consists of blinders. . . . It wilts before our complicity with evil. It is this innocence that cannot come to terms with the destructiveness in one's self or others . . . and hence, . . . becomes self-destructive."[17] Many "baby boomers" still cling to their pseudoinnocence, as do most Americans in general: We have no eyes for evil, which is what makes us so very vulnerable to it.

But the great discomfort felt around anger and rage reached well beyond any one age group or particular segment of the populace. As I slowly progressed through my psychotherapeutic training, supervision, and practice; moving from student counseling center, to clinic, to hospital emergency room; working with adults, adolescents, and children of different races, ethnicities, and wildly varying degrees of psychopathology, I was struck by how openly or surreptitiously angry my patients were; and how closely their unresolved anger—or in some cases, outright rage—correlated with their various psychological and behavioral problems. What was this widespread wrath about? And why was nobody addressing it? Generally speaking, for the vast majority of my patients, anger and rage was a taboo topic.

For most Americans, this remains the case. Anger and rage are still intensely taboo topics, to be avidly avoided however and whenever possible. We dare not deal with these nasty demons, this dark, destructive, or "negative" side of the daimonic. Instead, we are fascinated with the pure, symbolic *antithesis* of demons, namely angels—indeed, obsessed with them, if the recent spate of books, magazine articles, and television specials are any indication.[18] We are tenaciously unwilling to admit to ourselves or others our own anger and rage, nor our innate capacity for evil. In order to facilitate this falsely benevolent face, we establish intricate social rituals, say psychologists Herb Goldberg and George Bach, by which "each of us individually . . . disown[s] aggression as a reality existing within and between us, helping to maintain the taboos against its personal expression, and facilitating the maintenance of our own altruistic self-image."[19]

These unspoken and often unconscious collective collusions designed specifically to avoid authentic expressions of aggression, anger, or rage, can also be found in the consulting room. There may exist a tacit agreement between patient and therapist—never verbalized but nevertheless understood—to steer clear of the daimonic as much as possible, in what Bach and Goldberg dub a "dance around the beast." Religious or spiritual communities are another setting in which such suppressive rituals are rife. But, to cite May on this matter: "*Human beings can reach heaven only through hell. . . .* In America, we seem . . . to act on the wish that we could pass over the despair of mortification and know only the exaltation of ascent. We seem to believe we can be reborn without ever dying. Such is the spiritual version of the American Dream!"[20] Such is also, I would dare say, an accurate and damning statement of the 1990s "feel good— and as quickly as possible" approach to psychotherapy.

Exorcism and Psychotherapy

Exorcism is probably the primeval prototype of modern psychotherapy. The age-old practice of exorcism was—and still is—anchored in the equally ancient idea of *demonology*: the victim's problem is due to evil spirits that have penetrated and possessed his or her body. Catharsis or exorcism consists of forcefully "driving out . . . the spirit by conjurations or other psychic means."[21] As Ellenberger explains:

> Exorcism is the exact counterpart of possession and a well-struc-
> tured type of psychotherapy. Its basic characteristics are the fol-
> lowing: The exorcist does not, ordinarily, speak in his own name,
> but in the name of a higher being. He must have absolute
> confidence in this higher being and in his own powers, as well
> as in the reality of the possession and of the possessing
> spirit. . . . He dispenses encouragement to the possessed indi-
> vidual and saves his threats and admonitions for the
> intruder. . . . The exorcist must induce the intruder to speak, and
> after lengthy discussions, a bargain may sometimes take place.
> Exorcism is a struggle between the exorcist and the intruding
> spirit—often a long, difficult, and desperate struggle that may
> continue for days, weeks, months, or even years before a com-
> plete victory can be achieved. Not infrequently does the exor-
> cist meet with defeat; moreover, he is in danger himself of
> becoming infested with the very spirit he has just expelled from
> the patient. (p. 14)

Much the same may be said about modern psychotherapists! May observes that

> therapists belong to a strange profession. It is partly religion.
> Since the time of Paracelsus in the Renaissance the physician—

and afterward the psychiatrist and psychological therapist—has taken on the mantle of the priest. We cannot deny that we who are therapists deal with people's moral and spiritual questions and that we fill the role of father [or mother]—confessor as part of our armamentarium, as shown in Freud's position *behind* and unseen by the person confessing.[22]

Despite the ostensibly secular, scientific persona of most psychotherapeutic practitioners, simply scratching the surface of rationality and objectivity reveals—lo and behold!—a hidden exorcist: We, too, speak in the name of a "higher being," be it science or some metaphysical belief system; we firmly believe in the reality of the pathological problem, manifested in the patient's symptoms and suffering; and we dispense encouragement to our troubled patients while joining with them in a sacred, "therapeutic alliance" against the wicked forces bedeviling them. Notwithstanding the current economically driven, recklessly simplistic trend toward "brief psychotherapy" for all manner of psychological disturbances, sooner or later we discover in clinical practice strikingly similar principles to those educed by the exorcists: Psychotherapy can—of necessity—commonly consist of a prolonged, bitter, demanding, soul-wrenching, sometimes tedious battle *royale* with the patient's diabolically obdurate emotional "demons," at times waged over the course of years rather than months, and not necessarily with consummate success. Finally, there is growing recognition—no longer solely on the part of "psychodynamic" or depth psychologists, but by practitioners of diverse orientations—of the very real dangers and risks of *psychic infection* inherent in the practice of psychotherapy. "Counter-transference" is the technical term for this treacherous psychological phenomenon, which can cause the therapist to suffer disturbing, subjective symptoms of anxiety, depression, apathy, anger, or rage during the psychotherapy process—sometimes even as the patient progresses! Hence the ever-present importance for the exorcist or psychotherapist to perform his or her sacred duties within a formally ritualized structure, to make full use of collegial support, cooperation, and supervision, and to maintain inviolable personal boundaries—all this while keeping as consciously aware and clear of purpose as possible. To paraphrase Freud: No one wrestles with demons—even the demons of others—and comes away completely unscathed. Psychological "infestation" is an unavoidable "occupational hazard" shared by both the exorcist and psychotherapist, each of whom in his or her own way deals directly with the daimonic on a daily basis. We will be returning to this critical theme momentarily.

But first, let us consider the following brief description of exorcisms observed during 1953, on one of the small Ionian Islands scattered along the lovely western coast of Greece. In general, as the exorcisms get under way, there is predictably a

> sudden worsening of the . . . [symptoms] at the moment when the exorcist displays the holy relic. The manifestation can become so severe that some patients must be tied down for the duration of the exorcism. It is explained by the [Cephalonian] islanders as the rage of the demon, who antici- pates his expulsion. . . . The inhabitants of Cephalonia claim that the moment the demon is expelled a branch will fall in a mysterious way or a church window will break inexplicably, which is also ascribed to the expelled demon's rage. The more nasty and powerful the demon, the more likely he is to dem- onstrate his rage in such a manner.[23]

In such illustrative instances, the identification of the "demon" with the person's repressed rage seems self-evident. Indeed, the possessed "patients" are often restrained so as to prevent hurting themselves or others in a demonic fit of rage. Catharsis in this case involves the unbridled expression of the rage, or rather, the rage *expressing itself* through the possessed person. Note, however, that there is no conscious ownership of the rage required by this primitive process: the rage belongs to the demon, not the patient. Once the "patient" is purged of the demon— the repressed rage—he or she returns to a "normal" (albeit, I suspect, relatively unconscious) state of mind.

The case of an earlier, well-documented exorcism occurring during the course of almost two years, between 1842 and 1843, involved one Gottliebin Dittus, a twenty-eight-year-old European woman. Dittus had reportedly been "seeing visions," experiencing "violent convulsions," speak- ing in a voice different than her own, and vomiting various sharp objects such as nails and glass, along with—as we would suspect—blood.[24] In an attempt to save her, a Lutheran pastor, Reverend Blumhardt, undertook a lengthy and arduous exorcism, at the end of which, according to Blumhardt himself, the woman " 'was freed of spirits and demons.' "[25]

Blumhardt's confrontation with the demonic forces in this famous case has been the subject of intense study and scrutiny by modern-day medicine. One such study, published in 1960 by Italian psychiatrist Gaetano Benedetti, a then prominent expert in the psychotherapy of psychosis, compared Blumhardt's successful treatment of this desperately ill young woman to his own work with schizophrenic patients. Here, Henri Ellenberger does us the great favor of condensing Benedetti's analysis, which I present to you in its entirety:

> Blumhardt's first reaction was one of hesitation and defense, a necessary prelude to regarding a case in its full seriousness. The main effort was directed toward himself (prayer and fasting), just as the therapist of psychoses must give primary attention to his "counter-transference." . . . Blumhardt then throws himself into Gottliebin's demoniacal world, just as the modern therapist explores the inner world of his schizophrenic patient's delusions. The fact that the manifestations of possession kept getting worse is compared by Benedetti to the apparent worsening of psychotic symptoms through the effect of the patient's resistance. The patient tries to overcome the therapist, who must respond by frustrating such wishes, and this, says Benedetti, is exactly what Blumhardt did. Blumhardt also sharply differentiated his attitude toward the "victimized" spirits and evil spirits; in the same way, the therapist is very responsive to anything that comes from the healthy part of the patient's mind, while repudiating all sick manifestations. Blumhardt's acute psychological insight is shown in the fact that while resistance was taking increasingly absurd, exaggerated, and desperate forms, he was now setting conditions, testing his patient, and giving her orders. (We could add at this point that Blumhardt made full use of what existential therapists call the *kairos*, that is, the elective point for decisive intervention or decision.)[26]

Exorcists like Blumhardt presaged and foreshadowed, as we shall see, many of the highly specialized techniques employed today by those professionals who dare to treat that inordinately negative degree of daimonic possession known historically as "madness," "insanity," or "psychosis."

Clinical Approaches to Anger and Rage in Psychosis

Functional psychosis—psychotic conditions not demonstrably proven to be primarily organic in origin—is by far one of the most severe and devastating of all mental disorders; and thus demands the most daring and innovative therapeutic treatment available. Schizophrenia, which occurs in virtually all known cultures and across every socioeconomic strata, is a classic—and so far, for the most part, incurable—form of insanity or functional psychosis. It is likely that many—if not most—of those believed to be possessed by or in league with the devil or demons throughout history would be today diagnosed as "schizophrenic." However, in keeping with our paradigm of the daimonic, we could just as easily say that such patients are in an acute or chronic, consuming state of psychological "possession." Surely, no one having any personal experience with schizophrenic patients would argue that these ravaged individuals are in full possession of themselves. Yet, for all intents and purposes, psychotherapy is no longer deemed an appropriate treatment for schizophrenia by mainstream psychiatry, having been supplanted by the long-term use of anti-psychotic drugs to sedate the daimonic. There nonetheless still are psychologists and psychiatrists who believe that psychotherapy not only can be effective, but is essential in the proper treatment of schizophrenia and other psychotic disorders. Their methods are extremely controversial—so much so, that I am compelled to make the following disclaimer: *Despite certain theoretical affinities, the treatment methods discussed in this section do not reflect my own technical orientation to psychotherapy* (this will be presented toward the end of this chapter). *Nor do I recommend that these methods be adopted or experimented with by lay persons, or mental health professionals not specifically and formally trained in these hazardous techniques.* But to paraphrase Hippocrates, the revered namesake of that sacred oath to which physicians and other healers have for some twenty-five centuries sworn allegiance, *extreme illnesses require extreme remedies.* And psychotic disorders such as schizophrenia are the most extreme mental illnesses existent.

Wilhelm Reich's "Character Analysis"

One such controversial psychiatrist was Wilhelm Reich, of whom we spoke in the preceding chapter. In his classic work, *Character Analysis,* published in 1945, Reich relates a case history of a young, chronically schizophrenic woman, in whose treatment he applied his own, trail-blazing techniques. Reich was one of the first clinicians to, in effect, recognize the central role of the daimonic in schizophrenia. Having already witnessed the anger, rage, and destructive impulses underlying the characterological defenses of his neurotic patients, Reich took the following tack in treating this far-less-functional, psychotic patient:

The patient, a 32-year-old Irish girl, had been brought to me by her relatives. . . . I informed them of the great dangers of precipitating a breakdown. They were ready to take the risk and to sign an affidavit to this effect. I also warned them of the risk of a sudden outbreak of destructiveness. Since I was well acquainted with the manifestations preceding a destructive attack, I felt sure that I would sense the danger in time. Therefore, I undertook the experiment outside the institution under the strict condition that a nurse or relative should always be around the patient and that at the first sign of unrest and destructiveness the patient should be committed to the institution. . . . [27]

"Such precautions," Reich continues, "are indispensable if one wants to treat a schizophrenic outside an institution. One would prefer to rely on an institution . . . but, unfortunately, mental institutions—with very few exceptions—are not inclined to bother with new, hopeful medical efforts to treat schizophrenia" (ibid.). Sadly, this last remark of Reich's still largely holds true.

As this highly unorthodox therapy proceeded, Reich realized that whenever anger, rage, or hatred welled up in his patient, it was necessary to confront it "head on," instead of stopping the process. In response to Reich vigorously massaging her spastic "muscular armor," deepening her breathing, and assailing her psychological defenses, the patient experienced a rapid, undifferentiated flow of feelings—including both rage and crying—making it difficult to discern which one was more basic. Drawing on extensive clinical experience, Reich formulated the following technical approach:

In such situations, where different kinds of emotions are intermingled, it is necessary to separate the emotions from one another. This can be done by promoting the most superficial emotion, the one which fights off the deeper emotion, and by "pushing back" the latter. Accordingly, I encouraged her crying which blocked the rage, and after some tearful release of sorrow, I let her develop her rage by encouraging her to hit the couch. *This is a dangerous procedure if the patient, especially the schizophrenic, is not in perfect contact with the physician.* In order to secure this contact, one must explain to the patient that he must stop his rage action instantly when asked to do so. It is the task of the physician to decide when the patient is in danger of getting out of control. . . . One cannot proceed in such cases without releasing the rage, and one cannot release the rage without much experience previously gained in less emotional situations. (p. 409)

According to Reich—though it is virtually impossible to otherwise verify—following an intensive course of more than forty such treatments, marked by numerous self-destructive episodes, breakdowns, and regressions requiring multiple psychiatric hospitalizations, the patient eventually achieved "a full recovery, with freedom from psychosis for over five years after treatment" (p. 481).[28] Wilhelm Reich had become one of the first depth psychologists to directly confront the daimonic in schizophrenia with some putative success.

Alexander Lowen's "Bioenergetic Analysis"

Building upon and embellishing Reich's work, one of his former students and patients, American psychoanalyst Alexander Lowen, later developed a system of therapy he designated "bioenergetics,"[29] based on Reich's somatically oriented psychotherapy. Though he did not claim to specialize in the treatment of psychosis, Lowen ingeniously theorized that schizophrenia "is brought about by a block in the pathway of the aggressive impulses which prevents them from entering consciousness."[30] By "block," he meant some sort of physiological, musculo-skeletal, somatic inhibition, mirroring metaphorically a corresponding psychological suppression. So far as I am aware, Lowen no longer recommends his approach for the treatment of schizophrenia or other psychotic conditions. This would, in my view, make good sense. Having some familiarity with Lowen's techniques, I can testify that these methods are quite effective in forcefully inducing the daimonic; and, therefore, quite dangerous if not completely inappropriate, in my opinion, for use with psychotic or borderline psychotic patients—particularly in the hands of unsophisticated or inexperienced practitioners. Although Lowen's primary treatment focus is on enhancing the person's ability to experience pleasure and sexuality á la Reich, bioenergetics therapy includes sundry techniques, or so-called "stress-exercises," designed to induce and actively facilitate the expression of repressed anger and rage. For instance, the patient might be encouraged to angrily "strike out," by pummeling pillows or beating a bed or a couch. Or, he or she might be instructed to kick and hit a mattress violently while reclining upon it, in an attempt to reconnect with long-stifled feelings of infantile protest, fury, and defiance. Or, perhaps the bioenergeticist will provide the patient with a towel to twist, throttle, or strangle, in a relatively harmless yet powerful expression of suppressed angry, hostile, or sometimes murderous impulses. First these daimonic emotions are freed—via these and other physically manipulative, "hands-on" methods—from the "character armor" that once restrained them. Following this phase of treatment, Lowen (who first trained as a Freudian) would concurrently work with patients in a more orthodox fashion, helping them to integrate the daimonic on a psychological as well as physical level. Regrettably, this latter and absolutely imperative aspect of neo-Reichian or bioenergetic analysis—the cognitive integration of the daimonic— appears to have been devalued, curtailed, or completely abandoned by most practitioners today.

Robert Zaslow's "Rage Reduction" or "Z-Process"

Yet another highly contentious form of psychotherapy that arose during the revolutionary 1960s, around the same time as Janov's Primal Therapy, was psychologist Robert Zaslow's "Rage Reduction," later referred to as "the Z-Process."[31] Zaslow began his work mainly with disturbed children, specializing in the treatment of *autism*: a tragically debilitating, psychotic-like disorder, in which by age three the child cannot communicate normally (non-verbally or verbally), and is abnormally aloof and withdrawn, preferring to relate to mechanical, inanimate objects more than with people—including his or her own parents. In treating children with various problems including hyperactivity (now termed "attention-deficit/ hyperactivity disorder"), bed-wetting (enuresis), psychosomatic symptoms such as asthma, and autism—the most devastating psychiatric disorder of childhood—Zaslow discovered a common motif. He found that all of these disturbed children had formed inadequate emotional bonds or "attachments" to their primary caretakers. According to Zaslow, "the autistic child is an extreme form of the failure of normal attachment and represents the earliest form of the interpersonal disturbances leading to schizophrenia."[32]

Armed with this astute clinical observation, Zaslow developed a style of therapy which involved physically *holding* his small patients while he worked with them. Without exception, the children would grow agitated or irascible when unable to wriggle free from the firm but gentle grasp of the therapist, resist face-to-face contact, and finally, get *angry*. Zaslow viewed such behaviors as forms of "resistance," refusing to release the child at that point. When faced with the frustrating fact that there was no escaping the confining situation, these children would start to *rage*. But Zaslow would not back off or retreat from these ferocious displays of forthright rage, continuing to compassionately restrain the furious child. By the end of each session, however, this spontaneous rage had dissipated, and, paradoxically, a new, more positive attachment had developed between therapist and patient—a more human relationship. Most importantly, of course, is that according to Zaslow, many of these seriously disturbed and emotionally disabled children became better, their symptoms diminishing in apparent response to this unproven, radical method.

Encouraged by these results, Zaslow and his assistant, Marilyn Menta, went on to refine and apply this technique to adult mental disorders, including schizophrenia: "Our basic assumption is that schizophrenia results from poor attachment and inability to show constructive anger in the family. . . . The Z-Process . . . [is] a method whereby the disturbed person can experience feelings, including psychotic rage, if such is the case, and resolve them constructively in a controlled, safe manner."[33] Zaslow saw the chronically repressed rage of the schizophrenic or otherwise psychotic patient as the primary stumbling block in establishing a truly trusting, therapeutic alliance (or attachment) between doctor and patient. He held that depth psychologists like "Freud and Reich did not develop a methodology for handling rage, thereby limiting their abilities to handle resistance. . . . The Reichian rage is restrained, for it requires the patient to experience some measure of self-control for fear of its destructive effects. . . . The one-to-one situation of Reichian therapy and bioenergetics results in inadequate security for therapist and patient, thus producing a barrier to adequately handling resistances which may culminate in the full expression of adult rage."[34]

For Zaslow, the task of the therapist is to emancipate the enslaved patient from the destructive, negativistic resistances comprising and perpetuating his or her psychopathology. In order to do so successfully, these resistances must be frankly confronted. Such unequivocal confrontations or challenges to the patient's characterological defenses result, as Reich had discovered, in rage. Indeed, Zaslow asserts that this rage at times may itself be a sort of resistance, typically the final resistance encountered prior to some major therapeutic progress. In effect, Zaslow would use this intense psychophysiological state of arousal—the patient's daimonic rage—to systematically break through and dismantle pathological resistance, thereby redeeming his or her missing potency for rage. Curiously, reclaiming one's defensively renounced faculty for rage in this fashion, note Menta and Zaslow, often generalizes into orgasmic potency in adult patients, enhanced human attachment, and improved interpersonal relatedness, including the increased capacity to love and let oneself be loved.

The implications of Zaslow's critique of traditional depth psychology are provocative. He suggests that in the conventional "one-on-one" context, psychotherapy with psychotic patients—or even with much less severely disturbed "neurotics"—is inherently flawed and structurally inadequate; a situation in which excessive vulnerability and justifiable fear—on both sides—of the patient's potentially destructive rage, radically diminishes its curative power. Zaslow held that his method, unlike most other psychotherapies, "can handle aggression, rage and resistance to an effective degree, thereby removing one of the essential barriers and threats that exist for patient and doctor, or client and therapist in therapeutic work. Since the sense of threat exists in both client and therapist, it provides a common link of weakness in both, limiting the effectiveness of their therapeutic relationship."[35]

When employed in the treatment of adults, Zaslow's "rage reduction" therapy, during the first phase, requires the patient to be cradled comfortably in the laps of perhaps six or more supportive participants, for what could be a period of time in excess of several hours. During the session, the patient—who has almost always voluntarily agreed to submit to such treatment—is for all intents and purposes *physically* (via unpleasant "stimulation" or rubbing of the rib cage when offering resistance) and *psychologically* (via the therapist's staunch refusal to accept anything other than direct responses to specific questions posed) forced to confront unresolved conflicts around anger, rage, and attachment.[36] Skillfully, systematically, humanely yet relentlessly, the therapist proceeds to attack the patient's tangled defense mechanisms (resistances), sooner or later inducing a full, adult "rage reaction." Lovingly and safely restrained by the "holders," the patient is permitted to thoroughly and unreservedly verbalize his or her hostility, hatred, resentment, anger, and rage *face to face*— not only to the therapist, but, sometimes to significant others such as mother, father, spouse, sister, etc.

During the essential second phase of treatment—once the peak state of rage arousal has been reached, abreacted, and focused—"much of the interchange follows conventional psychotherapy patterns,"[37] including cognitive, systems-oriented, and psychoanalytic interpretation (though this phase may still of necessity include some "holding" within the controlled context of the therapeutic "community"). The therapist seeks—as in traditional depth psychology—to provide patients with insight as to the origins of their rage, the role of its repression in their psychological symptoms, their family and social interactions, and so forth. Based on their own informal survey, Zaslow and Menta proclaim their method capable of rendering dramatic results with psychotic patients in relatively short order. Due to the controversial nature of this therapy, there is, sadly, little interest or support in the scientific community for further investigation of its efficacy in the treatment of schizophrenia and other debilitating mental disorders. In my estimation, there should be. We Americans ought to be spending at least as much tax money, time, and effort on the search for sound psychotherapeutic solutions to psychosis as we presently pour into poorly premised, purely pharmacological approaches.

What follows is a condensed treatment summary by Zaslow and Menta of a sixteen-year-old schizophrenic patient named Ana, first published in *The Psychology of the Z-Process* in 1975. Ana had been psychiatrically hospitalized for one year following the insidious onset of her psychosis, which was marked by symptoms of autistic-like apathy, severe withdrawal, self-inflicted cigarette burns, delusions, and bizarre speech: she referred to herself as "a 'penguin,' classified people in terms of 'pica' or 'elite,' . . . and stated [that] she had died" (p. 40). Ana's psychiatrist requested that Zaslow work with this patient, who had thus far not responded to hospitalization, medication, nor psychotherapy:

> Ana was a slender, 16-year-old girl wearing jeans. She had long brown hair. . . . Her early history revealed that her biological father had been accidentally electrocuted when Ana was two. . . . After her father's death, Mother had gone into a state of shock which lasted for a period of one year . . . .
>
> Ana was described as a quiet and good child who was overly dominated by her [bright, articulate, yet perfectionistic, and emotionally aloof] mother. When Ana was six-years-old, her mother remarried a man who had several children of his own. [Ana's] mother stated that the relationship between the step-father and Ana was poor. . . .
>
> When Ana was about 12-years-old, her stepfather and mother divorced, . . . [but her mother remarried] when Ana was 14. . . . [Ana's schizophrenia started] shortly following [this] new marriage, and was undoubtedly a reaction to it. . . .
>
> . . . Five [Z-Process] sessions were given in a period of one month. The first session lasted five hours, without the parents present. . . .

Prior to her first session, Ana crouched between a chalkboard and wall and had to be led out. . . .

In the holding position, Ana was passive, but tension was obvious in her *face*. She closed her eyes and made strenuous attempts to turn her head away from the therapist, who gently but firmly, applied counterpressure on the sides of her face to maintain face contact. When asked a series of questions, such as "What is your name?," she casually and flippantly said she was a "penguin." But, when tactile stimulation began on the rib cage, to break through the schizophrenic resistances, she erupted with, "Would you stop putting I P rays into me!" She was then shown the finger which was stimulating her and asked, "What is this?" Ana at first insisted it was an "I P ray," but as the stimulation became intense, she [correctly] called it a finger. After further stimulation she said her name was Ana. This was the beginning of normalizing communication. . . . *The power of the tactile stimulation was critical in overcoming these first resistances.*

Later in the session, when the female therapist (Menta) was holding her head, Ana began to raise her voice and show real anger. (We felt that a tremendous amount of hidden rage had become frozen in her flat affect.) Her anger developed intensity, and she was confronted on her resistances in an escalating rhythm of intense verbal and tactile interactions. Ana became very angry as we [pursued] her resistances. Rage and intense hate surged out towards . . . [Menta] when the issues began to focus on [Ana's] feelings about being a girl and [toward] her mother. Ana exploded into "burning rage," screaming and verbalizing her inner feelings of hatred for [her] mother. She was encouraged and supported for her expressions of anger, loss, and alienation that had been buried inside of her. . . . After this outburst, her delusional system began to collapse, and her speech was calm and relevant toward the end of the session. When Ana . . . [arose from being held] she was now open to receive affection from others. . . . We met Ana the next day at the hospital, where she cheerfully showed us around, and then packed her belongings to go home.

Several days later, Ana came with her parents for the second session. [Her] mother was encouraged by the positive changes in Ana's behavior, and agreed to hold Ana's head in the session. Guided by the therapists, [Ana's] mother . . . confronted Ana about her [angry] feelings. Ana again erupted in a very intense and significant [psychotic] rage reaction . . . , [and] expressed [her] hate [directly] to her mother's face. Mother was encouraged to *face* Ana's anger, and . . . yelled back at Ana with [great] . . . intensity. This interchange enabled Ana and [her] mother to become *re-attached*, and they began to feel close and loving towards each other. (pp. 40–42)

"We had essentially broken through her *rage barrier*," write Zaslow and Menta, "which had prevented anger to be shown to her mother. . . . [Ana also] became reunited to her peer group, some of whom participated in sessions" (p. 42).

Subsequent to this intensive, month-long treatment process, Ana recovered from her tyrannical mental illness sufficiently to take a vacation trip to Mexico with friends, where, for the first time, she fell in love. But, as might be expected, this was not the end of Ana's psychological problems. Approximately one year after her "rage reduction" treatments, Ana became acutely anorexic, almost dying from malnutrition. Zaslow and Menta were recontacted, and successfully intervened in the case—this time, focusing on unresolved angers within the dynamics of Ana's dysfunctional family. It is significant to note that despite Ana's near-fatal bout with "anorexia nervosa"—a sign that her emotional difficulties had not been adequately addressed during the course of her first treatment—*her psychotic symptoms never returned*. According to her mother, Ana completed high school, earned excellent grades, obtained a driver's license, found a job—in short, she functioned as a "normal" teenager. A follow-up interview with Ana, then nineteen, was conducted three years after her initial treatment. Ana was apparently enjoying life, living with roommates, and travelling; she seems to have remained relatively free of schizophrenic symptoms. Six years after her treatment for psychosis, Menta reports that the patient was "thriving, after gaining genuine [emotional] support by both . . . parents."[38]

It is well nigh impossible, after reading a verbatim transcript of treatment sessions like these conducted by Zaslow and Menta with psychotic patients, to avoid comparing this powerful process to exorcism. Zaslow was himself well aware of the undeniable parallels, citing, for instance, the following native "treatment" of a deeply disturbed African villager by "witch doctors":

The man was tied down to a bed. Two male dancers, with tam-
bourine-like discs jingling on their bodies, began to dance in
rhythm. . . . In this manner, the strong rhythms of the dancers
began to dominate the deranged man's rhythms . . . ; that is,
the man could not ignore the influence of these
rhythms. . . . [He] then went into five distinct reactions: 1) an
exaggeration of his pathological behavior; 2) a reaction of great
fear and terror, accompanied by moaning and writhing; 3) a
long period of quiet, rigid resistance; 4) after rhythmical stimulation, a full blown rage reaction without fear and terror; and
5) a state of radiant calmness, peace and relaxation. . . . The
man was sent back to his village, apparently relieved of his
affliction.[39]

"It is remarkable," writes Zaslow, "how similar these psycho-biologi-
cal transformations are to the reactions of the individual undergoing the
Z-Process" (p. 66). He further reminds us that

the relationship between constructive anger, destructive hate,
and demonic possession is illustrated in ancient Jewish medieval tales of the *Dybbuk*, . . . a transmigrating demon who could
cause afflictions in individuals by inhabiting their bodies. On
the basis of this pre-scientific rationale, people afflicted by
physical or mental illness were brought into a synagogue and
surrounded by a *minyan,* or ten men required for Jewish
religious services. The group or minyan would surround the
afflicted one and then provoke him into extreme anger. . . . The
devil or demon would find that body uncomfortable to inhabit
and be forced to leave. (pp. 64–65)

But despite Zaslow's stress on the importance of abreacting anger
and rage, he recognizes that this sort of catharsis cannot, in and of itself,
constitute an adequate psychotherapy. Indeed, he is quite critical, for
example, of Janov's Primal Therapy, dismissing such procedures as
"essentially cathartic and not enduring." Janov, argues Zaslow, believes

that anger and rage come from feelings of pain and hurt, while
I view rage as an attempt to overcome . . . pain. . . . [Primal
Therapy may provide some] beneficial results . . . because
Janov's clients go into convulsive reactions during [Primal]
screaming in a manner that Mesmer induced a long time ago.
However, . . . these convulsive reactions are not sufficiently

controlled or regulated for enduring effects. . . . Janov's theory and technique would . . . produce more problems than solutions in the dissolution of neurotic [or psychotic] defense systems.[40]

Zaslow further contends that Janov's method does not deal well with the problem of anger, rage, and aggression in general. Moreover, he protests that Primal Therapy tends to strip away the patient's ego defenses, without replacing them with more constructive mechanisms. In fairness to Janov, however, it should be noted that Primal Therapy was one of the first alternative treatments to truly encourage the full expression of the daimonic in psychotherapy. Janov—who had worked for many years as a psychoanalytically oriented therapist prior to developing this method—maintains that anger and rage simply conceal the suffering of frustrated, unmet needs for love and acceptance. Hence, in the "Primal process," writes Janov, "the first Primals often deal with anger, the second group of Primals have to do with hurt, and the third with need for love."[41] Whereas Janov places "Primal Pain" at the heart of his therapeutic endeavors, Zaslow views pain as representing "in itself the last resistance to positive, assertive aggression which would reduce pain."[42] What Zaslow would not concede, is that while emotional pain may mask rage ("Hurt hides Hate" [p. 150]), the converse can also be true: Anger, rage, and hatred just as often *do* defensively hide hurt. As we have repeatedly seen, "The best defense is a good offense," whether during the course of psychotherapy or as part of one's everyday persona.

But, paradoxically, pathologically angry behavior patterns do not serve to reduce rage via ventilation. Nor can raucous carrying-on allow for any conscious resolution of the painful, emotional wounding which it cloaks. On the contrary, the habitual venting of spleen by characterologically hostile, vengeful, virulent individuals serves mainly to defensively intimidate others, and reinforces—rather than reduces—their rage. Bellicose folks who bully their way through life by way of their unceasing, offensive fury make horrendous role models for the constructive—let alone therapeutic—uses of anger and rage. Recovery counselor John Bradshaw rightly refers to these chronically choleric characters as "rage-aholics." For them, anger is an addiction, used—like any addiction—to avoid other intense feelings, like fear, sadness, or vulnerability.

Of course, the truth is that Zaslow and Janov are both right: Anger or rage can camouflage hurt feelings; or may instead be masked by them. Both emotions—anger and hurt—typically play some part in patients' problems. In either case, I submit that, sooner or later, the patient's anger or rage must somehow be broached by the psychotherapeutic process. Janov correctly understands anger and rage as primarily reactive, defensive emotions; maybe this is the reason he tends to minimize their role in psychopathology and psychotherapy, stressing rather the patient's repressed Primal Pain.[43] Once the patient has faced his or her childhood hurts, holds Janov, there is no more anger or rage. (Presumably, what he means is that the *pathological* anger and rage are resolved; hopefully, the patient is left with some access to *appropriate* anger, rage, and aggression.) At all events, partially accurate as it may be, the mere ranking of anger and rage as secondary reactions to Primal Pain does nothing to diminish their weight, nor the unavoidable challenge of effectively confronting these daimonic emotions during psychotherapy.

Jack Rosberg's "Direct Confrontation Therapy"

I would like next to present a verbatim transcript from another case of intensive psychotherapy performed by an altogether different clinician: psychologist Jack Rosberg. The year is 1974; the place is Los Angeles, California; the setting is a psychiatric hospital. The transcript that follows was contributed by Jack Rosberg for specific use in this chapter.

Rosberg specializes in the psychotherapeutic treatment of schizophrenia: probably the most intransigent, crippling, and bizarre type of psychotic disorder. For reasons that will soon become clear, Rosberg refers to his highly unconventional form of treatment as "Direct Confrontation Therapy." In essence it resembles exorcism, during which Rosberg relates to the patient in a distinctive, psychodramatic style. As readers will learn from the following vivid account, Rosberg carefully controls and directs the action during each session, utilizing trained staff members as well as other patients to create the proper milieu. Kelly, the seventeen-year-old, Caucasian, male recipient of Rosberg's unorthodox ministrations in this extraordinary session, had been recently diagnosed as "schizophrenic." As is so commonly the case, Kelly's malady evolved slowly, stealthily, until eventually, he became severely withdrawn, behaved bizarrely, could no longer function at home or at school, and was morbidly preoccupied with the devil; indeed, he flagrantly insisted there were "two devils" living within him. Strangely enough, such symptoms are commonplace in schizophrenia and certain other psychotic disorders. In the days of demonology, Kelly would surely have been said to be possessed by demons, if not the devil himself.

The dimly lit room in which this therapeutic encounter—the second of five—takes place, contains half-a-dozen patients and several staff members in addition to Kelly and Rosberg. Rosberg, sporting sleek, impenetrable sunglasses, chain-smoking, slowly engages Kelly in a primally mysterious, movingly symbolic ceremony—one which could best be compared to an exorcistic ritual. Even after having viewed this event on videotape several times, it is still truly difficult to describe the daimonic quality of this deeply disturbing—yet humane—procedure. One is unmistakably aware of an irrational—yet expertly orchestrated and regulated—primitive power permeating the participants; the hypnotic, pounding rhythms of distant drums in the primordial darkness are all but palpable, imparting the uncanny impression that this sacred ceremony has been performed, in some form or another, by shamans, witch doctors, medicine men, priests, priestesses, and assorted healers of the human spirit, soul, and body since time began.

We pick up the action—heavily edited for brevity's sake—as Kelly is confronted by Rosberg and his assistant, Chess Brodnick, about what they have inferred from the case history to be Kelly's suppressed rage toward his parents. Chess plays the provocative role of Kelly's father; Helen, herself another patient at the clinic, plays the part of Kelly's mother:

"DAD": I need to hear . . . the feelings that go with that hatred. . . . Tell me so that I can hear it.

ROSBERG: Let him have it, Kelly!

[Kelly is crying, but unwilling or unable to express any anger. His "father," Chess, continues to encourage Kelly to communicate his hatred directly toward him. Gradually, after a great deal of reluctance, Kelly haltingly expresses his secret feelings to his "father."]

KELLY: I just don't think that you are a good father, because you take things so technically. [Still sobbing.] You didn't tell me about sex.

Suddenly, Rosberg, having remained silent during most of the session until now, rises from his chair, and begins speaking loudly in his booming, bass voice.

ROSBERG: *No.* I think the devil—you [Chess] will move out of the chair, because the devil is still inside of him, and I have to get the devil out of him again. . . . I want you to feel the devil growing inside of you. Do you feel the devil growing inside of you? Taking over your mind? Taking over your soul? Taking over your body? Do you feel it now? Do you feel the devil inside of you? *Do you?*

Now Kelly is angry, but simultaneously continues to sob deeply.

KELLY: *Go to hell father! Go to hell!*

The emotional atmosphere turns electric.

ROSBERG: *Get the devil out of you! Get the devil out, out, out, out, out!!!* It's coming up. [He stands right next to Kelly, gesturing with his hands.] Now, I'm pushing the devil up, up, up your thighs. I am pushing it up.

KELLY: *Get out of here!* [Attempts to push Rosberg away from him.]

ROSBERG: *No! I'm going to get the devil out! The devil is going to get out of you! Now ... now ... now. ... Up ... up ... up. ... Out of your face. ... Open your mouth ... Get rid of the devil. ... The devil is in there. Open your mouth. Open your eyes. ...*

KELLY: *You fucking stupid devil! Get out of here! God damn it.*

ROSBERG: *Kill the devil! Kill the devil! Here. Here. There he is. Get him! Kill him! Destroy him! Get rid of him!*

Rosberg hands Kelly a piece of plain blank paper. Kelly is by now in a barely controlled rage, screaming violently at the imaginary paper "devil," tearing at it, twisting it as if strangling someone, and angrily stomping it with his feet. At one point, he even tries tearing it to pieces with his teeth. Rosberg continues to exhort this expression of rage until Kelly tires and starts to sob even more deeply than before. Rosberg's demeanor softens dramatically.

ROSBERG: Now look at me, Kelly. ... Is the devil still inside of you? ... The "she devil" and the "he devil," are they inside of you? [Kelly shakes his head indicating no.] I want you to talk [now] to your mother, and tell her what you feel about her.

At first, Kelly refuses to speak to his "mother," as played by a fellow patient. Finally, after some manipulative pleading from "mother" to speak to her, Kelly bitterly reacts.

KELLY: *Go back to where you belong!*

"MOM": Where do I belong?

KELLY: *In hell.*

"MOM": *Why?*

KELLY: *Because you are evil!*

"MOM": *But I can change!*

KELLY: *No you cannot; you cannot change!*

"MOM": Why?

KELLY: *Because God damned you!*

"MOM": Please forgive me, Kelly. I'll try to be good. I've been exorcised by Father John! [She continues to cajole Kelly to trust her, sometimes seductively.]

ROSBERG: Don't trust her Kelly. . . . She's trying to trick you again. . . . Tell her to get out of your life, to get out of your body.

KELLY: [Begins to breathe laboriously. Then, he fiercely explodes.] *Leave me alone! Get out of here! Go back to hell! Go back to hell!*

Having expressed some rage toward his mother, Kelly—still inflamed—is a few minutes later redirected toward his troubled relationship with his father.

ROSBERG: Okay. . . . Now we'll talk to the father devil.

KELLY: [Gasping for air.] You weren't a good father to me. *You weren't a good father to me! . . .* I hate you. *I don't even want to talk to you! Get out of here! I hate you! . . . Stay out of my life! . . .* I hate you as much as my mom. . . . *I hate you more!*

Dissatisfied with the quality of Kelly's response, Rosberg again actively intervenes.

ROSBERG: No, he still has it inside of him. Move aside. . . . He still has the devil in him. . . . I've got to get the devil out of you some more. Now let the devil grow inside of you again!

KELLY: *Noooooooooo!*

ROSBERG: Yes, let the devil grow inside of you again. Let it grow stronger and take over your mind. Let the devil take over your mind and your soul and your body. Do you feel him growing inside of you? Do you feel him now? . . . *Do you feel the devil?*

KELLY: *Yessss! Now get out of here!*

ROSBERG: Well, I'm going to take him out of you. Again. . . . It's going to come up here and it's coming up to your stomach, and it's coming up to your throat, *and let him out!*

KELLY: *Get back! God damn you! Oh shit!*

At this point Kelly seems to momentarily disintegrate, speaking in schizophrenic gibberish and convulsively rage crying. But again, Rosberg urges him to "kill" the paper "devil."

ROSBERG: Kill the devil. Kill him again! There's the devil on the floor [pointing to the paper]. Destroy the devil! *Harder!* . . . *Choke it!* . . . *Tear it to pieces!* [Kelly, cooperating, totally destroys the paper "devil."] *Get rid of it! The devil died! Die devil, devil die.*

KELLY: *Devil die! Devil die! Devil die!*

By now, Kelly is spent. Having vented his rage, it appears—for the moment—to have dissipated. However, he still sobs furiously as Rosberg, once more, in a much kinder, gentler, supportively paternal tone, speaks to him softly:

ROSBERG: All right, look at me, Kelly. . . . I want you to look at me. You can throw the devil on the floor. . . . See, the devil's gone. The devil's gone? [Kelly nods affirmatively.] Okay. You killed the devil. Congratulations. . . . Now let me talk to you. . . . I'm going to explain what the devil is. . . . Do you understand what I'm saying to you? . . . Is your head clear? [Kelly nods affirmatively again.] Do you feel crazy? [Kelly nods in the negative.] I know you're pretty tired. That was hard work! Do you know what the devil is? You had a "he" and a "she devil" inside of you, right? . . . When a child is born, a child has a mother and a father. . . . And when you grow up and up and up you take the mother and the father inside of your system, inside, and they become a part of you. They have good parts and they have bad parts. . . . And when you grow up and you mature, then you get rid of the bad parts and you keep the good parts.

Next, and for the remainder of the session, Rosberg continues to talk with Kelly—as a good therapist might with any adolescent patient—about his parents, the fact that they, like all of us, have both bad (evil) and good aspects; and about Kelly's will to be well, which Kelly convincingly confirms.

According to Rosberg—founder and former director of treatment at the Anne Sippi Clinic in Los Angeles, California, a freestanding residential treatment center for schizophrenia—after five equally confrontive sessions, Kelly recovered sufficiently to be released from the hospital, and was referred for ongoing outpatient psychiatric treatment. As of 1977, three years after his brief but stirring treatment, Kelly was still receiving outpatient psychiatric care, attending college, and functioning comparatively well, reports Rosberg. Kelly was one of the few fortunate victims of schizophrenia who found effective treatment early enough in the "disease" process to stave off disaster. Most are not as lucky.

Jack Rosberg did his clinical training in "direct analytic psychotherapy" with schizophrenics during the mid-1950s, under the supervision of psychiatrist John Rosen. He sees schizophrenia as a series of intricate, deeply-rooted defenses or resistances designed to fend off painful reality, and prevent others from gaining entry to the patient's subjective world. Rosberg believes—as do the majority of mental health professionals—that schizophrenia is virtually untreatable by traditional methods of psychotherapy. Yet, in contradistinction to most mainstream clinicians, he claims that constructive contact can be established by unwaveringly challenging and verbally piercing what he conceives of as the psychotic patient's expertly executed psychopathological defenses. The challenge in working with chronic schizophrenic patients, contends Rosberg, is to directly confront their bizarre behavior unequivocally, without being driven away by it—which is precisely what typically occurs in most cases: "Schizophrenics are often labelled treatment-resistant because the psychological treatment they receive is seldom appropriate for their needs. . . . [Mental health] professionals must learn that changes occur because the therapist is stronger than the psychotic defenses of the patient, i.e., the patient's resistance to treatment."[44] Penetrating this formidable—and almost always effective—fortress of psychotic "symptoms" protecting and precluding the schizophrenic person from intimate, meaningful human relatedness, entails an intense, intrusive, close encounter with these autistic and narcissistic defense mechanisms, *and the daimonic emotions underlying them.* Enormous stores of hatred, anger, and rage, as well as the ever-present possibility of violence, are regularly aroused, and are typically utilized by the patient as a form of resistance. If the psychotherapist—like the exorcist—is physically, spiritually, or emotionally unprepared for what can quickly become a venomous verbal (or even physical) defensive onslaught, he or she will withdraw, and the psychosis or "demonic possession" will have won. (Readers might remember the 1973 film version of William Peter Blatty's best-selling book *The Exorcist,* dramatically depicting the life and death battle between exorcists and the "demonic" forces against which they intervene on behalf of the "possessed" person.)

In this sense, the daimonic passions of anger and rage play a key role in Rosberg's direct confrontation therapy, for both patient and therapist. In effect, Rosberg, rather than retreating from the daimonic, actively exploits the vitriolic anger and rage of his patients—as well as at times his own anger—to aggressively attack and combat the psychological demons bedeviling them. Rosberg, in the words of one well-informed reporter, recognizes

> that the therapist, to work effectively, has to be able to understand [and constructively utilize] his own angers and rages, . . . [and] that his patients seem to benefit from open anger which is directed toward their illness, not them. We [the reporter] were reminded of the dramatic physical and oral struggle between Annie Sullivan and the young Helen Keller. The beneficial effects of that anger resulted in the breakdown of Helen's defenses. (The defenses of the therapist, unless understood, may also be obstacles to successful treatment.)[45]

The initial phase of treatment consists of establishing the fact—in no uncertain terms—that the therapist (and not the patient) is in complete control of the therapeutic situation:

> This is achieved by making a strong initial impression, both physically and orally, and by countering any aggression with a show of power. For example, if the patient is exhibiting aggressive behavior, the therapist . . . [may at times "give permission" to] the patient . . . to continue with his aggression!

bullets," nor technical tricks designed to dispel his rage, do not utilize hypnosis or dispense tranquilizers, and that he—not me—is responsible for mastering his rage. Disgusted with what he deemed my therapeutic impotence, he stormed out at the end of the hour still indignant, contemptuously exclaiming: "You call this therapy?"

As it turned out (at least from my perspective), this caustic encounter proved to be a pivotal point in his treatment. Rehashing the event at our next session, I explained that I felt he had wanted me to "take away" his rage, to soothe him as might a "good" mother, or perhaps to punitively proscribe his rage—as his real mother might have done. What needed to happen, it seemed to me, was for him to *tolerate* his rage *without destructively acting on it*, so as to become more conscious of its source and psychological significance. (The compulsive, reflexive "acting-out" of anger and rage behaviorally is more often than not a means of remaining unconscious of its real meaning.) By that time, we were both well aware of the far-reaching roots of his rage—the main component being his massive "negative mother complex," to put it in Jungian terms—and were able to discuss it rationally and in greater depth than had been previously possible. Upon describing to me in more detail these "rage attacks," he realized that his impulse to strike out and destroy inanimate objects—typically hurting himself in the process—served as a poor substitute for his true desire: to strike (and perhaps even kill) his mother. My patient bitterly described his mother's "dark side" as rigid, cold, unloving, overcontrolling, castrating, and blatantly prejudicial toward him for having been born a boy rather than a girl, like his favored sister. Gradually, he came to recognize—and accept—that, as an adult, he was the only person now responsible for his rage and for his self-destructive behavior. Moreover, he could now permit himself to more fully experience his resentment toward his mother, and to verbalize it, without necessarily becoming violent, matricidal, or going "crazy." Of course, the question of what to do with his arrant rage—how to redirect it into some positive pursuits in his life—remained to be seen.

There are, to be sure, certain patients who have such difficulty controlling their destructive impulses that they require active intervention to prevent them from harming themselves, the psychotherapist, or others. Limit-setting, immediate medication, police involvement, and psychiatric hospitalization are all viable and sometimes necessary options in such critical situations. However, in my view, it is preferable—whenever possible—*to resist any technique or action that would relieve patients of their own responsibility for themselves.*

During his arduous course of psychotherapy, this patient had already progressed to the point of being able, for the first time, to create and maintain a close, long-term love relationship with a woman: he had decided to risk intimacy, and she reciprocated. One major decision my patient made shortly after the above-mentioned discussion—and one he stuck to—was to stop smoking marijuana. As he was well aware, this would force him to face his emotional "demons" more directly and consciously, without the comforting daily buffer of this illicit, palliative drug. Psychotherapy could now proceed in earnest.[90] Briefly following his courageous resolution to cease using marijuana to suppress the daimonic, he had this dream:

> Demons were chasing me, trying to eat me. They were grotesque, surreal, and they just kept pursuing me wherever I went. I was fighting them with some kind of sword, hacking them to pieces. But each time I would cut one into small pieces, another would appear.

This dream once more calls to mind Hercules fighting the Hydra (see fig. 22). Obviously, the battle had been joined, but was far from being won. The Hydra had been confronted, as it must be if one is ever to learn to constructively cope with the daimonic, rather than remaining always at war with it—and with oneself. In this case, not only was my patient at war with himself, but with the whole world. The colossal resentment, anger, and rage he harbored had crystallized into a toxic negativity, a morbid bitterness toward life. This unresolved bitterness about his childhood had, in turn, poisoned his personality, pessimistically permeating his interpersonal and professional relations. For this patient, as for many, it would be necessary to squarely face his fury, and his prophetically self-fulfilling negativity toward life. Then—and only then—would a new, more constructive, positive attitude toward himself and his world be possible. As the Greek playright Aeschylus dramatizes so well in his cathartic conclusion to the *Oresteia* trilogy, the "Furies," the "angry ones," "the everlasting children of the Night," known also as the "Curses,"[91] must be confronted rather than "killed off" or fled from, and fully accepted as an integral part of one's unique personality—and of life. Only under such conditions can the hell-bent, hateful, demonic "furies" turn into the helpful, empowering, "kindly ones," as occurs in the classic tale of Orestes.

Orestes, readers may recall, is the angry, obsessed young man who murders his mother to avenge her having slain his father. As a result, he is incessantly and unremittingly hounded day and night by the Erinyes or Furies. Physically resembling the Gorgons—or the Harpies, those

Fig. 22. The Greek hero Hercules combatting the immortal Hydra. For every serpentine head he severed, two more took its place. However, with help and persistence, Hercules overcame the Hydra, and used its life-blood (daimonic energy) for his own purposes. From Ernst and Johanna Lehner, *A Fantastic Bestiary: Beasts and Monsters in Myth and Folklore* (New York: Tudor, 1969), p. 47.

repulsive winged creatures who tore "the feast away from Phineus"[92]— the Furies were angry, avenging spirits (daimons) of revenge and retribution, in the talionic tradition of "an eye for an eye." According to Bulfinch, "the heads of the Furies were wreathed with serpents, and their whole appearance was terrific and appalling."[93] The Furies finally catch up to Orestes in Athens, where he decides to stop running, and heroically confront his fiendish pursuers, defending himself in a murder trial proceeded over by Pallas Athena herself. Incensed, the Furies demand their "pound of flesh" for the unforgivable sin of matricide. Psychologically, the Furies can be seen as symbols of Orestes' horrific rage: first, fueling the vengeful, hot-headed murder of his hated mother; then, turning against himself in the form of guilt. When Orestes is found not guilty by the jury, and acquitted by Athena, the Furies are fit to be tied. The leader of the Furies threatens to abandon the Greeks altogether in protest: "But for me to suffer such disgrace. . . . I, the proud heart of the past, driven under the earth, condemned, like so much filth, and the fury in me breathing hatred."

But Athena wisely persuades them to stay on as honored goddesses. The leader demands to know: "And if I do, what honor waits for me?"

Athena replies: "No house can thrive without you." At which point the leader responds: "Your magic is working. . . . I can feel the hate, the fury slip away."[94]

By virtue of valuing the daimonic, and inviting the Furies to become sanctified members of the community—psychologically, we could say of the personality and society—their destructive power is dissipated. They are thus transmuted into the kindly Eumenides: "the well disposed goddesses,"[95] reminiscent of those genial spirits of creativity, the nine Muses, or the equally lovely three Graces: Brilliance, Joy, and Bloom.

Yet another patient of mine, a fifty-year-old female with a history of harsh psychological and physical abuse by her parents, tearfully recounted the following recurrent nightmare from her terrifying childhood:

> I dreamed about snakes. They were large, muscular, green creatures, like wheels, with gigantic jaws. The colors in the dream were garish, overly vibrant, surreal, and deeply disturbing. In my dream, the snakes would suddenly turn into people; and then the people turned into snakes; and this would happen over and over again: the snakes becoming people and then transforming back into snakes, and so on. I became more and more frightened.

As I have sought to illustrate, the daimonic can manifest itself in myriad images produced by the fecund human psyche. In this particular case, the daimonic assumed the archetypal shape of a serpent, cyclically sloughing its skin to take human form—and vice versa! The serpent, in addition to symbolizing sexuality and evil, as mentioned in chapter two, can also contain positive connotations. Consider, for example, the ancient medical symbol of healing, the *caduceus,* consisting of a winged staff entwined by two serpents. Or the fact that in the traditional practice of Kundalini Yoga, the "kundalini" (i.e., the daimonic) is pictured in the mind's eye as a coiled serpent sleeping at the base of the spine, waiting to be wakened. Moreover, the dragon—sometimes seen as symbolizing Satan—is a serpent-like, mythological monster which, in various cultures throughout history, has been both feared and revered. Serpents and dragons are implicit images of the daimonic. For my patient, the snake-people represented the daimonic mixture of good and evil, caring and cold-bloodedness she experienced in her family. At times, her father and mother seemed like "normal" people, and ostensibly loving parents; at other times, however, they would suddenly and unpredictably metamorphose into toxic, poisonous, serpentine creatures, viciously striking out at her when least expected with their venomous fangs. (See figs. 23 and 24.)

Fig. 23. Snake of the passions. An archetypal image of the daimonic drawn by a patient in analysis. The *Agathodaimon* serpent of the Gnostics and alchemists was typically depicted with rays of light emanating from its head, symbolizing a unity of nefarious and healing possibilities. From Jolande Jacobi, *The Psychology of C. G. Jung* (New Haven: Yale University Press, 1962), plate 2. Copyright © 1962 Jolande Jacobi. Courtesy Yale University Press.

Permit me to conclude this chapter with one last case from my own practice, this time illustrating the intricate interrelationship between evil, creativity, and rage. This patient is a thirty-seven-year-old Caucasian male,

Fig. 24. The assault by the dragon. From Vitruvius, *De Architectura,* Book 1 (Venice, 1511). In Carl Jung, *Symbols of Transformation,* vol. 5 of *The Collected Works of C. G. Jung* (Princeton, N.J.: Princeton University Press, 1967), p. 375.

with a long-standing hatred for his violently abusive, alcoholic father. He had grown up in a "blue-collar," urban environment, in which he was constantly and brutally "hacked off," as he put it, by his bellicose, bullying father for expressing any feelings, ideas, or opinions that dared dissent or dispute his dad's paternal authority. (Note the choice of words: being "hacked off" by one's father can be seen as a sort of psychological castration; in addition, the vernacular expression "to be hacked off" means to be angry or enraged.) He was thus coerced into a not uncommon childhood role reversal of taking care of his hard-drinking, irresponsible, and unsupportive father, while at the same time trying to protect himself and his sisters from his father's obstreperous rages. Highly intelligent, sensitive, and articulate, he had graduated from a prestigious university, and possessed a teaching credential. Yet, he presented a rough-and-tumble exterior, a tough "macho" persona to the world. At the time this patient first consulted me, he had been working as a carpenter for the past decade, sometimes making use of these skills to support prolonged periods of adventurous wanderings abroad. There had been—not surprisingly—some history of episodic physical violence, usually while under the influence of alcohol, though he was not technically alcoholic. He complained of dis-satisfaction with his work, tended to minimize his traumatic childhood experiences, and described what sounded like a chronic state of low-grade depression, for which he had ten years earlier half-heartedly tried some medication. His feelings of powerlessness, helplessness, apathy, and de-spair were so intolerable at times that he seriously considered suicide in the past, though he had never acted on such thoughts. He harbored an abject fear of "becoming my father," a fateful phenomenon he felt was already inexorably in motion.[96] This bedeviled individual also expressed a profound dread of his own rage, the full depth and breadth of which he was then only peripherally aware.

In our first meeting, he traced the onset of his depression to having dropped out of a graduate program in literature more than a decade ago. He believed this to have been the direct result of "shutting down" mentally and emotionally during his first year, a persistent condition we later came to descriptively call "brain clench." After quitting graduate school, he re-turned to his parents' home, and proceeded to "just lie on the couch" in a state of abysmal depression, discouragement, and dejection. He felt he had "gotten off track" after that, never recovered, and had been reeling from the blow ever since.

As we set about our work together, he incrementally became more conscious of his towering rage toward his father, and how pervasively it had been negatively impacting his life. He had always been vaguely aware of his venom toward his "old man," but he was surprised—and visibly frightened—at the full extent and vehemence of his fury. He had tried hard to hide his hateful feelings from his father, his family, and, maybe most of all, from himself. Over the years, he had toiled diligently to keep the "genie in the jar"; he had managed, with some success, to constrain the daimonic. However, as he was now painfully learning, the daimonic cannot be depotentiated indefinitely—at least, not without paying a dear price. He harbored what, in Jungian terminology, could be referred to as a "negative father complex," comprised largely—though not completely—

of unresolved, patricidal rage. This was the predominant demon that had dogged him for so long, the metaphorical "monkey on his back."

By the end of his first eighteen months of once-weekly therapy, this man had taken several courageous steps toward reaching some tentative resolution of his deeply troubling relationship with his father—both internally and externally. One technique he found helpful was expressing his rage in writing: First, in furious, raw, unexpurgated letters to his father he had no intention of ever sending, but which he would read to me aloud; later, in letters carefully, calmly, and conscientiously composed, thoughtfully designed to assert, as clearly and constructively as possible, his authentic feelings and latest position regarding their past, present, and future relationship. After painstakingly discerning the degree to which the refined letter lucidly expressed his true intentionality toward his father, he finally decided to send it: to take his "best shot" at honestly communicating his anger—though neither of us had much hope of the external circumstance suddenly changing dramatically. Nonetheless, as a consequence of addressing this "unfinished business," he was increasingly able to devote more time, energy, and attention to the crucial issues of his current lifestyle and future career goals. Having long been interested in literature, theater, and creative writing, he decided—with much trepidation—to return to school part-time to study acting and film-making. Here is an edited excerpt from one of our sessions around that time:

> PATIENT: When I first came in here I was depressed all the time. . . . I was stuck, I was angry. . . . Now I'm starting to get a handle on the anger. . . . Now I feel I can stand up for myself. . . . I think a lot of the anger . . . toward my father has been destructive. . . . For the past year I've had this blind rage at him, which I think is justified. But in terms of myself, to stay that way isn't going to do any good. It's true that he did impact my life, . . . but I'm just going to hang there if I don't get over it.

And, indeed, he *had* begun to "get over" it. But, as we all know, old demons like these do not just disappear—much as we might wish them to! What follows is a partial transcript of our next meeting, one week later:

> PATIENT: I read *The Bridges of Madison County* this weekend. . . . It struck a chord in me. . . . For years I thought I would be a writer. . . . That's the road I started out on. . . . Since I was little, I've fantasized about faraway lands. . . . I saw myself as

an explorer, travelling around the world and writing about it for *National Geographic.* . . . The book unsettled me. . . . I've gotten off that track, but I'm struggling to get back on it.

THERAPIST: You haven't been doing any writing, have you?

PATIENT: No. I guess that's what it set off in me. . . . It's the whole thing of *creating something* . . . or being creative while I'm on this Earth, . . . and having the courage to tell the truth and see the truth. I get scared that I won't be able to do it.

THERAPIST: It seems *something* about it scares you. . . . Maybe the possibility of really expressing yourself creatively somehow frightens you, as if your own *creative potential* scares you.

PATIENT: It seems I've gotten so far from living the truth, looking at it, and embracing it for so long, that I don't know if I can get to it. I don't let it out for some reason. It does scare me. . . . It's paralyzing. . . . [Long, silent pause.] When I start thinking that way, I feel really vulnerable; it's like the old self . . . that I can slip back into isn't there if I commit to that. . . . You make that choice and then you're hung out there. . . . It seems like a very lonely place at times. . . . I've always felt like I've never fit in. . . . When you see the world through your own eyes, and carve out your own philosophy of what you see as true, it seems that . . . you no longer have anything in common . . . with other people. It seems lonely. . . . [Another long, silent pause.]

THERAPIST: Let's just say that when Paul Tillich titled his book *The Courage To Be,* and Rollo May published *The Courage to Create,* they weren't just fashioning catchy phrases. . . . You want the *positive,* . . . *creative* aspects of the daimonic, the "angels" as the German poet Rilke said, but you don't want the "devils," the "negative" side of creativity: loneliness, anxiety, suffering, conflict. . . . *Of course* it's scary to consider . . . ; that's precisely why we *need* courage!

PATIENT: It seems to me I need to be able to slow the [daimonic] feelings down sufficiently to be able to make a conscious choice; it feels like I'm holding onto a rein of wild horses pulling me. . . . I had this wild dream last night. . . . I wasn't going to tell you. . . . It was so ugly. . . . I was afraid to tell you. In my dream, I wanted to see what it was like to *kill;* so I took my shotgun and wiped out twelve little kids [ages five or six]. . . . It was such a random act of violence that nobody had a clue where to start looking, why it was done, or who did it. There were no traces. I kept vacillating back and forth whether to keep my mouth shut and go on living with the demons: it was obviously haunting, because I was ashamed and disgraced with what I did. Another option was to spend my life in prison; or to go on and try to live with it, come to terms with having made a horrible mistake. I came in to you to talk about it. I was very vague. . . . I wanted to tell the truth, but I believed that if I told you, you would have to turn me in to the police. . . . I *mimed* the incident to you. . . . I didn't want to come out and say it. . . . The big struggle for me was to tell the truth or not tell the truth; or, could I go on and live with something like that. As the dream ended I was leaning more towards lying to you and getting out of the country to save my ass. . . . What I got out of . . . [the dream] is that there's this dark side to me—to *everyone*—and acting on it and then taking responsibility for it was the question: whether I would do that or not. I chose not to. I chose to flee from it. . . . The dark side was very powerful. I let it go and then I wished I hadn't.

The "dark side"—the daimonic, or the "shadow," as Jung preferred to call it—*is* very powerful. Clinically, this is always cause for concern. In reality, this *was* going to be our last session prior to his leaving on a previously planned, extended vacation abroad! How are we to interpret and respond to this patient's disturbing dream? Or dreams of violence in general? Existential depth psychology takes a *phenomenological* approach to the technique of dream interpretation. That is to say, we try not to prejudge or place our own preconceptions on the dream, so as to remain receptive to the infinite number of possible meanings—or, to the possibility of no meaning, or at least, of no immediately discernible meaning. The creator of the dream—the patient—must be allowed the final say as to the subjective meaning or meanings of the dream, and bears the ultimate responsibility for deciding how he or she will respond to the dream: pursue it or forget it; minimize its importance; ridicule it; gloss over it; sexualize, concretize, or spiritualize it; take it literally or symbolically; personally, collectively, or archetypally; whimsically or seriously, etc. The fact that this particular patient had this nightmare, this unsettling, vivid inner vision of violence, mayhem, and random murder—which, after some hesitation, he chose to share with me—did not necessarily cause me to presume any conscious intentions or intentionality of carrying out this morbid fantasy; though one is always obliged to soberly explore such very real destructive potentialities, and painstakingly rule them out in these situations as best one can. In my experience, it is more often the case that expressing the daimonic in dreams (i.e., in the subjective theater of imagination) and subsequently recalling and "confessing" the dream—experiencing in the process its profound emotional content and latent existential meaning—*lessens* the likelihood of patients needing to compulsively "act out" the daimonic in actuality.

Liliane Frey-Rohn writes perceptively that "evil is of fundamental importance also in the creative process. For although creativity is usually evaluated as exclusively positive, the fact is that *whenever creative expression becomes an inner necessity, evil is also constellated.*"[97] First, we note that my patient, just prior to reporting his dream, had been discussing his simultaneous fantasy and fear of becoming creative, his profound desire and dread of living artistically and "truthfully" in the world, "to be or not to be," as it were. Because the daimonic may be channelled both creatively and destructively, *both* possibilities are present to the patient. The as yet unformed, embryonic, basic choice, the decision, the total commitment toward creativity or evil is gestating within. The dream appears to be playing out—in a relatively harmless way—the *destructive* scenario, the human potentiality for radical evil. Generally speaking, working with dreams, conscious fantasies, and role-playing provides an unparalleled opportunity for patients to "try on" certain attitudes and behaviors in the consulting room—rather than recklessly experimenting in the "real" world—in order to see how they "fit." Techniques like these can greatly facilitate the paramount process of discernment: they permit patients to safely dabble in the daimonic, preparing them for the far riskier, but infinitely more satisfying task of creatively and responsibly directing their daimonic energies beyond the womb-like security of the consulting room.

Returning now to the case at hand, this complex, deeply divided individual had become adept at cutting himself off from the daimonic, from the truth of his own being, especially his consuming rage toward his father. One of his impromptu associations to the dream was that in it, he had done literally to those unlucky children exactly what he felt his father had done to him as a boy: "blown him away" by his constant cruelty, criticism, savage insensitivity, belittling, and brutality. His father had the nasty habit of "hacking him off" whenever he tried to authentically express himself, causing him to protectively hide his vulnerable true self behind a thorny, street-smart, tough-guy exterior. As a child, my patient had often witnessed his father fly into a drunken rage, during which he would verbally and physically abuse not only his son, but his daughters and wife as well. As a result, the passions of anger and rage—and the daimonic in general— came, for this patient to be negatively associated with pain, destructive-ness, evil, and his highly conflictual relationship with his father. Thus, disregarding the fact that he was justifiably furious with his father, he repressed the bulk of his own rage and righteous indignation, fearing that if these daimonic emotions were ever to surface and break out of their bonds, he would face stern—possibly even fatal—retribution. In Freud-ian terms, this can be understood symbolically (not literally) as a form of "castration anxiety."

Readers may recall that the drama of *Oedipus Rex* recounts another explosively angry young man who was also badly treated by his father: abandoned, exposed to the elements, and, mistakenly, left for dead. Later, as an adult, Oedipus unwittingly murders his estranged father (and sev-eral others) on the very road via which he was fleeing from home to avoid fulfilling the disastrous Delphic prophecy:

> I . . . turned to flight from the land of Corinth, . . . to some spot where I should never see fulfillment of the infamies foretold in my evil doom. . . . When in my journey I was near to the three roads there met me a herald and a man seated in a carriage drawn by colts . . . ; He who was in front, and the old man himself, were for thrusting me rudely from the path. Then, in anger I struck him who pushed me aside, the driver; and the old man, seeing it, watched the moment when I was passing, and from the carriage brought his goad with two teeth full down upon my head. But he was paid with interest; by one swift blow from the staff in this hand he was rolled right out of the carriage on his back. I slew every man of them.[98]

Note the use by Sophocles of the now familiar expression "the old man" in referring to the surly stranger whom he later learns to be his bio-logical father. It is as if at some level Oedipus recognized his father, *but was unable at that time to see him for who he really was.* When Oedipus does, at last, learn the truth of who he is and what he has done, he cannot tolerate reality, and so, destroys his eyes, the precious organs of sight, perception, and, symbolically, of psychological insight and *truth*. Victims of severe childhood abuse, like my patient, typically "put their eyes out" too, in the sense that they are often unable—or unwilling, even as adults— to see the terrible truth of their situation, nor admit the deleterious, diabolical aspects of their tormentors. Such individuals tend to *minimize* the burdensome facts of the matter, psychologically blinding themselves to the truth, much in the manner of poor Oedipus.

To further amplify my patient's own interpretation, we could say that the dream bespeaks his propensity to direct his hatred and rage toward himself—a self-abusive twist patterned after his father's demeaning treatment of him as a boy. But was it not his father he hated, and even wished to kill at times? Clearly, the dream presents a transposition. The children in the dream (who, incidentally, are all aged around the so-called "Oedipal stage" of psychosexual development) could conceivably symbolize this patient's as yet *underdeveloped creative potentialities.* After all, children are the future: unpredictable bundles of still unrealized possibilities and raw, daimonic energy. In the dream, he "kills off" his own creative potentialities—unwritten plays, scripts, articles, books, yet-to-be-acted roles, etc.—cutting them down before they can come to fruition. He effectively chooses *non-being* over *being,* death over life, evil over creativity. As May observes, human *"consciousness itself implies always the possibility of turning against one's self, denying one's self.* The tragic nature of human existence inheres in the fact that consciousness itself involves the possibility and temptation at every instant to kill itself."[99] But why did he "blow away" *twelve* children in his dream? Why not two? Or twenty? It may or may not be significant that the number of children in the dream—an even dozen—happened to be the total of what he felt at times to be "wasted" years since aborting his stillborn literary career.

It became conspicuous as therapy slowly progressed that, in his adult endeavors to express himself creatively and pursue his own aesthetic interests, my patient unconsciously continued to do to himself what his father had done: While reading, viewing films, attending theatrical performances, writing, or acting, he would—almost immediately and automatically—"hack off" his "gut reactions," feelings, and opinions, a proficient self-sabotaging process that prevented him from relating to the material in any real depth. He was unwilling to allow himself much range in the way of emotional responsiveness or real passion, for fear that his daimonic rage would rear its ugly head. But one cannot "cut off" or "cut down" one component of the daimonic without curtailing another. The inveterate repression of his unresolved rage toward his father was resulting in the hindrance of his own inchoate creative potential. In striving to squelch the destructive forces of the daimonic, he had inadvertently forfeited access to the creative possibilities equally present. Having so hermetically "clamped the lid down" on his still seething rage, he was unable to relax his habitual posture sufficiently to permit the potentially creative energies of the daimonic any meaningful outlet. He felt "paralyzed" with fear by the very activities that most stimulated him, or called forth his strongest passions. For instance, seized with anxiety at the mere thought of having to read and critique a script, he would procrastinate for as long as possible. My stymied patient surreptitiously believed that if he were truly to speak his heart and mind—as he had belatedly begun to do in some measure with his father—or permit his defenses to be breached by the sublime beauty and power of art and literature, he would lose all control of himself, go berserk, become mad, destructively and violently possessed by the daimonic. The dream denotes this ineffable dread. But what he most feared was the potentiality of *transformation*: He dreaded having to transform himself into the man he wanted to become. He feared having to transmute his familiar *myth* of himself, depart from his habitual *persona,* and he doubly feared the risk of failure. Considerable creative possibilities—his prodigious daimonic passions—were confined alongside the loathesome anger and rage he had so long sought to contain.

Finally, the dream seems to indicate the depth of this person's frustration and desperation to *feel* something, anything—even if that sensation is "to know what it is to kill." At least this would be an act of some masculine power and self-assertion, no matter how cowardly or dastardly. To kill or destroy someone or something is the antithesis of *to create,* i.e., to bring something or someone new into being. If once the daimonic has been wakened, no constructive or creative conduits can be found, violence, destructiveness, and evil provide the last alternatives to a return to total and utter apathy. Hence the perils and importance of assisting patients in pursuing their creative proclivities.

Several months later, back from his brief hiatus from therapy, and still struggling with his demons, my patient felt he had hit "a brick wall" by which he was blocked from pursuing his career goals:

> PATIENT: I've never looked at myself as being competent in the professional world. . . . It's been so difficult for me to *survive.* . . . My father always drove me to . . . be a professional, like a lawyer or writer. . . . But at the same time he undermined me. . . . I don't feel like I can do it on my own. . . .

THERAPIST: Why not?

PATIENT: I think I'm not good enough. . . . I'm not capable. . . . My father . . . never gave me credit for accomplishing anything. . . . This is all part of the "brick wall."

THERAPIST: It sounds like a double message: On the one hand, he was saying you weren't capable; on the other hand, he was pushing you to—and maybe even believed that you *could*—become a "professional." My question is: How much of this "brick wall" might have to do with you being so angry with him, that you're going *against* his wishes?

PATIENT: That's really a good question, because just today . . . my mother told me my father . . . has a spot on his lung. . . . The troubling thing is that I couldn't feel sympathy for him, . . . and I had this thought: What if he dies? Will I become successful? . . . I think that I don't want to give him the satisfaction of seeing his son make something of himself, because it will make all the driving and all the degrading seem right. . . . To take it a step further, I feel like I've grown up to be my "father's son." . . . I'm still saying: See what you've created!

THERAPIST: See what *you* created; not, See what *I* created! You seem to have a tendency to "cut off your nose to spite your face" when it comes to your father. . . . You get into a bind where you have a hard time saying: This is what *I* want; and *I* am going to pursue it, because it is what *I* want. . . . You get into the issue with your father because it's also what *he* wanted. *And I'll be damned if I'm going to give him what he wanted!* . . . Therefore I can't succeed . . . because that would give him too much satisfaction. . . . You're *spiting* him, but you're really hurting yourself.

My patient recognized for the first time that his rage toward his father had been working against himself, and that he can no longer blame what he has become—*and what he will become*—on his alcoholic father. He—and *only* he—is now responsible for deciding how to deal with his daimonic tendencies, as well as for the consequences of his actions. The dream reflects his lingering conflicts in this regard. Nevertheless, during the course of therapy, he came—little by little—to endure the daimonic in depth without resorting to physical violence, to discern his desires, to direct his will, to be constructively assertive, and to experience more excitement, optimism, and joy than before. As he grew stronger in his new-found sense of self, he felt better able to stand up to the daimonic—to fend off those internal demons that disparaged and harassed him, much as his father had always done. Indeed, he even became able at times to *use* the daimonic—his intense feelings of anger and rage—creatively in his acting, and as an impetus toward aggressively pursuing his career goals.

For now, this individual has decided to throw his weight toward creativity. But such decisions are always subject to anxiety, insecurity, and doubt, and require daily reaffirmation. Evil is forever just one step away, an ever-present possibility in each of us.

In summation, notwithstanding the patent utility of technique in psychotherapy, *technique can only be as therapeutic as the person employing it;* which is why computers will never be proficient psychotherapists. At bottom, it is the unadulterated encounter between two imperfect human beings working toward common goals that plays the preeminent role in redeeming our devils and demons. Indeed, psychotherapy is one way of coming to terms with the daimonic. By bravely voicing our inner "demons"—symbolizing those denied tendencies we most fear, flee from, and hence, are obsessed or haunted by—we transmute them into helpful allies, in the form of newly liberated, life-giving psychic energy, for use in constructive activity. During this alchemical process, we come to discover the surprising paradox that many artists perceive: That which we had previously run from and rejected turns out to be a redemptive source of vitality, creativity, and authentic spirituality.

As to the question of complete catharsis or "cure" in psychotherapy, May reminds us that

> our task is not to "cure" people. . . . *Our task is to be guide, friend, and interpreter to persons on their journeys through their private hells and purgatories. . . .*
> *All through history it is true that only by going through hell does one have any chance of reaching heaven.* The journey through hell is a part of the journey that cannot be omitted—indeed, what one learns in hell is prerequisite to arriving at any good value thereafter. Homer had Odysseus visit the underworld, and there—and only there—can he get the knowledge that will enable him to get safely back to Ithaca. Virgil has Aeneas go into the netherworld and there talk to his father, in which discussion he gets directions as to what to do and

what not to do in the founding of the great city of Rome. How fitting it is that *each of these gets a vital wisdom which is learned in the descent into hell!*[100]

Beyond this point, as with most problems in life, we reach the limits of what an existential depth psychology can provide. From here we are on our own. With luck, we go forth into the world in greater possession of our selves, with an improved ability to deeply love and to accept the daimonic in ourselves and others. And we carry with us our rediscovered or resurrected sense of wonder, enthusiasm, and our innate capacity for creativity. *Creativity can now be the best therapy.*

8

Creativity, Genius, and the Daimonic

Our culture requires that we repress most of our anger, and, therefore, we are repressing most of our creativity.
—Rollo May, "Rollo May: Man and Philosopher"

The *sublime* [is] the artistic conquest of the awful.
—Friedrich Nietzsche, "The Birth of Tragedy from the Spirit of Music"

[Art] . . . must be the axe for the frozen sea inside us.
—Franz Kafka, Letter to Oskar Pollack

What Is Creativity?

Art—and creative activities of all kinds—can provide comparatively healthy outlets for the constructive expression of anger and rage. Creativity cannot, however, always substitute for psychotherapy. Nevertheless, creativity is at the very core of the psychotherapeutic project: The patient is encouraged to become more creative in psychologically restructuring his or her *inner* world, and then to continue this creative process in the *outer* world, not only by accepting and adjusting to reality, but, whenever possible, by reshaping it. The "capacity to experience a gap between expectations and reality," writes Rollo May, and, with it, the capacity to bring one's expectations into reality, is the characteristic of all creative endeavor. . . .

But there is a radical difference between neurotic [or psychotic] and the healthy manifestations of this capacity. In . . . [psychopathology], the cleavage between expectations and reality is in the form of a *contradiction.* Expectation and reality cannot be brought together, and since nobody can bear the constant tension of the experiences of such a cleavage, the individual engages in a . . . distortion of reality. . . .

In productive activity, on the other hand, the expectations are not in contradiction to reality, but are used as a means of *creatively transforming reality.* The cleavage is constantly being resolved by the individual's bringing expectations and reality progressively into greater accord.[1]

We humans are the only creatures who can and must more or less create ourselves. "Individuation," as Jung termed the realization and consolidation of the Self, is a creative process par excellence, in which each person is obliged to consciously participate. The sense of self and the entire personality must be actively wrought, forged, sculpted, rendered, and steadfastly reaffirmed. In this sense, the creative, evolving individual and his or her life itself can be likened to an ongoing "work of art" in progress.

"Creativity" can be broadly defined as *the constructive utilization of the daimonic.* Creativity is called forth from each one of us by the inevitable conflicts and chaos inherent in human existence; it is not limited only to artistic pursuits such as sculpture, poetry, painting, composing, and so forth. "The creative process," muses poet Brewster Ghiselin, "is a process of change, of development, of evolution, in the organization of subjective life. . . . The creative process is not only the concern of specialists, however; it is not limited to the arts and to thought, but is as wide as life. Or perhaps it would be more correct to say that invention in the arts and in thought is a part of the invention of life, and that this invention is essentially a single process."[2]

Creativity can and does occur naturally, universally, perennially, in all people, in every walk of life, be they primitive or civilized, psychotic or neurotic, "gifted" or "normal." Like evil, creativity cannot be proclaimed the exclusive propensity of some particular portion of the population; nor of any specific profession, vocation, personality type, or pathological condition. Creativity—as much as evil—is a congenital potentiality in every individual.

Creativity—be it the creativity of the artist, the psychotherapist, or the psychotherapy patient—can be understood to some degree as the subjective struggle to give form, structure, and *constructive* expression to inner and outer chaos and conflict. It can also be one of the most dynamic methods of meeting and redeeming one's devils and demons. As May admits, "the daimonic is the daily companion—and if the truth were known, the inspiration—of artists of all kinds. . . . Art can, indeed, be defined from one side as a specific method of coming to terms with the depths of the daimonic."[3] And, as Kafka indicates, art from the *objective* side—from the perspective of the spectator—can be a similarly cathartic experience, reviving the viewer's denied or dormant daimonic sensibilities. Great art is art that makes us feel angry, anxious, scared, sexual, sad, serene, awed, or joyful; it piques the passions, while simultaneously transmuting—and thus transcending—them via the sublime creative process.

Freud first spoke of this alchemical process, *sublimation,* in reference to the generic deflection of frustrated sexual energy (libido) into acceptable social functions. But, more accurately, *creativity is the constructive sublimation or positive expression of the daimonic.*[4] Contrary to orthodox Freudian doctrine, we can never completely reduce creativity to being the by-product of pathological, personal, sexual conflicts as such. If this were so, all neurotics and psychotics would be very creative—which they are not; except, of course, for the impressive inventiveness of their symptomatology.

Nonetheless, the correlation between psychological disturbance and creativity is too strong to be dismissed. Artists of all types suffer greatly from grave emotional disorders like depression and manic-depressive illness. Indeed, some of the most outstanding creative artists in history, according to one recent study, seem to have been afflicted by some significant degree of neurotic or psychotic depression and/or mania: the poets Antonin Artaud, Charles Baudelaire, William Blake, Lord Byron, Emily Dickenson, T. S. Eliot, Sylvia Plath, Edgar Allen Poe, and Walt Whitman; authors Hans Christian Andersen, Samuel Clemens, Joseph Conrad, Charles Dickens, Ernest Hemingway, Hermann Hesse, Herman Melville, Eugene O'Neill, Mary Shelley, Robert Louis Stevenson, William Styron, and Virginia Woolf; composers Hector Berlioz, Anton Bruckner, Gustav Mahler, and Sergey Rachmaninoff; and painters Paul Gaugin, Vincent van Gogh, Michelangelo, Edvard Munch, Georgia O'Keefe, and Jackson Pollock each manifested psychopathological symptoms sufficient to interfere with their ability to function, require psychiatric hospitalization, or incite them to suicide.[5] What psychological sense can we make of the correlation between creativity and psychopathology? Could the frenetic creative activities of such prominent artists be their valiant attempts at coming to terms with the daimonic? We will be taking a much closer look at the psychological demons driving some of these—and a few as yet unmentioned—artists forthwith.

Unquestionably, creativity *is* the child of conflict. In the absolute absence of any psychological conflict, it seems doubtful that true creativity could ever emerge, due in part to lack of motivation. Constant bliss and inner harmony are antithetical to daimonic creativity. "The daimonic," writes May, "is apt to come out when we are struggling with an inner problem; it is the conflict which brings the unconscious dimensions closer to the surface where they can be tapped. Conflict presupposes some need for a shift, some change in *Gestalt,* within the person; he struggles for a new life, as it were. This opens up the channels to creativity."[6] But these psychological conflicts from which creativity comes are not necessarily neurotic; creativity can also ensue from the existential dilemmas ineluctably engendered by the daimonic, on both personal and collective, or transpersonal planes. Jung points out that

> every period has its bias, its particular prejudice and its psychic malaise. An epoch is like an individual; it has its own limitations of conscious outlook, and therefore requires a compensatory adjustment. This is effected by the collective unconscious when a poet or seer lends expression to the unspoken desire of his times and shows the way, by word or deed, to its fulfilment—regardless whether this blind collective need results in good or evil, in the salvation of an epoch or its destruction.[7]

The creative individual—especially the artist—is compelled not only by the need to resolve his or her personal problems, but by the collective cultural conflicts of the day, as well as the fundamental facts of the human condition. It is the inability to create, the chronic blockage of creative self-expression, the stagnant state of "stuckness," that best describes the psychologically disturbed person's predicament. Such a stymied person, May reminds us, is "caught between his incapacity to mold these conflicts into creative works on one hand and his inability to deny them on the other. As Otto Rank remarked, the neurotic is the 'artiste manqué,' the artist who cannot transmute his conflicts into art."[8] Rank's recent biographer, E. James Lieberman, adds that, from a clinical perspective, "the neurotic is not merely someone who failed to adjust to the world, but a potentially superior individual who fails at being creative. A good therapeutic result means that the patient adjusts himself, and also, sometimes, the circumstances—which involves creativity. His task is 'to create himself and then to go on and create externally.' "[9]

There exists as close (albeit much less obvious) a correlation between anger, rage, and *creativity* as there does between anger, rage, and *evil*. The determining factor depends upon what the individual does—or does not do—with his or her anger and rage. For instance, take Franco-American feminist-terrorist artist Niki de Saint Phalle (1930–). She found a fertile outlet for her ferocious rage toward men—and the dominant masculine art establishment—via the creative expression of violence in her highly controversial work. During the 1960s, de Saint Phalle created unique collages of commonly found, yet potentially castrating, hostile, assaultive objects such as scissors, razor blades, and sharp knives, symbolically—and hence, harmlessly—expressing her rage, vehement hatred, and admittedly murderous impulses toward men. Shortly thereafter, she took to using guns to create her avant-garde art. Her famous "shooting paintings" resulted from firing live ammunition at paint-filled, white-washed balloons mounted on a blank, virginal canvas. "The resulting *tir*," reports one writer, " . . . were born out of violence, or as de Saint Phalle would write, 'I shot against daddy, against all men—my brother, society.' "[10] Thus, rather than becoming a crazed killer or vengeful victimizer of men, de Saint Phalle's fury—some of which stemmed from having been sexually abused by her father—fostered a fecund creativity, that served her well throughout her prolific career.

In addition to the curious relationship between anger, rage, and creativity—one of the least comprehended psychological associations—is the equally perplexing *coexistence of creativity and evil in the same personality*. Evil *and* creativity; creativity *and* evil. At first glance, they seem contradictory; mutually exclusive; polar opposites. Yet, on closer inspection (as we saw in the preceding chapter), creativity and evil represent two possible responses to the daimonic, both of which are potentially present in every person. When we invite or induce the daimonic Muse—during the course of artistic creativity or psychotherapy—we set a place for both her creative and destructive inspiration. This is why May, concurring with Frey-Rohn, writes that "creating, actualizing one's possibilities, always involves destructive as well as constructive aspects. It always involves destroying the status quo, destroying old patterns within oneself, progressively destroying what one has clung to from childhood on, and creating new and original forms and ways of living. . . . Every experience of creativity has its potentiality of aggression or denial toward other persons in one's environment or towards established patterns within one's self."[11] Hence, creativity cannot be unequivocally equated with *good*— though the one is commonly perceived to include the other. On the contrary, no quantity—no matter how colossal—of creativity and good can ever completely preclude evil.

Consider Spanish sculptor and painter Pablo Picasso (1881–1973), one of the most creative, celebrated, and prolific artists in history. Picasso— the typical "temperamental artist," was prone to frequent fits of infantile rage. He harbored such pathological hatred for women that he was habitually violent and sadistically abusive toward his many lovers. Psycho-therapist C. Kate Kavanagh, speaking on the subject of Picasso's immense misogyny, notes that despite the great artist's obvious emotional prob-lems, Carl Jung, for one, "did not see Picasso as the narcissistic victim of his own rage. Though . . . [Jung] felt . . . [Picasso's] art reflected his psychic fragmentation, he saw him less as mad than as evil. . . . He de-scribed him during his lifetime as 'a man . . . who (did) not turn toward the day-world, but (was) fatefully drawn into the dark; who (followed) not the accepted ideals of goodness and beauty, but the demoniacal attraction of ugliness and evil.' "[12] Picasso was no doubt deeply immersed in and partially possessed by the daimonic. Animosity spurred so much of his behavior, in fact, that I believe even Jung underestimated the huge role unresolved anger and rage played in Picasso's creativity—and in the closely linked processes of psychopathology and creativity in general. In my opinion, Picasso was not an "evil genius," as Kavanagh suggests. He was, as we shall see, a sort of "dysdaimonic genius": his wanton destruc-tiveness and unconsciousness were counterbalanced—though by no means excused—by his exceptional creativity.

The notion that creativity cannot only be accompanied by baseness, but used (or misused) exclusively in the service of evil is embodied in the archetypal guise of the "evil genius" so ubiquitous in popular films such as *Star Wars* (1977) and the James Bond series. In the *Star Wars* trilogy, for instance, we see the demonic Darth Vader using "the Force" (i.e., the daimonic) to serve the power-hungry, hateful, diabolical aims of his evil Emperor. Darth Vader is a tragic, Faustian figure, a true pernicious ge-nius of the "dark side" of the daimonic, who—like all those that impru-dently take up this path to perdition—is destroyed by it. Evil, when not counterbalanced by at least some good, consumes itself. The same is true of too much goodness.

Great creativity is most often an amalgamation of many elements, including mental disorder, disease, and evil. Herman Melville, in his epic novel *Moby-Dick*, goes so far as to suggest that great women and men "are made so through a certain morbidness. . . . All mortal greatness is but disease."[13] May, commenting on the confusing interplay between creativity and that which is pathological, evil, and negative, is reminded "of Rilke, who found his devil necessary for his creativity, and William Blake, who in his drawings of God always put hoofs on the feet of the Almighty, and all the other artists and musicians who secretly believe their creativity requires the presence of the devil. [Thomas] Mann . . . [says] that if we cure all disease [evil, and psychopathology], we will have wiped out our creativity."[14] Could creativity ever occur were it not needed to overcome evil? To invent ways of counteracting destructiveness, disease, and—maybe most of all—death?[15]

Jeffrey Burton Russell writes that "in Blake's *Marriage of Heaven and Hell* (1790), Satan is the symbol of creativity, activity, and energy struggling to be free." He goes on to say that

> for Blake, no goods or evils are absolute. "All deities reside in the Human breast," and no element of the psyche is wholly good or evil. True evil arises from the lack of integration of psychic elements; true good from the balance, union, and integration of the opposites. For the title page of *The Marriage [of Heaven and Hell]*, Blake drew an angel and a demon embracing. Reason and energy, love and hatred, passive and active, apparent good and evil, must all merge in a transcendent, integrated whole of which creativity will be the leading spirit. The true god is poetic creativity—that spirit, poet, and maker who makes not only art but the entire cosmos.[16]

Paradoxically, it is precisely in responding to the "devil"—the existential fact of evil, death, and the disturbing reality of the daimonic—that the true creative process takes place at all. Majestic artists like Rilke, Blake, Mann, and Melville, saw the absolute necessity of acknowledging, accepting—and, when need be, doing fierce battle with—the destructive, daimonic elements in life and in themselves. For it is chiefly grappling with the forces of darkness, negation, and non-being that our anger and rage resurges, daimonic passion without which we would be powerless to surmount such adverse trends. When channelled properly, anger and rage are the champions of creativity.

The Meaning of Genius

Genius is defined by Webster as "a strong leaning or inclination . . . ; an essential nature or spirit . . . ; a singular strongly marked capacity or aptitude; notable talent; . . . or extraordinary native intellectual power especially as manifested in unusual capacity for creative activity of any kind; a person endowed with transcendent mental superiority, inventiveness, and ability."[17] This latter connotation is the one most commonly understood in our modern usage of the term "genius." But there is another, lesser known meaning, which regards *genius* to be "an attendant spirit of a person or place; [a] tutelary deity (every human being has a genius associated with him from the moment of conception . . .)."[18] This is the venerable idea of genius as a daimon.

Historically, the concepts of genius and daimon are almost identical. May informs us that

> the daimonic was translated into Latin as *genii* (or *jinni*). This is a concept in Roman religion from which our word "genius" comes and which originally meant a tutelar deity, an incorporeal spirit presiding over the destiny of a person, and later became a particular mental endowment or talent. As "genius" (its root being the Latin *genere*) means to generate, to beget, so the daimonic is the voice of the generative process within the individual. The daimonic is the unique pattern of sensibilities and powers which constitutes the individual as a self in relation to his world.[19]

Or, as Heraclitus said: "Man's character is his daimon."

"The genii of the ancient Romans," writes M. L. von Franz,

> were originally household gods of a kind. . . . The genius represented first of all the reproductive power of the father of a family and of the son and heir, much like the Egyptian Ka-Soul of the Pharaoh. The marriage bed was called *genialis lecturs;* this referred not only to sexual potency but also to the qualities that today we would call psychic vitality, temperament, resourcefulness, and a lively imagination. . . . Miserly and dry people allow their genius to waste away. That the genius represented much more than the merely sexual is shown by the fact that for the Romans even places in a landscape or fields or groves could possess their genius, the *genius loci*, which

assured the continuity of their existence. Used in this way the word *genius* referred more to the psychic atmosphere or to the mood that such a place can evoke.[20]

Conversely, in contemporary usage, the creative "genius" is one who, by virtue of his or her artistic endeavors, can evoke in the observer some specific psychological or emotional state: be it sadness, beauty, joy, fear, or abject horror. The "genius" is that extraordinarily gifted person capable of conveying the daimonic in a popular medium, like literature, film, music, theater, sculpture, etc. In so doing, the audience is permitted a vicarious experience of the daimonic at a safe distance.

Genius, then, it would seem, was originally the Roman counterpart for the Greek idea of the daimon:

> In the *Timaeus* (90B–90C), Plato sets forth his theory that every human being has a divine daimon that is the noblest component of his psyche. Whoever seeks wisdom and seriously concerns himself with divine and eternal things nourishes his daimon, whereas worldly trivialities abase and mortify him. . . .
> . . . In the opinion of Plutarch (died AD 125), only a pure man can hear the voice of this daimon, a completely bodiless being who is the mediator of supernatural, "parapsychological" knowledge to the human being he watches over. The Neoplatonists thought of this genius-daimon as immortal. . . .[21]

The "genius-daimon" is that incorporeal, imperishable spirit of a particular place or person, possessing an inimitable "character" all its own. Genuine creativity consists of discovering ways of recognizing, accepting, and making the best use of one's own natural genius. Indeed, we have today come to limit the application of the term "genius" to those talented and enviable individuals who have best learned to do so. But if *character* is our daimon, as Heraclitus suggests, we each must have a genius, since we each have character. Surely, we are born with widely divergent degrees of physical prowess, talent, or intelligence; this constitutes our psychobiological destiny. Nevertheless, we each contain in our congenital character some genius—small, medium, or great—for something. It is up to each person to conscientiously discern and develop this creative potentiality; to constructively incorporate and express his or her peculiar daimon or daimons. When we say that someone has a "genius" for cooking, or sewing, or socializing, we are making reference to the creative functions of the daimonic.

Once more we are reminded of the mysterious *daimonion,* said by Socrates to have guided his actions throughout life by serving to deter certain injudicious decisions or behaviors. According to Apuleius, in *De Deo Socratis,* such a daimon is

> "a private patron and individual guide, an observer of what takes place in the inner person, guardian of one's welfare, he who knows one most intimately, one's most alert and constant observer, individual judge, irrefutable and inescapable witness, who frowns on evil and exalts what is good." If one "watches him in the right way, seeks ardently to know him, honors him religiously," then he shows himself to be "the one who can see to the bottom of uncertain situations and can give warning in desperate situations, can protect us in dangerous situations, and can come to our rescue when we are in need." He can intervene "now through a dream and now through a sign [synchronistic event], or he can even step in by appearing personally in order to fend off evil, to reinforce the good, to lift up the soul in defeat, to steady our inconstancy, to lighten our darkness, to direct what is favorable toward us and to compensate what is evil."[22]

In this elegant description of the properly related-to genius, the beneficent daimonion of Socrates, we can clearly recognize the pagan, pre-Christian prototype of *guardian angels:* those divinely helpful, nurturing, and protective spirits that have so keenly taken hold of the popular imagination in recent years. Morton Kelsey tells us that Thomas Aquinas had a great concern for "angels," but not in the insipid, one-sided way in which we see them today: "To Aquinas, good angels are the carriers of revelation to people, while the evil ones are the source of most of people's problems and difficulties. It is a purely mental and not a physical reality to which he refers as an angel. . . . He calls them *intelligibilia intelligentia,* or 'thinking thoughts.' Like our own conscious thinking and thoughts, they were effective in bringing about changes in events in the corporeal world. But this is as far as he goes in discussing how an angel acts upon the soul or psyche."[23] Regrettably, angels have today become blandly emblematic only of the good, positive, or creative aspects of the daimonic; but like Cupid—their cherubic prototype—angels are really daimons.

Kelsey further explains that "the word *aggelos,* angel, is derived from the Greek word for messenger. It means, in both Old and New Testaments, one of the host of spirits that wait upon some spiritual ruler, some divine monarch. They can be either messengers or instruments and vassals of higher spiritual reality. Thus there are angels of God and angels of Satan; but unless qualified, an angel refers to a good spiritual messenger, a representative of God."[24] The fundamental dilemma, of course, in dealing with these daimonic messengers, these denizens of the deep, these other-worldly visitants, is always the aforementioned matter of *discernment*: How does one accurately discern whether the inner impulsion, instinct, emotion, "hunch," idea, "voice," or visitation derives principally from the destructive or the creative side of the daimonic, from angel or demon, God or the Devil? How could Socrates have been so unequivocally and faithfully trusting of his adored daimonion? It is at this deepest level of conscious psychological discernment that our decisions fundamentally take us toward good (creativity) or evil. And there is no pre-ordained formula to follow, much as we tend to seek some objective, prescribed, canon, law, or Ten Commandment–like code of ethics or morality by which to conform our behavior. We are on our own—but not necessarily in the Nietzschean sense. We are on our own in deciding how to relate to our daimons, angels, or genii. Shall we persist in ignoring and disregarding them? Continue to defame these daimonic images as meaningless, infantile, or pathological figments of fatuous fantasy? Ought we allow ourselves to be guided by them? Or, should we instead simply and indiscriminately say *no* to their shadowy urgings? To cite an extreme example from psychopathology, shall the schizophrenic patient—who, try as he or she might, is no longer able to ignore these daimonic "spirits"—obey the commands of their "voices," even when their "voices" urge them to harm themselves or others?[25] And what of the biblical Abraham, who was instructed by some unseen god or daimon to sacrifice his own son? Or the fundamentalist minister who feels constrained by God to blow away abortionists? How to know from whence such impulses arise, and whether or not to honor them? When to oppose the daimonic, and when to pay homage to it?

Confusion about such bewildering questions abounds. For to cite C. G. Jung on this sticky subject: "The moral reaction is the outcome of an autonomous dynamism, fittingly called man's daemon, genius, guardian angel, better self, heart, inner voice, the inner and higher man, and so forth. [But] close beside these, beside the positive, 'right' conscience, there stands the negative, 'false' conscience called the devil, seducer, tempter, evil spirit, etc. . . . "[26] This juxtaposition of good and evil is exactly what makes discernment so devilishly difficult.

Perhaps the simplest yet most useful counsel one could consider prior to making such momentous choices was offered by John, in his first epistle (94:1, quoted from the New English Bible): "But do not trust any and every spirit, my friends; test the spirits, to see whether they are from God." Alas, even with such worthy counsel, we are still left with the weighty responsibility of discerning that which derives from God—which, in turn, requires some unambiguous, distinguishing definition of "God"; or, perhaps, less ambitiously, of "good," "constructive," "creative," and "evil." The better we become at consciously discerning the destructive from the creative or constructive "voices" or impulses within us, the more trusting we can afford to be of the daimonic. Still, as Jung said, "good and evil are no longer so self-evident. We have to realize that each represents a *judgment*. . . . Nevertheless we have to make ethical decisions. The relativity of good and evil by no means signifies that these categories are invalid, or do not exist. . . . Nothing can spare us the torment of [fallible] ethical decision."[27] (See fig. 25.)

Dysdaimonia and Eudaimonia

Novelist Rudyard Kipling vividly recalls first meeting his "Personal Daemon":

> Most men, and some most unlikely, keep him under an alias which varies with their literary or scientific attainments. Mine came to me early when I sat bewildered among other notions, and said: 'Take this and no other.' I obeyed, and was rewarded. . . .
>
> After that I learned to lean upon him and recognize the sign of his approach. If ever I held back . . . anything of myself (even though I had to throw it out afterwards) I paid for it by missing what I *then* knew the tale lacked. . . .
>
> My Daemon was with me in the Jungle Books, *Kim*, and both Puck books, and good care I took to walk delicately, lest he should withdraw. I know that he did not, because when those books were finished they said so themselves with, almost, the water-hammer click of a tap turned off. . . . *Note here*. When your Daemon is in charge, do not try to think consciously. Drift, wait, and obey. . . . [28]

Philosopher Arthur Schopenhauer, in the introduction to his book *The Wisdom of Life*, announces—with characteristic arrogance—his intention to speak of the art

Fig. 25. The Lord and Satan vying for the soul of a man navigating the treacherous sea of Vices and Sin. From *Le Grand Kalendrier et Compost des Bergiers,* printed by Nicolas Le Rouge (Troyes, 1496). Courtesy of Ernst and Johanna Lehner, *A Picture Book of Devils, Demons and Witchcraft* (New York: Dover, 1971), p. 9.

of ordering our lives so as to obtain the greatest possible amount of pleasure and success; an art the theory of which may be called *Eudaemonology,* for it teaches us how to lead a happy existence. . . . The only book composed, as far as I remember, with a like purpose . . . is Cardan's *De utilitate ex adversis capienda,* which is well worth reading. . . . Aristotle, it is true, has a few words on eudaemonology in the fifth chapter of the first book of his *Rhetoric;* but what he says does not come to very much.[29]

Aristotle, as alluded to so dismissively by Schopenhauer, defined *eudaimonism* as the capacity to live happily and harmoniously with the daimonic. "Eudaimonism," writes psychiatrist M. Sperber, "refers to the integration of opposing forces within one's being—love and hate, creativity and destructiveness, power and impotence. In a state of eudaimonism, these forces coexist in dynamic equilibrium."[30] As May puts it: "The more I come to terms with my daimonic tendencies, the more I will find myself conceiving and living by a universal structure of reality. This movement toward the logos is *trans* personal. Thus we move from an impersonal through a personal to a transpersonal dimension of consciousness."[31] This evolution in consciousness is achieved by learning to discern and—as far as is humanly possible—meaningfully assimilate the daimonic constructively into our day-to-day existence. Or, in other words, learning to live creatively with the daimons.

Sperber provides the following helpful distinctions between the "daimonic," the "antidaimonic," the "eudaimonic," and the "dysdaimonic" character:

The daimonic individual experiences his state of being with unusual intensity. The antidaimonic person, in contrast, is anhedonic or apathetic; he has repressed his daimon. A comparison may also be made between the dysdaimonic person, whose entire personality is dominated by one or more components of the daimonic, and the eudaimonic, who has integrated the daimonic into all spheres of his being. The dysdaimonic is 'possessed' and responds with a blind, impersonal, self-assertive push that is disconnected from his consciousness, while the eudaimonic experiences ever-deepening and ever-widening dimensions of consciousness. . . .

The dysdaimonic may be destructive (one thinks of Hitler) or creative, like Michaelangelo [*sic*] or Van Gogh.[32]

What Sperber does not address is the confounding fact that the *dysdaimonic character* can be both creative *and* destructive. Of course, the same may be said of anyone, since all human life consists of some admixture of creativity and evil. But in the dysdaimonic character, these capacities are greatly magnified. On the other hand, those lucky individuals who learn to discern the daimonic properly, and to discover creative ways of coming to harmonious terms with it in their lives, can be thought of as mainly *eudaimonic characters.*

In addition to Sperber's distinctions, it may further serve our present purposes to speak in terms of "dysdaimonic" versus "eudaimonic" genius. In contrast to the *dysdaimonic genius,* the *eudaimonic genius* is a more conscious, integrated, whole, and self-possessed person. I propose these designations to represent two opposite poles on a continuum of *daimonic genius:* the vast majority of that which we commonly call "genius" occupies a place somewhere in between these two theoretical extremes. As illustrated in the previous chapter, the potentialities for both evil and creativity coexist in every person, are magnified in the "daimonic personality" described by Sperber, but attain their zenith in the dysdaimonic genius. (Readers may recall me using this term earlier, in reference to Picasso.) The dysdaimonic genius manifests a confounding combination of exceptional creative powers coalesced with equally strong tendencies toward psychopathology, perversity, destructiveness, and evil; a providentially rare amalgamation of daimonic power witnessed—in its negative extreme—in devious historical figures like Adolf Hitler, or in the fictional film character Darth Vader. Who would deny Hitler's evil genius for destructiveness? Typically—but not always—these diabolical individuals die at an unusually young age, laid low by their overweening arrogance, hubris, and unholy alliance with evil.

What happens, we must wonder in such cases, when the generative inner voice, the daimon, the "genius," goes awry? What makes one person (Picasso, for example) a primarily *creative genius,* and another (like Hitler) an *evil genius?* Let us start by scrutinizing the comparatively plebeian dysdaimonic character; and then, the far rarer and immensely more talented dysdaimonic genius. As we shall see, these ultimately self-defeating, yet incomparably charismatic characters can be said to operate routinely in a relatively unconscious, pathologically persistent state of daimonic possession.

Herman Melville's Mad Captain Ahab

One of the most memorable dysdaimonic characters in all of literature was created by Herman Melville, the great—some say the greatest—American novelist. Melville's chilling, daimonic character, Ahab, the obsessed captain of the ill-fated whaling ship, *Pequod,* is *mad:* insanely, rabidly, inconsolably enraged at having lost his leg to the legendary leviathan, Moby-Dick, and hell-bent on revenge at any cost. Some weeks following Ahab's first meeting with Moby-Dick,

> on the homeward voyage, after the encounter, . . . the final monomania seized him . . . , he was a raving lunatic; and though unlimbed of a leg, yet such vital strength yet lurked in his Egyptian chest, and was moreover intensified by his delirium, that his mates were forced to lace him fast, even there, as he sailed, raving in his hammock. In a strait-jacket, he swung to the mad rockings of the gales.[33]

Even once this psychotic stage of Ahab's infernal madness had subsided, however, "Ahab, in his hidden self, raved on. Human madness is oftentimes a cunning and most feline thing," observes Melville, that seafaring psychologist. "When you think it fled, it may have but become transfigured into some still subtler form . . . so that far from having lost his strength, Ahab, to that one end, did now possess a thousand fold more potency than ever he had sanely brought to bear upon any one reasonable object" (p. 129). That despised object was Moby-Dick.

Psychologically, we note that Ahab had been narcissistically injured: Bested by Moby-Dick, defeated by the mighty behemoth in battle, his pride was cut to the quick by this symbolic castration. Much like the biblical Jacob, Ahab had wrestled with the great white angel from the depths, and came away crippled and limping. Some fundamentally human part of himself was lost in that first fateful encounter: Ahab's leg, that stabilizing prop so essential for support, strength, mobility, balance, and grounding. But in contrast to Jacob, rather than having forced the great white whale to bless him, and becoming more whole *(holy),* Ahab had been broken, emasculated, cursed, and left mad, sailing away with only his inexhaustible hatred for the creature that took his limb and insulted his manhood. His hatred possessed him, compulsively driving Ahab to avenge his loss by tracking down and killing the white whale—despite the many cautions and contraindications that common sense and rational judgment dictated. These are the unmistakable hallmarks of the dysdaimonic personality. We can safely surmise that at least some measure of Melville's own virulent rage and dysdaimonic character are mirrored in his mad Captain Ahab.

Melville conveys the irresistible, contagious charisma of Ahab's anger on those around him as follows:

> How it was that they so aboundingly responded to the old man's ire—by what evil magic their souls were possessed, that at times his hate seemed almost theirs; the White Whale as much their insufferable foe as his; how all this came to be—what the White Whale was to them, or how to their unconscious understandings, also, in some dim, unsuspected way, he might have seemed the gliding great demon of the seas of life,—all this to explain, would be to dive deeper than Ishmael can go. (p. 130)

May suggests, as have others, that "Melville gives us a picture of Satan in the person of Captain Ahab. . . . "[34] But I take a slightly different tack. Ahab is not the devil personified; he is just a man. But the devil—i.e., the daimonic—has taken hold of him in the most destructive and dangerous way imaginable. Ahab has become a dysdaimonic man. Like Hitler, Ahab is an enduring emblem of the daimonic's inordinate power to perfectly possess someone—body, mind, and soul—and to impel that person into diabolically disintegrative, destructive pursuits. Ahab reflects our own human frailty and vulnerability to the vindictive, blinding forces of anger, rage, and hatred. Ahab hates Moby-Dick wholeheartedly; and it is this unmitigated enmity that fuels his demoniacal mission to annihilate the white whale.

"Ahab is a study in the psychology of resentment," writes Edward Edinger. "His image serves as a mirror, showing the true nature of our own resentments. Everyone has this problem, his inner Ahab, his monomania, whose means are sane but whose motive and object are mad. Resentment that strives to get even, that inflicts one hurt for another, that asserts one's personal power over anything that challenges it, or that withdraws in sullen, wounded majesty, disdaining to communicate with a world that doesn't recognize its sovereignty, these are expressions of the Ahab in every soul."[35] Ahab's undying wrath toward his *bête noire,* his inhuman nemesis, remains unredeemed, even unto death:

> "Towards thee I roll, thou all-destroying but unconquering whale; to the last I grapple with thee; from hell's heart I stab at thee; for hate's sake I spit my last breath at thee. . . . Thou damned whale."[36]

Ahab—unlike Picasso, for instance—had committed his life to destroying rather than creating. He had chosen death over life. His unresolved resentment and rage had turned demonic. And, in the end, it was him—Ahab, and all those around him—who were obliterated by his bitterness.

But what of the great white whale himself, the immortal Moby-Dick? Was not this ghostly denizen of the depths the very source and object of Ahab's mad obsession? Whales are enormous, mysterious mammals, the largest and one of the most awesome and impressive life forms in nature. They embody immeasurable energy, power, and vitality. Even after whales were hunted down and harpooned commercially in Melville's day, their rendered blubber became a much-needed source of light and heat; their indestructible energy having thus been transmuted into yet another useful form. Much as we may humanely oppose whaling in this day and age, Edinger writes that "the whaling industry is . . . a paradigm of the heroic effort of human consciousness to confront and transform the raw and aboriginal energies of the psyche."[37] In a psychological sense, we are all whalers to the degree that we strive to creatively convert the dark contents of the daimonic into the life-giving light of consciousness.

Moby-Dick—the great white whale—*is the daimonic*. Indeed, he is life itself, that ambiguous, archetypal Being that can never be killed, but only given expression in some creative or destructive form: "Whales are the primitive, undifferentiated energies of nature,"[38] writes Edinger. Melville calls Moby-Dick "a 'Job's whale' (Chapter 41), referring to Leviathan in the book of Job, one of the manifestations of Yahweh. The whale is remarked to be one of the incarnations of Vishnu in the Matse Avatar (Chapter 55). The mad sailor, Gabriel, pronounces the white whale to be the Shaker God incarnated. . . . [Moby-Dick] is associated with Jupiter . . . [and] is called a 'grand god' (Chapter 133)." But most convincing is Melville's description (via Ahab) of Moby-Dick as "representing the transcendental reality behind the appearance of things. And such transcendental reality is another name for God."[39]

Moby-Dick is undeniably the reigning god of the great seas, the unconscious. But this inhuman monster is no beneficent, loving, or even neutral deity: it is daimonic—both *divine* and *diabolic*. It is nature, in all its beautiful and abhorrent reality. And it is eternal, indefatigable, and indestructible. It is a brute force to be both feared and revered; but never to be turned against, rejected, or repudiated. The daimonic melds both the positive and negative qualities of life, without making them mutually exclusive.

Melville expresses the numinous psychological meaning Moby-Dick held for Ahab in the following lucid passage:

Small reason was there to doubt, then, that ever since that almost fatal encounter, Ahab had cherished a wild vindictiveness against the whale, all the more fell for that in his frantic morbidness he at last came to identify with him, not only all his bodily woes, but all his intellectual and spiritual exasperations. The White Whale swam before him as the monomaniac incarnation of all those malicious agencies which some deep men feel eating in them, till they are left living on with half a heart and half a lung. That intangible malignity which has been from the beginning; to whose dominion even the modern Christians ascribe one-half of the worlds; which the ancient Ophites of the east reverenced in their statute devil;—Ahab did not fall down and worship it like them; but deliriously transferring its idea to the abhorred White Whale, he pitted himself, all mutilated, against it. All that most maddens and torments; all that stirs up the lees of things; all truth with malice in it; all that cracks the sinews and cakes the brain; all the subtle demonisms of life and thought; all evil, to crazy Ahab, were visibly personified, and made practically assailable in Moby-Dick. He piled upon the whale's white hump the sum of all the general rage and hate felt by his whole race from Adam down; and then, as if his chest had been a mortar, he burst his hot heart's shell upon it.[40]

Hence, for hateful Ahab, the daimonic had become the demonic, in the spectral image not of the devil, but of Moby-Dick. Similar projections of the daimonic may be found in the mythological motif of fire-breathing dragons, and many other monstrous imaginings of the human mind.[41] As Edinger comments, Captain Ahab "thinks he had discovered the nature of the deity—thinks it to be no more than destructive malice toward man. In fact, however, he is only seeing the reflected image of himself."[42] Moby-Dick was Ahab's own personal Satan; and Ahab sought to disgorge his gall by destroying this ungodly white devil—a deluded course of action destined to lead to his own demise. For the daimonic can never be done away with, extirpated or eradicated. At best, we can merely try to redeem and reclaim our devils and demons, and coexist with them as peaceably as possible.

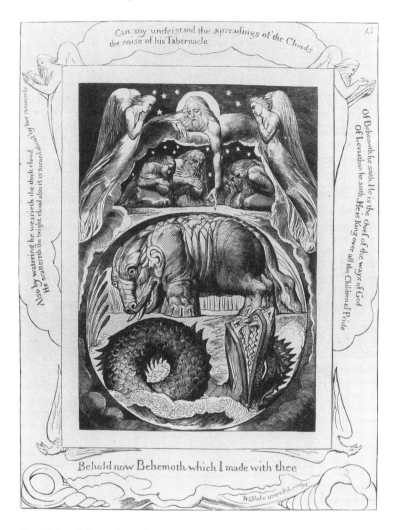

Fig. 26. *Behemoth and Leviathan* by William Blake. Daimonic
reality as revealed to Job in its inseparably divine and infernal aspects.
From *Illustrations to Book of Job* (1825). Courtesy Tate Gallery/Art
Resource, New York.

> Behold Behemoth which I made as I made you; . . .
> Can you draw out Leviathan with a fishhook,
> Or press down his tongue with a cord? . . .
> Can you fill his skin with harpoons, or
> His head with fishing spears? . . .
> No one is so fierce that he dares to stir him up.
> Who then is he that can stand before me?
> (Job 40:15–41:10 RSV)

It may well be that by living out Ahab's dysdaimonic character in his writing, Melville spared himself the fate of becoming Ahab in actuality. "It is a way I have of driving off the spleen," as Ishmael says of sailing in the opening chapter of *Moby-Dick*.[43] Born in New York City in 1819, by all accounts Melville lived a more or less normal, uneventful life through the age of eleven; at that time his father suffered a psychotic breakdown precipitated by financial difficulties, and died shortly thereafter. With no father to support the family, and no money, Melville was forced by the age of twelve to discontinue school in order to work, floundering about at various vocations until finally, at the age of twenty-one, he set out to sea on a four-year whaling voyage.

In his superb psychological study, *Melville's Moby-Dick: A Jungian Commentary,* Edinger tells us that

at the conclusion of his whaling voyage Melville was twenty-five years old. In a letter to [Nathaniel] Hawthorne, seven years later, he wrote, "Until I was twenty-five, I had no development at all. From my twenty-fifth year I date my life. Three weeks have scarcely passed at any time between then and now, that I have not unfolded within myself." What had Melville been doing during those seven years of growth? The answer is, writing. From age twenty-five to thirty-two, he completed six books, the last one his masterpiece, *Moby-Dick*.[44]

Edinger goes on to describe Melville as "a difficult man to live with. Like his fictional figure Ahab, he was gifted with the high perception, but lacked the low, enjoying power. He was frequently moody and withdrawn. On the evidence of his wife's letters, he was such a cause of apprehension to her that at one period she feared for his sanity. Melville's relation to the personal, practical aspects of life was always poor" (p. 13).

Psychologist Kay Jamison points out the pattern of mental illness in Melville's family, which may have made Melville himself more prone to madness: "He suffered from severe mood swings that ranged from expansive, energetic, and highly productive states to irascible, bitterly morbid, withdrawn, and listless periods in which little was done and he was obsessed with death and filled with pessimism.[45]

By the time Melville entered mid-life, around the age of thirty-five, after the consummation of *Moby-Dick,* he slipped into a decade-long "period of extreme psychic distress and reorientation. His mental and physical health were in jeopardy, and at times he was close to psychosis or suicide."[46] Eventually, he somehow learned to live with his unruly demons. Toward the end of this tumultuous mid-life crisis (which may have more than coincidentally paralleled the pandemonium of the American Civil War), Melville settled into a stable, steady job as a customs agent in New York City. But he continued to write, completing his crowning book, *Billy Budd,* in 1891, just before his death at the ripe age of seventy-two.

"Melville died in obscurity," says Edinger, but "by the middle of the twentieth century. . . it was beginning to dawn on Americans that Herman Melville is the greatest literary genius our country has yet produced."[47] And *Moby-Dick*—the mythic tale of the great white whale—was Melville's masterpiece. Much more than an exhilarating, high-seas adventure yarn, *Moby-Dick* marked the start of Melville's incipient, inner voyage into the murky, unplumbed, dangerous depths of the daimonic. During that treacherous period, Melville—unlike his pathological alter ego, Ahab—appears to have discovered a way, through his art, to safely navigate past the savage schools of devils and demons assailing him. More like Ishmael—the youthful protagonist and narrator of *Moby-Dick*—Melville miraculously survived the stormy seas of life, and found some precious peace of mind in the process. Whereas Ahab surely represents some pathological, shadowy part of Melville's own dysdaimonic personality—his submerged rage and resentment—Melville has Ishmael, the sole survivor of and witness to the Pequod's infernal fate, at some point say: "No more my splintered heart and maddened hand were turned against the wolfish world."[48] Perhaps the process of creating *Moby-Dick*—a work once described by Melville in a letter to Nathaniel Hawthorne as "a wicked book"—had similarly soothing, mollifying effects on Melville's angry inner Ahab.

Let us turn next to the following non-fictional, contemporary account of another dysdaimonic character, one which well illustrates our inordinate naiveté and confusion concerning the daimonic nature of evil and creativity—and their intricate interrelationship.

Jack Henry Abbott: In the Belly of Behemoth

In 1981, author Norman Mailer championed the publication of an extraordinary book by Jack Henry Abbott, entitled *In the Belly of the Beast: Letters from Prison.* At that time, Abbott was an inmate at the Utah State Penetentiary, awaiting parole. His criminal history reads like that of thousands of other sociopaths:

Half Irish, half Chinese, Jack Abbott was born January 21, 1944, in Oscoda, Michigan. He spent his childhood in foster homes throughout the Midwest. At the age of twelve he was committed to a juvenile penal institution—the Utah State Industrial School for Boys—for "failure to adjust to foster home," and was released five years later. At eighteen he was convicted of "issuing a check against insufficient funds," and was incarcerated . . . on a sentence of up to five years. By the age of twenty-nine Abbott had killed an inmate and wounded another in a fight behind bars; had escaped from Maximum Security; had committed bank robbery as a fugitive; and had served time in such federal penitentiaries as Leavenworth, Atlanta and Marion.[49]

By the time he turned thirty-seven, also in 1981, Abbott had "been free a total of only nine and a half months," and had "served a total of more than fourteen years in solitary confinement."[50] He had become what we today call a "career criminal."

Notwithstanding this classic criminal profile, there was something different about Abbott, something that set him apart from the other pimps, perverts, cons, and killers inhabiting that living hell we call "prison." Unlike most inmates, he never surrendered to the authoritarian penal system, resisting the oppressive reality of his situation like some furious, wild stallion refusing to be ridden. As a result, he was severely punished for his rebelliousness: isolated from prison society in prolonged solitary confinement. Nothing out of Dante could be more dauntingly purgatorial. Then, at some indeterminate moment, during the darkest night of his unendingly lonely vigil, something "clicked"—and Abbott began to *read*. He read everything, voraciously consumed it, as if compelled by some unquenchable passion to know, to learn, to comprehend his hellish predicament.

Ultimately, he took to *writing*, writing like a man possessed, or as Mailer later put it, "like a devil."[51] Abbott wrote intensely, powerfully, violently, like a demon unleashed. He had discovered a creative outlet for his boundless rage. He began corresponding with Mailer, who found his prose so ferociously mesmerizing that he helped to compile the missives into what became Abbott's first book. Mailer, a man not personally unfamiliar with the creative as well as destructive aspects of the daimonic, perceived its undeniable presence in the work of this precipitously poetic prisoner: "I felt all the awe one knows before a phenomenon. Abbott had his own voice. I had heard no other like it. At his best, when he knew exactly what he was writing about, he had an eye for the continuation of his thought that was like the line a racing car driver takes around a turn. He wrote like a devil, which is to say (since none of us might recognize the truth if an angel told us) that he had a way of making you exclaim to yourself as you read, 'Yes, he's right. My God, yes, it's true.' "[52]

So enthralled was Mailer with his new literary discovery that, in addition to arranging for the publication of Abbott's letters, and contributing an introduction to the book, he somehow managed to arrange for Abbott's early release from prison. Forgiving and forgetting the glaring facts of his extensive and violent criminal history, his life-long immersion in the shadowy, bestial underbelly of society, many of Mailer's colleagues agreed that Jack Henry Abbott was indeed a man possessed of wildly potent literary talent—possibly even genius. Upon Abbott's discharge from prison, the literary community welcomed him with open arms, and rave reviews. One critic in the *New York Times Book Review* wrote that "Jack Abbott is no Saint Genet. He is too precise about evil and human ugliness for that kind of self-conscious role. . . . Out of nowhere comes an exceptional man with an exceptional literary gift. His voice is sharp-edged and hurling with rage. Mailer saw this immediately, and we must be grateful to him for getting these letters into publishing form and—a job more difficult—for helping to get Abbott out on parole."[53]

But, as fate would have it, Abbott's freedom was short-lived. Several weeks subsequent to his parole from prison, after a warm, adoring, and gracious initiation into New York's elite literary society, he was once again in trouble and on the run from the law: sought for the fatal stabbing of a young, unarmed waiter outside a trendy Manhattan restaurant. Following several months as a fugitive, Abbott was finally apprehended, brought to trial, and convicted of manslaughter. He is still serving out this latest prison sentence, and—so far as I know—has not been creatively heard from since.

Mailer and company were understandably stunned. Novelist Jerzy Kosinski, one of Abbott's staunchest supporters, expressed his horror this way: " 'I feel guilty, terribly guilty. . . . We had chosen to ignore that we had a violent man in our midst. Instead I think we preferred to see him as a man who is going to become an intellectual of violence. . . . Maybe I share with my intellectual friend Norman Mailer the feeling that talent redeems. . . . How could we disregard the 25 years of his prison, his past which was still his present, and instead talk about his forthcoming bestsellership, his week-old career as a writer?' "[54]

What the sophisticated literati failed to see—or, perhaps, as Kosinski suggests, preferred not to see—was the deadly, malignant, destructive power of the daimonic still present in this sociopathic personality. For despite his new-found writing career, Abbott remained as antisocial, angry, belligerent, hateful, and potentially violent as ever, a classic dysdaimonic character, who happened to have hit upon—at least temporarily—his hidden creative genius. He had unearthed in himself a latent talent for expressing rage in raw, robust, sinewy writing. But his rage had by then become so rancid, pathological, and deeply rooted that it could never have been exorcised, redeemed, or transmuted merely by making this brief foray into creativity. Why could Mailer and other artists not see this simple fact? Why would they turn a blind eye to the evil tendencies in someone like Abbott? I submit that their unwarranted optimism about Abbott's apparent jailhouse conversion from evil to creativity can be linked to the complex, confounding phenomenon of "dysdaimonic genius": the simultaneous presence of evil *and* creativity in the same person. "His prose," wrote reviewer Terence Des Pres of Abbott, "is most penetrating, most knife-like, when anger is its occasion. . . . But if, finally, his genius as a writer does depend upon anger and rage, that need not be a problem."[55] Yet, as we now know, Abbott's anger and rage *was* a problem, a lethal two-sided sword, cutting a swath of considerably more destruction than creativity. We humans have a devil of a time reconciling the co-existence of both *creativity* (or beauty, success, affability) and *evil* in a single individual: we childishly try to separate the two. This *pseudoinnocence*, says Rollo May, consists of our inability to perceive evil in ourselves and others, and results from a denial or misunderstanding of the daimonic: "Innocence that cannot include the daimonic becomes evil."[56] Such innocence played a major role in the unwillingness or inability of Mailer and others to discern the daimonic destructiveness of Jack Henry Abbott, despite his dazzling creativity—as if the presence of creativity could ever preclude evil! As a result, these reputable and well-meaning artists became—like all of us in one way or another—unwitting participants in evil.

Vincent van Gogh: Dysdaimonic Genius

A classic example of dysdaimonic genius was bedeviled Dutch painter Vincent van Gogh. The brief but brilliant career of van Gogh

(1853–1890), one of the most remarkable creative geniuses of the nineteen (or any) century, has been described by Anna Freud as "a high-
minded individual's struggle against the pressures within himself." She goes
on to observe that "even the highly prized and universally envied gift of
creative activity may fail tragically to provide sufficient outlets or acceptable solutions for the relief of intolerable internal conflicts and overwhelming destructive powers active within the personality."[57]

What were these "overwhelming destructive powers," these
unpropitiated demons dwelling in the valiant heart and mind of Vincent
van Gogh? From whence did they come? And what part did they play in
van Gogh's incomparable genius, his volcanic creativity? A voluminous
amount has already been written about van Gogh. Born in Holland to
the Reverend Theodore van Gogh and Anna Cornelia Carbentus, Vincent
was named after an ill-starred predecessor: his brother, who died during
childbirth the previous year. There are indications that Vincent's mother
may have suffered from postpartum depression following the loss of her
stillborn son. Psychoanalyst Barry Panter points out that "in his letters
to his brother Theo, Vincent referred to their mother as 'Mater Dolorosa'
(Mother of Sorrow). Because of her depression, she was probably withdrawn and emotionally unavailable to the young Vincent for much of the
time. From this ongoing experience with her, during these formative years
of his life, Vincent may have developed the ideas and feelings of unworthiness and isolation that plagued him constantly."[58] Moreover, Vincent
had a violently stormy relationship with his father, a Protestant minister.

Vincent's adult activities selling both books and art; his discouraging disappointments in love; his preoccupation with religion and brief stint
as an evangelical preacher; his burgeoning fascination for drawing and
painting, which led him to Arles in southern France; his exceedingly close
relationship with his younger brother, Theo; and his ensuing mental
breakdowns, culminating in suicide at the age of thirty-seven, have all been
well documented. Humberto Nagera, who has done one of several psychoanalytic studies of van Gogh, writes that

> the assessment of psychopathology in the genius poses special
> questions. . . . Eissler remarks in his book on *Leonardo da Vinci,*
> 'It is no longer disputed that in the study of genius a surpris-
> ingly large amount of psychopathology is encountered. The
> question, however, has not been answered what connection
> exists between the genius' psychopathology and his achieve-
> ments. . . . Psychopathology, in general, is looked upon as a
> defect, though most forms of psychopathology have a useful

function in so far as they spare the psychic apparatus a damage that would be greater than that caused by the psychopathology (primary gain). Observation of the genius, however, suggests the possibility that psychopathology is indispensable to the highest achievements of certain kinds'.[59]

Prior to conceding this distinct possibility, however, I hasten to pose this polemical—and, perhaps, unanswerable—question: Precisely what comprises so-called "pathological" as opposed to "ontological" or existential conflicts in the genius, and in general?

At all events, the fact that van Gogh suffered from severe psychopathology—including substance dependence—is indisputable. Indeed, the presence of marked psychopathology is one of the defining hallmarks of *dysdaimonia*. According to Dr. Panter, "more than 150 different diagnoses have been given to Vincent—both organic and psychological, including manic-depressive psychosis, schizophrenia, Meuniere's Disease, brain tumor, organic brain syndrome secondary to absinthe poisoning or syphilis, and many others."[60] Judging from the available evidence, including his prolific correspondences to friends and family, van Gogh's demons consisted of profound feelings of melancholy, sadness, anxiety, despair, loneliness, and—notably—anger or rage. To make matters worse, says Panter, "probably as an attempt to control the anger that welled up in him with closer contact with people, he began drinking heavily. He drank absinthe—a drink that has since been banned in most countries because it is known to cause permanent brain damage."[61] Abusing this drug was one negative way in which van Gogh tried to contend with his unendurable daimonic conflicts.

There were several suicide attempts at St. Remy—the mental institution where van Gogh was confined for close to twelve months—in which Vincent deliberately consumed his highly poisonous oil paints. During these daimonic seizures of suicidal insanity, he experienced what appear to have been hallucinations, accompanied by horrendous fits of anxiety and rage. Indeed, van Gogh had always been prone to barely controlled attacks of anger and rage. Once, notes Nagera,

> he threw a glass of absinthe into Gauguin's face. According to Gauguin [Vincent's housemate at the time] on the evening of December 24, 1889, he went out of the house and Vincent followed him in the dark, armed with a razor. Gauguin became aware of being followed, turned around and looked at Vincent. The latter stopped and finally went away back to the yellow house where he severed the lower part of his ear lobe

with the razor. He proceeded to wrap it up and took it as a present to the girl at the brothel that he used to visit occasionally.[62]

Panter infers that "Vincent's misfortune with Gauguin is an expression of his difficulties with many people throughout his life. He desperately wanted a close intimate relationship. But his feelings of unworthiness and unacceptability made him extremely vulnerable to narcissistic injuries. When these occurred, as they inevitably will, Vincent reacted with anger and sometimes rage, which eventually led to failure of every one of his relationships, even with his saint-like brother, Theo."[63] But might Vincent's violent temper also have been in some way related to his frenzied creativity? Was not his frenetic creative activity a clever means of constructively funnelling frustration, anger, and rage into effervescent, ebullient works of art?

Psychoanalytic interpretations of van Gogh's mental illness make much of his unconscious hostility and aggression against his father, his beloved brother, Theo, and his brother's wife, Jo. Some theorize that Vincent's repressed resentment, anger, and rage toward his family was expressed passively or indirectly, detrimentally aimed instead at friends like Gauguin, and—ultimately—at himself. Unresolved frustration, ire, and indignation almost certainly comprised a great portion of van Gogh's debilitating emotional problems; these were some of the persistent, eventually overpowering psychological demons against which he was in the end unable to defend himself, and which at times took possession of him so ruinously. Yet, despite the pervasive, and finally fatal, self-destructive features of van Gogh's dysdaimonic genius, he somehow managed—mostly by sheer force of will, the unmistakable sign of true genius—to turn his turbulent inner war with his personal demons into creativity of the highest order. Van Gogh's genius was for painting, painting the likes of which the world had never seen before nor probably ever will again. His god-given genius would never have become as highly developed and fully expressed, however, had he not completely committed himself to his art, choosing to direct his astounding daimonic energies—and extraordinary talent—into *creative work:* hard, detailed, draining, painstaking work. It was this conscious decision, and his active pursuit of painting despite his crippling personal problems, that enabled van Gogh to harness his wild, raging demons to the fiery carriage of his creative toil with such astonishing results. Or, as van Gogh wrote in a letter to his brother Theo: "The notion that painting is inborn [is naive]. Yes, it *is* inborn, but not as is generally supposed; one must put out one's hands and grasp it; that grasping is a difficult thing—one must not wait till it reveals itself. There is something to be discovered, but not what most people suppose. By painting, one becomes a painter."[64] Creativity, Vincent tells us, does not simply happen; it is a course of action, a calling which must be consciously valued, chosen, willed, and committed to with all one's daimonic passion, strength, and courage.

Jackson Pollock: "Pissed-Off" Expressionist

Speaking of van Gogh inevitably evokes the name of another intensely dysdaimonic artist: abstract American expressionist, Jackson Pollock (1912–1956). A chronic alcoholic who—unlike van Gogh—underwent years of psychotherapy, Pollock nevertheless could not redeem his raging demons. As a boy, Pollock was emotionally disturbed, began drinking by age nine, and developed a violent temper. He suffered from profound depression for most of his life, and was first hospitalized psychiatrically in 1937, at the age of twenty-five. Between hospitalizations, Pollock worked with several different psychotherapists, including two well-known Jungian analysts; but he never overcame that most devious of demons: alcoholism. Nor did he ever come to conscious terms with the real roots of his rage. "In reminiscences by Pollock's acquaintances," writes artist and art therapist Evelyn Virshup, "they said he would react with rage when he couldn't do well, when he couldn't control people. . . . People remembered him ripping headlights off parked cars, punching his fist through panes of glass, crushing a drinking glass in his hand, and breaking down doors."[65] After attaining unprecedented notoriety for his original "drip" style of painting, an intoxicated Pollock drove his car into a tree, killing himself and one of his two female passengers. He was forty-four. Perhaps on account of his untreated alcoholism, as Virshup suggests, neither his art nor analysis could save him from his own inner "furies."

Barry Panter comments that

> Pollock was certainly an angry man. His urinating in public, his frequent fights, can be seen as angry reactions following feelings of humiliation and inferiority. His drinking may have been . . . an attempt to quell the rage that arose in him so frequently.

His paintings and his painting technique are expressive of his inner chaos, the attempt to create a self, and his rage. By externalizing his inner demons onto the canvas, he had the chance to free himself momentarily of them, and possibly to begin to master them. By dripping, "urinating" on the canvas, as he did on the world, he was attacking the canvas. If this had occurred in a man of lesser talent, the work would be simply bizarre. However, Pollock, in his attempts to externalize his inner chaos and his anger on canvas, has given the world great works of art.[66]

But truly "mastering" and overcoming one's demons first requires understanding their psychological significance, a comprehension Pollock violently resisted throughout his life, with ultimately tragic consequences. In refusing to face his demons directly—to unveil and gaze upon the personal and transpersonal meaning of the daimonic—Pollock was destroyed by them: a disastrous destiny shared by many a dysdaimonic genius before and since.

Richard Wright's Daimonic Wrath

Based in part on my reading of the intimate biographical work *Richard Wright: Daemonic Genius,* by award-winning poet and novelist Margaret Walker, I propose that Wright—unlike Pollock—may be thought of as an artist whose relationship with his own genius resided somewhere midway between the dysdaimonic and eudaimonic sides of the spectrum. Richard Wright, the brilliant black American author best known for his books *Uncle Tom's Children* (1938), *Native Son* (1940), *Black Boy* (1945), and *The Outsider* (1953), was born in backwoods Mississippi, in the year 1908. At that time, writes Walker, "the state of Mississippi . . . was a veritable hell. . . . Richard Wright came out of hell. All his life devils were pursuing him. Anger was the name of one fiend."[67]

Here were sown the bitter seeds of Wright's suffering; the existential roots of his rage; and the fructifying kernels of his future creativity. Lynchings, poverty, beatings, and extreme prejudice against blacks were but a few of the prevalent horrors Wright—who was partially white—had to endure during boyhood. This inhumanely hostile environment, coupled with difficult personal circumstances, such as his father's early desertion of the family, and subsequent physical abuse by his mother, molded Wright's wrathful destiny. "He would grow up to become an angry man," notes Walker, "and he would learn to write as a means of expressing that anger. His anger would have many targets: his family, the society, the white man, [women,] the white race, and the more fortunate" (p. 23).

As a sensitive, vulnerable "black boy" in the violent white South, Wright learned—the hard way—to hide his hatred toward his tormenters and to stifle his spiralling anger. He dreamed of only one thing: someday escaping the suffocating South and becoming a writer. All the while, writes Walker, "he would keep bottled within him a terrible and explosive rage that he himself would not always understand. It was the beginning of a neurotic anger which would become a part of his expressed daemonic genius" (ibid.).

By the time Wright turned seventeen, he had managed to move as far north as Memphis, where, scuffling to save money from menial jobs, he happened upon the writings of H. L. Mencken. "That night," recalls Wright in his autobiographical book, *Black Boy: A Record of Childhood and Youth,*

> in my rented room, while letting the hot water run over my can of pork and beans in the sink, I opened *A Book of Prefaces* and began to read. I was jarred and shocked by the style, the clear, clean, sweeping sentences. Why did he write like that? And how did one write like that? I pictured the man as a raging demon, slashing with his pen, consumed with hate, denouncing everything American, extolling everything European or German, laughing at the weaknesses of people, mocking God, authority. What was this? . . . This man was fighting, fighting with words. He was using words as a weapon, using them as one would use a club. Could words be weapons?[68]

Wright, too, like Mencken, would himself discover artful ways of using words as weapons, wielding them like cudgels to lash out angrily against all that galled him so greatly. Somehow, this gifted young man survived the bleak conditions of his childhood, and eventually fled, via Memphis, to Chicago, New York, and, finally, Paris, where he died in 1960. But Wright was never able to outrun his earliest traumatic exposure to virulent racism. To cite William Gardner Smith on the subject: "Richard Wright was a wounded man, therefore a distorted man—that is, different from what he would have been without the wound. The wound was the result of his race and youthful poverty in hate-filled Mississippi; it cut deep—neither fame, nor money, nor 14 years in Paris where he was idolized, could heal it."[69]

As previously mentioned, the same may be said of each of us to some degree or another: Some childhood wounding or trauma is inevitable in this imperfect world of ours, and such fateful psychic damage becomes our daimon—part of our destiny—forming our character and more or less informing our future actions. In adulthood, emotional laceration may be recognized, made conscious, placed in a wider perspective, and, sometimes, even healed. But "healing" does not mean forgetting, for to become conscious is to remember and to know. Healing entails the mature acceptance of the traumatic facts of one's emotional mortification, the causes and the consequences, as well as a resolute willingness to swallow the following bitter pill: We cannot change the past nor undo the wound. Nor can we realistically hope as adults to now magically receive that which, in so many cases, brought about the original wounding by dint of its absence during infancy, childhood, or adolescence. We can, nonetheless, allow ourselves to feel our rage and grief over this irretrievable loss. We have the power to determine our attitude toward the past. We may even—with some good fortune, time, and grace—find within ourselves the capacity to *forgive* those who we feel inflicted our agonizing injuries. But we cannot ever expect to totally exorcise such demons. They have taken up permanent residence; turned into an integral part of us; molded our personality; made us who we are. To deny them or try to eradicate them is tantamount to self-renunciation. To live *with* them is what is required, and for this, *creativity* is key.

Walker—who knew Wright personally—insists that, despite the devastating effects of his harrowing youth, "I am convinced that the best of Richard Wright's fiction grew out of the first nineteen years of his life. All he ever wrote of great strength and terrifying beauty must be understood in this light. . . . These stories grew out of his bitterness and anger, even rage, born during those painful and frustrating years."[70] Without this daimonic wrath, Wright would never have written as he did. His writing provided a positive outflow for his resentment, a blessed release which permitted him—more so than Pollock—to maintain some measure of balance and equanimity during most of his life. "Understanding Wright's anger helps us to understand his daemonic genius," suggests Walker. For

> Richard Wright had two kinds of anger: realistic and neurotic. The realistic anger was based on situations of fact and circumstances in his family life and early formative environment—the problems of a broken home, a displaced family, and extreme poverty marked by hunger and deprivation. This anger he

surely possessed and understood. The neurotic anger was something else. It fed upon that psychic wound of racism, that irrational world of race prejudice and class bigotry, of religious fanaticism, and sexual confusion, inversion, and revulsion. . . . This neurotic anger and fear grew in Wright from a pit to a peak of rage, but it was part of his unconscious, which he could never understand though he constantly sought to express it. Out of these two angers a daemonic genius of great creative strength and power was born, his tremendous creative drive to write and to express himself, his daemonic demi-urges, his deepest and most suffering self. (pp. 43–44)

I, for one, would restate this subtle yet essential distinction between "realistic" or existential anger, and "neurotic" or pathological anger slightly differently: Richard Wright's "neurotic" rage resulted from the life-long repression of his ontologically "realistic" rage, with which he was never able to consciously come to terms. Nonetheless, in a very real sense, we could say that Wright's unrelenting and inconsolable rage—coupled with his considerable talent—was indeed an integral aspect of his genius, his daimon, his "Fury," or perhaps even his Muse. He could have picked a different path, a course of destructiveness, criminality, or apathy, as do so many others with similar demons. He did not, however, surrender to this perennial tempta-tion. Nor did he endeavor to ignore the demands of his insatiable inner daimon, as did Jonah by refusing to journey to Nineveh.[71] But let us not overlook a most crucial point: Wright—like Pollock and van Gogh—was, for the most part, an *unconscious genius*, one who never came to consciously comprehend his own demons. This critical character trait, this "fatal flaw," links him—again, like Pollock and van Gogh—more closely with dysdaimonic than eudaimonic genius, the latter category being distinguished by a much healthier degree of conscious assimilation. The primarily uncon-scious or dysdaimonic genius, like van Gogh, Picasso, Pollock, or Wright, as Walker rightly recognizes, is "driven by the soul possessed of devils. The demons possess him and drive him and give him no rest until he is dead. This is compulsive genius, self-destructive and tormented and difficult to control. Unless the demons are exorcised, as they are aroused, the genius becomes restless to create. Once the process of creation is complete, the demons are quiescent for a time until the process begins again. This is the daemonic genius, and perhaps the greatest of all" (p. 96).

Though he had little consciousness of what was happening to him and why, Wright as an artist was subconsciously guided—or, rather, irresistably driven—by an inner daimon, not unlike the one known to Socrates: "One day as Wright and I walked together . . . ," recounts Walker, "he turned to me and said, 'Margaret, if a voice speaks within you, you can live.' " . . .

> This statement was the key to that daemonic genius already exploding within him, the god-maker, his creativity, the genii voices of the demons within him, the sure indication of a rich and fecund inner life that gave him inner strength and passion out of which he would make powerful creations. . . .
> . . . This is his daimon, daemon, demon—any way you spell it, his creative urge—his compulsion, the force behind his creativity. (pp. 93–94)

Wretchedly predominant for Wright were the restless demons of resentment, anger, and rage, whose inextinguishable heat he learned to wield so well in forging the works that made him famous. During his final years, worldwide success and adulation seem to have sated, and hence, diminished the once fiercely inventive, torrid, even violent daimonic energy of Wright's earlier work, as is so often true of fame. Yet, his unredeemed demons still haunted him; perhaps even more so when he stopped sublimating his neurotic rage into prose as poignantly as in days past. When denied adequate creative expression, the desecrated *genius* turns more demonic than daimonic. Disaster awaits the one who dares deny the daimonic its due.

In Paris, Wright reportedly might have become clinically "paranoid" (a form of psychosis), believing himself to be harassed by the CIA, and complaining of being poisoned. His health rapidly deteriorated, and he passed away prematurely—in what Walker suggests may have been mysterious, even suspicious circumstances—of a supposed heart attack. He was fifty-two. His lamentably dysdaimonic genius had at last extracted its tragic toll.

Ludwig van Beethoven: Belligerence and Beauty

In his excellent little book *Beethoven: His Spiritual Development*, J. W. N. Sullivan speaks to the significant distinction between the conscious, eudaimonic genius and the comparatively unconscious, dysdaimonic genius. He concludes that, in the case of Beethoven, "we are left with no evidence that he was an unconscious genius in any extraordinary degree."[72] In other words, the incomparable German composer was, for the most part, a *eudaimonic genius*.

Goethe—another eudaimonic genius of the first order—assessed Beethoven's extraordinary personality as follows:

> The ordinary human mind might, perhaps, find contradictions in it; but before that which is uttered by one possessed of such a daemon, an ordinary layman must stand in reverence, and it is immaterial whether he speaks from feeling or knowledge, for here the gods are at work strewing seeds for future discernment and we can only wish that they may proceed undisturbedly to development. But before they can become general, the clouds which veil the human mind must be dispersed. . . . To think of teaching him would be an insolence even in one with greater insight than mine, since he has the guiding light of his genius, which frequently illumines his mind like a stroke of lightning while we sit in darkness and scarcely suspect the direction from which daylight will break upon us.[73]

Throughout his tempestuous life, Ludwig van Beethoven (1770–1827) heroically transformed his heartfelt frustration, anger, and rage into the farthest reaches of human creativity. By all reports, Beethoven was badly treated by his alcoholic father. Physically and emotionally neglected as a boy, he was extremely introverted and withdrawn, even as a child. His isolation increased with age, as did his pugnaciousness, earning him a notorious reputation for being brusque, irascible, acerbic, uncouth, and outright offensive to those with whom he had social or professional contact. In brief, Beethoven was a bad-tempered and belligerent young man. Frustrated at every turn in his first attempts to earn a living as a musician, and to establish a "normal" life of marriage and family, he withdrew ever further into himself—and his music. Told—at the tender age of twenty-eight, just as his musical star was rising—that he was losing his hearing, Beethoven became deeply depressed, morose, and discouraged. "It would appear," writes Sullivan, "that Beethoven first noticed symptoms of his deafness in 1798. His first reference to it, however, occurs in a letter . . . dated June 1, 1801. The letter is most interesting as showing us Beethoven's attitude, at this time, towards the impending calamity. His first reaction, as we should expect, is rage at the *senselessness* of the hideous affliction. That he, of all men, should lose this particular sense must, indeed, have seemed the most abominable of ironies" (pp. 67–68).

In this letter, a most miserable Beethoven, being "at strife with nature and Creator," (p. 68), fearing that "the most beautiful years of my life must pass without accomplishing the promise of my talent and powers," nevertheless hopes against hope, bitterly resolving somehow "to rise superior to every obstacle" (p. 72). Six months later, a second correspondence provides Beethoven's combative response: "No! I cannot endure it. I will take Fate by the throat; it shall not wholly overcome me. Oh, it is so beautiful to live—to live a thousand times! I feel that I am not made for a quiet life" (ibid.). Having taken this defiant posture to turn his towering rage toward challenging and transcending the terrible tragedy of his deafness, Beethoven went on—despite his limitations—to compose his most heroic and beautiful music, silenced only by death, at the age of fifty-seven.

From all appearances, Beethoven—the mature Beethoven, that is— was, as Sullivan and Goethe suggest, essentially a eudaimonic genius: one who knew his own inner conflicts, frustrations, and neurotic tendencies, and had gradually grown to consecrate them through coming to creative terms with the daimonic in his life and work. By the closing years of his life, says Sullivan,

> Beethoven had come to realize that his creative energy, which he at one time opposed to his destiny, in reality owed its very life to that destiny. It is not merely that he believed that the price was worth paying; he came to see it as necessary that a price should be paid. To be willing to suffer in order to create is one thing; to realize that one's creation necessitates one's suffering, that suffering is one of the greatest of God's gifts, is almost to reach a mystical solution of the problem of evil. . . . (p. 155)

It was a *spiritual* solution. When I speak of "spirituality," I mean *psychological growth* and *emotional maturation.* In this sense, spirituality is the antithesis of pseudoinnocence: Spirituality entails the capacity to see life as it is—wholly, including the existential realities of evil, suffering, and the daimonic—and to love life nonetheless. This was Beethoven's titanic accomplishment: He accepted the absolute necessity of the daimonic in his life and art; he came to love it as part of his personal fate; and he embraced that fate as the driving force behind his great creative destiny. This *amor fati,* as Friedrich Nietzsche—that ill-fated, dysdaimonic genius— phrased it, is a spiritual achievement of the highest magnitude. Indeed, *spirituality* can fundamentally be defined as *a capacity to love the daimonic.* "For God," Diotima tells Socrates, "mingles not with man; but through a spirit [daimon] all the intercourse and converse of god with man, whether awake or asleep, is carried on. The wisdom which understands this is spiritual."[74]

We detect the exquisite presence of this assenting attitude toward life in Beethoven's last string quartets, composed joyfully just before his death, despite his total deafness, isolation, and intense physical suffering. Clearly, he had arrived at some sublime conciliation with his demons, with his difficult, lonely life, and with death. Indeed, he strove valiantly most of his life to express the daimonic in his music. As Erich Neumann observes, eminent eudaimonic artists like Beethoven "seem to have attained the image and likeness of a primal creative force, prior to the world and outside the world, which, though split from the very beginning into the polarity of nature and psyche, is in essence one undivided whole."[76] And this "undivided whole" is the daimonic.

Eudaimonism always implies a conscious, spiritual development, wherein the daimonic is acknowledged, accepted, and constructively integrated into the lifestyle and personality. Eudaimonic genius can be defined by the extent to which creativity and spirituality cumulatively evolve during the artist's career. It is a very rare occurrence: "Few men, even amongst artists, manifest a true spiritual growth. Their attitude towards life is relatively fixed; it may be exemplified with more richness and subtlety as they mature, but it does not develop."[77]

The eudaimonic genius utilizes his or her art to meet, accept, and assimilate the daimonic, a process from which we all could learn more about living creatively. For each of us faces essentially the same task: To assertively and constructively affirm ourselves and our lives; to muster the requisite courage to confront existence and to accept—even embrace—life on its own terms, including our own and others' intrinsic daimonic tendencies. Such an acceptance requires the conscious recognition of *being* as ineluctably incorporating *non-being*—in all its demonic, noxious, negative, multifarious forms forever threatening the annihilation, degradation, defeat, or death of the individual.

"The capacity to confront non-being," writes Rollo May, "is illustrated in the ability to accept anxiety, hostility, and aggression. By 'accept' we mean here to tolerate without repression and so far as possible to utilize constructively. Severe anxiety, hostility and aggression are states and ways of relating to one's self and others which would curtail or destroy being."[78] These latter psychopathological states—so frequently the focus of psychotherapy—are precisely those which, when left unexamined, prove fatal for the dysdaimonic character, but are kept in check, controlled, and creatively counterbalanced in the eudaimonic character.

As Paul Tillich once said, " 'The self is stronger the more non-being it can take into itself.' " "Thus," responds May, "if we can accept normal anxiety and guilt, if we can live with our anger, we become the stronger; but we also find, as in the psychotherapeutic confronting of anger, that feelings of love also increase."[79] That is to say, the more willing we are to meet our devils and demons head on, the more likely we are to have access to our angels. To turn again to Tillich on this topic:

> The affirmation of one's essential being in spite of desires and anxieties creates joy. Lucillus is exhorted by Seneca to make it his business "to learn how to feel joy." It is not the joy of fulfilled desires to which he refers, for real joy is a "severe matter"; it is the happiness of a soul which is "lifted above every circumstance." Joy accompanies the self-affirmation of our essential being in spite of the inhibitions coming from the accidental elements in us. Joy is the emotional expression of the courageous Yes to one's own true being.[80]

And, I would add, to Being—to life—itself.

The eudaimonic genius or eudaimonic character—an ideal state of conscious development more often aspired to than attained—has come to courageously say yes to him or her self, yes to the daimonic, and yes to life, despite the indwelling difficulties; and thus, to appreciate and enjoy his or her work, being, world and all they have to offer. But even for the multitude of us who have yet to reach such lofty spiritual heights, creativity can serve as a pragmatic means of approximating this sort of healthy, integrated, well-balanced eudaimonism. In any case, the incremental movement toward *eudaimonia,* when consciously willed and assiduously sought, is, for every imperfect human being, always a creative work of art—a symphony—in progress.

Finally, we note that Beethoven never surrendered his daimonic fire, his anger, his belligerent rage—even on his death bed. Near the end, a terrific winter storm arose, lashing out with wind, thunder, and lightning—the full daimonic fury of nature. It is said that as his dying gesture, Beethoven defiantly—or perhaps harmoniously—shook his fist at the very heavens themselves.

Ingmar Bergman: Residing with Demons

Master film-maker Ingmar Bergman seems to be one modern artist of unexcelled caliber who has progressed over the course of his cinematic career from dysdaimonic toward eudaimonic genius. Born in 1918, in Stockholm, Sweden, he recalls in his candid autobiography, *The Magic Lantern,* one of his earliest memories, the momentous birth of his baby sister in 1922:

> When I was four, my sister was born and the situation changed radically. A fat monstrous creature had suddenly acquired the main rôle. I was banished from my mother's bed and my father beamed over this bawling bundle. The demon of jealousy fastened its claws into my heart. I raged, wept, crapped on the floor and messed myself. My older brother and I, usually mortal enemies, made peace and planned various ways of killing this repulsive wretch.[81]

With equally brutal honesty, Bergman goes on to describe in minute, vivid detail how he attempted to act (unsuccessfully) on his infantile, daimonic urges toward his helpless sibling, and how he subsequently struggled all his life with such wicked demons.

By the time he became a director, the adult Bergman had found ways—like most of us—to drive the daimonic down into unconsciousness: concealing his "constant tumult"[82] within from others, while rigidly insisting upon an emotionally sterile environment in which to work and live. He cites an ex-lover who "scorned my cleanliness theory and maintained that theatre is shit, lust, rage, and wickedness. 'The only boring thing about you, Ingmar Bergman,' she said, 'is your passion for the wholesome. You should abandon that passion. It's false and suspect. It sets limits you daren't exceed. Like Thomas Mann's Doctor Faustus, you should seek out your syphilitic whore.' " (p. 35). As this insightful female rightly recognized, Bergman had by then neurotically dissociated himself from the daimonic, and therefore could not tolerate such distasteful emotions in his associates either. *Perfectionism* provided the compulsive method by which he endeavored to exclude the daimonic from consciousness; it too became a neurotic tendency which, in his own retrospective judgment, had eventually "driven out life and spirit" (p. 63) from his later work.

What Bergman was unaware of as yet was the price one must pay for repressing the daimonic—for devaluing its raw, earthy, unrefined, crude, and messy imperfection. Bergman's penalty first took the form of worrisome somatic symptoms such as an incessantly "nervous stomach," diarrhea, and chronic insomnia, which persisted all his life. However, unlike most sufferers of such distressing symptoms, he understood them metaphorically as "demons," explaining that "over the years I have patiently taught myself to master my troubles sufficiently to be able to carry on working without all too obvious disturbances. It is like housing an evil demon in the most sensitive core of your body. With strict rituals, I can keep my demon under control. His power lessened considerably when *I* was the one to decide my actions, not *him*" (p. 63).

Bergman learned not only to listen attentively to his demons, but to deny them autocratic rule over his behavior. On the subject of his insomnia, for instance, he confesses that "for more than twenty years, I have suffered from chronic insomnia. . . . The wear and tear comes with the vulnerability of night, the altered proportions, the harping on stupid or humiliating situations, regrets over thoughtless or deliberate malice. Flocks of birds often come and keep me company: anxiety, rage, shame, regret and boredom" (pp. 62–63). In order to outmaneuver the numerous demons that still visit him nightly, those uninvited nocturnal disturbers of sleep, Bergman created his own counteractive rituals: "changing beds, switching on the light, reading a book, listening to music, eating biscuits or chocolate, drinking mineral water" (p. 63).

But Bergman's ability to abide the company of demons was hard won. In 1949, at the age of thirty-one, already a financially and artistically successful theatrical director, he suffered a "breakdown." As Bergman himself dramatically describes it:

> I was sitting at home . . . reading a book and listening to music. . . .
> The music ceased and the tape stopped with a small bang. It was absolutely quiet, the roofs on the opposite side of the street white and the snow falling slowly. I stopped reading. Anyhow, I was finding it hard to take anything in. The light in the room was sharp, with no shadows. A clock struck a few times. Perhaps I was asleep, perhaps I had taken that short step from the accepted reality of the senses into the other reality. I didn't know and now I was deep down in a motionless vacuum, painless and free of emotions. I closed my eyes. I thought I had closed my eyes, then sensed there was someone in the room and opened my eyes. In the sharp light, a few metres away, I myself was standing looking at myself. The experience was concrete and incontestable. I was standing on the yellow rug looking at myself sitting in the chair. I was sitting in the chair looking at myself standing on the yellow rug. So far, the I who was sitting in the chair was the one in charge

of reactions. This was the end, there was no return. I could hear myself wailing. . . .

. . . I sounded like an injured dog. I got up out of my chair to leave through the window. (pp. 90–91)

Fortunately for theater and film fans around the world, the distinguished director did not "leave through the window," but was instead psychiatrically hospitalized for three weeks and put under heavy sedation: "I read no papers, and neither saw nor heard any news programmes. Slowly and imperceptibly, my anxiety disappeared—my life's most faithful companion, inherited from both my mother and my father, placed in the very centre of my identity, my demon but also my friend spurring me on. Not only the torment, the anguish and the feeling of irreparable humiliation faded, but the driving force of my creativity was also eclipsed and fell away" (pp. 92–93).[83] Without the insistent goading of the daimonic—now subdued by medication—Bergman no longer felt the *need* to create. He grew impassive, apathetic, torpid, as the drugs went about their work of dulling the daimonic.

But once released from the clinic, he abruptly—against medical advice—quit taking his tranquilizers: "My suppressed anxiety shot up like the flame of a blowlamp, insomnia was total, my demons raging. I thought I would be torn apart by internal detonations. . . . I went on to the attack against the demons with a method that had worked well in previous crises. . . . Only by rigidly following my day and night programme could I maintain my sanity against torments so violent that they became interesting. To put it briefly, I returned to planning and staging my life with great care" (p. 94).

Despite his obsessive-compulsive defenses designed to ward off the dreaded invaders, Bergman, over the course of the next several months, verged on being overrun by the daimonic. Synchronously, he became more conscious of "a stifled rage, compressed and silenced for some considerable time, . . . moving down in my darkest corridors" (p. 95). Rather than suppressing it, as always, he allowed his long-denied anger to surface, redeeming the daimonic rage that proved to be his salvation: "To put it simply, I was so furiously angry that I recovered immediately" (p. 99). His despised daimonic anger was his angelic savior.

Bergman had won this critical life-or-death battle with his obdurate demons by reclaiming his repressed rage; but the war waged on, as it does in all of us to one degree or another. "Salvation" is not normally a singular, isolated victory, but rather an ongoing series of successful skirmishes with the daimonic. Slowly, perhaps ploddingly, Bergman devised ways of *hon-oring*—sometimes submitting, other times opposing—rather than desecrating his demons, and as a result, was transformed.

Honoring the daimonic does not consist of slavishly obeying its every injunction or desideratum, just as honoring one's parents, or spouse, or government, ought never mean blind, indiscriminate compliance. To "honor" or "consecrate" the daimonic—in the best sense of these words—is not necessarily to submit, but to take its reality seriously, to consider its significance, and the possible social and emotional implications of saying 'yea' or 'nay' to it. Now, saying 'nay' to the daimonic is not tantamount to denying it: *denial,* in the psychological sense, means making ourselves unconscious or unaware of some painful fact. On the contrary, denying or opposing the destructive impulsions of the daimonic means to consciously stand against such urgings, *while at the same time remaining fully aware of their presence and psychological implications.* It requires the capacity to tolerate the tension of this willful opposition: we may refuse to act on the bidding of the daimonic, but we sanctify it still by permitting the demons to reside in consciousness.

Looking back on his prolific life, the great film-maker admits that "I do not recognize the person I was forty years ago. . . . I was alone and raging. . . " (p. 146). He unabashedly confesses further that "ghosts, demons and other creatures with neither name nor domicile have been around me since childhood" (p. 202), and that these "ghosts, devils, demons, good, evil or just annoying, . . . have blown in my face, pushed me, pricked me with pins, plucked at my jersey. They have spoken, hissed or whispered," says Bergman. "Clear voices, not particularly comprehensible but impossible to ignore" (p. 204). Even now, concedes this chronic insomniac, he is still

> often drawn up in a spiral out of deep slumber, an irresistible force which makes me wonder where it hides itself. . . . Worst are the "hours of the wolf" in the small hours between three and five. That is when the demons come: mortification, loathing, fear, and rage. There is no point in trying to suppress them, for that makes it worse. . . . I close my eyes and listen with concentration and give the demons free rein: come on then, I know you, I know how you function, you just carry on until you tire of it. After a while the bottom falls out of them and they become foolish, then disappear, and I sleep for a few hours. (pp. 226–227)

It was not until his later years that the mature Bergman could comfortably say: "I had learnt to deal with my demons" (p. 233). Undoubtedly, most of this tortuous progression from dysdaimonia to eudaimonia was accomplished by virtue of his artistic activities.

Bergman's close—apparently palpable—contact with the daimonic dimension may be seen in such sublime works as *The Seventh Seal* (1956), *Cries and Whispers* (1972), *Scenes from a Marriage* (1973), and his final film, *Fanny and Alexander* (1982). Referring to an American television interview granted by Bergman during the 1960s, psychologist Ira Progoff remarked that

> the question of psychological demons in relation to the process of creation as it occurs in Bergman's work is of the widest implication. . . . As an artist Bergman seems to have hit upon a way of working with his demons. It is a method altogether valid from the point of view of depth psychology. . . .
>
> "I always have been interested in those voices inside you," Bergman said. . . . "I think everybody hears those voices and those forces." "And I have always wanted to put them in 'reality,' to put them on the table."
>
> "To put them on the table," means, for Bergman, to accord them the same respect that we give to every other fact of our life. It means to treat the inner demons not as though they were unreal imaginings but to treat them as facts, and therefore to relate to them in a serious way. Bergman has . . . done this, . . . especially in making certain of his movies like *Through a Glass Darkly* and *Hour of the Wolf.*
>
> In these films Bergman let the demons come out so that they could speak and act. That was the only way he could establish a relationship with them so they could be free to speak in dialogue and reveal their desires. Only then too, when they had expressed their needs could their negative potency be neutralized. In other words, only then could the demons of the psyche be exorcised. Bergman has been able to let this happen, and thus it has been possible for his involvement in his artworks . . . to serve as a means of spontaneous therapy.[84]

Ingmar Bergman happily found a creative medium for expressing his daimonic genius. We each must find our own. Nonetheless, as if to underscore the tenacious obstinacy of devils and demons—particularly ones which have not been fully brought to light by way of intensive introspection and/or psychotherapy—Bergman's tormenters once more made their undiminished power known to him with a vengeance in 1985, around the time he reached his fateful decision to retire from film-making. He had begun preparing a new script, but

> after three weeks of good work, I suddenly fell violently ill. . . . I seemed to have been poisoned and was rent with anguish and contempt in the presence of my misery. I realized I would never again make a film. . . .
>
> Sometimes I perceived clearly, almost physically, a primaeval monster, half-beast, half-man, moving inside me to which I was about to give birth. One morning I was chewing on a rough evil-smelling beard. . . . Sometimes I dreamt I was losing my teeth and was spitting out worn yellow stumps.
>
> I decided to retreat before my actors and collaborators caught sight of this monster and were seized with disgust or pity.[85]

The renewed creative process resurrected the daimonic in ways with which Bergman was psychologically and physically unwilling to contend. Whatever this strange, gestating creature represented was ready to be born; but Bergman could not at that time submit to the laborious birth of this intimidating, daimonic "monster." Regrettably, the pregnancy was aborted. We can only wonder now, in hindsight, what might have happened—for better or worse—had Bergman been more directly involved with depth psychology during his career; and what revitalizing, primal, creative energies could have been liberated by bravely bringing forth rather than running from this rejected, neglected, half-buried being longing for release.[86]

9

Conclusion

Some Final Reflections on Anger, Rage, Guilt, and Responsibility

We have finally come full circle: The epidemic of anger and violence reported at the outset of our investigation still rages on around and within us. Teetering on the verge of a new millennium, we find ourselves staring into the impenetrable depths of a vast, uncharted chasm outstretched before us. Despite the damnable darkness surrounding us, and the undeniably dangerous demons of the night nipping at our heels, this perilous—yet completely unprecedented—perch provides an unparalleled perspective, and a precious opportunity for positive change. Behind us, illuminated by its own undying energy, stands the entire story of human history, in all its gory and glorious details. Before us lies the unforeseeable future. The path directly ahead cannot be clearly discerned nor predicted. We are, to some significant degree, all responsible for defining that yet obscured way which will lead us to our destiny: not only our individual personal or professional destinies, but the collective destiny of this country.

Since it can be overtaxing to peer too far into either direction, it may be helpful for us to purposely limit our gaze for the moment, surveying merely the most immediately perceptible past and future. Despite the indubitable technological strides and humanitarian reforms in our free society, the past hundred years serve notice as a microcosmic messenger regarding the future: Man's inhumanity to man *must* be mitigated if we wish to survive through the end of the twenty-first century intact. This is surely a global truism, but one especially salient for the United States, where mean-spirited mayhem threatens to rend even further the already torn and tattered tapestry of beleaguered American life. The violent, anarchic disintegration of democratic America would not bode well for the rest of the world.

There is a natural, human reflex to try to "fix" the pandemic violence and evil around us at political, national, or even international levels; or to find socioeconomic or sociocultural solutions to the spreading scourge. As indicated in my introductory chapter, there has been a great deal of heated public rhetoric concerning the sources of the blight, including a befitting emphasis on the deterioration of so-called family values. But, germane as it may be, a clarion call to return to these traditional "family values"—however they might be defined—does not adequately address the indigenous dilemma of our deeply ensconced *devaluation of the daimonic.* In my estimation, macroscopic social approaches—though admirably idealistic—are inherently restricted and doomed to failure, as evidenced, for instance, by the abysmal breakdown of the simplistic "war on drugs," or the ineffective—even iatrogenic—American penal system.

The same may be said of our misdirected national mental health policies and programs: they have been drifting in the wrong direction for decades now, promulgating the mechanistic *biomedical* model over the far more sophisticated and holistic *biopsychosocial* model of mental disorders.[1] In effect, such attitudes and policies actually promote mental illness and violence, by supporting the suppression of rage and anger, rather than their conscious sublimation into constructive personal and collective action.[2] These misperceptions of psychopathology and psychotherapy are in themselves iatrogenic: The daimonic is not a disease the symptoms of which require suppressive medical therapy. On the contrary, as I have sought to show, it is the chronic suppression of the daimonic that has so insidiously engendered the currently diseased state of the union.[3]

What are we to do? Right now, the most valuable intervention we Americans, as a people, could possibly implement—at the various governmental, societal, community, and family levels in this troubled land—would be to revise our misguided attitudes regarding the real genesis of anger, violence, and psychopathology. *We must somehow admit into our thinking the archetypal paradigm of the daimonic.* Such a vital cognitive shift would, in turn, revolutionize the way we tend to think about the proper "treatment" of mental problems, and psychotherapy in general. Now, more than ever, we need *real* psychotherapy in America, not some watered-down, superficial, monetarily motivated, "revolving door" mental health system, focused as narrowly as possible on minimal symptom management. Psychotherapy is no longer a middle or upper-class luxury for the privileged few, or the stigmatic secret of the psychologically "sick," as in days past. Nor can we as a nation in good conscience permit it to ever return to that status. America can no longer afford to make the mental health of its citizenry—and by "mental health," I mean not only *psychological,* but *spiritual* health as well—any less of a priority than their inseparable physical health. I am speaking not only of community, county, or state hospitals and clinics, but of private practitioners, too. Independent providers of psychotherapy services—psychologists, psychiatrists, social workers, and other mental health counselors—must reconsider their own preconceived attitudes, values, and priorities. Psychotherapy services have become prohibitively expensive. At the same time, there is decreasing funding available for it, growing resistance on the part of private and governmental insurance programs to pay even partially for it, and therefore, mounting financial hardship on those who honestly seek the help that competent psychotherapy can provide—all at a time when so many Americans so desperately need it. For federal, state, and private health care officials to respond to this national crisis by curtailing psychological services, discouraging the professional practice of depth psychology, and making sweeping decisions on mental health treatment driven mainly by cold economics, is to further aggravate the gathering storm cloud surrounding us. This pertains to the profit-driven purveyors of "managed mental health care," as well as to we clinicians cowed by them into accepting an unacceptable state of affairs. In this regard, we are all morally and ethically guilty of participating in—and thereby supporting—the negative and destructive cycle of pathological anger, rage, and violence in America.

The Paradox of Personal Responsibility

How much responsibility must we ultimately bear for managing our anger and rage? Psychiatry and psychology have for some time now been guilty of allowing individual responsibility for one's behavior to be slowly eroded, to the point that we no longer—legally or morally—hold the adult person fully responsible for his or her actions. But, reversing the pathological trend of anger, rage, and violence is primarily the responsibility of the *individual.* Any collective efforts that reinforce—even tacitly—the relinquishing of individual responsibility for good and evil are guilty of complicity in per-petuating the very problem such social programs seek to solve. The real quandary is this: If we as adults are not responsible for our behavior, then who is? The government? The psychiatrist or psychologist? The police? The legal system? The devil or demons? And, if we do not *hold* each other accountable for how we deal with the daimonic and how we act—and I concur with those who claim that this sort of responsibility for one's behavior is best inculcated by the nuclear family—how can we reasonably expect ourselves, on balance, to be primarily productive rather than destructive citizens? Each time a psychiatric defense is inappropri-ately introduced by high-powered attorney's in the courts to defend or excuse self-evident evil-doing—as, for instance, in the first Menendez brothers defense, or Lorena Bobbitt's castration trial, or the proposed "black rage" mass murder defense of Colin Ferguson—we run the risk of taking yet another step down the slippery slope of chaos and anarchy.[4] We remove the admittedly onerous burden of responsibility from the bowed back of the individual—a cumbersome personal cross we each must be willing to bear—and deem the individual not guilty of behaving as she or he did, due to some diagnosable mental disorder or psychological condition. Or, we come to view such individuals as hapless victims of circumstances: bad genes, dysfunctional families, physical or sexual abuse, alcoholism, drug addiction, poverty, racism, etc. Hence, we hold them to a lower standard of responsibility than others presumably less encum-bered by such psychobiological baggage: either we believe their violent behavior *justifiable* by the special circumstances surrounding it; or deem their responsibility *diminished* due to some mental disturbance. As one prominent Lutheran theologian has said: " 'As a society, we seem to believe that if our behavior is biologically determined, then the genes we inherit—not we ourselves—can be held responsible for what we do. Confronted by moments of moral crisis, we are often quick to scapegoat our genes.' "[5] As more and more emphasis is placed on *biological* over *psychological* factors in human destructiveness and violence, we shall soon from all quarters hearken the plaintive cry: "My genes made me do it!" Indeed, this de-monic trend has already begun in courts throughout the country.

Of course, there is strong literary and legal precedent for consid-ering the presence of mitigating circumstances in determining an individual's personal responsibility and guilt. Orestes, readers might re-member from chapter seven, was found not guilty in a trial by jury of matricide, despite the fact that he had incontestably murdered his mother. His acquittal hinged on the special circumstances justifying his action:

namely, that his mother, having killed his father, also intended to kill him, and that he—according to the god of truth, Apollo, his divine "defense attorney"—had been impelled by Zeus himself to avenge his father's death. Yet in the *Oresteia,* there is never really any question of Orestes' guilt: he freely admits his guilt, never once denying his deadly deed. The Furies represent his guilty conscience about murdering his mother. Like most guilt feelings in general, the Furies are comprised of vengeful anger and condemnation directed toward himself for the evil he has irrevocably and knowingly done.

The metaphorical Furies who so ferociously chase Orestes, however, are not neurotic guilt, or pathological anger turned inwards. Orestes *is* guilty, *knows* he is guilty, and suffers from his guilt, even as he tries to evade it. His is an *existential* guilt, for which there is no "cure" other than conscious acknowledgment, acceptance of personal responsibility, repentance, and, perhaps in time, self-forgiveness. For to be human is to be flawed; and to be flawed is to be guilty. This phenomenon of *existential guilt* leads us to one last root—possibly the ontological taproot—of the existential anger and rage explicated heretofore: Whenever we commit some act which violates our own values or fundamental nature; when we somehow dishonor or desecrate our own being or the being of others, by going against our better judgment or instincts; whenever we vainly or naively deny our potentialities for *both* good and evil, or slough off our inborn responsibility to direct our daimonic impulses as constructively as possible, there develops—often subconsciously, buried deep in the psyche of even the most ostensibly conscienceless criminal—a natural, existential sense of anger with one's self; an inner outrage at one's failure to follow one's most noble—not basest—impulses. Sartre has spoken of such states of self-betrayal as *mauvaise foi,* or "bad faith."[6] We have "sinned" or "missed the mark," and, at some level, we know it, have inwardly registered it, and bitterly condemn ourselves for it. If, we further compound the problem by denying our existential shame and guilt, refusing to face it without the cowardly cushion of excuses, we call forth from the depths the tormenting demons of *neurotic guilt*—a ruthlessly shameful, largely unconscious, self-loathing. The psychological process of which I speak applies not only to our malicious actions or misbehaviors, but to our "sins of omission" as well: those *self* defining situations in which we fail to act with integrity, for lack of courage, fear, laziness, greed, self-centeredness, etc. In the hardened heart of every sinner, no matter how evil, the capacity—maybe even an abysmally imbedded proclivity—for *good* endures despite the habitude toward evil. And it is precisely this innate inclination toward good which, when thwarted, generates guilt feelings—though feelings of guilt, it must be granted, can, like any other human emotion, be repressed, and thereby, rendered unconscious. We witness this phenomenon most clearly in the so-called sociopath or "antisocial personality disorder."[6]

Orestes finds the courage to confront his guilt, and hence, redeems his self-directed rage. As a result, he is permitted to go free, rather than being punished by his community. *Guilt* and *punishment* are two different principles: "Guilt" refers to culpability for one's behavior. "Punishment" refers to the negative consequences imposed either by oneself or by the community on the guilty party, usually for some violation of another's rights. But how one "behaves" toward or treats *oneself* is also a crucial aspect of guilt. When we behave in subtle, sometimes imperceptible ways that work toward the disintegration, diminution, or detriment of our selves, *we are guilty;* when we decline to confront the daimonic consciously, *we are guilty.* We—at least at that moment in time—lack integrity, and surreptitiously or outwardly suffer from our insufficiency. But, does guilt *always* merit punishment? Surely, there are always consequences for our behavior, whether we are aware of them or not. *Consequences,* from a psychological perspective, are the natural, organic sequelae to the actions of one individual or group on the systemically interconnected psyches of others. *Punishment* may be defined as the subsequent imposition of a noxious stimulus or consequence designed to deter, modify, or correct undesirable behavior. Punishment is but one kind of consequence—and probably the least effective as a behavior modifier—for what we humans deem evil, inappropriate, or undesirable conduct.[7] The madman or madwoman may be guilty of murder; but do they deserve the identical legal punishment and consequences as the so-called "sane" person? Or, might there be mitigating circumstances contributing to one's guilt, and hence, diminishing, tempering, or perhaps even negating *not* one's guilt, but rather, one's punishment?

Such matters are immeasurably complicated by the fact that there are *always* mitigating circumstances contributing to one's guilt or innocence. The difference between an act of evil and an act of good can be infinitismally small, decided by the slightest nudge in either direction. No one exists in a vacuum. We are all—to some extent or another—victims of circumstance, fate, and destiny. For this reason, any determination of the appropriate punishment for a violent act must be made in the full light of all relevant facts leading up to that act. And—since every situation has not only its commonly occurring patterns, but also its unique confluence of contributing factors—each and every act of violence must still be judged on a case-by-case basis.

Nonetheless, *even victims are responsible for their behavior.* We are responsible for how we cope with our victimhood, how we interpret it, and how we learn from it. While there are countless evils beyond our control that can befall us at any time, there are others which we sometimes unwittingly invite or make more likely. Moreover, we must continually grapple with the question of whether "unconsciousness"—that is, not knowing what one is doing, or why—automatically exculpates. Christ's famous sentiment from the cross, "Father, forgive them; for they know not what they do" (Luke 23:34 AV), appears at first to condone exoneration for "not knowing" the full implications of ones actions. Yet, there is a big difference between "not knowing" the objective facts of a given situation, and being psychologically *unconscious.* In the latter case, one is existentially guilty of not knowing the pertinent, *subjective* facts about one's self, one's psyche, and the idiosyncratic significance of one's own comportment in the past, present, and future. To once more summon up May on this subject: "We are responsible for the effect of our actions, and we are also responsible for becoming as aware as we can of these effects."[8]

Reconsider, for instance, the calamitous story of Oedipus, discussed in chapter seven.[8] Victimized by his parents' fear of him fulfilling the Delphic prophecy to kill his father and marry his mother, he is deliberately tied by his foot to a stake, exposed to the elements, and left to die. Nevertheless, the divination eventually comes true. Oedipus is now guilty of murdering his father and marrying his mother; however, he *did not know it!* Psychologically, we could say that he is "in denial" about his behavior, unconscious, and desires desperately to remain so even when finally confronted with the inconceivable facts of his situation. He vehemently rejects the truth he hears, bitterly resists becoming more conscious of his sordid history. This is why May writes that, for Oedipus, the central "issue in the drama is whether he will recognize what he has done. The tragic issue is that of seeking the truth about one's self; it is the tragic drama of a person's passionate relation to truth. *Oedipus' tragic flaw is his wrath against his own reality.*"[9]

But is not this "wrath against reality" to some extent an existential plight for every person? I have sought in the foregoing pages to suggest so. Oedipus, at this juncture in his life, is yet a dysdaimonic young man, "distempered by self-wrought woes"[10]: he cannot reckon with the daimonic, turning his "wrath against reality" first toward others, and then, toward himself. It is not until a lifetime later that the mature Oedipus masters the daimonic, as Sophocles—by then himself a ripe octogenarian—suggests in *Oedipus at Colonus.*

"This subsequent drama," says May, "is Oedipus' stage of reconciliation with himself and his fellow men. . . . The first theme we find in Oedipus' meditation at Colonus is *guilt*—the difficult problem of the relation of ethical responsibility to self-consciousness. Is a man guilty if the act was unpremeditated, done unknowingly? In the course of his probing old Oedipus comes to terms with . . . [his guilt]."[11]

Oedipus has by now forgiven himself his youthful folly—actions driven in part by cosmic forces beyond his control or conscious ken—keenly defending himself against the harsh condemnations of Creon:

> Tell me now, if an oracle had prophesied a divine doom coming upon my father, that he should die by a son's hand, how could you justly reproach me with it, me who was then unborn, whom no sire had yet begotten, no womb conceived? And if when born to woe—as I was born—I met my father in strife and slew him, all ignorant of what I was doing and to whom, how could you justly blame the unknowing deed?[12]

Venerable Oedipus has at last learned to live with his demons—the fiery murder of his father and impassioned marriage to his mother—but not in the sense of having suppressed them, or the daimonic in general. He has now become *eudaimonic.* But his eudaimonism does not consist of unadulterated absolution, lightness, and love, though loving and gracious he has surely become. He is, at the same time, still able to get angry when necessary, passionately standing up for himself and those he loves. "His sharp and violent temper," writes May,

> present at the crossroads where he killed his father years [before] . . . is still much in evidence in this last drama, unsubdued by suffering or maturity. The fact that Sophocles does not see fit to remove or even soften Oedipus' aggression and anger—the fact, that is, that the "aggression" and the "angry affects" are not the "flaws" he has old Oedipus get over— . . . illustrate[s] . . . that . . . [his] maturity is not at all a renouncing of [daimonic] passion to come to terms with society, not a learning to live "in accord with the reality requirements of civilization." It is Oedipus' reconciliation with himself, with the special people he loves, and with the . . . [spiritual] meaning of his life.[13]

The aged Oedipus found a way to forgive himself for his sins, *while at the same time taking full responsibility for his unconscious behavior and its consequences.* Oedipus thus provides a splendid illustration of the process of spiritual and psychological growth evolving slowly, over time, from *dysdaimonia* to *eudaimonia.* He has creatively come to terms with his own daimonic tendencies. So must we all.

Let us not forget, however, that as a result of his impulsivity, Oedipus had spent the better part of his life in self-imposed exile, ostracized from society, a beggar, and blind by his own maddened hand. He had done his proper penance; he had paid a high price for his unconscious, hot-headed deeds. The subject of appropriate *penance* is thus separate from legal guilt or innocence. "Penance" is a *psychological sacrament,* a symbolic act of contrition and self-absolution. Since there are always mitigating circumstances molding and influencing our behavior—from various conscious and unconscious, internal and external sources—applying the *appropriate* penance is of the utmost importance in sentencing guilty violent offenders. Mere prolonged imprisonment, for example, is probably not the most appropriate penance for the vast majority of individuals convicted of committing a violent crime. There can be no true atonement or absolution without proper penance. Punishment is for the most part a meaningless form of penance; and without some personal meaning, there can be no real rehabilitation or inner transformation. To be truly therapeutic, penance must be chosen, accepted, actively willed, rather than imposed on one from without.

One of the most moving portrayals of appropriate penance in recent memory can be found in the disturbingly beautiful film, *The Mission* (1986), starring Jeremy Irons and Robert De Niro. De Niro—surely a daimonic character in real life—plays a South American mercenary, who murders his brother in a fit of jealous rage. Following the murder—for which there are no clear legal consequences beyond incarceration—he withdraws from the world in a state of inconsolable depression, guilt, and remorse. His fate is turned over to a saintly Jesuit missionary (Jeremy Irons), who strives to save this suffering soul. As part of his penance, the murderer must tow the tied-up trappings of his violent life—armor, sword, guns, and so forth—behind him as he and the priest ascend the sheer (but spectacularly breathtaking) cliffs and waterfalls separating the primeval rain forest (and the far-flung Jesuit mission of the film's title) from so-called civilization. The contrite soldier accepts his Sisyphus-like penance with a vengeance, purging his sin, jettisoning his former persona, and becoming first a nonviolent—but, finally, true to form, a militant—Jesuit monk. Even the most effective penance is powerless to eradicate the daimonic.

But I am just a psychologist and psychotherapist, not a priest, lawyer, or jurist. As such, my concern is with *preventing*—as far as possible—the commission of destructive violence by my patients, while, at the same time, promoting and encouraging their emotional welfare, psychological integrity, and creative evolution. Violence has fatal fallout for both victims *and* perpetrators. Part of my own responsibility as a psychologist requires that I sometimes actively intervene in preventing patients from visiting violence upon themselves or others. Still, under most circumstances, it must be my patients themselves who decide whether or not to act on their daimonic dispositions. It is their responsibility to become as aware of their daimonic inclinations and capacity for evil as possible, in order to better be able to choose their behavior more consciously—based on a mature, realistic perception of the probable remote and immediate consequences, both inner and outer. More than this, one cannot do. When patients come to me for consultation or psychotherapy, this is what is asked of them. If they are unready or unwilling to pursue this path, I will probably be of little use to them. If, on the other hand, they desire to become more cognizant of the daimonic, and are prepared more or less to commit themselves to this arduous descent—the duration of which may be artificially prescribed or indeterminate—we are ready to begin: together, to initiate that unpredictable trek toward discovering revivifying meaning, even in the dreadful demons of resentment, anger, and rage. I have the utmost respect and admiration for anyone authentically willing to embark on such a daunting journey—no matter what manner of evil they may previously have committed. Redemption must always remain in our minds and hearts an ever-present—albeit sometimes highly unlikely—human potentiality. "Let he [or she] who is without sin cast the first stone," was how Jesus expressed the pitfalls of pharisaical or legalistic judgment, and the diabolical hypocrisy of collective condemnation (see John 8:7).

Considering the dearth of alternative methods, rites, or rituals for redeeming our raging devils and demons in modern American culture, psychotherapy—especially the sort of "existential depth psychology" I have herein tried to describe—has, in my opinion, the most potential for facilitating this much needed process. But given the appalling direction psychotherapy, as a field, has taken of late, there seems little hope of reaching any more than the smallest segment of people imaginable. Americans interested in such psychotherapy are instead being financially forced into the "fast-food" model of "brief therapy." Hence the urgency to stem and counterbalance the surging tide of those therapeutic approaches philosophically or financially unwilling—or clinically unable—to work constructively with the daimonic. This presents an unprecedented call to arms to American psychotherapists, and to the health-conscious American consumer.

We, as a nation, are faced with a moral, ethical, and—dare I say?—spiritual dilemma of the first degree. We stand at a philosophical crossroads, where we are forced to make a difficult, fateful choice. In a sense, we must choose between two very different, rudimentary myths. *Myths,* as already mentioned, are the ways in which we see ourselves, imagine ourselves, conceptualize ourselves in relation to the world—not only individually, but culturally as well. What will we become? What myths will inform and guide our lives, and the lives of our children and grandchildren? Myths always embody basic truths about ourselves and the world we live in. In order to reach new levels of psychological integration, consciousness, and emotional maturity, we must be willing periodically to modify, redefine, or completely replace our personal myth, moving through several different developmental "incarnations" during the long course of a lifetime. As we grow and change, so must the myths of who and how we are in the world. Myths become obsolete when they no longer make adequate sense of our personal, cultural, or existentially *human* experience. At such a point—and we have unquestionably arrived at that pressing point—we are confronted with the weighty task of creating new, more adequate myths to live by, lest we totally succumb to the postmodern experience of life as merely chaotic, nonsensical, meaningless, and absurd. *Nihilism* is the negative net result of a life devoid of meaningful myths; indeed, devoid of all philosophical values. Nihilism, to its credit, does not deny the dark, demonic side of life; but it disregards the daimonic. Contrary to the common misconceptions about existential philosophy and psychology, the negation called "nihilism" is not a viable or constructive long-term solution for coping with the human condition. It is, rather, an angry, bitter and resentful refusal and failure to accept the reality of the daimonic. "Courage," writes Tillich, "is the power of life to affirm itself in spite of . . . [its daimonic] ambiguity, while the negation of life because of its negativity is an expression of cowardice."[14]

Nations, religions, and professions are subject to the same laws of growth and change as are individuals. Psychotherapy, as a profession, is in the painful process of shedding its old identity in favor of a new, more streamlined, cost effective myth. But, for the most part, this new, monstrous, postmodern myth disregards the daimonic. Staying the current course more than flirts with disaster: it courts catastrophe. What alternative is there? Rather than roundly rejecting the practice of "depth psychology" (as I have, for our purposes, herein redefined it) in favor of more economically efficient, short-term modalities that gloss over the real genesis of psychopathology and violence, we might try to integrate the holistic, humanistic myth of the daimonic into time-limited psychotherapy, community mental health programs, and national mental health policies. As I have tried to demonstrate, the daimonic is an archetypal *symbol* par excellence of our collective dilemma, especially as it pertains to the pernicious problems of runaway anger, rage, and violence. As a true symbol, it demands that we take some stand for or against it. Like all bona fide symbols, it arises out of a tremendous internal conflict, brewing in ourselves and in our national psyche. The daimonic symbolizes the perennial conflict between the cultural pressures of repression, rationality, adjustment, and conformity on one side, and the vital forces of freedom, individuality, integrity, passion, and creativity on the other. Any time the latter values are too long frustrated or suppressed, anger, rage—and eventually, violence—are sure to follow. This is the salient social significance of the daimonic paradigm: it symbolically bespeaks our mishandling of anger and rage, as well as *pointing the way past the present danger.* But are we ready to hear the hopeful message borne by this symbol?

The daimonic myth is a psychological and philosophical signpost, pointing in a particular direction, and provoking from us some personal decision. Like symbols and myths in general, it is both regressive and progressive at the same time, which is what makes the model of the daimonic so dynamically controversial and powerfully healing. "The healing power of the symbol and myth," as May points out,

> has two aspects. This power resides, on one hand, in the fact that the symbol and myth elicit and bring into awareness the repressed, unconscious, archaic urges, longings, dreads and other psychic content. This is the *regressive* function of symbols and myths. But on the other hand, the symbol and myth reveal new goals, new ethical insights and possibilities; they are a breaking through of greater meaning which was not present before. The symbol and myth in this respect are ways of working out the problem on a higher level of integration. This we call the *progressive* function of symbols and myths.[15]

It is just this quality of "creative ambiguity" that causes the concept of the daimonic to be so anxiety provoking, threatening, and readily dismissed in political, theological, and scientific circles as regressive, anachronistic, blasphemous, irrational, unscientific, or simply impractical. But, as I by now hope to have evinced, the daimonic is an eminently prag-matic myth for both comprehending and remediating many of the per-vasive social problems facing us today. What our present predicament calls for is a cultural and personal reclamation of the daimonic, rather than its continued denigration and rejection. But how prepared are we to take up this intimidating psychological task? And what fate awaits us if we refuse?

Radically altering our attitude toward the daimonic, from disdain and derogation to one of respect and valuation, involves an encounter with the Sphinx-like puzzle the daimonic poses. The Sphinx, writes mytholo-gist Edith Hamilton, was a "frightful monster, . . . a creature shaped like a winged lion, but with the breast and face of a woman. She lay in wait for the wayfarers along the roads to [Thebes] . . . and whomever she seized she put a riddle to, telling him if he could answer it, she would let him go. No one could, and the horrible creature devoured man after man until the city was in a state of siege."[16]

Such is the sorry state we find ourselves in today. Our land is being ravaged by the destructive side of the daimonic. America, like the ancient city of Thebes, is in a violent state of siege. Anger and rage are rampaging across the land; every man, woman, and child is at risk. But, reading on, we learn that Thebes survived the Sphinx's murderous reign of terror:

> So matters stood when there came into the stricken country a stranger, a man of great courage and great intelligence, whose name was Oedipus. . . . "What creature," the Sphinx asked him, "goes on four feet in the morning, on two at noonday, on three in the evening?" "Man," answered Oedipus. "In childhood he creeps on hands and feet; in manhood he walks erect; in old age he helps himself with a staff." It was the right answer. The Sphinx, inexplicably, but most fortunately, killed herself; the Thebans were saved.[17]

Still other accounts attribute the Sphinx's self-destruction to a combination of mortification and rage.[18] At all events, the terrible Sphinx was outsmarted *by taking the riddle she posed seriously.* The enigma of the daimonic is our modern Sphinx. Today it is we, like Oedipus on his way to Thebes, who are met with a similar riddle to solve, a riddle requiring a right decision, and rather quickly, lest we too be consumed piecemeal by this beastly, carnivorous demon of violence. The life-or-death decision our current circumstance calls forth is whether to ally ourselves with the collective forces that would serve to *suppress* the daimonic; or, instead, to work toward the redemption of our anger and rage in any constructive

ways we can. For as our old friend Oedipus, that daimonic man, found
in his triumphant meeting with the terrible Sphinx, "man," mankind, or
much better, *humankind*—the indomitable human will and spirit to
survive, create, individuate, transcend, to find truth and bestow meaning—
is the only sensible response to the paradox posed by "senseless" violence
and evil. To learn to creatively live *with* the daimonic or be violently
devoured by it. We will decide our own destiny. Let us choose wisely.

Fig. 27.   Oedipus explaining the engima to the Sphinx. Attic medallion cup
(Viticcio Painter-School of Douris, circa 470 B.C.). Museo Gregoriano Etrusco,
Vatican Museums, Vatican State. Courtesy Alinari/Art Resource, New York.

Notes

Chapter 1. The Angry American

1. Despite the fact that, according to FBI data, there was a 4% *decrease* in violent crime in America in 1994, reaching the lowest level since 1989, savvy criminologists take small comfort in such deceptive statistics: They recognize that violent crime in this country is increasingly committed by troubled teens, whose numbers are rapidly growing. FBI Director Louis Freeh recently cautioned that " 'the ominous increase in juvenile crime, coupled with population trends, portend future crime and violence at nearly unprecedented levels.' " (Fox Butterfield, "FBI Reports Lower Crime Rate, But Warns of New Surge," *San Francisco Examiner*, Nov. 19, 1995, p. A–12.)

2. On October 2, 1995, in a Los Angeles courtroom, a jury of his peers acquitted O. J. Simpson of all charges, a controversial verdict that outraged some Americans, and amplified preexisting racial animus. Simpson still faces several pending civil suits.

3. *San Jose Mercury News*, Oct. 31, 1994.

4. *San Francisco Chronicle*, Sept. 14, 1994.

5. Sara Martin, "Workplace Is No Longer a Haven from Violence," *The APA Monitor* 27, no. 10 (Oct. 1994): 29.

6. See ibid.

7. James Clarke, *On Being Mad or Merely Angry: John W. Hinckley, Jr., and Other Dangerous People* (Princeton, N.J.: Princeton University Press, 1990), p. 94.

8. Ibid., pp. 93–94, including note, p. 94.

9. For more on this tragedy, see, for instance, Jonathan Foster (*London Independent*), "British Boys Shared a Murderous Urge," in the *San Francisco Examiner*, Nov. 25, 1993, p. A-1.

10. *International Crime Rates* (Washington, D.C.: Bureau of Justice Statistics, 1988): 1.

11. Rollo May, *Love and Will* (New York: W. W. Norton, 1969), pp. 163–164. As we shall discuss in depth throughout this book, May defined the *daimonic* as "*any natural function which has the power to take over the whole person*" (p. 123). Anger and rage—while the exclusive concern of our current inquiry—are but two examples of numerous emotions, impulsions, instincts, drives, or tendencies that can also participate in this possessive quality deemed by May as *daimonic*. (See chapters five and six in *Love and Will*, and chapters three and four of this volume for a thorough discourse on "the daimonic.")

12. Walter Cannon, *Bodily Changes in Panic, Hunger, Fear, and Rage* (New York: Appleton-Century, 1915). See also W. Cannon, *The Wisdom of the Body* (New York : W. W. Norton, 1963). Hans Selye, "The General Adaption Syndrome and the Diseases of Adaption," *Journal of Clinical Endocrinology* 6 (1946).

13. John Klama, *Aggression: The Myth of the Beast Within* (New York: John Wiley and Sons, 1988).

14. Ibid., p. 58.

15. Carol Tavris, *Anger: The Misunderstood Emotion* (New York: Simon and Schuster, 1982), p. 32.

16. Erich Neumann, "Fear of the Feminine," *Quadrant* (a publication of the C. G. Jung Foundation for Analytical Psychology) 19, no. 1 (Spring 1986): 31.

17. Rollo May, *Freedom and Destiny* (New York: W. W. Norton, 1981), p. 41.

18. Charles Spielberger, Susan Krasner, and Eldra Solomon, "The Experience, Expression, and Control of Anger," in *Health Psychology : Individual Differences and Stress*, ed. M. P. Janisse (New York: Springer Verlag, 1988), p. 91.

19. Spielberger, Jacobs, Russell, and Crane cited in ibid.

20. Willard Gaylin, *The Rage Within: Anger in Modern Life* (New York: Penguin Books, 1989), p. 75.

21. Ibid., p. 76.

22. Robert Zaslow and Marilyn Menta, *The Psychology of the Z-Process: Attachment and Activation*, rev. ed. (San Jose, Calif.: San Jose State University, 1975), p. 58.

23. William Shakespeare, *The Tragedy of Hamlet Prince of Denmark* in The Harvard Classics, registered ed., ed. C. Eliot (New York: P. F. Collier and Son, 1938), p. 166.

24. *Webster's Third New International Dictionary* , unabridged (Springfield, Mass.: Merriam-Webster, 1986), p. 82.

25. Zaslow and Menta, *The Psychology of the Z-Process,* p. 255.

26. Rollo May, *Power and Innocence : A Search for the Sources of Violence* (New York: W. W. Norton, 1972), p. 167.

27. Zaslow and Menta, *The Psychology of the Z-Process,* pp. 60-61.

28. May, *Power and Innocence,* p. 179.

29. Ibid., p. 189.

30. Ibid., p. 191.

31. *Webster's Desk Dictionary of the English Language* (New York: Portland House, 1990), p. 1001.

32. May, *Power and Innocence,* p. 97.

33. Herman Melville, *White-Jacket or The World in a Man-of-War* in *Herman Melville: Redburn, White-Jacket, Moby-Dick* (New York: Literary Classics of the United States, 1983), p. 645. We will be taking a closer look at Melville's immensely creative life later, in chapter eight.

34. *San Francisco Examiner,* Dec. 19, 1993, p. 1.

35. See Oliver Stone's sardonic film, *Natural Born Killers* (1994) on the iconization of mass murderers by the media.

36. As we know, the human immune system consists in part of white blood cells, which vigorously attack and devour any alien or threatening life forms.

37. The updated figures are six dead and nineteen wounded.

38. Robert D. McFadden, "N.Y. Railway Shooting Suspect: A Man Obsessed," *San Francisco Sunday Examiner and Chronicle,* Dec. 12, 1993, p. B-7. Originally published in the *New York Times* as "A Tormented Life—A Special Report; A Long Slide from Privilege Ends in Slaughter on a Train," Dec. 12, 1993.

39. "Competency" is a legal term referring to the defendant's *current* mental condition, as reflected by his or her ability to comprehend the nature and significance of the proceedings, and the capacity to constructively cooperate with defense counsel. Unlike the plea of "not guilty by reason of insanity," competency refers not to the defendant's state of mind at the time of the crime, but only to his or her mental state at the time of the trial.

40. For more on the subject of narcissistic rage, see chapter six.

41. May, *Love and Will,* p. 112.

42. Shakespeare, *Hamlet,* p. 144.

43. May, *Freedom and Destiny*, p. 47.

44. Alexander Lowen, *Fear of Life* (New York: Macmillan, 1980), p. 49.

45. May, *Freedom and Destiny*, p. 90.

46. Otto Rank, *The Trauma of Birth* (New York: Harper Torchbooks, 1929).

47. Carl Jung, *Symbols of Transformation : An Analysis of the Prelude to a Case of Schizophrenia*, 2nd ed., vol. 5 of *The Collected Works of C. G. Jung*, trans. R. F. C. Hull, ed. Herbert Read et al., Bollingen Series XX (Princeton, N.J.: Princeton University Press, 1967), p. 235.

48. Buddha (c. 560–480 B.C.) taught that the source of all human suffering and frustration stems from "attachment" or "desire," both being types of *expectation:* We expect, or demandingly desire certain specific outcomes or results of our actions; when these fail to occur, we suffer frustration. Buddhism advocates relinquishing all such worldly attachments or "cravings," hence eliminating frustration and, consequently, anger or rage. While there is much of value for Westerners to learn from Buddhist teachings, we should not expect to attain the perfectly serene detachment of Buddha, even after a lifetime of practice. For most humans, existential frustration persists so long as we retain our attachment to life itself.

49. May, *Freedom and Destiny*, p. 47.

50. J. Dollard, N. Doob, N. Miller, and R. Sears, *Frustration and Aggression* (New Haven, Conn.: Yale University Press, 1939).

51. Tavris, *Anger: The Misunderstood Emotion*, p. 154.

52. Research supports my point. Averill (1982, 1983) found that, on average, adult subjects reported experiencing "anger" at least once daily; and "annoyance" several times per day. See J. R. Averill, *Anger and Aggression: An Essay on Emotion* (New York: Springer Verlag, 1982), and "Studies on Anger and Aggression: Implications for Theories on Emotions," *American Psychologist* 38 (1983): 1145–1160.

53. Clarke, *On Being Mad or Merely Angry*, p. 96.

54. May, *Love and Will*, pp. 30-31.

55. See Clarke, *On Being Mad or Merely Angry*. See also Oliver Stone's strong statement on violence and the American media in *Natural Born Killers* (1994). Assassin Sirhan Sirhan is said to have told his captors that in the brief seconds it took to shoot and kill Robert F. Kennedy, he attained the fame Kennedy had worked for his whole life.

56. Viktor Frankl, *The Will to Meaning: Foundations and Applications of Logotherapy* (New York: The New American Library, 1969). In *Man's Search for Meaning*, rev. ed. (New York: Washington Square Press, 1985), Frankl writes that "there are three main avenues on which one arrives at meaning in life. The first is by creating a work or doing a deed. The second is by experiencing something or encountering someone; in other words, meaning can be found not only in work but also in love. . . . Most important, however," holds Frankl, "is the third avenue to meaning in life: even the helpless victim of a hopeless situation, facing a fate he cannot change, may rise above himself, may grow beyond himself, and by so doing change himself. He may turn a personal tragedy into a [meaningful] triumph" (p. 170).

57. Frankl, *Man's Search for Meaning*. See pp. 128–130.

58. May, *Power and Innocence*, p. 36.

59. William Grier and Price Cobbs, *Black Rage* (New York: Basic Books, 1992), p. xvi. See also E. Cose, *The Rage of a Privileged Class* (New York: Harper Collins, 1993).

60. Ibid., pp. 3–4.

61. Ibid., p. 213.

62. Prior to his death in 1995, celebrated civil rights attorney William Kunstler had announced plans to defend Ferguson on appeal. He intended to use what he dubbed a "black rage" defense: that is, he hoped to successfully argue that Ferguson was, at the moment of the fatal shootings, in the irresistible grips of a murderous rage resulting from insurmountable racial discrimination against him. The critical question as to wherein resides one's personal responsibility for constructively channelling his or her anger or rage—and for any evil deeds arising from failure to do so—is a subject we will revisit, particularly in chapter nine.

63. May, *Power and Innocence*, p. 182.

Chapter 2. Sex Wars

1. See, for instance, Susan Faludi, *Backlash: The Undeclared War Against American Women* (New York: Crown, 1991).

2. Christine Hoff Sommers, *Who Stole Feminism?; How Women Have Betrayed Women* (New York: Simon and Schuster, 1995), p. 41.

3. Cannon, *The Wisdom of the Body*.

4. Gaylin, *The Rage Within*, p. 56.

5. *San Francisco Examiner*, Dec. 19, 1993, p. A-2.

6. According to psychoanalyst Wolfgang Lederer in *The Fear of Women* (New York: Harcourt Brace Jovanovich, Inc., 1968), "the myth of the *vagina dentata* is incredibly prevalent. Thompson gives some 30 pertinent references relating to North American Indian tribes, and Metraux relates how the first women of the Chaco Indians were said to have had teeth in their vaginas. . . " (p. 44). He reports comparable myths in Indian folklore. In many cases, the male hero of the story must break the vaginal teeth prior to attempting sexual intimacy.

7. Eugene Monick, *Castration and Male Rage: The Phallic Wound* (Toronto: Inner City Books, 1991), pp. 10–11.

8. Ibid., p. 51.

9. Karen Horney, *Feminine Psychology* , ed. Harold Kelman (New York: W. W. Norton, 1967), p. 145.

10. Ibid., Harold Kelman, from his introduction, p. 30.

11. Taoism is attributed mainly to the philosophical writings of Lao Tzu (500 B.C.), and teaches "the Way": the path of creative balance, unity, and virtuous conduct in complete harmony with the natural flow of the cosmos. See, for instance, *The Way of Life: Lao Tzu,* trans. R. B. Blakney (New York: The New American Library, 1955).

12. Irene Claremont de Castillejo, *Knowing Woman: A Feminine Psychology* (New York: Harper Colophon, 1973), p. 15.

13. Rollo May, "Psychotherapy and the Daimonic," in *Myths, Dreams, and Religion*, ed. Joseph Campbell (New York: E. P. Dutton, 1970), pp. 200–201.

14. James Hillman, *Anima: An Anatomy of a Personified Notion* (Dallas: Spring Publications, 1985), pp. 13-15.

15. Claire Douglas, "Christiana Morgan's Visions Reconsidered: A Look Behind *The Visions Seminars*," *The San Francisco Jung Institute Library Journal* 8, no. 4 (1989): 10–15. See also Douglas' "The Animus," *The San Francisco Jung Institute Library Journal* 6, no. 3 (1986): 1–20; Mary Ann Mattoon and Jennette Jones, "Is the Animus Obsolete?", *Quadrant* (a publication of the C. G. Jung Foundation for Analytical Psychology) 20, no. 1 (1987): 5–22; and, for a sympathetic male perspective, Gareth Hill, *Masculine and Feminine: The Natural Flow of Opposites in the Psyche* (Boston: Shambhala, 1992).

16. Neumann, "Fear of the Feminine," p. 13. See also Neumann's *Fear of the Feminine and Other Essays on Feminine Psychology* (Princeton, N.J.: Princeton University Press, 1994).

17. Neumann's analysis of homosexuality as psychopathology—like Freud's—has fallen from favor. Since 1973, male or female homosexuality has been deleted from the *Diagnostic and Statistical Manual of Mental Disorders*, published by the American Psychiatric Association. Most experts today emphasize the biological and genetic factors determining sexual preference, over psychological determinants. In my estimation, the complex matter of sexual preference and attraction is still one of the greatest unsolved mysteries—and may always remain so.

18. Neumann, "Fear of the Feminine," p. 13.

19. According to psychoanalyst Heinz Kohut (1913–1981), *mirroring* is a process whereby the mother empathically "mirrors" the intrinsic value and lovability of the infant in her facial features, smile, twinkling eyes, etc. *Modeling* involves the viewing of (in this case) the mother as a "role model" the daughter can identify with and emulate.

20. Neumann, "Fear of the Feminine," p. 23.

21. There are, of course, those women who have no interest whatsoever in achieving heterosexual intimacy. Again, Neumann's views are dismissed by most today as old-fashioned, biased, and outmoded.

22. *The APA Monitor* 25, no. 9 (Sept. 1994) : 1.

23. See C. H. Sommers, *Who Stole Feminism?*, pp. 192-194. Sommers suggests that these figures may be exaggerated by feminists and the media. More conservative estimates confirm, however, that at least 2 million women annually are in fact battered by boyfriends or husbands.

24. Paul Carus, *The History of the Devil and the Idea of Evil* (La Salle, Ill.: Open Court, 1974), p. 328.

25. See Felix Morrow in his foreword to Montague Sommers, *The History of Witchcraft and Demonology* (New Hyde Park, N.Y.: University Books, 1956), p. viii.

26. May, *Freedom and Destiny*, p. 113.

27. This archetypal fear of the opposite sex—and of one's own anima or animus—may be seen in the idea of *succubi* and *incubi:* female (succubus) and male (incubus) demons believed from biblical times to sexually overpower people while asleep, and therefore, most vulnerable. See chapter five, note 1.

28. Wendy Doniger O'Flaherty, *The Origins of Evil in Hindu Mythology* (Berkeley: University of California Press, 1976), p. 27.

29. Homer, *The Odyssey : The Story of Odysseus*, trans. W. H. D. Rouse (New York: New American Library, 1937), p. 138.

30. Thomas Bulfinch, *Bulfinch's Mythology*, illus. ed. (New York: Avenel Books, 1979), pp. 13-14.

31. Edith Hamilton, *Mythology* : *Timeless Tales of Gods and Heroes*, illustrated by Steele Savage (New York: New American Library, 1969), pp. 143–144.

32. Sam Keen, *Faces of the Enemy: The Psychology of Enmity* (New York: Harper and Row, 1988), p. 131.

33. C. H. Sommers, *Who Stole Feminism?*, pp. 41–42.

34. This remarkable process has been intelligently discussed by Sam Keen (1986) as already mentioned, and in far greater depth by Robert Jay Lifton (*The Nazi Doctors* : *Medical Killing and the Psychology of Genocide* [New York: Basic Books, 1986]) and Hannah Arendt among others. Lifton speaks of "doubling" as the dissociative psychological defense mechanism whereby Nazi physicians participated in the evils conducted in German concentration camps. Lifton's archetypal notion of "doubling" is derived in part from Otto Rank's writings on "the double," and, as we shall see, corresponds closely to Jung's conception of "the shadow."

35. See chapter five, for example, in *Who Stole Feminism*.

36. See Richard Gelles and Murray Straus, *Physical Violence in American Families* : *Risk Factors and Adaptations to Violence in 8, 145 Families* (New Brunswick, N.J.: Transaction Publishers, 1990).

37. Anne Campbell, *Men, Women, and Aggression* (New York: Basic Books, 1993), p. 1. In other recent studies, female researchers found—much to their surprise—that college women were reportedly *more* likely to behave violently toward their male partners than vice versa. See *The APA Monitor* 12, no. 9 (Sept. 1995): 48.

38. Ibid., p. 144.

39. Ibid., p. 160.

Chapter 3. The Psychology of Evil

1. *Webster's New Collegiate Dictionary* (Springfield, Mass.: G. and C. Merriam, 1977), p. 396.

2. *Webster's Third New International Dictionary*, unabridged (Springfield, Mass.: Merriam-Webster, 1986), p. 789.

3. There have, however, been some recent exceptions. For example, immediately following the 1995 bombing of a federal building in Oklahoma City, President Clinton called the deed "evil," and the perpetrators "evil cowards." (The men

accused of this mass murder of almost two hundred fellow Americans—some children— are reported to be "outraged" at the federal government.) And, of course, many recall President Reagan's infamous remarks about Russia, the "evil empire."

4. Liliane Frey-Rohn, "Evil from the Psychological Point of View," in *Evil*, Studies in Jungian Thought Series (Evanston, Ill.: Northwestern University Press, 1967), p. 153.

5. N. Sanford, C. Comstock, and associates, *Sanctions for Evil: Sources of Social Destructiveness* (San Francisco: Jossey-Bass, 1971), p. 5.

6. See, for example, Karl Menninger, *Whatever Became of Sin?* (New York: Bantam Books, 1978).

7. Frey-Rohn, "Evil from the Psychological Point of View," p. 160.

8. See Jung's excellent essay "Good and Evil in Analytical Psychology" (1959), in *Civilization in Transition,* 2d ed., vol. 10 of *The Collected Works of C. G. Jung,* trans. R. F. C. Hull, Bollingen Series XX (Princeton N.J.: Princeton University Press, 1970), as well as my discussion of *discernment* in the closing chapters of this volume.

9. William Shakespeare, *The Tragedy of Hamlet Prince of Denmark*, act 2, scene 2, p. 132.

10. Justin Martyr, *First Apology* 28. Cited by Elaine Pagels in *The Origin of Satan* (New York: Random House, 1995), p. 122.

11. Carus, *The History of the Devil and the Idea of Evil*, p. 440.

12. While some well-known interpreters of Asian religions (like Alan Watts, for instance) have suggested that evil is dismissed by most as merely illusory, Wendy Doniger O'Flaherty, in her book *The Origins of Evil in Hindu Mythology* (Berkeley: University of California Press, 1976), refutes this common misconception, corroborating the universality of *theodicy* (the existential problem of evil and its attempted resolution).

13. John A. Sanford, *Evil: The Shadow Side of Reality* (New York: Crossroad, 1990), p. 142.

14. M. Scott Peck, *People of the Lie: The Hope for Healing Human Evil* (New York: Simon and Schuster, 1983), p. 67.

15. For more on "malignant narcissism," see Erich Fromm, *The Anatomy of Human Destructiveness* (New York: Fawcett Crest Books, 1973).

16. Ibid., see p. 128, for example.

17. Rollo May, "Reflections and Commentary," in Clement Reeves, *The Psychology of Rollo May: A Study in Existential Theory and Psychotherapy* (San Francisco: Jossey Bass, 1977), p. 305.

18. Sigmund Freud, "Psychopathology of Everyday Life," in *The Basic Writings of Sigmund Freud*, trans. and ed. A. A. Brill (New York: The Modern Library, 1938), p. 165.

19. Sigmund Freud, "Totem and Taboo," in *The Basic Writings of Sigmund Freud*, pp. 857–858.

20. G. van der Leeuw, *Religion in Essence and Manifestation*, trans. J. E. Turner (Princeton, N.J.: Princeton University Press, 1986), pp. 134–135.

21. Freud, "Totem and Taboo," in *The Basic Writings of Sigmund Freud*, p. 858.

22. O'Flaherty, *The Origins of Evil in Hindu Mythology*, p. 57.

23. In James Hillman, *Healing Fiction* (New York: Station Hill, 1983), p. 63. See chapter two, "The Pandaemonium of Images—*Jung's Contribution to Know Thyself*," pp. 53–81.

24. Carl Jung, *Psychological Types*, vol. 6 of *The Collected Works of C. G. Jung* (1971), p. 109.

25. My statement about the archetypal contents of delusions in psychotic patients is not meant to discount the existence of U.F.O.'s (unidentified flying objects) nor their possible physical reality. For those interested in a psychological perspective on this fascinating phenomenon, see Carl Jung, "Flying Saucers: A Modern Myth" in *Civilization in Transition*, pp. 589–824.

26. B. C. Dietrich, *Death, Fate and the Gods* (London: University of London, Athlone Press, 1965), p. 358.

27. This description of daimons as "invisible and wrapped in mist" can be found in B. C. Dietrich, *Tradition in Greek Religion* (Berlin: Walter de Gruyter, 1986), p. 95. According to James Hillman: "Daimon is the original Greek spelling for these figures who later became *demons* because of the Christian view and *daemons* in positive contradistinction to that view" (*Healing Fiction*, p. 55). However, for our purposes in this volume, *daimon* (the Greek spelling) and *daemon* (the Latin spelling) can, in most cases, be considered similar—if not identical—terms, in contradistinction to the contemporary, unipolar conception of *demons*.

28. May, *Love and Will*, p. 123.

29. Ibid., p. 130.

30. R. H. Barrow, *Plutarch and His Times* (Bloomington, Indiana: Indiana University Press, 1967), p. 86.

31. M. L. von Franz, *Projection and Re-Collection in Jungian Psychology: Reflections of the Soul* (La Salle, Illinois: Open Court, 1985), p. 108.

32. Barrow, *Plutarch and His Times*, pp. 90–91.

33. E. R. Dodds, *The Greeks and the Irrational* (Berkeley: University of California Press, 1951), pp. 10–11.

34. Translation by E. R. Dodd's of Plato's *Symposium*, in E. R. Dodds, *Pagan and Christian in an Age of Anxiety: Some Aspects of Religious Experience from Marcus Aurelius to Constantine* (Cambridge, England: Cambridge University Press, 1965), pp. 86–87. In most other English translations of Plato's *Symposium*, the unique Greek word δαιμων (daimon) is replaced with terms such as "spirit," "divinity," or even "higher force" or "power." However, none of these quite captures the dual yet indivisible quality of "daimon." See, for example, the revised version of the Jowett translation, which has Diotima speak of " ' . . . a great spirit, (*daimon*) . . . ' " in *Plato: Euthyphro, Crita, Apology, and Symposium*, A Gateway Edition (Chicago: Henry Regnery Company, 1953), p. 117.

35. Cited in ibid., pp. 89–90.

36. Paul Friedlander, *Plato: An Introduction*, trans. Hans Meyerhoff, Bollingen Series LIX, Bollingen Foundation (New York: Pantheon Books, 1958), pp. 34–35.

37. D. O'Brien, *Empedocles' Cosmic Cycle*, 2d ed. (Cambridge, England: Cambridge University Press, 1953), p. 331.

38. Dodds, *Pagan and Christian in an Age of Anxiety*, p. 38.

39. Dietrich, *Death, Fate and the Gods*, pp. 49–50.

40. von Franz, *Projection and Re-Collection in Jungian Psychology*, p. 108. See also Rudolf Otto's classic study, *The Idea of the Holy*, trans. John W. Harvey (Oxford: Oxford University Press, 1958) for a further description of this "daemonic dread."

41. Carl Jung, *Aion: Researches Into the Phenomenology of the Self*, 2d ed., vol. 9, part 2 of *The Collected Works of C. G. Jung* (1968), p. 27.

42. Jeffrey Burton Russell, *The Prince of Darkness* : *Radical Evil and the Power of Good in History* (Ithaca, N.Y.: Cornell University Press, 1988), p. 25.

43. May, *Love and Will*, p. 138.

44. Russell, *The Prince of Darkness*, pp. 29, 45.

45. From the foreword by Felix Morrow in *The History of Witchcraft and Demonology* by M. Sommers, p. vii.

46. *The Holy Bible* containing the Old and New Testaments, rev. standard ed. (New York: Thomas Nelson and Sons, 1952), pp. 789–790. Note that this biblical "demoniac" appears to have been in an unremitting state of rage.

47. Elaine Pagels, *The Origin of Satan* (New York: Random House, 1995), pp. 40, 143.

48. Hillman, *Healing Fiction*, p. 65.

49. van der Leeuw, *Religion in Essence and Manifestation*, p. 137.

50. David Manning White, *Eternal Quest: The Search for God*, vol. 1, The Paragon Treasury of Inspirational Quotations and Spiritual Wisdom (New York: Paragon House, 1991), p. 248.

51. Russell, *The Prince of Darkness*, pp. 5-7.

52. *Psychology Today* 22, no. 12 (Dec. 1988): 8.

53. "Satan," *Life* 12, no. 7 (June 1989): 48.

54. See Sigmund Freud, "A Neurosis of Demoniacal Possession in the Seventeenth Century," in vol. 4 of *Collected Papers*, The International Psycho-Analytical Library, no. 10, ed. Ernest Jones, trans. under the supervision of Joan Riviere (London: Hogarth Press, 1959). Originally published in *Imago* (1923).

55. Ibid., pp. 451–452n.

56. Louis Berkowitz, "The Devil Within," *Psychoanalytic Review* 55, no. 1 (1968): 28.

57. Ibid., pp. 28, 32.

58. See, for instance, Mario Jacoby, Verena Kast, and Ingrid Riedel, *Witches, Ogres, and the Devil's Daughter: Encounters with Evil in Fairy Tales*, trans. Michael H. Kohn (Boston: Shambhala, 1992).

59. May, "Reflections and Commentary," p. 304.

60. May, *Love and Will*, p. 138.

61. Russell, *The Prince of Darkness*, pp. 10–28. For more on the Hindu idea of *Brahman*, see, for instance, *The Song of God: Bhagavad-Gita*, trans. Swami Prabhavananda and Christopher Isherwood, introduction by Aldous Huxley (New York: New American Library, 1972).

62. Rudolf Otto (1958) writes that " 'ferocity' is the origin of Lucifer, in whom the mere potentiality of evil is actualized. . . . It might be said that Lucifer is 'fury', . . . the *mysterium tremendum* cut loose from the other elements and intensified to *mysterium horrendum*. . . . It is a horror that is in some sort numinous, and we might designate the object of it as the negatively numinous. . . . In all religions, 'the devilish' plays its part and has its place as that which, opposed to the divine, has yet something in common with it" (*The Idea of the Holy*, pp. 106–107n.).

63. Hermann Hesse, *Demian: The Story of Emil Sinclair's Youth*, trans. Michael Roloff and Michael Lebeck, introduction by Thomas Mann (New York: Bantam Books, 1965), p. 78.

64. Ibid., p. 93. As regards the drawbacks of giving concrete form to living myths like "Abraxas" or "the daimonic," recall one of the first commandments communicated to Moses on Mount Sinai: "Thou shalt not make unto thee any graven image, or any likeness *of any thing* that *is*. . . " (Exodus 20:4 AV). We will discuss further the definite dangers of reification in chapter four.

65. Jung, *Aion*, p. 10.

Chapter 4. Myths of the Unconscious

1. *Materialism* is the philosophical doctrine deeming matter the only reality, even in mental phenomena.

2. See chapter two for definitions of "masculine" and "feminine."

3. May, "Psychotherapy and the Daimonic," p. 210.

4. Rollo May, *The Cry for Myth* (New York: W. W. Norton, 1991), p. 15.

5. Aniela Jaffé, *The Myth of Meaning* : *Jung and the Expansion of Consciousness,* trans. R. F. C. Hull (New York: Penguin Books, 1975), p. 18.

6. See Rudolf Otto, *The Idea of the Holy* : *An Inquiry into the Non-Rational Factor in the Idea of the Divine and Its Relation to the Rational,* trans. John W. Harvey (Oxford: Oxford University Press, 1958). According to Otto: "Representations of spirits and similar conceptions [such as derived from "imaginative 'myth' " and "intellectualist Scholasticism"] are . . . all . . . modes of 'rationalizing' a precedent experience, to which they are subsidiary. They are attempts in some way or other, it little matters how, to guess the riddle it propounds, and their effect is at the same time always to weaken and deaden the experience itself. . . " (pp. 26–27). Nevertheless, I would argue, we *need* such myths to make sense of our "daemonic dread," despite their drawbacks. The critical question, of course, is which myths or scientific models have the fewest drawbacks, and which serve to encourage rather than to suppress our experience of the daimonic.

7. Jung, *Psychological Types,* vol. 6 of *The Collected Works of C. G. Jung,* p. 475.

8. Henri F. Ellenberger, *The Discovery of the Unconscious: The History and Evolution of Dynamic Psychiatry* (New York: Basic Books, 1970), p. 562n. For an exceedingly lucid (but somewhat dated) explication and comparative analysis

of the evolution of depth psychology, see also Ira Progoff, *The Death and Rebirth of Psychology: An Integrative Evaluation of Freud, Adler, Jung and Rank and the Impact of Their Culminating Insights on Modern Man* (New York: The Julian Press, 1956). For Freud's own version of events, see Sigmund Freud, *On the History of the Psycho-Analytic Movement*, vol. 14 of *The Standard Edition of the Complete Psychological Works of Sigmund Freud*, trans. James Strachey, in collaboration with Anna Freud, assisted by Alix Strachey and Alan Tyson, and Angela Richards (London: Hogarth Press and the Institute of Psycho-Analysis, 1914). For his part, Progoff defines "depth psychology" as "the study of man and all that pertains to him in terms of the magnitude of the human personality and the dimensions of experience that underlie and transcend consciousness" (p. 23).

9. Sigmund Freud, "Psycho-analysis," in vol. 5 of *Collected Papers*, The International Psycho-Analytical Library, no. 37, ed. Ernest Jones and James Strachey (New York: Basic Books, 1959), p. 127.

10. Sigmund Freud, *Introductory Lectures on Psychoanalysis* (formerly titled *General Introduction to Psychoanalysis*), trans. and ed. James Strachey (New York: Liveright Publishing Corporation, 1966), p. 113.

11. Josef Breuer and Sigmund Freud, *Studies on Hysteria*, trans. and ed. James Strachey, in collaboration with Anna Freud (New York: Basic Books, 1957), p. 250.

12. Sigmund Freud, *A General Introduction to Psychoanalysis*, trans. and rev. Joan Riviere, preface by Ernest Jones and G. Stanley Hall (New York: Washington Square Press, 1952), pp. 268–269.

13. Sigmund Freud, *The Ego and the Id*, The International Psycho-Analytical Library, no. 12, sixth impression, ed. Ernest Jones, trans. Joan Riviere (London: The Hogarth Press, 1950), p. 9.

14. Freud, *Introductory Lectures on Psychoanalysis*, p. 113.

15. Carl Jung, *The Structure and Dynamics of the Psyche*, 2d ed., vol. 8 of *The Collected Works of C. G. Jung* (1969), p. 185.

16. Ibid., pp. 133–134 .

17. Rollo May, in R. May, E. Angel, H. Ellenberger, eds., *Existence : A New Dimension in Psychiatry and Psychology* (New York: Simon and Schuster, 1958), pp. 90–91.

18. Otto Rank, *Beyond Psychology* (New York: Dover, 1958), pp. 39, 38.

19. Georg Groddeck, *Das Buch vom Es: Psychoanalytische Briefe an eine Freundin* (Vienna: Internationaler Psychoanalytischer Verlag, 1923). Translated into English as *The Book of the Id* (New York: Nervous and Mental Disease

Publishing Co., 1928). For more on Freud's friend, Georg Groddeck, see Martin Grotjahn, *The Voice of the Symbol* (New York: Dell Publishing, 1971), chapter seven.

20. Freud, *The Ego and the Id*, p. 28n.

21. Ellenberger, *The Discovery of the Unconscious*, p. 844.

22. Freud, *The Ego and the Id*, p. 30.

23. Sigmund Freud, "Analysis Terminable and Interminable," in vol. 5 of *Collected Papers*, p. 337.

24. Sigmund Freud, *New Introductory Lectures on Psychoanalysis and Other Works*, vol. 22 of *The Standard Edition of the Complete Psychological Works of Sigmund Freud*, trans. and ed. James Strachey, in collaboration with Anna Freud, assisted by Alix Strachey and Alan Tyson, and Angela Richards (London: Hogarth Press and the Institute for Psycho-Analysis, 1932–36), p. 73.

25. See Sigmund Freud, *Beyond the Pleasure Principle*, vol. 18 of *The Standard Edition of the Complete Psychological Works of Sigmund Freud* (1920–22).

26. Sigmund Freud, *Moses and Monotheism, an Outline of Psycho-Analysis and OtherWorks*, vol. 23 of *The Standard Edition of the Complete Psychological Works of Sigmund Freud* (1937–39), p. 300.

27. Carl Jung, *The Symbolic Life*, 2d ed., vol. 18 of *The Collected Works of C. G. Jung* (1980), p. 128.

28. Jung, *Aion*, p. 266.

29. Aniela Jaffé in C. G. Jung, *Memories, Dreams, Reflections*, recorded and ed. Aniela Jaffé, trans. R. and C. Winston (New York: Pantheon Books, 1961), pp. 386–387.

30. Jung, *Aion*, p. 266.

31. Russell, *The Prince of Darkness*, pp. 246–247.

32. Jung, *Memories, Dreams, Reflections*, pp. 336–337.

33. Ellenberger, *The Discovery of the Unconscious*, p. 707.

34. Jung, *The Symbolic Life*, p. 648.

35. May, *Love and Will*, p. 123.

36. Ibid., p. 143. See also May's fond reminiscences of his friendship with former mentor, Paul Tillich, in *Paulus: Tillich as Spiritual Teacher*, rev. ed. (Dallas: Saybrook Publishing, 1988).

37. See, for example, Paul Tillich, *The Courage to Be* (New Haven: Yale University Press, 1952): "The courage to affirm oneself must include the courage to affirm one's own demonic depth. . . . This could happen [in some circles, such as the Romantics and Bohemians] because the demonic was not considered unambiguously negative but was thought to be part of the creative power of being" (p. 122). Though Tillich still spells it "demonic," and elsewhere employs this term in the negative sense, he is obviously speaking here of the "daimonic."

38. May, "Reflections and Commentary," p. 305.

39. Jung, *Memories, Dreams, Reflections*, pp. 331-332.

40. May in R. May, E. Angel, and H. Ellenberger, eds., *Existence: A New Dimension in Psychiatry and Psychology*, p. 86.

41. Jaffé, in *Memories, Dreams, Reflections*, p. 387.

42. Frey-Rohn, "Evil from the Psychological Point of View," pp. 176–177.

43. Jung, *The Structure and Dynamics of the Psyche*, pp. 368, 287; and Carl Jung, *Psychology and Alchemy*, 2d ed., vol. 12 of *The Collected Works of C. G. Jung* (1968), p. 46.

44. Frey-Rohn, "Evil from the Psychological Point of View," p. 162.

45. May, *Love and Will*, p. 152.

46. Rollo May, *Psychology and the Human Dilemma* (Princeton, N.J.: D. Van Nostrand, 1967), p. 136.

47. Rollo May in R. May and L. Caligor, *Dreams and Symbols: Man's Unconscious Language* (New York: Basic Books, 1968), pp. 6, 8.

48. Rollo May in R. May, ed., *Existential Psychology*, 2d ed. (New York: Random House, 1969), p. 34.

49. Rollo May, *The Discovery of Being : Writings in Existential Psychology* (New York: W. W. Norton, 1986), p. 96.

50. Paul Tillich, *Morality and Beyond*, Religious Perspectives Series, ed. Ruth Nanda Anshen, vol. 9 (New York: Harper and Row, 1963), pp. 20–21.

51. May, *Love and Will*, p. 139.

52. Rollo May, "Existential Bases of Psychotherapy," in May, ed., *Existential Psychology*, p. 82.

53. May, *Love and Will*, p. 308.

54. Jung, *The Symbolic Life*, p. 690.

55. Rollo May, *The Meaning of Anxiety*, rev. ed. (New York: W. W. Norton, 1977), p. 159. Specifically, May alludes to Jung's opening chapter "The Autonomy

of the Unconscious," from *Psychology and Religion: West and East*, 2d ed., vol. 11 of *The Collected Works of C. G. Jung* (1969).

56. May, *Love and Will*, p. 196.

57. May, "Reflections and Commentary," p. 305.

58. *Repression* is, by definition, an *unconscious* defense mechanism, meaning we have no awareness of the content nor the process of the repression. *Suppression* is considered a *conscious* defense mechanism, wherein we are aware of the fact that we choose to suppress rather than attend to or express something. As in all such matters, there is no absolute dividing line distinguishing the former from the latter.

59. May, *Psychology and the Human Dilemma*, p. 175.

60. May, *Love and Will*, p. 124.

61. von Franz, *Projection and Re-Collection in Jungian Psychology*, p. 145.

62. Jung, *Psychology and Alchemy*, p. 41; and Jung, *Psychological Types*, p. 460.

63. May in R. May, E. Angel, and H. Ellenberger, eds., *Existence: A New Dimension in Psychiatry and Psychology*, p. 11.

64. May, *Love and Will*, p. 136.

65. Ibid., p. 130.

66. In Plato's *Symposium*, Diotima tells Socrates that "only through the daimonic is there intercourse and conversation between men and gods, whether in the waking state or during sleep. And the man who is expert in such intercourse is a daimonic man, compared with whom the experts in arts or handicrafts are but journeymen" (trans. E. R. Dodds in *Pagan and Christian in an Age of Anxiety*, p. 37). For the full context, readers are referred directly to Plato, *The Symposium*. See also Jung's recounting of his prolonged and dangerous encounter with the daimonic in his autobiography, *Memories, Dreams, Reflections*, as well as my own discussion of "eudaimonic genius" in chapter eight.

67. Frey-Rohn, "Evil from the Psychological Point of View," pp. 175–176. We must remember, however, that there is a limit to which we can—or should—claim personal responsibility in life, as later discussed in chapter nine.

68. J. Sanford, *Evil: The Shadow Side of Reality*, p. 110.

Chapter 5. The Possession Syndrome

1. See, for example, T. K. Oesterreich, *Possession and Exorcism Among Primitive Races in Antiquity, the Middle Ages, and Modern Times* (New York:

Causeway Books, 1974). For more on modern manifestations of possession or "demonopathy," read P. M. Yap, "The Possession Syndrome: A Comparison of Hong Kong and French Findings," *The Journal of Mental Science (The British Journal of Psychiatry)* 106, no. 442 (Jan. 1960): 114–137. Yap, a psychiatrist, compared and contrasted the extensive clinical documentation of possession in the French psychiatric literature with his observations of psychiatric patients in Hong Kong, noting that in certain French cases, possession is believed to be not by Satan, but rather by "succubi, incubi and animal familiars," and that these cases "are probably closer to those that are seen in Hong Kong" (p. 125). The *succubus* is a female demon believed to possess men with lust; the *incubus* is her male counterpart. Here, writes Gerardus van der Leeuw, "we see the *sexual* root of the idea of the demon; for the sexual or ejaculatory dream called into existence the countless forms of *incubi* and *succubi*. Thus the Babylonian *ardat lile*, the 'maid of the night', persisted in Jewish tradition as Lilith, 'Adam's first wife' " (*Religion in Essence and Manifestation*, p. 138). See fig. 1, which some believe to be an image of Lilith, the first female. Also, see note 27 in chapter two.

2. Esther Leonard De Vos, "Voodoo: Our Link with the Occult," in *The Analytic Life: Personal and Professional Aspects of Being a Jungian Analyst*, ed. the New England Society of Jungian Analysts (Boston: Sigo Press, 1988), p. 45.

3. M. Sommers, *The History of Witchcraft and Demonology*, p. 202.

4. Carl Jung, *The Spirit in Man, Art, and Literature*, vol. 15 of *The Collected Works of C. G. Jung* (1966), p. 42.

5. Harold Kaplan and Benjamin Sadock, *Synopsis of Psychiatry: Behavioral Sciences; Clinical Psychiatry*, 6th ed. (rev.) (Baltimore: Williams and Wilkins, 1991), pp. 406–407.

6. Freud, "A Neurosis of Demoniacal Possession in the Seventeenth Century," in vol. 4 of *Collected Papers*, p. 451.

7. Jung, *The Structure and Dynamics of the Psyche*, 2d ed., vol. 8 of *The Collected Works of C. G. Jung*, pp. 304–305.

8. M. Sommers, *The History of Witchcraft and Demonology*, p. 198. Note the emphasis on the individual's role in the matter of how the daimonic manifested itself.

9. Morton Kelsey, *Discernment: A Study in Ecstasy and Evil* (New York: Paulist Press, 1978), pp. 59–60.

10. *The Holy Bible* containing the Old and New Testaments, Authorized King James Version (Boston: The Christian Science Publishing Society, n.d.), p. 1267.

11. Jung, *The Structure and Dynamics of the Psyche*, p. 368. Jung misspeaks here by saying that such a person is "not legitimately ill." For we know (as did

he) that the demoniac or possessed person may be very ill indeed, both in body and soul. But theirs is predominantly a *spiritual* or *psychological* disease that sometimes manifests somatically, rather than a primarily biological or physically caused affliction. Such "psychosomatic" syndromes are discussed summarily in chapter six.

12. See the *Diagnostic and Statistical Manual of Mental Disorders*, 4th ed. (Washington, D.C.: American Psychiatric Association, 1994).

13. Jon Allen, *Bulletin of the Menninger Clinic* 57, no. 3 (1993): 405–406.

14. *Diagnostic and Statistical Manual of Mental Disorders*, 3d ed. rev. (Washington, D.C.: American Psychiatric Association, 1987), p. 269.

15. Ellenberger, *The Discovery of the Unconscious*, p. 13.

16. Jung, *The Structure and Dynamics of the Psyche*, p. 121. See Breuer and Freud, *Studies on Hysteria*.

17. Carl Jung, *Psychology and Religion: West and East*, 2d ed., vol. 11 of *The Collected Works of C. G. Jung* (1969), p. 14.

18. See J. Sanford's fine analysis of Stevenson's story in "The Problem of the Shadow and Evil in *The Strange Case of Dr. Jekyll and Mr. Hyde*," in *Evil: The Shadow Side of Reality*.

19. *ICD-10: The ICD-10 Classification of Mental and Behavioural Disorders* (Geneva: World Health Organization, 1992), p. 156.

20. See Jung, "The Definition of Demonism," in *The Symbolic Life*, vol. 18 of *The Collected Works of C. G. Jung*, p. 648.

21. D. J. Henderson, "Exorcism, Possession, and the Dracula Cult: A Synopsis of Object-Relations Psychology," *Bulletin of the Menninger Clinic* 40, no. 6 (Nov. 1976): 603.

22. Ibid., p. 627.

23. For those interested in further readings in this area, see, for example, Peter Buckley, ed., *Essential Papers on Object Relations* (New York: New York University Press, 1986).

24. Jung, *Memories, Dreams, Reflections*, p. 347.

25. May, *Love and Will*, p. 125.

26. M. Cramer, "Psychopathology and Shamanism in Rural Mexico: A Case Study of Spirit Possession," *The British Journal of Medical Psychology* 53 (1980): 67.

27. Oesterreich, *Possession and Exorcism,* p. 17.

28. Peck, *People of the Lie,* p. 192.

29. F. D. Whitwell and M. G. Barker, "Possession in Psychiatric Patients in Britain," *The British Journal of Medical Psychology* 53 (1980): 287.

30. Ibid., p. 293.

31. Oesterreich, *Possession and Exorcism,* p. 121.

32. R. Spitzer, M. Gibbon, A. Skodol, J. Williams, M. First, *DSM-111-R CaseBook,* rev. ed. (Washington, D.C.: American Psychiatric Press, 1989), p. 391.

33. *Diagnostic and Statistical Manual of Mental Disorders* (*DSM-III-R*), pp. 449–450.

34. Whitwell and Barker, "Possession in Psychiatric Patients in Britain," p. 292.

35. May, "Psychotherapy and the Daimonic," p. 203.

36. Jung, *The Structure and Dynamics of the Psyche,* p. 98.

37. Alfred Ribi, *Demons of the Inner World: Understanding Our Hidden Complexes,* trans. M. Kohn (Boston: Shambhala, 1990), pp. 48–49.

38. Erich Fromm, *The Anatomy of Human Destructiveness* (New York: Fawcett Crest, 1973), p. 308.

39. Tom Mcintyre, "Millennium Witness," *San Francisco Examiner Magazine,* Oct. 9, 1994, pp. 13–24.

40. Robert A. Johnson, *We: Understanding the Psychology of Romantic Love* (San Francisco: Harper and Row, 1983), p. xiii.

41. Rollo May, *The Courage to Create* (New York: Bantam Books, 1976), p. 49.

42. M. Sommers, *The History of Witchcraft and Demonology,* pp. 200–201.

43. Kay Redfield Jamison, *Touched with Fire: Manic Depressive Illness and the Artistic Temperament* (New York: The Free Press, 1993), p. 7.

44. Following the Greek philosopher Heraclitus (530–470 B.C.), Jung termed the shifting of one extreme into its opposite or compensatory polarity "enantiodromia."

45. Cramer, "Psychopathology and Shamanism in Rural Mexico," p. 68.

46. For readers dubious about the modern belief in Voodoo and "possession" here in high-tech America, consider the following gruesome story, reported in the *San Francisco Examiner* on Sunday, July 10, 1994 by David Usborne: Three sisters in Arcadia, Louisiana claimed that, while driving on a Texas freeway, the

steering wheel of their car came alive, "mutating into a monstrous demon" (p. A-3). The demon then took possession of the driver, causing her to career recklessly down the road. By the time the bizarre episode ended, she was admitted to a hospital emergency room *with both eyes torn out*. As the twisted tale unfolded, it was learned that one of the sisters had been told by a local "hoodoo" (a variant of *voodoo*) healer that the source of her headaches was demons trying to possess her. Terrified, she and her two sisters fled their Louisiana home in a panic, hoping to elude the evil demons. But to no avail. Though the sisters claimed it was the demonic steering wheel that scratched out the driver's eyes, the more likely explanation is perhaps still more disturbing: It seems that in hoodoo lore, introduced to this country some two centuries ago, eye-gouging is believed to exorcise the evil spirit from the possessed person.

47. De Vos, "Voodoo: Our Link with the Occult," p. 36.

48. Ibid., p. 39.

49. Ibid., pp. 39, 45.

50. Ribi, *Demons of the Inner World*, p. 68.

51. M. Esther Harding, *Psychic Energy: Its Source and Its Transformation*, with a foreword by C. G. Jung, Bollingen Series X (Princeton, N.J.: Princeton University Press, 1973), p. 152.

52. Ibid., pp. 152–154.

Chapter 6. Madness, Mental Disorders, and the Daimonic

1. See Heinz Ansbacher and Rowena Ansbacher, eds., *The Individual Psychology of Alfred Adler: A Systematic Presentation in Selections from His Writings* (New York: Harper and Row, 1956), p. 111. See also Viktor Frankl, *The Will to Meaning: Foundations and Applications of Logotherapy* (1969), as well as *Man's Search for Meaning: An Introduction to Logotherapy* (1985), Frankl's finest treatment of this subject.

2. Ellenberger, *The Discovery of the Unconscious*, p. 275.

3. Friedrich Nietzsche, *Ecce Homo: How One Becomes What One Is*, trans. Clifton P. Fadiman in *The Philosophy of Friedrich Nietzsche*, introduction by Willard Huntington Wright (New York: The Modern Library, n.d.), pp. 15–16.

4. Ellenberger, *The Discovery of the Unconscious*, p. 274.

5. George Bach and Herb Goldberg, *Creative Aggression: The Art of Assertive Living* (New York: Avon Books, 1974), p. 128.

6. Sigmund Freud, "The Libido Theory," in vol. 5 of *Collected Papers*, pp. 134–135.

7. See R. Zaslow and M. Menta, *The Psychology of the Z-Process*, on the role of repressed rage in psychosis.

8. Sigmund Freud, "Why War?", in vol. 5 of *Collected Papers*, pp. 280–281.

9. See Ansbacher and Ansbacher, eds., *The Individual Psychology of Alfred Adler*, p. 30; and Carl Jung, *Wandlungen und Symbole der Libido*, later published as *Psychology of the Unconscious* (1916), and *Symbols of Transformation* (1952).

10. Freud, "Analysis Terminable and Interminable," in vol. 5 of *Collected Papers*, pp. 349–350.

11. Michael Stone, "Aggression, Rage, and the 'Destructive Instinct,' Reconsidered from a Psychobiological Point of View," *Journal of the American Academy of Psychoanalysis* 19, no. 4 (1991): 510–511.

12. Ibid., pp. 520–521.

13. Ibid., p. 521.

14. Fromm, *The Anatomy of Human Destructiveness*, p. 462.

15. Ansbacher and Ansbacher, eds., *The Individual Psychology of Alfred Adler*, p. 34.

16. Ibid., p. 48.

17. Ibid., p. 38. High blood pressure can also sometimes have purely physiological causes.

18. Edward Hitschmann, "The History of the Aggression-Impulse," *Samiksa* 1 (Calcutta, India: 1947): 139–140.

19. Freud quoted in ibid., pp. 138–139.

20. Jung, *Symbols of Transformation*, 2d ed., vol. 5 of *The Collected Works of C. G. Jung*, p. 136.

21. See, for instance, Carl Jung, *Freud and Psychoanalysis*, vol. 4 of *The Collected Works of C. G. Jung* (1961), p. 303n.

22. Jung, *Symbols of Transformation*, p. 112.

23. Wilhelm Reich, *The Function of the Orgasm : The Discovery of the Orgone; Sex-Economic Problems of Biological Energy*, vol. 1, trans. Theodore P. Wolfe (New York: World Publishing, 1971), p. 128. As we shall see in the next chapter, this is even more pertinent to the problem of anger and rage in psychotherapy: What does one do with it?

24. Wilhelm Reich, *Character Analysis*, 3d enlarged ed., trans. Vincent R. Carfagno (New York: Simon and Schuster, 1972), p. 368.

25. Reich, *The Function of the Orgasm*, p. 122.

26. Ibid.

27. Ibid., p. 123.

28. May, *The Meaning of Anxiety*, p. 231.

29. Ibid., p. ix.

30. Donald Klein, "Anxiety Reconceptualized," in *Anxiety: New Research and Changing Concepts*, ed. Donald F. Klein and Judith G. Rabkin (New York: Raven Press, 1981), p. 235. In defense of May's position in particular—and the significant degree of truth contained in this theory—I would add the crucially important adjective "functional" to Klein's reference to psychosis, which precludes clearly organically caused mental disorders. However, even in the latter, anxiety can have an exacerbatory—though not necessarily causal—effect on psychopathological symptomatology.

31. May, *The Meaning of Anxiety*, pp. 3–4.

32. The term "pandemonium" derives from the Greek words *pan* (all) and *daimon*. In *Paradise Lost* (1667), Milton names the hub of hell *Pandaemonium:* Satan's palace and meeting place for all daimons.

33. See, for instance, Karen Horney, *The Neurotic Personality of Our Time* (New York: W. W. Norton, 1937).

34. May, *The Meaning of Anxiety*, pp. 164, 165.

35. Freud, *A General Introduction to Psychoanalysis*, p. 410.

36. May, *The Meaning of Anxiety*, p. xv.

37. See Rudolf Otto, *The Idea of the Holy*; and Sören Kierkegaard, *The Concept of Dread*, trans. Walter Lowrie (Princeton, N.J.: Princeton University Press, 1957), and *Fear and Trembling*, trans. Walter Lowrie in *A Kierkegaard Anthology*, ed. Robert Bretall (New York: The Modern Library, 1946).

38. May, *The Meaning of Anxiety*, p. xiv.

39. Readers might remember Ariadne from Greek mythology. It was she who helped her beloved, Theseus, escape the Minotaur's labyrinth by giving him a ball of thread with which to retrace his steps.

40. Stephen M. Johnson, *Humanizing the Narcissistic Style* (New York: W. W. Norton, 1987), p. 39.

41. Heinz Kohut, "Thoughts on Narcissism and Narcissistic Rage," in *The Search for the Self: Selected Writings of Heinz Kohut: 1950–1978* (New York: International University Press, 1978), pp. 637–638.

42. Otto F. Kernberg, *Aggression in Personality Disorders and Perversions* (New Haven: Yale University Press, 1992), pp. viii, 21.

43. Kohut, "Thoughts on Narcissism and Narcissistic Rage," in *The Search for the Self*, p. 652.

44. May, *Freedom and Destiny*, p. 145.

45. See, for instance, the writings of Zaslow and Menta in *The Psychology of the Z-Process*.

46. Mario Jacoby, "Reflections on Heinz Kohut's Concept of Narcissism," in *Psychopathology: Contemporary Jungian Perspectives*, ed. with an introduction by Andrew Samuels (London: The Guilford Press, 1991), p. 143.

47. Psychotherapists have a name for this phenomenon: "projective iden-tification," an unconscious process wherein the patient manages to subtly manipu-late the situation in such a way as to make the therapist feel the patient's unwanted (therefore, "projected") emotions.

48. May, *Freedom and Destiny*, p. 145.

49. *The Complete Grimm's Fairy Tales*, introduction by Padraic Colum, commentary by Joseph Campbell (New York: Pantheon Books, 1972), p. 237.

50. The actual quote from Congreve, the English playwright, reads:

> Heaven has no rage like love to hatred turned,
> Nor hell a fury like a woman scorned.

From *The Mourning Bride* (1697), quoted in *Bartlett's Familiar Quotations* by John Bartlett, ed. Justin Kaplan, 16th ed., rev. (New York: Little Brown and Co., 1992), p. 291.

51. *The Complete Grimm's Fairy Tales*, p. 240.

52. Bruno Bettelheim, *The Uses of Enchantment* (New York: Vintage Books, 1977), p. 234.

53. *The Complete Grimm's Fairy Tales*, p. 240.

54. May, *The Cry for Myth*, p. 204.

55. *The Complete Grimm's Fairy Tales*, p. 240.

56. W. R. D. Fairbairn, "A Revised Psychopathology of the Psychoses and Psychoneuroses," in *Essential Papers on Object Relations,* ed. Peter Buckley (New York: New York University Press, 1986), pp. 95, 97.

57. Jung, *Symbols of Transformation,* p. 404.

58. May, *Freedom and Destiny,* p. 46.

59. See Martin Seligman, "Depression and Learned Helplessness," in *The Psychology of Depression: Contemporary Theory and Research,* ed. R. J. Friedman and M. M. Katz (New York: Wiley and Sons, 1974).

60. See Aaron Beck and Marjorie Weishar, "Cognitive Therapy," in *Current Psychotherapies,* ed. Raymond J. Corsini and Danny Wedding, with the assistance of Judith W. McMahon, 4th ed. (Itasca, Illinois: F. E. Peacock Publishers, 1989), p. 295; and Albert Ellis, "Rational-Emotive Therapy," in *Current Psychotherapies,* p. 197.

61. Harold Mosak, "Adlerian Psychotherapy," in *Current Psychotherapies,* p. 66. According to May, who studied with Adler, this "myth" of oneself may be formed within the first few years of life, and lived out unconsciously into adulthood. Moreover, this "myth" may be composed, as Jung said, of both *personal* and *transpersonal* (i.e., collective or archetypal) material.

62. Paraphrased by Schopenhauer from *The Enchiridion,* by Epictetus, in "The Wisdom of Life," *Complete Essays of Schopenhauer,* trans. T. Bailey Saunders (New York: Willey Book Co., 1942) p. 18.

63. Kaplan and Sadock, *Synopsis of Psychiatry,* p. 405.

64. May, *Love and Will,* p. 175.

65. Kaplan and Sadock, *Synopsis of Psychiatry,* p. 649.

66. Maurizio Fava, et al., "Anger Attacks in Depressed Outpatients and Their Response to Fluoxetine," *Psychopharmacology Bulletin* 27, no. 3 (1991): 275.

67. Peter D. Kramer, *Listening to Prozac: A Psychiatrist Explores Antidepressant Drugs and the Remaking of the Self* (New York: Penguin Books, 1993), p. 147.

68. *Diagnostic and Statistical Manual of Mental Disorders* (*DSM-III-R*), pp. 127–128.

69. Robert Louis Stevenson, *The Strange Case of Dr. Jekyll and Mr. Hyde,* with an introduction by B. Allen Bentley (New York: Airmont, 1964), pp. 88–89.

70. *DSM-IV Draft Criteria,* Task Force on DSM-IV (Washington, D.C.: American Psychiatric Association, 1993), p. H:8. See also *ICD-10: The ICD-10*

Classification of Mental and Behavioural Disorders; Clinical Descriptions and Diagnostic Guidelines (Geneva: World Health Organization, 1992), p. 74.

71. Jerome Jaffe, Thomas Babor, and Diana Fishbein, "Alcoholics, Aggression and Antisocial Personality," *Journal of Studies on Alcohol* 49, no. 3 (1988): 211, 215.

72. Reproduced with permission of author and publisher from: Simón, A. The Berserker/Blind Rage Syndrome as a Potentially New Diagnostic Category for the DSM-III. *Psychological Reports*, 1987, 60, 131–135. Copyright © Psychological Reports 1987. In the Middle Ages, the Berserker Vikings were elite Scandinavian warriors and devotees of Odin who displayed fiercely intimidating fits of rage before and during battle.

73. *Diagnostic and Statistical Manual of Mental Disorders (DSM-IV)*, p. 609.

74. *The APA Monitor* 27, no. 10 (Oct. 1994): 32.

75. Reproduced with permission of author and publisher from: Simón, A. The Berserker/Blind Rage Syndrome as a Potentially New Diagnostic Category for the DSM-III. *Psychological Reports*, 1987, 60, 131–135. Copyright © Psychological Reports 1987, p. 133. Simón does not clearly specify the number of episodes he deems necessary to warrant his diagnosis. It is, in my opinion, doubtful that such a diagnosis of a mental disorder would be appropriate for single, isolated instances, with no previously established pattern of such behavior. The current criteria set by the American Psychiatric Association for "intermittent explosive disorder" include "several discrete episodes of failure to resist aggressive impulses that result in serious assaultive acts or destruction of property" (*Diagnostic and Statistical Manual of Mental Disorders* [*DSM-IV*], p. 612).

76. See, for instance, H. Klüver and P. C. Bucy, "Preliminary Analysis of Functions of the Temporal Lobes in Monkeys," *Archives of Neurology and Psychiatry* 42 (1939); P. Bard and V. B. Mountcastle, "Some Forebrain Mechanisms Involved in Expression of Rage with Special Reference to Suppression of Angry Behavior," *Research Publications of the Association for Research in Nervous and Mental Disease* 27 (1947); J. M. R. Delgado, "Aggression and Defense Under Cerebral Radio Control," in *Aggression and Defense : Neural Mechanisms and Social Patterns,* ed. C. D. Clemente and D. B. Lindsley (Los Angeles: University of California Press, 1967); and J. P. Flynn, "The Neural Basis of Aggression in Cats," in *Neurophysiology and Emotion*, ed. D. C. Glass (New York: Rockefeller University Press, 1967). I further refer those readers interested in delving more deeply into this perplexing matter to such distinguished authors as Konrad Lorenz (*On Aggression,* trans. Marjorie Kerr Wilson [New York: Harcourt Brace Jovanovich, 1966]), and Ashley Montagu (in his rejoinder, *The Nature of Human Aggression* [New York: Oxford University Press, 1976]) for a fuller discussion of the "nature vs. nurture" controversy still confounding the literature.

77. Reproduced with permission of author and publisher from: Simón, A. The Berserker/Blind Rage Syndrome as a Potentially New Diagnostic Category for the DSM-III. *Psychological Reports,* 1987, 60, 131–135. Copyright © Psychological Reports 1987, p. 132.

78. *Testosterone,* for instance, is an androgen which has been associated with aggressiveness in males. Some studies suggest that the presence of an extra Y chromosome in men may intensify aggression and criminal violence by overstimulating testosterone production. (See P. A. Jacobs, M. Brunton, and M. M. Melville, "Aggressive Behavior, Mental Sub-normality, and the XYY Male," *Nature* 208 [1965]: 131–152; also see the analysis by L. F. Jarvik, V. Klodin, and S. S. Matsuyama, "Human Aggression and the Extra Y Chromosome: Fact or Fantasy?", *American Psychologist* 28, no. 8 [1973]: 674–682.) Androgenic (anabolic) *steroids* are sometimes used by athletes to enhance strength and stamina; they influence testosterone levels and can, when taken in very large doses, result in marked anger (so-called "roid rage") and violent—even murderous—behavior.

79. I say that these "twin studies" are inherently flawed because the vast majority of cases fail to take into account the influence of "nurture" (versus "nature") on these genetically identical or similar subjects, who have usually been brought up in the same environment by the same set of parents, had comparable life experiences, psychologically identify with each other, etc.

80. Kaplan and Sadock, *Synopsis of Psychiatry,* p. 325.

81. Gaylin, *The Rage Within,* p. 119.

82. Tavris, *Anger,* pp. 56–57.

83. Ibid., p. 59.

84. *Diagnostic and Statistical Manual of Mental Disorders (DSM-IV),* p. 290.

85. Ibid., p. 302.

86. Kaplan and Sadock, *Synopsis of Psychiatry,* p. 360.

87. *Diagnostic and Statistical Manual of Mental Disorders (DSM-IV),* p. 845.

88. In the *Diagnostic and Statistical Manual of Mental Disorders (DSM-III-R),* p. 444.

89. Ibid., p. 404.

90. The confusing term "psychosomatic" classically connotes the presence of a verifiable medical disorder involving some objective degree of tissue disturbance or damage, exacerbated or brought on by some sort of psychological stress or emotional disturbance. In a less technical, clinical sense, *psychosomatic* refers to the integral, convoluted interconnection between mind *(psyche)* and body *(soma).*

91. Kaplan and Sadock, *Synopsis of Psychiatry*, p. 504.

92. Redford Williams and Virgina Williams, *Anger Kills: Seventeen Strategies for Controlling the Hostility that Can Harm Your Health* (New York: Harper Perennial, 1994), p. 47.

93. Robert Zaslow and Marilyn Menta, *Rage, Resistance, and Holding: Z-Process Approach* (San Jose, Calif.: San Jose State University, 1977), pp. 263–264. "Attention-deficit/hyperactivity disorder," as it is called today, is a complex syndrome believed to be neurological in origin, and often treated with the drug Ritalin. But, based on my own limited clinical experience with this disorder, suppressed anger or rage certainly appear to play some etiological role, both in children and adults.

94. John P. Hatch, et al., "Anger and Hostility in Tension-type Headache," *Headache* 31, no. 5 (1991): 302.

95. Ibid., p. 304.

96. Franz Alexander, *Psychosomatic Medicine: Its Principles and Applications* (New York: W. W. Norton, 1950), pp. 160–162.

97. Gaylin, *The Rage Within*, pp. 55–56.

98. P. H. D. d'Holbach (1822) cited in Erich Fromm, *The Anatomy of Human Destructiveness*, p. 30.

99. Ibid., p. 98.

100. May, *The Discovery of Being*, p. 50.

Chapter 7. Redeeming Our Devils and Demons

1. See David L. Miller, "Orestes: Myth and Dream as Catharsis," in *Myths, Dreams, and Religion*, ed. Joseph Campbell, Essays Sponsored by the Society for the Arts, Religion and Contemporary Culture (New York: E. P. Dutton, 1970).

2. *Holism* is the philosophical principle holding that the part can be comprehended only as it pertains to the whole; and that the whole is synergistically and systemically greater than the sum of its separate parts.

3. See Ira Progoff, *The Death and Rebirth of Psychology: An Integrative Evaluation of Freud, Adler, Jung and Rank and the Impact of Their Culminating Insights on Modern Man* (New York: The Julian Press, 1956).

4. For instance, advocates of "brief therapy" point to statistical studies in which rate of improvement during psychotherapy appears to level off dramatically

somewhere between the eighth and twenty-sixth weekly session. But the intervening variables in such research are numerous, notoriously elusive, and differ from patient to patient and therapist to therapist. Current research indicates that though brief therapy may be sufficient for certain "high-functioning" individuals in situational crises, for the majority of patients, brief therapy has not been proven preferable to more "open-ended" approaches. (See B. Steenbarger, "Duration and Outcome in Psychotherapy," *Professional Psychology* 25, no. 2 [1994]: 111–119.) Moreover, one recent survey conducted by *Consumer Reports* revealed that patients who remained in treatment for more than six months reported more improvement than those who stopped sooner; and that the "people who stayed in treatment for more than two years reported the best outcomes of all" *(Consumer Reports* 60, no. 11 [Nov. 1995]: 739).

5. M. Sperber, "The Daimonic: Freudian, Jungian and Existential Perspectives," *Journal of Analytical Psychology* 20, no. 1 (1975): 49. While I generally agree with Sperber's statement, my own clinical position regarding techniques such as electroshock therapy (which, following a decade-long decline, appears to be coming back into favor) and psychotropic medication may be slightly different. Psychiatric medications, when properly and moderately utilized as an *adjunct* to psychotherapy, can be of great help in the treatment of many disorders. Electroconvulsive therapy (ECT) is admittedly an extreme remedy for an extreme disease—like a severe depression that does not respond to psychotherapy or medication—but can be life saving. (We will be examining several other equally extreme treatments later in this chapter.) Behavior modification may be enormously useful in the treatment of phobic and anxiety disorders, behavior disorders in children, or when working with developmentally disabled individuals. But I believe that even in such cases, these techniques can and should be viewed as methods of assisting patients to confront, rather than avoid, the daimonic conflicts contributing to their problems.

6. Therapists are not the only helping professionals vulnerable to escalating violence. Attorneys report a rising incidence of physical assaults against them by their angry clients. See, for example, Harriet Chiang, "Violent Times, Angry Clients: 'More Dangerous to Be a Lawyer'," in the *San Francisco Chronicle*, May 15, 1995, p. 1.

7. Carl Jung, *Two Essays on Analytical Psychology*, 2d ed., vol. 7 of *The Collected Works of C. G. Jung* (1966), pp. 152–153.

8. *Webster's Third New International Dictionary*, unabridged. (Springfield, Mass.: Merriam-Webster, 1986), p. 353.

9. Miller, "Orestes," p. 29.

10. Ellenberger, *The Discovery of the Unconscious*, p. 46.

11. May, *The Cry for Myth,* p. 162.

12. We will be reviewing some of Rank's contributions later in this chapter.

13. Breuer and Freud, *Studies On Hysteria,* p. 8.

14. See *The Primal Scream* (New York: Delta, Dell, 1970), or *The New Primal Scream: Primal Therapy Twenty Years On* (Wilmington, Del.: Enterprise Pub., 1991), in which Janov reviews the preeminent role of repression in mental and physical disorders.

15. See Aldous Huxley, *The Doors of Perception* and *Heaven and Hell* (New York: Harper Colophon, 1963), wherein Blake is cited: " 'If the doors of perception were cleansed everything would appear to man as it is, infinite.' "

16. Tavris, *Anger,* pp. 43–44.

17. May, *Power and Innocence,* pp. 49–50.

18. According to a poll conducted and published by *Time* magazine (December 27, 1993) 69 percent of Americans believe angels literally exist. On one recent visit to a bookstore, I found an entire section dedicated to books about angels! But what about demons, those other residents of the daimonic? I will be exploring the psychological implications of "angelology" in the next chapter.

19. Bach and Goldberg, *Creative Aggression,* p. 125.

20. May, *The Cry for Myth,* pp. 166–167.

21. Ellenberger, *The Discovery of the Unconscious,* p. 13.

22. May, *The Cry for Myth,* p. 151.

23. Ellenberger, *The Discovery of the Unconscious,* p. 17.

24. Ibid., pp. 18–19. I am presuming that she deliberately swallowed these sharp—and potentially lethal—objects for reasons about which we can only speculate, rather than accepting a more metaphysical explanation, such as their spontaneous materialization.

25. Reverend Blumhardt quoted in ibid., p. 19.

26. Ibid., pp. 21–22. See Gaetano Benedetti, "Blumhardts Seelsorge in der sicht heutiger psychotherapeutischer Kenntnis," *Reformatio* 9 (1960): 474–487, 531–539.

27. Reich, *Character Analysis,* p. 404.

28. For a full explication of the course of this treatment see Reich's chapter 15, "The Schizophrenic Split," pp. 399–503. One immediate question that could be raised—besides the issue of the reliability of Reich's report—is whether this

patient might have been misdiagnosed in the first place. For instance, perhaps she was not schizophrenic at all, but suffered instead from some other sort of psychosis or severe borderline personality disorder. We will probably never know, though this does not necessarily negate the efficacy of Reich's clinical efforts in this extremely difficult case.

29. See Alexander Lowen, *Bioenergetics* (New York: Penguin Books, 1976).

30. Alexander Lowen, *The Language of the Body* (New York: Collier, 1971), p. 352.

31. See R. Zaslow and M. Menta, *The Psychology of the Z-Process*.

32. Ibid., p. 4.

33. Robert Zaslow and Marilyn Menta, *Face to Face with Schizophrenia: Z-Process Approach* (San Jose, Calif.: San Jose State University, 1976), pp. 2–3.

34. Zaslow and Menta, *The Psychology of the Z-Process*, p. 75.

35. Ibid., p. 77. But I would pose the following question: What truly intimate human relationships are without "weakness," vulnerability, and risk? This seems to me an existential given—if not an absolute precondition—of interpersonal intimacy. And it is precisely this interpersonal relationship—with all its foibles, limitations, shortcomings, and potential pitfalls—that plays the paramount part in dealing with the daimonic. If there is to be any comfort at all, it can only come from the unique relationship between therapist and patient, as we shall shortly see.

36. One serious drawback of this "tactile stimulation" technique—a deliberate rubbing of the ribs relied upon to prod the patient into responding to the therapist's posed questions—is the fact that it can cause bruising when engaged in during the lengthy course of extended sessions. Moreover, since this method is physically stressful in general, it is contraindicated for patients with diagnosed physiological vulnerabilities like heart conditions. Indeed, even without the existence of such systemic conditions, these techniques are physically as well as psychologically risky. But as Jung once remarked, some risk is required if treatment for neurosis and psychosis is going to be anything more than ineffectual.

37. Zaslow and Menta, *The Psychology of the Z-Process*, p. 23.

38. Marilyn Menta, personal correspondence, June 30, 1995.

39. Zaslow and Menta, *The Psychology of the Z-Process*, pp. 65–66.

40. Ibid., pp. 150–151.

41. Janov, *The Primal Scream*, p. 322.

42. Zaslow and Menta, *The Psychology of the Z-Process*, p. 149.

43. In Janov's most recent book, *The New Primal Scream: Primal Therapy Twenty Years On* (1991), the word *rage* is referred to only once in the index; *anger* is not mentioned there at all.

44. J. Rosberg and A. A. Stunden, "The Use of Direct Confrontation: The Treatment-Resistant Schizophrenic Patient," *Acta Psychiatr Scand* 81 (1990): 352.

45. Susi George in *The Caduceus,* the Newspaper for San Diego County's Health Care Professional 1, no. 11 (Dec. 1981).

46. Ibid.

47. May, "Psychotherapy and the Daimonic," p. 202.

48. George in *The Caduceus.*

49. Ibid. Unlike Rosberg, Zaslow believes that virtually all forms of psychotherapy with all manner of patients—even "normal neurotics"—are seriously limited by their lack of physical (and therefore, psychological) security around the issue of expressing rage. We will return to this matter toward the end of this chapter.

50. Peck, *People of the Lie,* p. 185.

51. Rosberg believes Zaslow to be "incorrect in his [general] view of [the] limitation of individual therapy." Personal correspondence, December 29, 1981.

52. Malachi Martin is the author of, among other works, *Hostage to the Devil* (New York: Bantam Books, 1977).

53. E. James Lieberman, *Acts of Will: The Life and Work of Otto Rank,* with a new preface (Amherst: University of Massachusetts Press, 1993), p. 404. For more on Rank, see, for instance, Ira Progoff, *The Death and Rebirth of Psychology,* and Ernest Becker, *The Denial of Death* (New York: The Free Press, 1973).

54. Jesse Taft in *Psychoanalytic Review* 18, no. 4 (October 1931): 454–462.

55. See Otto Rank, *Technik der Psychoanalyse,* trans. into English by Jesse Taft as *Will Therapy* (New York: Knopf, 1936).

56. Progoff, *The Death and Rebirth of Psychology,* p. 205.

57. Otto Rank, "The Psychological Approach to Personal Problems," *Journal of the Otto Rank Association* 1, no. 1 (Fall 1966): 17.

58. Lieberman, *Acts of Will,* p. 333.

59. Most existentially oriented or depth psychologists disagree with me on the value and importance of proper diagnosis. My position is that—despite the infamous philosophical pitfalls—formal psychodiagnosis and a well-founded familiarity with psychopathology is an essential basis for successful psychotherapy,

whatever the practitioner's theoretical orientation happens to be. The trick is not to take the diagnostic terminology too terminally, literally, or concretely, always bearing in mind its phenomenological and *metaphorical* meaning.

60. Lieberman, *Acts of Will*, p. 333.

61. Ibid., p. 66.

62. May, *The Discovery of Being*, p. 47.

63. See Irvin Yalom's excellent textbook, *Existential Psychotherapy* (New York: Basic Books, 1980).

64. May, *The Discovery of Being*, p. 153.

65. Jung, *Civilization in Transition*, 2d ed., vol. 10 of *The Collected Works of C. G. Jung*, p. 159.

66. William Barrett, *Irrational Man: A Study in Existential Philosophy* (Garden City, N.Y.: Doubleday Anchor, 1962), p. 220.

67. Jung, *Memories, Dreams, Reflections*, p. 386. The Hebrew prayer "Hear, O Israel, the Lord our God, the Lord is One" may be making reference to the supremacy and divinity of the Self.

68. May in R. May, E. Angel, and H. F. Ellenberger, eds., *Existence*, p. 44.

69. The "ego" is encompassed by the "self." The concept of "ego strength," or the heroic "will"—an important, indeed essential feature of personality development and spiritual growth—is commonly (and erroneously) considered anathema by Western adherents of Oriental psychologies like Hinduism or Buddhism, in which the goal is to eliminate the ego. But the much maligned personal ego cannot simply be bypassed on the path toward "enlightenment," the attaining of the Self. As the equally maligned Indian philosopher-turned-guru, Bhagwan Shree Rajneesh, succinctly states: "First you have to attain a *very* crystallized ego, and then you have to drop it. If you don't attain to a crystallized ego, surrender can never happen to you. How can you surrender something which you have not got? . . . The first part of life for a rightly maturing person is to attain the ego, and the second part—then the circle becomes complete—is to renounce it" (from *The Mustard Seed* [San Francisco: Harper and Row, 1975], pp. 143–144).

70. See May's foreword at the beginning of this book.

71. Quoted in May, *The Discovery of Being*, p. 99.

72. May, *Power and Innocence*, p. 122.

73. *Epilepsy*, a neurological disease, frequently coincides with psychiatric syndromes such as psychosis and personality disorders. The etiology of epilepsy is now believed by most physicians to be primarily organic, rather than emotional,

possibly stemming from a lesion in the brain. Nevertheless, the true cause of most epileptic conditions is still not known. (Such common conditions are called "idiopathic epilepsy.") It is interesting to note, however, that there is a correlation between anger, violent behavior, and *temporal lobe epilepsy*, and that these patients respond well to psychotherapy. Moreover, there is yet another type of epilepsy—presumed to originate in the *limbic system* of the brain—characterized by rage attacks. The behavioral descriptions of these supposed epileptic "seizures" are strikingly similar to those described earlier, in chapter six, as "the Berserker/Blind Rage Syndrome." But there is no demonstrable proof that such violent behavior is caused by a neurological condition per se. Indeed, according to the *Synopsis of Psychiatry* (6th ed., 1991): "Only in very rare cases should violence of an epileptic patient be attributed to the seizure itself" (p. 266).

74. See Dr. May's foreword in this book.

75. See chapter two for my summary discussion of the "masculine" and "feminine" modes.

76. May, *Love and Will*, p. 261.

77. Again, in fairness to Arthur Janov, I refer the reader to chapter 18, "The Basis of Fear and Anger," in *The Primal Scream*, pp. 322–350. Janov recounts being consulted by a prim and proper young woman complaining of chronic muscle tension. In therapy, she would spontaneously become very angry, and violently pound a pillow. This, however, provided her only transitory relief. Finally, Janov prevented her from pummelling the pillow, and encouraged her instead to verbalize the feeling—which she did with a vengeance. This helped her to consciously connect her "free-floating" rage with her resentment toward her parents; and to recognize that her muscular tension resulted from having to constantly suppress her impulse to physically pummel *them*. As Janov notes, "she pounded a pillow because she had not yet made the mental connection. The pillow punching was symbolic acting out. The anger was felt but not [appropriately] directed (which is why any persistent anger goes on)" (p. 324). Once this patient could verbalize—rather than "act out"—her rage toward her parents in therapy, her physical symptoms, says Janov, subsided, as did her anger. "We must feel . . . anger fully to eradicate it," he writes (p. 326). But can anger ever really be "eradicated"? Is the eradication of anger and rage a realistic—or even desirable—therapeutic endeavor?

78. May, "Psychotherapy and the Daimonic," p. 207.

79. Tavris, *Anger*, p. 45.

80. Ibid., p. 127.

81. *Webster's Third New International Dictionary*, p. 644.

82. Kelsey, *Discernment*, p. 101.

83. See F. S. Perls, *Ego, Hunger and Aggression: The Beginning of Gestalt Therapy* (New York: Vintage Books, 1969) and *Gestalt Therapy Verbatim* (New York: Bantam Books, 1971) for examples.

84. May, *The Discovery of Being*, p. 21n. For a more extensive explication of *intentionality* see May, *Love and Will*, chaps. 9 and 10.

85. May, *Love and Will*, p. 234.

86. Ibid., pp. 260–261.

87. For those interested in learning more about the evolution of this method since Jung, see Barbara Hanna, *Encounters with the Soul: Active Imagination* (Boston: Sigo Press, 1981), and June Singer, *Boundaries of the Soul: The Practice of Jung's Psychology*, rev. ed. (New York: Doubleday, 1994), chap. 10.

88. Edward F. Edinger, *Ego and Archetype: Individuation and the Religious Function of the Psyche* (New York: Penguin Books, 1973), pp. 113–114.

89. May, *Power and Innocence*, p. 87.

90. As a rule, traditional psychotherapy is contraindicated, in my judgment, for patient's actively abusing psychoactive substances such as alcohol, cocaine, amphetamine, marijuana, etc. Such patients seem to do much better by availing themselves of Alcoholics Anonymous style support groups, along with outpatient or inpatient structured treatment programs. One reason is that the drugs interfere with the psychotherapy process. Another is that psychotherapy is inherently stressful: it exacerbates daimonic emotions, driving the drug-dependent patient to take even more of the drug in order to mitigate them. In this particular case, however, the patient desperately needed therapeutic support, but was, at first, unwilling to pursue any of these other avenues. Rules are made to be broken on occasion.

91. Aeschylus, "The Eumenides," in *The Oresteia*, trans. Robert Fagles, introduction, notes, and glossary by R. Fagles and W. B. Stanford (New York: Penguin Books, 1977), p. 249.

92. Ibid., p. 233.

93. Bulfinch, *Bulfinch's Mythology*, p. 9.

94. Aeschylus, *The Oresteia*, pp. 268–270.

95. *Great Classical Myths*, ed. with an introduction by F. R. B. Godolphin (New York: The Modern Library, 1964), p. 443.

96. This phenomenon is commonly seen in psychotherapy patients. Much to our dismay, it is often the case that when we psychologically reject the destructive, "negative" characteristics of a parent—especially the same-sex parent—vowing

"never to be like him or her when I grow up," we unwittingly constellate similar behavior patterns in our adult selves. Why? Because we have denied in ourselves the daimonic tendencies we so disliked, feared, or despised in our father or mother. Anger and rage are good examples. Sooner or later this reactive suppression of the daimonic comes back to haunt us.

97. Frey-Rohn, "Evil from the Psychological Point of View," p. 188.

98. Sophocles, *Oedipus the King*, in *The Complete Plays of Sophocles*, trans. Richard Claverhouse Jebb, ed. with an introduction by Moses Hadas (New York: Bantam Books, 1982), pp. 96–97.

99. May, *The Discovery of Being*, pp. 33–34.

100. May, *The Cry for Myth*, pp. 165–166.

Chapter 8. Creativity, Genius, and the Daimonic

1. May, *The Meaning of Anxiety*, pp. 389–390.

2. Brewster Ghiselin in Brewster Ghiselin, ed., *The Creative Process: A Symposium* (New York: The New American Library, 1955), pp. 12–24.

3. May, *Love and Will*, p. 128.

4. "Positive expression" is not the same as "pretty" or "beautiful." The daimonic, as we have seen, is not always pretty; it is often ugly or grotesque. Thus the *content* of creativity can be disturbing. What defines creativity is how well the individual or "artist" conveys the daimonic in his or her work without being compelled to act it out in the outer world.

5. For a powerful subjective account of profound depression, see Styron's autobiographical book *Darkness Visible: A Memoir of Madness* (New York: Random House, 1990). Styron portrays his daimonic descent with Baudelaire's haunting, poetic image: " 'I have felt the wind of the wing of madness' " (p. 46). He further recalls how his depression "gradually took full possession of [his] . . . system. . . " (p. 47). Beset by demons, despondent, and actively suicidal, Styron was eventually psychiatrically hospitalized, which, for him, served as a healing experience: "THE HOSPITAL WAS A WAY STATION, A PURGATORY" (p. 69). (See also note 83 in this chapter for more on psychiatric hospitalization.) Styron—like Jonah, but unlike countless other casualties—survived his close encounter with the daimonic, and came back to tell us about it. (See note 71 in this chapter.) But his book raises some question, at least in my own mind, about the degree to which Styron consciously *assimilated*—as opposed to *reinterring*—the daimonic. Still, sometimes simply *surviving* such

dire situations is sufficient; the necessary work of psychologically integrating the offending demons can come later. See also Kay Redfield Jamison, *Touched with Fire*, pp. 267–270.

6. May, *Love and Will*, p. 170.

7. Jung, *The Spirit in Man, Art, and Literature*, vol. 15 of *The Collected Works of C. G. Jung*, p. 98.

8. May, *Love and Will*, pp. 23–24.

9. Lieberman, *Acts of Will*, p. 282.

10. Cynthia Robins, "A Rage for Art," *San Francisco Examiner* Magazine, September 17, 1995, p. 20.

11. May, *The Meaning of Anxiety*, p. 44.

12. C. Kate Kavanagh, "Picasso: The Man and His Women," in *Creativity and Madness: Psychological Studies of Art and Artists*, ed. B. Panter, M. Panter, E. Virshup, and B. Virshup (Burbank, Calif.: AIMED Press, 1995), p. 277. It should be noted that Kavanagh quotes Jung out of context on this point.

13. Herman Melville, *Moby-Dick; or, The Whale* in *The Best of Herman Melville* (Secaucus, N.J.: Castle, 1983), p. 61.

14. Edward F. Edinger, *Melville's Moby-Dick: A Jungian Commentary* (New York: New Directions, 1975), p. 261.

15. For much more on the connection between death and creativity, see Ernest Becker, *The Denial of Death* (New York: The Free Press, 1973).

16. Russell, *The Prince of Darkness*, p. 224.

17. *Webster's Third New International Dictionary*, p. 946.

18. Ibid.

19. May, *Love and Will*, p. 125.

20. von Franz, *Projection and Re-Collection in Jungian Psychology*, p. 146.

21. Ibid., p. 147.

22. Cited in ibid., pp. 148–149.

23. Kelsey, *Discernment*, pp. 70–71.

24. Ibid., p. 57.

25. The technical term for such "psychotic" phenomena is "command hallucinations."

26. Jung, *Civilization in Transition*, 2d ed., vol. 10 of *The Collected Works of C. G. Jung*, p. 447.

27. Jung, *Memories, Dreams, Reflections*, pp. 329–330. The psychology of evil was discussed in more detail in chapter three of this book.

28. Rudyard Kipling, "Rudyard Kipling: Working Tools," in *The Creative Process: A Symposium*, ed. Brewster Ghiselin (New York: The New American Library, 1955), pp. 157–158.

29. *Complete Essays of Schopenhauer*, trans. T. Bailey Saunders (New York: Wiley Book Company, 1942), pp. 1–2.

30. Sperber, "The Daimonic: Freudian, Jungian and Existential Perspectives," p. 47.

31. May, *Love and Will*, p. 177.

32. Sperber, "The Daimonic: Freudian, Jungian and Existential Perspectives," p. 41.

33. Melville, *Moby-Dick*, pp. 128–129.

34. May, *The Cry for Myth*, p. 277.

35. Edinger, *Melville's Moby-Dick*, p. 65.

36. Melville, *Moby-Dick*, p. 359.

37. Edinger, *Melville's Moby-Dick*, p. 75.

38. Ibid., pp. 76–77.

39. Ibid., pp. 77–78.

40. Melville, *Moby-Dick*, p. 128.

41. See, for instance, chapters two and seven for some discussion of serpents, dragons, and similar images of the daimonic.

42. Edinger, *Melville's Moby-Dick*, p. 90.

43. Melville, *Moby-Dick*, p. 17.

44. Edinger, *Melville's Moby-Dick*, p. 11.

45. Jamison, *Touched with Fire*, p. 217.

46. Edinger, *Melville's Moby-Dick*, pp. 13–14. A similar fate befell C. G. Jung, shortly following his professional separation from Freud, and persisted for many years prior to his psychological stabilization during his mid-forties.

47. Ibid., p. 14.

48. Melville, *Moby-Dick*, p. 47.

49. From the dustjacket of *In the Belly of the Beast: Letters from Prison*, with an introduction by Norman Mailer (New York: Random House, 1981).

50. Ibid.

51. Norman Mailer, introduction to *In the Belly of the Beast*, by Jack Henry Abbott, p. x.

52. Ibid.

53. Terence Des Pres, "A Child of the State," *New York Times Book Review*, July 19, 1981, p. 3.

54. Jerzy Kosinski, quoted by Joyce Wadler in "The Short, Unhappy Career of Jack Henry Abbott," *The Washington Post*, reprinted in the *San Jose Mercury*, Aug. 18, 1981, p. 1C.

55. Des Pres, "A Child of the State," pp. 14–15.

56. May, *Power and Innocence*, p. 50.

57. Anna Freud, from the foreword to *Vincent van Gogh: A Psychological Study*, by Humberto Nagera (London: George Allen and Unwin Ltd., 1967), p. 5.

58. Barry Panter, "Vincent van Gogh: Creativity and Madness," in *Creativity and Madness*, p. 2.

59. Nagera, *Vincent van Gogh*, p. 114.

60. Panter, "Vincent van Gogh: Creativity and Madness," p. 10. See also Jamison, *Touched with Fire*.

61. Panter, "Vincent van Gogh: Creativity and Madness," p. 7.

62. Nagera, *Vincent van Gogh*, pp. 116–117.

63. Panter, "Vincent van Gogh: Creativity and Madness," p. 9.

64. Vincent van Gogh, in Irving Stone, with Jean Stone, *Dear Theo: The Autobiography of Vincent Van Gogh* (New York: Signet, The New American Library, 1969), p. 251.

65. Evelyn Virshup, "Jackson Pollock: Art Versus Alcohol," in *Creativity and Madness*, p. 30.

66. Barry M. Panter in ibid., p. 38.

67. Margaret Walker, *Richard Wright: Daemonic Genius; A Portrait of the Man, A Critical Look at His Work* (New York: Amistad, 1993), p. 13.

68. Richard Wright, *Black Boy: A Record of Childhood and Youth* (New York: Harper and Row, 1945), pp. 271–272.

69. William Gardner Smith, "The Compensation for the Wound," *Two Cities* 6 (Summer 1961): 67–69.

70. Walker, *Richard Wright: Daemonic Genius,* p. 43.

71. When Jonah's inner daimon urged him to angrily chastise the wicked in the town of Nineveh, he went instead to Tarshish. On the way, as Jonah lay "asleep" (i.e., unconscious), "there was a mighty tempest on the sea," and he was swallowed by a "great fish." After three hellish days in the whale's brackish belly—and a repentant recognition of his wrongdoing—Jonah was released, and theretofore transformed by this brief, unbidden descent into daimonic possession (Jonah: 1, 2).

72. J. W. N. Sullivan, *Beethoven: His Spiritual Development* (New York: Vintage Books, 1960), p. 86.

73. Goethe, quoted in *Beethoven: Impressions By His Contemporaries,* ed. O. G. Sonneck (New York: Dover Publications, 1967), p. 83.

74. Plato's *Symposium* in *Plato: Euthyphro, Crito, Apology, and Symposium,* p. 117.

75. Especially the String Quartet No. 14, in C Sharp Minor, Op. 131.

76. Erich Neumann, *Art and the Creative Unconscious: Four Essays,* trans. Ralph Manheim, Bollingen Series LXI (Princeton, N.J.: Princeton University Press, 1971), p. 103.

77. Sullivan, *Beethoven: His Spiritual Development,* p. 173.

78. May in R. May, E. Angel, and H. Ellenberger, eds., *Existence,* p. 49.

79. Paul Tillich quoted in Rollo May, *Paulus: Tillich as Spiritual Teacher,* rev. ed. (Dallas, Tex.: Saybrook, 1988), p. 83. (Originally published as *Paulus: Reminiscences of a Friendship* [New York: Harper and Row, 1973].) May, ibid., p. 83.

80. Paul Tillich, *The Courage To Be* (New Haven: Yale University Press, 1952), p. 14.

81. Ingmar Bergman, *The Magic Lantern: An Autobiography,* trans. Joan Tate (New York: Penguin Books, 1989), p. 2.

82. Ibid., p. 33.

83. I am not at all opposed to the appropriate use of psychiatric hospitalization. Under some circumstances, as here, for instance, where the patient was acutely suicidal, hospitalization is clinically necessary, and can be a constructive, life-preserving aspect of the patient's treatment. Again, see for example Styron's account

of the beneficial effects of temporary hospitalization in his book, *Darkness Visible: A Memoir of Madness*. In hindsight, Styron states: "I'm convinced I should have been in the hospital weeks before" (p. 68). (See also note 5 in this chapter.)

84. Ira Progoff, "Waking Dream and Living Myth," in *Myths, Dreams, and Religion*, ed. Joseph Campbell, Essays Sponsored by the Society for the Arts, Religion and Contemporary Culture (New York: E. P. Dutton, 1970), pp. 189–190.

85. Bergman, *The Magic Lantern*, pp. 61–63.

86. It is unknown to me the extent to which Bergman has been personally involved in psychotherapy. I have the impression that while intellectually interested, he may (like many other artists) have avoided it, for fear of having his daimons—and hence, his creativity—exorcised forever. "No more conflict, no more creativity" is what the artist is ostensibly concerned about. But this bestows too much power on the capacity of psychotherapy to preclude all conflict, and to finally neutralize the daimonic. Bergman's American admirer, director Woody Allen, for instance, makes no secret of his own decades-spanning psychoanalysis. Maybe Allen—like the late, great Italian film-maker, Federico Fellini—has a bit more faith than Bergman in the ability of the daimonic—and its infinitely creative (and destructive) possibilities—to withstand and outlive any reductive analysis and rationalization, no matter how thoroughly exhaustive or penetrating.

Chapter 9. Conclusion

1. The "biopsychosocial" model of psychiatry was introduced by George Engel. It consists of a comprehensive, integrated, systemic way of thinking about and treating mental disorders, taking into consideration the *biological, psychological*, and *social*—or *systemic*—contributions to psychiatric problems.

2. As previously stated, *sublimation* is a term made popular by Freud; Jung called it *displacement*. I think it important to discriminate between conscious sublimation and unconscious sublimation, since both occur continuously. "Conscious sublimation" is the earmark of eudaimonic character or genius. I see it as a creative choice, rather than, according to Freud, yet another psychological "defense mechanism" replacing unacceptable, unconscious impulses with "socially acceptable" behaviors. Conscious, creative sublimation of the daimonic does not necessarily translate into social conformity—quite the contrary—though such creative individuals do tend to make more constructive than destructive contributions to society.

3. According to a survey conducted in 1982, only 63 percent of first-year medical residents "considered the ability to perform psychotherapy the most crucial tool in psychiatry. In 1993, the figure dropped to 37 percent" (*New York Newsday*, Jan. 31, 1995, p. B27).

4. See chapters one and two for a synopsis of some of these notorious cases.

5. Rev. Ted Peters cited by Willmar Thorkelson in "The Genes Made Me Do It: Sin and Responsibility," *San Jose Mercury News,* Aug. 6, 1994, p. 10C.

6. See Jean-Paul Sartre, *Existential Psychoanalysis,* trans. Hazel E. Barnes, introduction by Rollo May, A Gateway Edition (Chicago: Henry Regnery Co., 1962), pp. 153–210.

7. In order to be effective, *punishment* must be applied immediately after the decried behavior, and should be discontinued as soon as the misbehavior ceases. For these and several other reasons, research suggests that the long-term effects of punishment—as opposed to penance—are extremely limited, a fact apparently lost on our overburdened penal system.

8. May, *Power and Innocence,* p. 259.

9. May, *The Cry for Myth,* p. 78.

10. Sophocles, *Oedipus at Colonus,* in *The Complete Plays of Sophocles,* trans. and ed. Richard Jebb, with an introduction by Moses Hadas (New York: Bantam Books, 1982), p. 238.

11. May, *The Cry for Myth,* p. 82.

12. Sophocles, *Oedipus at Colonus,* p. 244.

13. May, *The Cry for Myth,* p. 85.

14. Tillich, *The Courage To Be,* p. 27.

15. Rollo May, "The Significance of Symbols," in *Symbolism in Religion and Literature,* ed. and with an introduction by Rollo May (New York: George Braziller, 1960), p. 45.

16. Hamilton, *Mythology: Timeless Tales of Gods and Heroes,* p. 257.

17. Ibid.

18. See Bulfinch, *Bulfinch's Mythology.*

Bibliography

Abbott, Jack Henry. *In the Belly of the Beast: Letters from Prison*. With an introduction by Norman Mailer. New York: Random House, 1981.

Aeschylus. *The Oresteia*. Translated by Robert Fagles. Introduction, notes, and glossary by R. Fagles and W. B. Stanford. New York: Penguin Books, 1977.

Alexander, Franz. *Psychosomatic Medicine: Its Principles and Applications*. New York: W. W. Norton, 1950.

Allen, Jon. *Bulletin of the Menninger Clinic* 57, no. 3 (1993): 405–406.

American Psychiatric Association. *Diagnostic and Statistical Manual of Mental Disorders*. 3rd ed., rev. Washington, D.C.: American Psychiatric Association, 1987.

———. *DSM-IV Draft Criteria*. Task Force on DSM-IV. Washington, D.C.: American Psychiatric Association, 1993.

———. *Diagnostic and Statistical Manual of Mental Disorders*. 4th ed. Washington, D.C.: American Psychiatric Association, 1994.

American Psychological Association. *APA Monitor* 25, no. 9 (September 1994): 1.

———. *APA Monitor* 27, no. 10 (October 1994): 32.

———. *APA Monitor* 12, no. 9 (September 1995): 48.

Ansbacher, Heinz, and Rowena Ansbacher, eds. *The Individual Psychology of Alfred Adler: A Systematic Presentation in Selections from His Writings*. New York: Harper and Row, 1956.

Averill, J. R. *Anger and Aggression: An Essay on Emotion*. New York: Springer Verlag, 1982.

———. "Studies on Anger and Aggression: Implications for Theories on Emotions." *American Psychologist* 38 (1983): 1145–1160.

Bach, George, and Herb Goldberg. *Creative Aggression: The Art of Assertive Living.* New York: Avon Books, 1974.

Bard, P., and V. B. Mountcastle. "Some Forebrain Mechanisms Involved in Expression of Rage with Special Reference to Suppression of Angry Behavior." *Research Publications of the Association for Research in Nervous and Mental Disease* 27 (1947).

Barrett, William. *Irrational Man: A Study in Existential Philosophy.* Garden City, N.Y.: Doubleday Anchor, 1962.

Barrow, Reginald H. *Plutarch and His Times.* Bloomington, Indiana: Indiana University Press, 1967.

Beck, Aaron, and Marjorie Weishar. "Cognitive Therapy." In *Current Psychotherapies,* 4th ed., edited by Raymond J. Corsini and Danny Wedding, with the assistance of Judith W. McMahon. Itasca, Ill.: F. E. Peacock Publishers, 1989.

Becker, Ernest. *The Denial of Death.* New York: The Free Press, 1973.

Benedetti, Gaetano. "Blumhardts Seelsorge in der sicht heutiger psychotherapeutischer Kenntnis." *Reformatio* 9 (1960): 474–487; 531–539.

Bergman, Ingmar. *The Magic Lantern: An Autobiography.* Translated by Joan Tate. New York: Penguin Books, 1989.

Berkowitz, Louis. "The Devil Within." *Psychoanalytic Review* 55, no. 1 (1968): 28–36.

Bettelheim, Bruno. *The Uses of Enchantment.* New York: Vintage Books, 1977.

Breuer, Josef, and Sigmund Freud. *Studies on Hysteria.* Translated and edited by James Strachey, with the collaboration of Anna Freud, assisted by Alix Strachey and Alan Tyson. New York: Basic Books, 1957. Originally published in 1895 as *Studien über Hysterie* (Leipzig and Vienna: Deuticke).

Buckley, Peter, ed. *Essential Papers on Object Relations.* New York: New York University Press, 1986.

Bulfinch, Thomas. *Bulfinch's Mythology.* Illustrated ed. New York: Avenel Books, 1979.

Butterfield, Fox. "FBI Reports Lower Crime Rate, But Warns of New Surge." *San Francisco Examiner* (November 19, 1995): A-12.

Campbell, Anne. *Men, Women, and Aggression*. New York: Basic Books, 1993.

Cannon, Walter. *Bodily Changes in Panic, Hunger, Fear, and Rage*. New York: Appleton-Century, 1915.

———. *The Wisdom of the Body*. New York: W. W. Norton, 1963.

Carus, Paul. *The History of the Devil and the Idea of Evil, From the Earliest Times to the Present Day*. La Salle, Ill.: Open Court, 1974.

Charcot, J. M., and Paul Richer, *Les Démoniaques dans l'Art*. Paris: A. Delahaye and E. Lecrosnier, 1887.

Chiang, Harriett. "Violent Times, Angry Clients: 'More Dangerous to Be a Lawyer.' " *San Francisco Chronicle* (Monday, May 15, 1995): 1.

Claremont de Castillejo, Irene. *Knowing Woman: A Feminine Psychology*. New York: Harper Colophon, 1973.

Clarke, James. *On Being Mad or Merely Angry: John W. Hinckley, Jr., and Other Dangerous People*. Princeton, N.J.: Princeton University Press, 1990.

Collin de Plancy, J. A. S. *Dictionnaire Infernal*. 6th ed. Drawings by M. L. Breton. Paris: Henri Plon, 1863. Reprint, Genéve: Slatkine Reprints, 1980.

Consumer Reports. "Mental Health: Does Therapy Help?" 60, no. 11 (November 1995): 734–739.

Cose, E. *The Rage of a Privileged Class*. New York: Harper Collins, 1993.

Cramer, M. "Psychopathology and Shamanism in Rural Mexico: A Case Study of Spirit Possession." *British Journal of Medical Psychology* 53 (1980): 67–73.

De Vos, Esther Leonard. "Voodoo: Our Link with the Occult." In *The Analytic Life: Personal and Professional Aspects of Being a Jungian Analyst,* edited by the New England Society of Jungian Analysts. With an introduction by Sidney Handel. Boston: Sigo Press, 1988.

Delgado, J. M. R. "Aggression and Defense Under Cerebral Radio Control." In *Aggression and Defense: Neural Mechanisms and Social Patterns,* edited by C. D. Clemente and D. B. Lindsley. Los Angeles: University of California Press, 1967.

Des Pres, Terence. "A Child of the State." Review of *In the Belly of the Beast: Letters from Prison,* by Jack Henry Abbott. *New York Times Book Review,* July 19, 1981.

Diamond, Stephen A. "Rediscovering Rank." Review of *Acts of Will: The Life and Work of Otto Rank,* by E. James Lieberman. *The San Francisco Jung Institute Library Journal* 7, no. 3 (1987): 1–10.

———. Review of *Aggression: The Myth of the Beast Within,* by John Klama. *Readings* (published by the American Orthopsychiatric Association) 4, no. 1 (March 1989): 29.

———. "The Psychology of Evil." Review of *People of the Lie: The Hope for Healing Human Evil,* by M. Scott Peck. *The San Francisco Jung Institute Library Journal* 9, no. 1 (1990): 5–26.

———. "Redeeming Our Devils and Demons." Chapter 38 in *Meeting the Shadow: The Hidden Power of the Dark Side of Human Nature,* edited by C. Zweig and J. Abrams. New York: Tarcher/Putnam, 1991.

Dietrich, Bernard C. *Death, Fate and the Gods: The Development of a Religious Idea in Greek Popular Belief and in Homer.* London: University of London, Athlone Press, 1965.

———. *Tradition in Greek Religion.* Berlin: Walter de Gruyter, 1986.

Dodds, Eric R. *The Greeks and the Irrational.* Berkeley: University of California Press, 1951.

———. *Pagan and Christian in an an Age of Anxiety: Some Aspects of Religious Experience from Marcus Aurelius to Constantine.* Cambridge, England: Cambridge University Press, 1965.

Dollard, J., N. Doob, N. Miller, and R. Sears. *Frustration and Aggression.* New Haven, Conn.: Yale University Press, 1939.

Douglas, Claire. "The Animus." *The San Francisco Jung Institute Library Journal* 6, no. 3 (1986): 1–20.

———. "Christiana Morgan's Visions Reconsidered: A Look Behind *The Visions Seminars.*" *The San Francisco Jung Institute Library Journal* 8, no. 4 (1989): 10–15.

Edinger, Edward F. *Ego and Archetype: Individuation and the Religious Function of the Psyche.* New York: Penguin Books, 1973.

———. *Melville's Moby-Dick: A Jungian Commentary.* New York: New Directions, 1975. See also 2d ed., with index (Toronto: Inner City Books, 1995).

Ellenberger, Henri F. *The Discovery of the Unconscious: The History and Evolution of Dynamic Psychiatry.* New York: Basic Books, 1970.

Ellis, Albert. "Rational-Emotive Therapy." In *Current Psychotherapies,* 4th ed., Raymond J. Corsini and Danny Wedding, with the assistance of Judith W. McMahon. Itasca, Ill.: F. E. Peacock Publishers, 1989.

Encyclopedia of Witchcraft and Demonology. Introduction by Hans Holzer. London: Octopus Books Limited, 1974.

Fairbairn, W. R. D. "A Revised Psychopathology of the Psychoses and Psychoneuroses." In *Essential Papers on Object Relations,* edited by Peter Buckley. New York: New York University Press, 1986.

Faludi, Susan. *Backlash: The Undeclared War Against American Women.* New York: Crown, 1991.

Fava, Maurizio, et al. "Anger Attacks in Depressed Outpatients and Their Response to Fluoxetine." *Psychopharmacology Bulletin* 27, no. 3 (1991): 275–279.

Flynn, J. P. "The Neural Basis of Aggression in Cats." In *Neurophysiology and Emotion,* edited by D. C. Glass. New York: Rockefeller University Press, 1967.

Foster, Jonathan. "British Boys Shared a Murderous Urge." *San Francisco Examiner* (November 25, 1993).

Frankl, Viktor. *The Will to Meaning: Foundations and Applications of Logotherapy.* New York: The New American Library, 1969.

———. *Man's Search for Meaning.* Revised and updated. New York: Washington Square Press, 1985.

Freud, Anna. From the foreword to *Vincent van Gogh: A Psychological Study* by Humberto Nagera. London: George Allen and Unwin Ltd., 1967.

Freud, Sigmund. *On the History of the Psycho-Analytic Movement.* Vol. 14 of *The Standard Edition of the Complete Psychological Works of Sigmund Freud.* Translated by James Strachey, in collaboration with Anna Freud, assisted by Alix Strachey and Alan Tyson, and Angela Richards. London: Hogarth Press and the Institute of Psycho-Analysis, 1914.

———. *Beyond the Pleasure Principle.* Vol. 18 of *The Standard Edition of the Complete Psychological Works of Sigmund Freud.* Translated under the general editorship of James Strachey, in collaboration with Anna Freud, assisted by Alix Strachey and Alan Tyson, and Angela Richards. London: Hogarth Press and the Institute of Psycho-Analysis, 1920–1922.

———. *New Introductory Lectures on Psychoanalysis and Other Works.* Vol. 22 of *The Standard Edition of the Complete Psychological Works of Sigmund Freud.* Translated and edited by James Strachey, in collaboration with Anna Freud, assisted by Alix Strachey and Alan Tyson, and Angela Richards. London: Hogarth Press and the Institute for Psycho-Analysis, 1932–1936.

———. *Moses and Monotheism, an Outline of Psycho-Analysis and Other Works.* Vol. 23 of *The Standard Edition of the Complete Psychological Works of Sigmund Freud.* Translated under the general editorship of James Strachey, in collaboration with Anna Freud, assisted by Alix Strachey and Alan Tyson, and Angela Richards. London: Hogarth Press and the Institute of Psycho-Analysis, 1937–1939.

———. *Psychopathology of Everyday Life.* In *The Basic Writings of Sigmund Freud,* translated and edited by A. A. Brill. New York: The Modern Library, 1938.

———. *Totem and Taboo.* In *The Basic Writings of Sigmund Freud,* translated and edited by A. A. Brill. New York: The Modern Library, 1938.

———. *The Ego and the Id.* The International Psycho-Analytical Library. No. 12. Sixth impression. Edited by Ernest Jones, translated by Joan Riviere. London: The Hogarth Press, 1950.

————. *A General Introduction to Psychoanalysis*. Authorized English translation of the rev. ed. by Joan Riviere. Preface by Ernest Jones and G. Stanley Hall. New York: Washington Square Press, 1952.

————. "A Neurosis of Demoniacal Possession in the Seventeenth Century." Vol. 4 of *Collected Papers*. London: Hogarth Press, 1953. Originally published in *Imago* (1923).

————. Vol. 5 of *Collected Papers*. The International Psycho-Analytical Library. No. 37. Edited by Ernest Jones. Edited by James Strachey. New York: Basic Books, 1959.

————. *Introductory Lectures on Psychoanalysis* (formerly titled *General Introduction to Psychoanalysis*). Translated and edited by James Strachey. New York: Liveright Publishing Corporation, 1966.

Frey-Rohn, Liliane. "Evil from the Psychological Point of View." In *Evil*, translated by Ralph Manheim and Hildegard Nagel, edited by the Curatorium of the C. G. Jung Institute, Zürich. Studies in Jungian Thought Series. Evanston, Ill.: Northwestern University Press, 1967. Originally published in translation by H. Nagel in *Spring Journal* (1965): 5–48.

Friedlander, Paul. *Plato: An Introduction*. Translated by Hans Meyerhoff. Bollingen series LIX, Bollingen Foundation. New York: Pantheon Books, 1958.

Fromm, Erich. *The Anatomy of Human Destructiveness*. New York: Fawcett Crest Books, 1973.

Gaylin, Willard. *The Rage Within: Anger in Modern Life*. New York: Penguin Books, 1989.

Gelles, Richard, and Murray Straus. *Physical Violence in American Families: Risk Factors and Adaptations to Violence in 8,145 Families*. New Brunswick, N.J.: Transaction Publishers, 1990.

George, Susi. In *The Caduceus*, the Newspaper for San Diego County's Health Care Professional 1, no. 11 (December 1981).

Ghiselin, Brewster. Introduction to *The Creative Process: A Symposium*, edited by Brewster Ghiselin. New York: The New American Library, 1955.

Godolphin, F. R. B., ed. *Great Classical Myths*. New York: The Modern Library, 1964.

Grier, William, and Price Cobbs. *Black Rage*. With a new introduction by the authors. Foreword by former United States Senator Fred R. Harris. New York: Basic Books, 1992.

Grimm Brothers. *The Complete Grimm's Fairy Tales*. Introduction by Padraic Colum. Commentary by Joseph Campbell. New York: Pantheon Books, 1972.

Groddeck, Georg. *Das Buch vom Es: Psychoanalytische Briefe an eine Freundin*. Vienna: Internationaler Psychoanalytischer Verlag, 1923. Translated into English as *The Book of the Id*. New York: Nervous and Mental Disease Publishing Co., 1928.

Grotjahn, Martin. *The Voice of the Symbol*. New York: Dell Publishing, 1971.

Hamilton, Edith. *Mythology: Timeless Tales of Gods and Heroes*. Illustrated by Steele Savage. New York: New American Library, 1969.

Hanna, Barbara. *Encounters with the Soul: Active Imagination*. Boston: Sigo Press, 1981.

Harding, M. Esther. *Psychic Energy: Its Source and Its Transformation*. With a foreword by C. G. Jung. Bollingen Series X. Princeton, N.J.: Princeton University Press, 1973.

Hatch, John P., Lawrence S. Schoenfeld, Nashaat N. Boutros, Ermias Seleshi, Patricia J. Moore, and Margaret Cyr-Provost. "Anger and Hostility in Tension-type Headache." *Headache: The Journal of the American Association for the Study of Headache* 31, no. 5 (1991): 302–304.

Henderson, D. J. "Exorcism, Possession, and the Dracula Cult: A Synopsis of Object-Relations Psychology." *Bulletin of the Menninger Clinic* 40, no. 6 (November 1976): 603–628.

Hesse, Hermann. *Demian: The Story of Emil Sinclair's Youth*. Translated by Michael Roloff and Michael Lebeck. Introduction by Thomas Mann. New York: Bantam Books, 1965.

Hill, Gareth. *Masculine and Feminine: The Natural Flow of Opposites in the Psyche*. Boston: Shambhala, 1992.

Hillman, James. *Healing Fiction*. New York: Station Hill, 1983.

————. *Anima: An Anatomy of a Personified Notion*. Dallas: Spring Publications, 1985.

Hitschmann, Edward. "The History of the Aggression-Impulse." *Samiksa* 1, Calcutta, India (1947): 137–141.

Homer, *The Odyssey: The Story of Odysseus*. Translated by W. H. D. Rouse. New York: New American Library, 1937.

Horney, Karen. *The Neurotic Personality of Our Time*. New York: W. W. Norton, 1937.

————. *Feminine Psychology*. Edited with an introduction by Harold Kelman. New York: W. W. Norton, 1967.

Huxley, Aldous. *The Doors of Perception* and *Heaven and Hell*. New York: Harper Colophon, 1963.

International Crime Rates. Washington, D.C.: Bureau of Justice Statistics (1988): 1.

Jacobi, Jolande. *The Psychology of C. G. Jung: An Introduction with Illustrations*. Translated by Ralph Manheim. 6th ed. New Haven: Yale University Press, 1962.

Jacobs, P. A., M. Brunton, and M. M. Melville. "Aggressive Behavior, Mental Sub-normality, and the XYY Male." *Nature* 208 (1965): 131–152.

Jacoby, Mario. "Reflections on Heinz Kohut's Concept of Narcissism." In *Psychopathology: Contemporary Jungian Perspectives*, edited with an introduction by Andrew Samuels. London: The Guilford Press, 1991.

Jacoby, Mario, Verena Kast, and Ingrid Riedel. *Witches, Ogres, and the Devil's Daughter: Encounters with Evil in Fairy Tales*. Translated by Michael H. Kohn. Boston: Shambhala, 1992.

Jaffé, Aniela. *The Myth of Meaning: Jung and the Expansion of Consciousness*. Translated by R. F. C. Hull. New York: Penguin Books, 1975. Originally published in German under the title *Der Mythus vom Sinn im Werk von C. G. Jung* by Rascher Verlag, Zurich.

Jaffe, Jerome, Thomas Babor, and Diana Fishbein. "Alcoholics, Aggression and Antisocial Personality." *Journal of Studies on Alcohol* 49, no. 3 (1988): 211–218.

Jamison, Kay Redfield. *Touched with Fire: Manic Depressive Illness and the Artistic Temperament.* New York: The Free Press, 1993.

Janov, Arthur. *The Primal Scream; Primal Therapy: The Cure for Neurosis.* New York: Delta, Dell, 1970.

————. *The New Primal Scream: Primal Therapy Twenty Years On.* Wilmington, Del.: Enterprise Publishing, 1991.

Jarvik, L. F., V. Klodin, and S. S. Matsuyama. "Human Aggression and the Extra Y Chromosome: Fact or Fantasy?" *American Psychologist* 28, no. 8 (1973): 674–682.

Johnson, Robert A. *We: Understanding the Psychology of Romantic Love.* San Francisco: Harper and Row, 1983.

Johnson, Stephen M. *Humanizing the Narcissistic Style.* New York: W. W. Norton, 1987.

Jung, Carl G. *Memories, Dreams, Reflections.* Recorded and edited by Aniela Jaffé. Translated by R. and C. Winston. New York: Pantheon Books, 1963.

————. *Freud and Psychoanalysis.* Vol. 4 of *The Collected Works of C. G. Jung.* Translated by R. F. C. Hull. Edited by Herbert Read, Michael Fordham, Gerhard Adler, and William McGuire. Bollingen Series XX. Princeton, N.J.: Princeton University Press, 1961.

————. *The Spirit in Man, Art, and Literature.* Vol. 15 of *The Collected Works of C. G. Jung.* Translated by R. F. C. Hull. Edited by Herbert Read, Michael Fordham, Gerhard Adler, and William McGuire. Bollingen Series XX. Princeton, N.J.: Princeton University Press, 1966.

————. *Two Essays on Analytical Psychology.* 2d ed., rev. Vol. 7 of *The Collected Works of C. G. Jung.* Translated by R. F. C. Hull. Edited by Herbert Read, Michael Fordham, Gerhard Adler, and William McGuire. Bollingen Series XX. Princeton, N.J.: Princeton University Press, 1966.

————. *Symbols of Transformation: An Analysis of the Prelude to a Case of Schizophrenia.* 2d ed. Vol. 5 of *The Collected Works of C. G. Jung.* Translated by R. F. C. Hull. Edited by Herbert Read, Michael Fordham, Gerhard Adler, and William McGuire. Bollingen Series XX. Princeton, N.J.: Princeton University Press, 1967. Originally published in 1912 as *Wandlungen und Symbole der Libido* (Leipzig and Vienna: Franz Deuticke).

———. *Aion: Researches into the Phenomenology of the Self.* 2d ed. Vol. 9, part 2 of *The Collected Works of C. G. Jung.* Translated by R. F. C. Hull. Edited by Herbert Read, Michael Fordham, Gerhard Adler, and William McGuire. Bollingen Series XX. Princeton, N.J.: Princeton University Press, 1968.

———. *Psychology and Alchemy.* 2d ed. Vol. 12 of *The Collected Works of C. G. Jung.* Translated by R. F. C. Hull. Edited by Herbert Read, Michael Fordham, Gerhard Adler, and William McGuire. Bollingen Series XX. Princeton, N.J.: Princeton University Press, 1968.

———. *Psychology and Religion: West and East.* 2d ed. Vol. 11 of *The Collected Works of C. G. Jung.* Translated by R. F. C. Hull. Edited by Herbert Read, Michael Fordham, Gerhard Adler, and William McGuire. Bollingen Series XX. Princeton, N.J.: Princeton University Press, 1969.

———. *The Structure and Dynamics of the Psyche.* 2d ed. Vol. 8 of *The Collected Works of C. G. Jung.* Translated by R. F. C. Hull. Edited by Herbert Read, Michael Fordham, Gerhard Adler, and William McGuire. Bollingen Series XX. Princeton, N.J.: Princeton University Press, 1969.

———. *Civilization in Transition.* 2d ed. Vol. 10 of *The Collected Works of C. G. Jung.* Translated by R. F. C. Hull. Edited by Herbert Read, Michael Fordham, Gerhard Adler, and William McGuire. Bollingen Series XX. Princeton, N.J.: Princeton University Press, 1970.

———. *Psychological Types.* Vol. 6 of *The Collected Works of C. G. Jung.* Translated by R. F. C. Hull. Edited by Herbert Read, Michael Fordham, Gerhard Adler, and William McGuire. Bollingen Series XX. Princeton, N.J.: Princeton University Press, 1971.

———. *The Symbolic Life.* 2d ed. Vol. 18 of *The Collected Works of C. G. Jung.* Translated by R. F. C. Hull. Edited by Herbert Read, Michael Fordham, Gerhard Adler, and William McGuire. Bollingen Series XX. Princeton, N.J.: Princeton University Press, 1976.

Kaplan, Harold I., and Benjamin J. Sadock, Jack A. Grebb, assistant to the authors. *Synopsis of Psychiatry: Behavioral Sciences; Clinical Psychiatry.* 6th ed., rev. Baltimore: Williams and Wilkins, 1991.

Kavanagh, C. Kate. "Picasso: The Man and His Women." In *Creativity and Madness: Psychological Studies of Art and Artists,* edited by B. Panter, M. Panter, E. Virshup, and B. Virshup. Burbank, Calif.: AIMED Press, 1995.

Keen, Sam. *Faces of the Enemy: The Psychology of Enmity.* New York: Harper and Row, 1988.

Kelsey, Morton. *Discernment: A Study in Ecstasy and Evil.* New York: Paulist Press, 1978.

Kernberg, Otto F. *Aggression in Personality Disorders and Perversions.* New Haven: Yale University Press, 1992.

Kierkegaard, Sören. *Fear and Trembling.* Translated by Walter Lowrie in *A Kierkegaard Anthology,* edited by Robert Bretall. New York: The Modern Library, 1946.

———. *The Concept of Dread.* Translated by Walter Lowrie. Princeton, N.J.: Princeton University Press, 1957.

Kipling, Rudyard. "Rudyard Kipling: Working Tools." In *The Creative Process: A Symposium,* edited by Brewster Ghiselin. New York: The New American Library, 1955, pp. 157–159.

Klama, John. *Aggression: The Myth of the Beast Within.* New York: John Wiley and Sons, 1988.

Klein, Donald. "Anxiety Reconceptualized." In *Anxiety: New Research and Changing Concepts,* edited by Donald F. Klein and Judith G. Rabkin. New York: Raven Press, 1981.

Klüver, H., and P. C. Bucy. "Preliminary Analysis of Functions of the Temporal Lobes in Monkeys." *Archives of Neurology and Psychiatry* 42, no. 6 (December 1939): 979–1000.

Kohut, Heinz. "Thoughts on Narcissism and Narcissistic Rage." In *The Search for the Self: Selected Writings of Heinz Kohut: 1950–1978.* New York: International University Press, 1978.

Kosinski, Jerzy. Quoted by Joyce Wadler in "The Short, Unhappy Career of Jack Henry Abbott." *Washington Post,* reprinted in the *San Jose Mercury* (August 18, 1981): 1C.

Kramer, Peter D. *Listening to Prozac: A Psychiatrist Explores Antidepressant Drugs and the Remaking of the Self.* New York: Penguin Books, 1993.

Lederer, Wolfgang. *The Fear of Women*. New York: Harcourt Brace Jovanovich, Inc., 1968.

Lehner, Ernst, and Johanna Lehner. *A Fantastic Bestiary: Beasts and Monsters in Myth and Folklore*. New York: Tudor, 1969.

———. *A Picture Book of Devils, Demons and Witchcraft*. New York: Dover, 1971.

Lieberman, E. James. *Acts of Will: The Life and Work of Otto Rank*. With a new preface. Amherst: University of Massachusetts Press, 1993.

Life. "Satan." 12, no. 7 (June 1989): 48–56.

Lifton, Robert Jay. *The Nazi Doctors: Medical Killing and the Psychology of Genocide*. New York: Basic Books, 1986.

Lorenz, Konrad. *On Aggression*. Translated by Marjorie Kerr Wilson. New York: Harcourt Brace Jovanovich, 1966.

Lowen, Alexander. *The Language of the Body*. New York: Collier, 1971.

———. *Bioenergetics*. New York: Penguin Books, 1976.

———. *Fear of Life*. New York: Macmillan, 1980.

Mailer, Norman. Introduction to *In the Belly of the Beast: Letters from Prison,* by Jack Henry Abbott. New York: Random House, 1981.

Martin, Sara. "Workplace Is No Longer a Haven from Violence." *The APA Monitor* (a publication of the American Psychological Association) 27, no. 10 (October 1994): 29.

Mattoon, Mary Ann, and Jennette Jones. "Is the Animus Obsolete?" *Quadrant* (a publication of the C. G. Jung Foundation for Analytical Psychology, New York) 20, no. 1 (1987): 5–22.

May, Rollo. "The Significance of Symbols." In *Symbolism in Religion and Literature*, edited and with an introduction by Rollo May. New York: George Braziller, 1960.

———. *Psychology and the Human Dilemma*. Princeton, N.J.: D. Van Nostrand, 1967.

———. *Love and Will*. New York: W. W. Norton, 1969.

———. "Psychotherapy and the Daimonic." In *Myths, Dreams, and Religion,* edited by Joseph Campbell. Essays Sponsored by the

Society for the Arts, Religion and Contemporary Culture. New York: E. P. Dutton, 1970.

———. *Power and Innocence: A Search for the Sources of Violence.* New York: W. W. Norton, 1972.

———. *Paulus: Tillich as Spiritual Teacher.* Rev. ed. Dallas: Saybrook Publishing, 1988. Originally published as *Paulus; Reminiscences of a Friendship* (New York: Harper and Row, 1973).

———. *The Courage to Create.* New York: Bantam Books, 1976.

———. *The Meaning of Anxiety.* Rev. ed. New York: W. W. Norton, 1977. Originally published in 1950 by The Ronald Press Company.

———. *Freedom and Destiny.* New York: W. W. Norton, 1981.

———. "Rollo May: Man and Philosopher, with contributions from his colleagues." *Perspectives: Humanistic Psychology Institute,* special issue 2, no. 1 (Summer 1981).

———. *The Discovery of Being: Writings in Existential Psychology.* New York: W. W. Norton, 1983, 1986.

———. *The Cry for Myth.* New York: W. W. Norton, 1991.

May, R., and L. Caligor. *Dreams and Symbols: Man's Unconscious Language.* New York: Basic Books, 1968.

May, R., E. Angel, H. F. Ellenberger, eds. *Existence: A New Dimension in Psychiatry and Psychology.* New York: Simon and Schuster, 1958.

May, Rollo, ed. *Existential Psychology.* 2d ed. New York: Random House, 1969.

McFadden, Robert D. "N.Y. Railway Shooting Suspect: A Man Obsessed." *San Francisco Sunday Examiner and Chronicle* (December 12, 1993): B-7. Originally published in The *New York Times* under the title "A Tormented Life—A Special Report; A Long Slide from Privilege Ends in Slaughter on a Train" (December 12, 1993).

Mcintyre, Tom. "Millennium Witness." *San Francisco Examiner Magazine* (October 9, 1994): 13–24.

Melville, Herman. *Moby-Dick; or, the Whale* in *The Best of Herman Melville.* Secaucus, N.J.: Castle, 1983.

————. *White-Jacket or The World in a Man-of-War.* In *Herman Melville: Redburn, White-Jacket, Moby-Dick.* Notes, chronology, and text selection by G. Thomas Tanselle. Literary Classics of the United States, Inc., 1983.

Menninger, Karl. *Whatever Became of Sin?* New York: Bantam Books, 1978.

Miller, David L. "Orestes: Myth and Dream as Catharsis." In *Myths, Dreams, and Religion,* edited by Joseph Campbell. Essays Sponsored by the Society for the Arts, Religion and Contemporary Culture. New York: E. P. Dutton, 1970.

Monick, Eugene. *Castration and Male Rage: The Phallic Wound.* Toronto: Inner City Books, 1991.

Montagu, Ashley. *The Nature of Human Aggression.* New York: Oxford University Press, 1976.

Morrow, Felix. Foreword to *The History of Witchcraft and Demonology,* by Montague Sommers. New Hyde Park, N.Y.: University Books, 1956.

Mosak, Harold. "Adlerian Psychotherapy." In *Current Psychotherapies,* 4th ed., edited by Raymond J. Corsini and Danny Wedding, with the assistance of Judith W. McMahon. Itasca, Ill.: F. E. Peacock Publishers, 1989.

Nagera, Humberto. *Vincent van Gogh: A Psychological Study.* Foreword by Anna Freud. London: George Allen and Unwin Ltd., 1967.

Neumann, Erich. *Art and the Creative Unconscious: Four Essays.* Translated by Ralph Manheim. Bollingen Series LXI. Princeton, N.J.: Princeton University Press, 1971.

————. "Fear of the Feminine." Translated by Irene Gad, with the assistance of Ruth Horine, and with editing by Jeanne Walker. *Quadrant* (a publication of the C. G. Jung Foundation for Analytical Psychology, New York) 19, no. 1 (Spring 1986): 7–30. See also Neumann, Erich, *Fear of the Feminine and Other Essays on Feminine Psychology.* Princeton, N.J.: Princeton University Press, 1994.

New York Newsday (January 31, 1995).

Nietzsche, Friedrich. *Ecce Homo: How One Becomes What One Is*. Translated by Clifton P. Fadiman in *The Philosophy of Nietzsche*. Introduction by Willard Huntington Wright. New York: The Modern Library, Random House, n.d.

———. *The Birth of Tragedy from the Spirit of Music*. Translated by Clifton P. Fadiman in *The Philosophy of Nietzsche*. Introduction by Willard Huntington Wright. New York: The Modern Library, Random House, n.d.

O'Brien, D. *Empedocles' Cosmic Cycle*. 2d ed. Cambridge, England: Cambridge University Press, 1953.

Oesterreich, T. K. *Possession and Exorcism Among Primitive Races in Antiquity, the Middle Ages, and Modern Times*. New York: Causeway Books, 1974.

O'Flaherty, Wendy Doniger. *The Origins of Evil in Hindu Mythology*. Berkeley: University of California Press, 1976.

Otto, Rudolf. *The Idea of the Holy: An Inquiry into the Non-Rational Factor in the Idea of the Divine and Its Relation to the Rational*. 2d ed. Translated by John W. Harvey. Oxford: Oxford University Press, 1958.

Pagels, Elaine. *The Origin of Satan*. New York: Random House, 1995.

Panter, Barry M. "Vincent van Gogh: Creativity and Madness." In *Creativity and Madness: Psychological Studies of Art and Artists*, edited by B. Panter, M. Panter, E. Virshup, and B. Virshup. Burbank, Calif.: AIMED Press, 1995.

Peck, M. Scott. *People of the Lie: The Hope for Healing Human Evil*. New York: Simon and Schuster, 1983.

Perls, F. S. *Ego, Hunger and Aggression: The Beginning of Gestalt Therapy*. New York: Vintage Books, 1969.

———. *Gestalt Therapy Verbatim*. New York: Bantam Books, 1971.

Plato. *The Works of Plato*. Selected and edited by Irwin Edman. Translated by Benjamin Jowett. New York: The Modern Library, 1928.

———. *The Symposium*. Translated by Walter Hamilton. New York: Penguin Books, 1951.

———. *Plato: Euthyphro, Crito, Apology, and Symposium.* The Jowett translation, revised, with an introduction by Moses Hadas. A Gateway Edition. Chicago: Henry Regnery Co., 1953.

Progoff, Ira. *The Death and Rebirth of Psychology: An Integrative Evaluation of Freud, Adler, Jung and Rank and the Impact of Their Culminating Insights on Modern Man.* New York: The Julian Press, 1956.

———. "Waking Dream and Living Myth." In *Myths, Dreams, and Religion,* edited by Joseph Campbell. Essays sponsored by the Society for the Arts, Religion and Contemporary Culture. New York: E. P. Dutton, 1970.

Psychology Today 22, no. 12 (December 1988): 8.

Rajneesh, Bhagwan Shree. *The Mustard Seed: Discourses on the Sayings of Jesus taken from the Gospel According to Thomas.* Compilation by Swami Amrit Pathik. Edited by Swami Satya Deva. San Francisco: Harper and Row, 1975.

Rank, Otto. *The Trauma of Birth.* New York: Harper Torchbooks, 1929.

———. *Technik der Psychoanalyse.* Translated into English by Jesse Taft as *Will Therapy.* New York: Knopf, 1936.

———. *Beyond Psychology.* New York: Dover, 1958.

———. "The Psychological Approach to Personal Problems." *Journal of the Otto Rank Association* 1, no. 1 (Fall 1966): 12–25.

Reeves, Clement. *The Psychology of Rollo May: A Study in Existential Theory and Psychotherapy.* San Francisco: Jossey-Bass, 1977.

Reich, Wilhelm. *The Function of the Orgasm: The Discovery of the Orgone; Sex-Economic Problems of Biological Energy.* Vol. 1 of a two-vol. series entitled *The Discovery of the Orgone.* Translated by Theodore P. Wolfe. New York: World Publishing, 1971.

———. *Character Analysis.* 3d enl. ed. Translated by Vincent R. Carfagno. New York: Simon and Schuster, 1972.

Ribi, Alfred. *Demons of the Inner World: Understanding Our Hidden Complexes.* Translated by M. Kohn. Boston: Shambhala, 1990.

Rosberg, J., and A. A. Stunden. "The Use of Direct Confrontation: The Treatment-Resistant Schizophrenic Patient." *Acta Psychiatr Scand* 81 (1990): 352–358.

Russell, Jeffrey Burton. *The Prince of Darkness: Radical Evil and the Power of Good in History.* Ithaca, N.Y.: Cornell University Press, 1988.

San Francisco Examiner (December 19, 1993): A-2.

Sanford, John A. *Evil: The Shadow Side of Reality.* New York: Crossroad, 1990.

Sanford, Nevitt, Craig Comstock, and associates. *Sanctions for Evil: Sources of Social Destructiveness.* San Francisco: Jossey-Bass, 1971.

Sartre, Jean-Paul. *Existential Psychoanalysis.* Translated by Hazel E. Barnes. Introduction by Rollo May. A Gateway Edition. Chicago: Henry Regnery Company, 1953, 1962.

Schopenhauer, Arthur. "The Wisdom of Life." In *Complete Essays of Schopenhauer.* Translated by T. Bailey Saunders. New York: Willey Book Co., 1942.

Seligman, Martin. "Depression and Learned Helplessness." In *The Psychology of Depression: Contemporary Theory and Research,* edited by R. J. Friedman and M. M. Katz. New York: Wiley and Sons, 1974.

Selye, Hans. "The General Adaption Syndrome and the Diseases of Adaption." *Journal of Clinical Endocrinology* 6 (1946).

Shakespeare, William. *The Tragedy of Hamlet Prince of Denmark.* The Harvard Classics. Registered ed. Edited by C. Eliot. New York: P. F. Collier and Son, 1938.

Simón, A. "The Berserker/Blind Rage Syndrome as a Potentially New Diagnostic Category for the DSM-III." *Psychological Reports* 60 (1987): 131–135.

Singer, June. *Boundaries of the Soul: The Practice of Jung's Psychology.* Rev. ed. New York: Doubleday, 1994.

Smith, William Gardner. "The Compensation for the Wound." *Two Cities* 6 (Summer 1961): 67–69.

Sommers, Christine Hoff. *Who Stole Feminism?: How Women Have Betrayed Women.* New York: Simon and Schuster, 1995.

Sommers, Montague. *The History of Witchcraft and Demonology.* New Hyde Park, N.Y.: University Books, 1956.

The Song of God: Bhagavad-Gita. Translated by Swami Prabhavananda and Christopher Isherwood. Introduction by Aldous Huxley. New York: New American Library, 1972.

Sonneck, O. G., ed. *Beethoven: Impressions by His Contemporaries.* New York: Dover Publications, 1967.

Sophocles. *Oedipus the King.* In *The Complete Plays of Sophocles,* translated and edited by Richard Claverhouse Jebb. With an introduction by Moses Hadas. New York: Bantam Books, 1982.

———. *Oedipus at Colonus.* In *The Complete Plays of Sophocles.* Translated by Richard Claverhouse Jebb. Edited with an introduction by Moses Hadas. New York: Bantam Books, 1982.

Sperber, Michael A. "The Daimonic: Freudian, Jungian and Existential Perspectives." *Journal of Analytical Psychology* 20, no. 1 (January 1975): 41–49.

Spielberger, Charles, Susan Krasner, and Eldra Solomon. "The Experience, Expression, and Control of Anger." In *Health Psychology: Individual Differences and Stress,* edited by M. P. Janisse. New York: Springer Verlag, 1988.

Spitzer, R., M. Gibbon, A. Skodol, J. Williams, M. First. *DSM-111-R CaseBook.* Rev. ed. Washington, D.C.: American Psychiatric Press, 1989.

Steenbarger, B. "Duration and Outcome in Psychotherapy." *Professional Psychology* 25, no. 2 (1994): 111–119.

Stevenson, Robert Louis. *The Strange Case of Dr. Jekyll and Mr. Hyde.* With an introduction by B. Allen Bentley. New York: Airmont, 1964.

Stone, Irving, with Jean Stone. *Dear Theo: The Autobiography of Vincent Van Gogh.* New York: Signet, The New American Library, 1969.

Stone, Michael. "Aggression, Rage, and the 'Destructive Instinct,' Reconsidered From a Psychobiological Point of View." *Journal of the American Academy of Psychoanalysis* 19, no. 4 (1991): 507–529.

Styron, William. *Darkness Visible: A Memoir of Madness.* New York: Random House, 1990.

Sullivan, J. W. N. *Beethoven: His Spiritual Development.* New York: Vintage Books, 1960.

Taft, Jesse. Review of *Die Analyse des Analytikers*, by Otto Rank. *Psychoanalytic Review* 18, no. 4 (October 1931): 454–462.

Tavris, Carol. *Anger: The Misunderstood Emotion*. New York: Simon and Schuster, 1982.

Thorkelson, Willmar. "The Genes Made Me Do It: Sin and Responsibility." *San Jose Mercury News* (August 6, 1994): 10C.

Tillich, Paul. *The Courage To Be*. New Haven: Yale University Press, 1952.

———. *Morality and Beyond*. Religious Perspectives Series. Edited by Ruth Nanda Anshen. Vol. 9. New York: Harper and Row, 1963.

Time. "Angels Among Us." 142, no. 27 (December 27, 1993): 56–65.

Usborne, David. "Eerie Tale of Voodoo Ends in Blindness." *San Francisco Examiner* (July 10, 1994): A:3.

van der Leeuw, Gerardus. *Religion in Essence and Manifestation*. Translated by J. E. Turner with appendices incorporating the additions to the second German edition by Hans H. Penner. With a new foreword by Ninian Smart. Princeton, N.J.: Princeton University Press, 1986.

Virshup, Evelyn. "Jackson Pollock: Art Versus Alcohol." In *Creativity and Madness: Psychological Studies of Art and Artists*, edited by B. Panter, M. Panter, E. Virshup and B. Virshup. Burbank, Calif.: AIMED Press, 1995.

von Franz, M. L. *Projection and Re-Collection in Jungian Psychology: Reflections of the Soul*. Translated by William H. Kennedy. The Reality of the Psyche Series. La Salle, Ill.: Open Court, 1985. Originally published as *Spiegelungen der Seele: Projektion und innere Sammlung* (Stuttgart: Kreuz Verlag, 1978).

Walker, Margaret. *Richard Wright: Daemonic Genius; A Portrait of the Man, A Critical Look at His Work*. New York: Amistad Press, 1993.

White, David Manning. *Eternal Quest: The Search for God*, vol. 1. The Paragon Treasury of Inspirational Quotations and Spiritual Wisdom. New York: Paragon House, 1991.

Whitwell, F. D., and M. G. Barker. " 'Possession' in Psychiatric Patients in Britain." *The British Journal of Medical Psychology* 53 (1980): 287–295.

Williams, Redford, and Virginia Williams. *Anger Kills: Seventeen Strategies for Controlling the Hostility That Can Harm Your Health.* New York: Harper Perennial, 1994.

World Health Organization. *ICD-10: The ICD-10 Classification of Mental and Behavioural Disorders; Clinical Descriptions and Diagnostic Guidelines.* Geneva: World Health Organization, 1992.

Yalom, Irvin. *Existential Psychotherapy.* New York: Basic Books, 1980.

Yap, P. M. "The Possession Syndrome: A Comparison of Hong Kong and French Findings." *The Journal of Mental Science* (The British Journal of Psychiatry) 106, no. 442 (January 1960): 114–137.

Zaslow, Robert W., and Marilyn Menta. *The Psychology of the Z-Process: Attachment and Activation.* 2nd ed., rev. San Jose, Calif.: San Jose State University, 1975.

———. *Face to Face with Schizophrenia: Z-Process Approach.* San Jose, Calif.: San Jose State University, 1976.

———. *Rage, Resistance, and Holding: Z-Process Approach.* San Jose, Calif.: San Jose State University, 1977.

Zilboorg, Gregory. "Masculine and Feminine: Some Biological and Cultural Aspects." *Psychiatry: Journal of the Biology and the Pathology of Interpersonal Relations* 7 (1944): 257–296.

Zweig, Connie, and Jeremiah Abrams, eds. *Meeting the Shadow: The Hidden Power of the Dark Side of Human Nature.* New York: Jeremy P. Tarcher/G. P. Putnam's Sons, 1991. Originally published by Jeremy P. Tarcher, Inc., a division of G. P. Putnam's Sons.

Index